Role-Based Access Control

For quite a long time, computer security was a rather narrow field of study that was populated mainly by theoretical computer scientists, electrical engineers, and applied mathematicians. With the proliferation of open systems in general, and of the Internet and the World Wide Web (WWW) in particular, this situation has changed fundamentally. Today, computer and network practitioners are equally interested in computer security, since they require technologies and solutions that can be used to secure applications related to electronic commerce. Against this background, the field of computer security has become very broad and includes many topics of interest. The aim of this series is to publish state-of-the-art, high standard technical books on topics related to computer security. Further information about the series can be found on the WWW at the following URL:

http://www.esecurity.ch/serieseditor.html

Also, if you'd like to contribute to the series by writing a book about a topic related to computer security, feel free to contact either the Commissioning Editor or the Series Editor at Artech House.

Recent Titles in the Artech House Computer Security Series

Rolf Oppliger, Series Editor

Computer Forensics and Privacy, Michael A. Caloyannides

Demystifying the IPsec Puzzle, Sheila Frankel

Developing Secure Distributed Systems with CORBA, Ulrich Lang and Rudolf Schreiner

Implementing Electronic Card Payment Systems, Cristian Radu

Implementing Security for ATM Networks, Thomas Tarman and Edward Witzke

Information Hiding Techniques for Steganography and Digital Watermarking, Stefan Katzenbeisser and Fabien A. P. Petitcolas, editors

Internet and Intranet Security, Second Edition, Rolf Oppliger

Non-repudiation in Electronic Commerce, Jianying Zhou

Role-Based Access Control, David F. Ferraiolo, D. Richard Kuhn, and Ramaswamy Chandramouli

Secure Messaging with PGP and S/MIME, Rolf Oppliger

Security Fundamentals for E-Commerce, Vesna Hassler

Security Technologies for the World Wide Web, Second Edition, Rolf Oppliger

Software Verification and Validation for Practitioners and Managers, Second Edition, Steven R. Rakitin

Role-Based Access Control

David F. Ferraiolo
D. Richard Kuhn
Ramaswamy Chandramouli

Artech House
Boston • London
www.artechhouse.com

Library of Congress Cataloging-in-Publication Data
Ferraiolo, David.
   Role-based access control / David F. Ferraiolo, D. Richard Kuhn, Ramaswamy Chandramouli.
     p.   cm. — (Artech House computer security series)
   Includes bibliographical references and index.
   ISBN 1-58053-370-1 (alk. paper)
    1. Computers—Access control.   2. Computer security.   3. Computer networks—Access control.
    I. Kuhn, D. Richard.   II. Chandramouli, Ramaswamy.   III. Title.   IV. Series.
   QA76.9.A25F47 2003
   005.8—dc21   2003041492

British Library Cataloguing in Publication Data
Ferraiolo, David F.
   Role-based access control. —(Artech House computer security series)
   1. Computers—Access control
   I. Title II. Kuhn, D. Richard III. Chandramouli, Ramaswamy
   005.8
   ISBN   1-58053-370-1

Cover design by Christina Stone

© 2003 ARTECH HOUSE, INC.
685 Canton Street
Norwood, MA 02062

All rights reserved. Printed and bound in the United States of America. No part of this book may be reproduced or utilized in any form or by any means, electronic or mechanical, including photocopying, recording, or by any information storage and retrieval system, without permission in writing from the publisher.
   All terms mentioned in this book that are known to be trademarks or service marks have been appropriately capitalized. Artech House cannot attest to the accuracy of this information. Use of a term in this book should not be regarded as affecting the validity of any trademark or service mark.

International Standard Book Number: 1-58053-370-1
Library of Congress Catalog Card Number: 2003041492

10 9 8 7 6 5 4 3

*In memory of my father, who died too soon, and to my wife, Hildegard,
and son, Michael, for the time I spent at my computer instead of with them.*
—DFF

*To my parents, Richard and Jane Kuhn, and
my children, Gary, Christine, and Kevin, with love.*
—DRK

*To my dear father, late mother, loving wife, Mira, and
dear daughters, Dipika and Divya.*
—RC

Contents

Preface		*xv*
Acknowledgments		*xvii*
1	**Introduction**	**1**
1.1	The purpose and fundamentals of access control	2
	1.1.1 Authorization versus authentication	3
	1.1.2 Users, subjects, objects, operations, and permissions	4
	1.1.3 Least privilege	5
1.2	A brief history of access control	6
	1.2.1 Access control in the mainframe era	6
	1.2.2 Department of Defense standards	8
	1.2.3 Clark-Wilson model	9
	1.2.4 Origins of RBAC	9
1.3	Comparing RBAC to DAC and MAC	16
1.4	RBAC and the enterprise	18
	1.4.1 Economics of RBAC	18
	1.4.2 Authorization management and resource provisioning	20
	References	23
2	**Access Control Policy, Models, and Mechanisms—Concepts and Examples**	**27**
2.1	Policy, models, and mechanisms	27
2.2	Subjects and objects	30

2.3	Reference monitor and security kernel	31
	2.3.1 Completeness	33
	2.3.2 Isolation	33
	2.3.3 Verifiability	34
	2.3.4 The reference monitor—necessary, but not sufficient	35
2.4	DAC policies	35
2.5	Access control matrix	36
	2.5.1 ACLs and capability lists	37
	2.5.2 Protection bits	38
2.6	MAC policies and models	39
2.7	Biba's integrity model	41
2.8	Clark-Wilson model	42
2.9	The Chinese wall policy	44
2.10	The Brewer-Nash model	45
2.11	Domain-type enforcement model	46
	References	48

3 Core RBAC Features 51

3.1	Roles versus ACL groups	53
3.2	Core RBAC	55
	3.2.1 Administrative support	55
	3.2.2 Permissions	56
	3.2.3 Role activation	58
3.3	Mapping the enterprise view to the system view	59
	3.3.1 Global users and roles and indirect role privileges	62
	3.3.2 Mapping permissions into privileges	63

4 Role Hierarchies 67

4.1	Building role hierarchies from flat roles	68
4.2	Inheritance schemes	69
	4.2.1 Direct privilege inheritance	69
	4.2.2 Permission and user membership inheritance	70
	4.2.3 User containment and indirect privilege inheritance	72
4.3	Hierarchy structures and inheritance forms	75
	4.3.1 Connector roles	76
	4.3.2 Organization chart hierarchies	79

Contents

	4.3.3 Geographical regions	81
4.4	Accounting for role types	83
4.5	General and limited role hierarchies	84
4.6	Accounting for the Stanford model	87
	References	89

5 SoD and Constraints in RBAC Systems . . 91

5.1	Types of SoD	94
	5.1.1 Static SoD	94
	5.1.2 Dynamic SoD	98
	5.1.3 Operational SoD	99
	5.1.4 History and object-based SoD	100
5.2	Using SoD in real systems	101
	5.2.1 SoD in role hierarchies	102
	5.2.2 Static and dynamic constraints	103
	5.2.3 Mutual exclusion	104
	5.2.4 Effects of privilege assignment	105
	5.2.5 Assigning privileges to roles	107
	5.2.6 Assigning roles to users	108
5.3	Temporal constraints in RBAC	112
	5.3.1 Need for temporal constraints	112
	5.3.2 Taxonomy of temporal constraints	113
	5.3.3 Associated requirements for supporting temporal constraints	116
	References	117

6 RBAC, MAC, and DAC 121

6.1	Enforcing DAC using RBAC	122
	6.1.1 Configuring RBAC for DAC	123
	6.1.2 DAC with grant-independent revocation	124
	6.1.3 Additional considerations for grant-dependent revocation	125
6.2	Enforcing MAC on RBAC systems	125
	6.2.1 Configuring RBAC for MAC using static constraints	126
	6.2.2 Configuring RBAC for MAC using dynamic constraints	127
6.3	Implementing RBAC on MLS systems	130
	6.3.1 Roles and privilege sets	132
	6.3.2 Assignment of categories to privilege sets	133

		6.3.3	Assignment of categories to roles	134
	6.4		Running RBAC and MAC simultaneously	136
		6.3.4	Example of MLS to RBAC mapping	134
			References	138

7 NIST's Proposed RBAC Standard 141

7.1	Overview	141
7.2	Functional specification packages	142
7.3	The RBAC reference model	144
7.4	Functional specification overview	145
7.5	Functional specification for core RBAC	146
	7.5.1 Administrative functions	146
	7.5.2 Supporting system functions	146
	7.5.3 Review functions	147
7.6	Functional specification for hierarchical RBAC	147
	7.6.1 Hierarchical administrative functions	147
	7.6.2 Supporting system functions	149
	7.6.3 Review functions	149
7.7	Functional specification for SSD relation	150
	7.7.1 Administrative functions	150
	7.7.2 Supporting system functions	151
	7.7.3 Review functions	151
7.8	Functional specification for a DSD relation	152
	7.8.1 Administrative functions	152
	7.8.2 Supporting system functions	152
	7.8.3 Review functions	153
	Reference	153

8 Role-Based Administration of RBAC . . . 155

8.1	Background and terminology	155
8.2	URA02 and PRA02	158
8.3	Crampton-Loizou administrative model	162
	8.3.1 Flexibility of administrative scope	163
	8.3.2 Decentralization and autonomy	164
	8.3.3 A family of models for hierarchical administration	164
8.4	Role control center	169

	8.4.1	Inheritance and the role graph	170
	8.4.2	Constraints	172
	8.4.3	Role views	172
	8.4.4	Delegation of administrative permissions	173
	8.4.5	Decentralization and autonomy	176
	References		178

9 Enterprise Access Control Frameworks Using RBAC and XML Technologies 179

9.1	Conceptual view of EAFs		179
9.2	Enterprise Access Central Model Requirements		182
	9.2.1	EAM's multiple-policy support requirement	183
	9.2.2	EAM's ease of administration requirement	183
9.3	EAM specification and XML schemas		184
9.4	Specification of the ERBAC model in the XML schema		186
	9.4.1	XML schema specifications for ERBAC model elements	187
	9.4.2	XML schema specifications for ERBAC model relations	190
9.5	Encoding of enterprise access control data in XML		193
9.6	Verification of the ERBAC model and data specifications		197
9.7	Limitations of XML schemas for ERBAC model constraint representation		198
9.8	Using XML-encoded enterprise access control data for enterprisewide access control implementation		202
9.9	Conclusion		208
	References		208

10 Integrating RBAC with Enterprise IT Infrastructures. 211

10.1	RBAC for WFMSs		212
	10.1.1	Workflow Concepts and WFMSs	212
	10.1.2	WFMS components and access control requirements	213
	10.1.3	Access control design requirements	214
	10.1.4	RBAC model design and implementation requirements for WFMSs	216
	10.1.5	RBAC for workflows—research prototypes	219
10.2	RBAC integration in Web environments		220
	10.2.1	Implementing RBAC entirely on the Web server	221

	10.2.2	Implementing RBAC for Web server access using cookies	222
	10.2.3	RBAC on the Web using attribute certificates	224
10.3	RBAC for UNIX environments		231
	10.3.1	RBAC for UNIX administration	231
	10.3.2	RBAC implementation within the NFS	236
10.4	RBAC in Java		239
	10.4.1	Evolution of Java security models	240
	10.4.2	JDK 1.2 security model and enhancement	241
	10.4.3	Incorporating RBAC into JDK 1.2 security model with JAAS	244
10.5	RBAC for FDBSs		246
	10.5.1	IRO-DB architecture	247
	10.5.2	RBAC model implementation in IRO-DB	248
10.6	RBAC in autonomous security service modules		249
10.7	Conclusions		251
	References		251

11 Migrating to RBAC—Case Study: Multiline Insurance Company 255

11.1	Background		256
11.2	Benefits of using RBAC to manage extranet users		256
	11.2.1	Simplifying systems administration and maintenance	258
	11.2.2	Enhancing organizational productivity	259
11.3	Benefits of using RBAC to manage employees (intranet users)		259
	11.3.1	Reduction in new employee downtime	259
	11.3.2	Simplified systems administration and maintenance	260
11.4	RBAC implementation costs		260
	11.4.1	Software and hardware expenses	261
	11.4.2	Systems administrators' labor expenses	261
	11.4.3	Role engineering expenses	261
11.5	Time series of benefits and costs		262
	Reference		264

12 RBAC Features in Commercial Products . 265

12.1	RBAC in relational DBMS products		266
	12.1.1	Informix Dynamic Server version 9.3 (IBM)	267

		12.1.2	Oracle Enterprise Server version 8i (Oracle)	269
		12.1.3	Sybase adaptive server version 12.5 (Sybase)	271
	12.2	RBAC in enterprise security administration software		274
		12.2.1	CONTROL-SA (BMC software)	276
		12.2.2	DirXmetaRole version 1.0 (Siemens)	280
		12.2.3	SAM Jupiter (Systor)	284
		12.2.4	Tivoli Identity Manager version 1.1 (IBM)	289
	12.3	Conclusions		292
		References		293

Appendix A 295

Appendix B 299

About the Authors 303

Index 305

Preface

Role-based access control (RBAC) is a technology that is attracting a great deal of attention, particularly for commercial applications, because of its potential for reducing the complexity and cost of security administration in large networked applications. Under RBAC, security administration is greatly simplified by using roles, hierarchies, and constraints to organize privileges. RBAC reduces costs within an organization, because it takes into account that employees change much more frequently than the duties within positions. Under RBAC, if, for example, an employee moves within an organization, only his or her role assignment is changed. Accordingly, it is unnecessary to revoke his or her existing privileges and assign a completely new set of privileges. RBAC can be configured to support a wide variety of access control policies, including traditional discretionary access control (DAC) and mandatory access control (MAC), as well as organization-specific policies. Recently, RBAC has also been found to be a natural access control facility for workflow management systems. The concept and design of RBAC make it perfectly suited to a wide variety of application and system software environments, for both stand-alone and distributed deployments. It provides a safe and effective way to manage access to an organization's information, while reducing administration costs and minimizing errors.

Over the past decade, interest in RBAC has increased dramatically, with most major information technology (IT) vendors offering a product that incorporates some form of role-based access. The profusion of new RBAC products offers many advantages for security administrators and software developers, but sorting out the capabilities of different products can be challenging. Until now, RBAC research has been documented in hundreds of research papers, but not consolidated in book form. This book explains RBAC and its administrative and cost advantages and implementation issues and the migration from conventional access control methods to RBAC.

Specialized topics—including role hierarchies, separation of duties, combining RBAC with military security models, and recent efforts toward standardization—are detailed. To enable system integrators to integrate RBAC into the various IT infrastructures found in an enterprise-like Web applications, such as Java and Federated Database Systems, the book provides an analysis of research ideas and prototypes built so far. The book also describes RBAC implementations in various commercial products and includes a case study documenting a large organization's migration to a role-based security architecture.

Intended audience

This book is designed to be useful to three groups of readers: (1) security professionals, technology managers, and users in industry, government, and military organizations, including system administrators responsible for security, policy officials, and technology officers; (2) software developers for database systems, enterprise management, security, and cryptographic products; and (3) computer science and IT students and instructors. The treatment is not excessively formal; mathematical descriptions of RBAC properties are included as sidebars, but the text is understandable without reference to them. Because computer security is such a rapidly changing field, we have included a discussion of research and commercial product documentation through this year.

Acknowledgments

First of all, we want to thank Tim Grance of the National Institute of Standards and Technology (NIST). Much of NIST's contribution to RBAC research can be traced to Tim's early persistent and continuing support, leadership, and counsel. We would also like to thank Andrew Marshall of TD Bank in Canada for his detailed review of material in Chapters 3 and 4 and his great insight regarding the application of role hierarchies to commercial business structures, and Leann Michaels for advice and counsel regarding medical applications, functions, and roles that were applied throughout this book. The authors also thank Dr. Martin Kuhlmann and Axel Kern of Systor Security Solutions, Mr. Wiley Vasquez and Gary Holland of BMC Software, and Harald Kopper of Siemens AG for providing technical documentations pertaining to "Enterprise Security Administration" product offerings from their respective organizations. We are grateful to Michael Gallaher, Alan O'Connor, and Brian Kropp of the Research Triangle Institute and Greg Tassey of NIST for their excellent analysis of the economic impact of RBAC.

Finally, we also thank the many contributors to the RBAC field from the public, academic, and private sectors, such as Gail-Joon Ahn, Vijay Atluri, Elena Ferrari, Arif Ghafoor, James Joshi, Trent Jaeger, Serban Gavrila, Virgil Gligor, Bill Majurski, Tony Cincotta, Wayne Jansen, Janet Cugini, Elisa Bertino, and Konstantin Beznosov.

CHAPTER 1

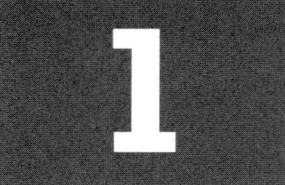

Contents

1.1 The purpose and fundamentals of access control

1.2 A brief history of access control

1.3 Comparing RBAC to DAC and MAC

1.4 RBAC and the enterprise

References

Introduction

Access control—or authorization, in its broadest sense—has existed as a concept for as long as humans have had assets worth protecting. Guards, gates, and locks have been used since ancient times to limit individuals' access to valuables. A need for access control in fact prompted the invention of what can be regarded as the world's first secure computing system. In 1879, a Dayton, Ohio, saloonkeeper named James Ritty invented the "incorruptible cashier," which later became known as the cash register. Ritty's invention reduced the common problem of employee pilfering by permitting access to the cash drawer only when a sale was rung up by entering the amount of the sale in full view of the customer. By recording the amount of sales and keeping a running total, the register made it possible for store-owners to ensure that the cash drawer contents matched the total sales made during the day.

In today's information technology, authorization is concerned with the ways in which users can access resources in the computer system, or informally speaking, with "who can do what." Access control is arguably the most fundamental and most pervasive security mechanism in use today. Access control shows up in virtually all systems and imposes great architectural and administrative challenges at all levels of enterprise computing. From a business perspective, access control has the potential to promote the optimal sharing and exchange of resources, but it also has the potential to frustrate users, impose large administrative costs, and cause the unauthorized disclosure or corruption of valuable information.

Access control can take many forms. In addition to determining whether a user has rights to use a resource, the access control system may constrain when and how the resource may be used. For example, a user may have access to a network only during working hours. Some organizations may establish more complex controls, such as requiring that two staff members conduct certain high-risk operations such as opening a vault or launching a missile. The definition and modeling of access control stem from seminal papers of the early 1970s, the early standardization efforts of the 1980s, and the emergence of RBAC that began in the early 1990s, and it continues to this day. This chapter introduces the origins, history, and central concepts of access control, reviews popular forms of access controls in use today, and introduces the basic concepts of RBAC and its advantages for system, application, and network security.

1.1 The purpose and fundamentals of access control

Access control is only one aspect of a comprehensive computer security solution, but it is one of the most visible. Every time a user logs on to a multiuser computer system, access control is enforced. To gain a better understanding of the purpose of access control, it is worth reviewing the risks to information systems. Information security risks can be broadly categorized into the following three types, *confidentiality, integrity,* and *availability,* which can be remembered with the convenient mnemonic "CIA." These categories are described as follows:

- *Confidentiality* refers to the need to keep information secure and private. This category may include anything from state secrets to confidential memoranda, financial information, and security information such as passwords.
- *Integrity* refers to the concept of protecting information from being improperly altered or modified by unauthorized users. For example, most users want to ensure that bank account numbers used by financial software cannot be changed by anyone else and that only the user or an authorized security administrator can change passwords.
- *Availability* refers to the notion that information is available for use when needed. Attacks that attempt to overload corporate Web servers, widely reported in the popular press, are attacks on availability.

1.1 The purpose and fundamentals of access control

Access control is critical to preserving the confidentiality and integrity of information. The condition of confidentiality requires that only authorized users can read information, and the condition of integrity requires that only authorized users can alter information in authorized ways. Access control is less obviously central to preserving availability, but it clearly has an important role: An attacker who gains unauthorized access to a system is likely to have little trouble bringing it down.

1.1.1 Authorization versus authentication

Authorization and authentication are fundamental to access control. They are distinct concepts but often confused. Part of the confusion stems from the close relationship between the two; proper authorization in fact is dependent on authentication.

Authentication is the process of determining that a user's claimed identity is legitimate. Every computer user is familiar with passwords, the most common form of authentication. If Alice logs in as alice46 and then provides the correct password for user identification (ID) alice46, she has authenticated herself to the system. Less common forms of authentication include biometrics (e.g., fingerprint readers) and smart cards. Authentication is based on one or more of the following factors:

- Something you know, such as the password, personal identification number (PIN), or lock combination;
- Something you have, such as a smart card, automatic teller machine (ATM) card, or key;
- Something you are, or a physical characteristic, such as a fingerprint or retinal pattern, or a facial characteristic.

Clearly, authentication is normally stronger if two or more factors are used. A password can be guessed; a key can be lost; and face-recognition systems have a significant false positive rate, so using only one of these authentication methods may not provide an acceptable level of security. This is why banks require both cards and PINs to access ATMs rather than only a password, or only a key or card. If the card were lost, a thief would have to guess the PIN in only three tries to beat the authentication system.

While authentication is a process of determining who you are, authorization determines what you are allowed to do. Authorization refers to a yes or no decision as to whether a user is granted access to a system resource. An information system must maintain some relationship between user IDs and system resources, possibly by attaching a list of authorized users to resources, or by storing a list of accessible resources with each user ID. Note that authorization necessarily depends on proper authentication. If the system cannot be certain of a user's identity, there is no valid way of determining if the user should be granted access.

1.1.2 Users, subjects, objects, operations, and permissions

A reasonably consistent terminology has developed over the past 3 decades for describing access control models and systems. Almost any access control model can be stated formally using the notions of *users, subjects, objects, operations,* and *permissions,* and the relationships between these entities. It is important to understand these terms, because the reader will encounter them not only in this book but also in most of the literature on access control and computer security.

The term *user* refers to people who interface with the computer system. In many designs, it is possible for a single user to have multiple login IDs, and these IDs may be simultaneously active. Authentication mechanisms make it possible to match the multiple IDs to a single human user, however.

An instance of a user's dialog with a system is called a *session*.

A computer process acting on behalf of a user is referred to as a *subject*. Note that in reality, all of a user's actions on a computer system are performed through some program running on the computer. A user may have multiple subjects in operation, even if the user has only one login and one session. For example, an e-mail system may be operating in the background, fetching e-mail from a server periodically, while the user operates a Web browser. Each of the user's programs is a subject, and each program's accesses will be checked to ensure that they are permitted for the user who invoked the program.

An *object* can be any resource accessible on a computer system, including files, peripherals such as printers, databases, and fine-grained entities such as individual fields in database records. Objects are traditionally viewed as passive entities that contain or receive information, although even early access control models included the possibility of treating programs, printers, or other active entities as objects [1].

An *operation* is an active process invoked by a subject. Early access control models that were concerned strictly with information flow (i.e., read-and-write access) applied the term subject to all active processes, but RBAC models require a distinction between subject and operation. For example, when an ATM user enters a card and correct PIN, the control program operating on the user's behalf is a subject, but the subject can initiate more than one operation—deposit, withdrawal, balance inquiry, or others.

Permissions (or privileges) are authorizations to perform some action on the system. As used in this book, and in most computer security literature, the term permission refers to some combination of object and operation. A particular operation used on two different objects represents two distinct permissions, and similarly, two different operations applied to a single object represent two distinct permissions. For example, a bank teller may have permissions to execute debit and credit operations on customer records, through transactions, while an accountant may execute debit and credit operations on the general ledger, which consolidates the bank's accounting data.

1.1.3 Least privilege

Least privilege is the time-honored administrative practice of selectively assigning permission to users such that the user is given no more permission than is necessary to perform his or her job function. The principle of least privilege avoids the problem of an individual having the ability to perform unnecessary and potentially harmful actions merely as a side effect of granting the ability to perform desired functions. The question then becomes how to assign the set of system permissions to the aggregate of functions or duties that correspond to a role of a user or subject acting on behalf of the user. Least privilege provides a rationale for where to install the separation boundaries that are to be provided by the access control mechanism. Ensuring adherence to the principle of least privilege is largely an administrative challenge that requires the identification of job functions, the specification of the set of permissions required to perform each function, and the restriction of the user to a domain with those privileges and nothing more.

Strict adherence to least privilege requires an individual to have different levels of permission at different times, depending on the task or function being performed. It must be recognized that in some environments and with some permissions, restricting permission because it is nominally unnecessary may inconvenience the user or place an additional burden on administrators. However, granting of excess privilege that potentially can be exploited to circumvent protection, whether for integrity or confidentiality, should be avoided whenever possible. It is also important that permissions not persist beyond the time that they are required for performance of duties.

1.2 A brief history of access control

Although security issues had been addressed in some early time-sharing computer systems from the 1960s, the discipline of computer security began to progress rapidly in the early 1970s. At this time large resource-sharing systems were becoming commonplace in government, military, and large commercial organizations. The field developed both in government and military systems, and in the commercial arena where applications such as ATMs required strong security.

1.2.1 Access control in the mainframe era

The growth in multiuser computer systems and the increased dependence of defense systems on computers led to efforts by the U.S. Defense Science Board to investigate the vulnerability of government systems in the late 1960s. University researchers also considered the problem. The earliest work in defining a formal, mathematical description of access control is that of Lampson [2], who introduced the formal notions of *subject* and *object* and an access matrix that mediated the access of subjects to objects. An access matrix is a simple conceptual representation in which the (i,j) entry in the matrix specifies the rights that subject i has to object j. An example is shown in Figure 1.1. Subjects (processes invoked by users) are allowed to access objects such as files or peripherals according to the rights specified in the matrix. For example, user Bob is allowed read and write access to the payroll file, and read access to the accounts receivable and accounts payable file.

A RAND Corporation report from 1970 [3] provided a comprehensive analysis of security for DoD computer systems. Included in the report was the definition of a method to implement multilevel—relating to documents classified by a security level, such as confidential, secret, or top-secret—access control on a resource-sharing system, with separate considerations for local access and remote access where password-based authorization would be required. This document also discussed the basic requirements for

	General ledger	Payroll	Accounts receivable	Accounts payable
Alice	R,W		R	R
Bob		R,W	R	R
Charles	R		R	R

Figure 1.1 Access matrix.

1.2 A brief history of access control

controlling access to information based on a user's clearance level and the classification level of files stored on the system. Proposals for a multi-level secure system were extended in a U.S. Air Force report [4] that included engineering development plans for such a system along with communications.

Bell and LaPadula [5] formalized military access control rules into a mathematical model suitable for defining and evaluating computer security systems. As formulated in this model, multilevel secure systems implement the familiar government document classification rule: Users are only allowed to access information that is classified at or below their own clearance level. Conceptually, this is a very simple policy, readily understood and followed by humans. However, as with much in information technology, implementing this seemingly simple policy on a computer system can be tricky. Unexpected loopholes and nonobvious interactions between different components of the system can leave a computer security system vulnerable. The Bell-LaPadula model was significant because it provided a formal (i.e., mathematical) model of the multilevel security policy, making it possible to analyze properties of the model in detail.

Two basic rules are required in the formal model: the simple security rule and the *-property, commonly known as "no read up" and "no write down." The simple security rule is obvious: A user with a particular clearance level cannot be allowed to read information above that level (e.g., a user with secret clearance cannot read top-secret documents). The *-property, which is essentially the reverse of the simple security rule, is required to maintain system security: A user operating at a particular clearance level can write information only at that level or above. For example, if a user is logged in at secret level, programs or processes operated by that user are not permitted to write information at the confidential level, although it could be written to a higher level, such as top-secret. (Note that this rule makes sense where we are concerned with processes operating on a computer. Obviously, a human being could log in at a high level, then print out or memorize information and re-enter it after logging in at a lower level.) Also included in the Bell-LaPadula model was the notion of categories, which refers to a vertical breakdown of security compartments across levels. In addition to having the proper clearance level, a user is required to be cleared for all of the categories attached to a classified document. For example, a document might be classified [Secret, nuclear, NATO]. To access the document, a user would need a clearance of secret or above and must also be cleared for the two categories—nuclear and NATO. (Chapter 2 provides a more detailed discussion of these rules.) This policy ensures that information cannot be downgraded either through unintentional or malicious actions of a process.

A 1976 paper by Harrison, Ruzzo, and Ullman showed that safety is inherently undecidable in a conventional access matrix view of security [6]. In other words, it is impossible to know whether a given configuration considered "safe" with respect to some security requirement would remain safe. If the system is started with a set of access rights to objects, it is impossible to know that the system will not eventually grant access rights that are not in the original matrix. Although the proof of this result is somewhat technical, the underlying reason for the undecidability is that users can give away access rights. If the system has no control over what rights are passed from one user to another, there is no way to be sure that an unauthorized user will not eventually receive rights improperly, through some chain of rights delegation.

1.2.2 Department of Defense standards

Codification of access control models in standards took a significant step forward in 1983, when the U.S. Department of Defense (DoD) published its *Trusted Computer System Evaluation Criteria* (TCSEC) [1], commonly known as the "Orange Book," for its orange cover. This standard defined in detail two important access control modes for military systems: discretionary access control (DAC) and mandatory access control (MAC). As the name suggests, DAC is a mode in which the creators or owners of files assign access rights, and a subject with discretionary access to information can pass that information on to another subject.

By itself, DAC is insufficient for implementing the document classification scheme used by the military. Since users in the DAC model of security can give away rights to access objects, the Harrison, Ruzzo, Ullman undecidability result applies to DAC. To provide a truly secure scheme in which a system is guaranteed to remain secure, MAC is required.

As usually implemented, MAC controls provide the multilevel security policy as formalized by the Bell-LaPadula model described in Section 1.2.1. (Chapter 2 provides a more detailed treatment of DAC and MAC policies.) The key feature of MAC is that, as its name implies, it is required for the mediation of all accesses of objects on the system. Since the access control system mediates all access to objects using rules imposed externally, users cannot give away permissions for object access. Since users are limited in the actions they can take, the access controls can ensure that the system will remain in a secure state regardless of user actions.

1.2.3 Clark-Wilson model

One goal of the TCSEC was to encourage a market for secure operating systems and computer security products. Many writers argued that systems meeting the lower levels of TCSEC requirements would be sufficient for commercial use. The hope was that a uniform market for security products would develop, with the TCSEC providing guidance for both commercial and military security.

Despite efforts to promote TCSEC-compliant systems as commercial security solutions, most commercial firms recognized that DAC and MAC were not sufficient for their needs. TCSEC-oriented systems are focused on the information flow and confidentiality of information. In a widely referenced 1987 paper, Clark and Wilson [7] argued that while confidentiality was important to commercial users, their primary concern pertains to integrity (i.e., ensuring that information is modified only in appropriate ways by authorized users).

When Clark and Wilson formalized business security practices into a security model, the result was quite different from the military security model formalized by Bell and LaPadula. The two central concepts in the Clark-Wilson model are the well-formed transaction and separation of duty (SoD). Well-formed transactions constrain the user to change data only in authorized ways. For example, a bank teller cannot modify an arbitrary part of a customer record, only those data fields that are incorporated into the particular transaction being run, such as a savings deposit or withdrawal. Complementing the well-formed transaction is the ancient principle of SoD, which ensures the consistency of changes made to critical data. A division manager, for example, can request an expenditure, but another person must approve it, and a third audits the completed transaction to ensure that fraud has not occurred. Implementing these rules in a computer system has been found to be as challenging as implementing information flow policies. One of the motivations of RBAC was to make commercial security policies easier to manage.

1.2.4 Origins of RBAC

Like the multilevel security policy formalized by Bell and LaPadula, RBAC has its roots in historical practices that predate the formal model, except that RBAC's features stem primarily from the commercial world. Also like multilevel security, RBAC is conceptually simple: Access to computer system objects is based on a user's role in an organization. Roles with different privileges and responsibilities have long been recognized in business organizations, and commercial computer applications dating back to at least the 1970s implemented limited forms of access constraints based on the user's role within the organization. For example, on-line banking applications in that period included both teller and teller supervisor roles that could execute different sets of transactions, while simultaneously users at ATMs were able to execute another set of transactions against the same databases.

In the late 1980s and early 1990s researchers began recognizing the virtues of roles as an abstraction for managing privileges within applications and database management systems. A role was seen as a job or position within an organization. A role exists as a structure separate from that of the users who were assigned to the roles. Dobson and McDermid [8] used the term functional roles. Baldwin [9] called these structures named protection domains (NPDs) and stated that they could be related and organized into hierarchies based on NPD permission subsets. Also recognized was the use of roles in support of the principle of least privilege in which a role is created with minimum permissions in specification of duty requirements [10]. The Brewer and Nash model [11] presented a basic theory for use in implementing dynamically changing access permissions. The model is described in terms of a particular commercial security policy, known as the *Chinese wall*. The model is developed by first defining what a Chinese wall means and then defining a set of rules (SoD requirements) such that no user can ever access data from the wrong side of the wall. Nash and Poland [12] discussed the application of role-based security to cryptographic authentication devices commonly used in the banking industry.

These role-based systems were relatively simple and application-specific. That is, there was no general-purpose model defining how access control could be based on roles, and little formal analysis of the security of these systems. The systems were developed by a variety of organizations, with no commonly agreed upon definition or recognition in formal standards.

In 1992, NIST initiated a study [13] of both commercial and government organizations, and found that access control needs were not being met by products on the market at the time, many of which implemented only TCSEC-style discretionary controls, considered by many organizations as the "standard of due care." In many enterprises within industry and civilian government, end users do not "own" the information for which they are allowed access as assumed by DAC. For these organizations, the corporation or agency is the actual "owner" of system objects, and discretionary control on the part of the users may not be appropriate. Conventional MAC, focused on preserving confidentiality, is also inadequate for these organizations. Although enforcing a need-to-know policy is important where classified information is of concern, there existed a general need to support

1.2 A brief history of access control

subject-based security policies, such as access based on competency, the enforcement of conflict-of-interest rules, or access based on a strict concept of least privilege. Supporting such policies requires the ability to restrict access based on a user function or role within the enterprise.

A solution to meet these needs was proposed in 1992 by Ferraiolo and Kuhn [14], integrating features of existing application-specific approaches into a generalized RBAC model. This paper described, in a simple formal manner, the sets, relations, and mappings used in defining roles and role hierarchies, subject-role activation, and subject-object mediation, as well as the constraints on user-role membership and role-set activation. Three basic rules were required:

1. *Role assignment:* A subject can execute a transaction only if the subject has selected, or been assigned to, a role. The identification and authentication process (e.g., login) is not considered a transaction. All other user activities on the system are conducted through transactions. Thus, all active users are required to have some active role.

2. *Role authorization:* A subject's active role must be authorized for the subject. With rule 1, this rule ensures that users can take on only roles for which they are authorized.

3. *Transaction authorization:* A subject can execute a transaction only if the transaction is authorized for the subject's active role. In concert with rules 1 and 2, this rule ensures that users can execute only transactions for which they are authorized.

The formal description of the model is given in Figure 1.2. A key feature of this model is that all access is through roles. A role is essentially a collection of permissions, and all users receive permissions only through the roles to which they are assigned, as shown in Figure 1.3. Within an organization, roles are relatively stable, while users and permissions are both numerous and may change rapidly. Controlling all access through roles therefore simplifies the management and review of access controls.

The most common method of implementing access control in a computer system is through access control lists (ACLs). All system resources, such as files, printers, and terminals, have a list of authorized users attached. This makes it easy and quick to answer the per object review question: "What users have access to object X?" Much more difficult is the per subject review question: "What objects can user X access?" Answering this question requires scanning all objects on the computer system, which may number in the millions; recording their access control lists; and finally reporting on

Original formal description of RBAC
For each subject, the active role is the one that the subject is currently using: $AR(s : subject) = \{$the active role for subject $s\}$
Each subject may be authorized to perform one or more roles: $RA(s : subject) = \{$authorized roles for subject $s\}$
Each role may be authorized to perform one or more transactions: $TA(r : role) = \{$transactions authorized for role $r\}$
Subjects may execute transactions. The predicate $exec(s,t)$ is true if and only if subject s can execute transaction t at the current time; otherwise it is false: $exec(s:subject,t:tran) = \{$true iff subject s can execute transaction $t\}$ 1. Role assignment: A subject can execute a transaction only if the subject has selected or been assigned a role: $\forall s : subject, t : tran \cdot exec(s,t) \Rightarrow AR(s) \neq \varnothing$ 2. Role authorization: A subject's active role must be authorized for the subject: $\forall s : subject \cdot AR(s) \subseteq RA(s)$ 3. Transaction authorization: A subject can execute a transaction only if teh transaction is authorized for teh subject's active role: $\forall s : subject, t : tran \cdot exec(s,t) \Rightarrow t \in TA(AR(s))$
Note that because the conditional in rule 3 is "only if," this rule allows for the possibility that additional restrictions may be placed on transaction execution. That is, the rule does not guarantee a transaction to be executable just because it is in $TA[AR(s)]$. The set of transactions potentially executable by the subject's active role. For example, a trainee for a supervisory role may be assigned the role of *supervisor* but may have restrictions applied to his or her role that limit accesible transactions to a subset of those normally allowed for the supervisor role.

Figure 1.2 Formal description of RBAC from Ferraiolo and Kuhn [14].

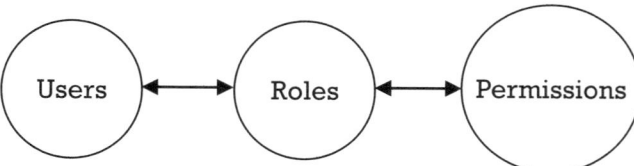

Figure 1.3 RBAC relationships.

user X. Measurements of real systems have shown that this process can take more than a day. A side effect of this scheme is that ACLs make it easy to add permissions to an object but hard to revoke all of a particular user's

1.2 A brief history of access control

permissions. In many systems, users are combined into groups, which are then used as entries in ACLs.

Readers familiar with conventional group mechanisms will recognize a superficial similarity between RBAC and groups. As normally implemented, a group is a collection of users, rather than a collection of permissions, and permissions can be associated with both users and the groups to which they belong, as shown in Figure 1.4. Because users may access objects based on either their user or group ID, it is possible for users to retain access permissions that should be revoked when group permission is removed from the object. The permission based on the individual user ID is in effect a loophole in the enforcement of the security policy. The RBAC requirement that all access be through roles helps to strengthen security significantly in real applications by eliminating this loophole.

A second important feature of the Ferraiolo-Kuhn model is that roles are hierarchical—roles can inherit permissions from other roles (Figure 1.5) —while groups are normally treated as flat collections of users. Also included in this model was a provision for constraints on role membership, although specific types of constraints were not proposed.

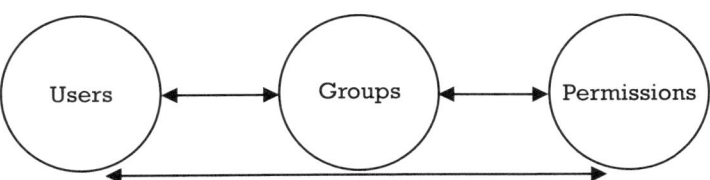

Figure 1.4 Group access control relationships.

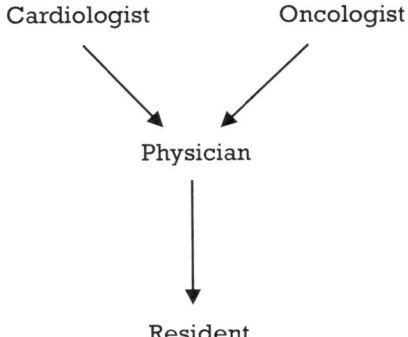

Figure 1.5 Example of a functional role hierarchy.

The 1992 paper showed that this model subsumes the Clark-Wilson model (i.e., the Clark-Wilson model is included as a special case). A subsequent NIST publication [15] investigated RBAC in more detail, proposing additional functions beyond those included in the 1992 model, and included specific forms for constraints to implement separation-of-duty requirements.

George Mason University Professor Ravi Sandhu, a well-known and influential security expert, described the Ferraiolo-Kuhn RBAC model as "an important innovation, which makes RBAC a service to be used by application.... Instead of scattering security in application code, RBAC will consolidate security in a unified service which can be better managed while providing the flexibility and customization required by individual applications" [16]. Dr. Sandhu went on to conduct extensive research and publish numerous papers in the area of RBAC. Several of his students have joined him in this research, and some have produced doctoral theses in areas related to RBAC.

In 1994, Nyanchama and Osborn [17] proposed a very generalized form of role organization called a role graph model. The authors showed that roles could be organized based on three role relationships: partial, shared, and augmented privileges. The role graph model is particularly useful in analyzing privilege sharing, which is critical in detecting and preventing conflict of interest relationships between roles. Gligor introduced the notion of "role types," which allow role administration to be simplified with parameterized types that are instantiated to produce roles. This work became the subject of the first U.S. patent in the area of RBAC [18].

In 1996, Sandhu and colleagues [19] introduced a framework of RBAC models, *RBAC96*, breaking down RBAC into four conceptual models. Shown in Figure 1.6, this framework specified a base model, RBAC0, that contains the minimal features of a system implementing RBAC. Two advanced models, RBAC1 and RBAC2, include RBAC0, but add (respectively) support for hierarchies and for constraints such as SoD. A fourth component, RBAC3, includes all aspects of the lower-level models. The Sandhu et al. RBAC96 framework established a modular structure for RBAC systems, providing for simplified commercial implementations that could offer basic RBAC0 functionality, or more advanced features as required by customers.

Largely due to a series of conferences sponsored by the Association for Computing Machinery (ACM), founded by Professor Sandhu and David Ferraiolo of NIST, a robust RBAC research community had developed, and today commercial implementations are providing ever more sophisticated RBAC systems. RBAC began to see application in a wide variety of areas. Early work by Barkley [20] showed that RBAC has a natural application in

1.2 A brief history of access control

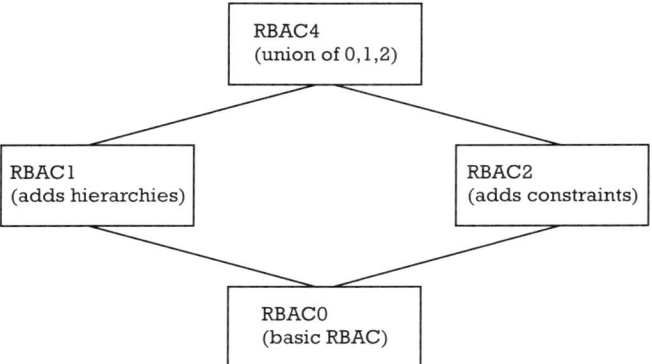

Figure 1.6 Sandhu et al. RBAC96 framework.

health care. Workflow management, an economically important field that deals with the automation of business processes, is another area where RBAC seems to be ideally suited to not only provide security, but serve as a framework for workflows as well. Barkley and Cincotta [21] and Bertino, Ferrari, and Atluri [22] introduced RBAC-based workflow systems.

In 2000, NIST initiated an effort to establish an international consensus standard for RBAC, publishing a proposal [23] in the ACM RBAC workshop. The proposed standard follows the RBAC96 structure and incorporates features developed out of subsequent discussions and formal comments received from the research and commercial vendor communities. In 2002 the proposed standard was submitted to the international standards process, and commercial firms have already begun building products that will conform to the RBAC standard.

What is most striking about RBAC's history is its rapid evolution from a concept to its commercial implementation and deployment. Although this success can be attributed to a variety of factors, recognition of RBAC's dual policy and productivity advantages have undoubtedly contributed to its present stature. In this respect, RBAC differs from many other security concepts, in that its costs of deployment need not be justified based solely on perceived threats and system vulnerabilities. Although RBAC allows for the enforcement of a wide variety of important access control policies that are either impractical or even impossible to enforce in its absence, RBAC's productivity advantages alone are often sufficient in justifying its deployment. When taken together, these dual motivators can lead to a strong business justification. To improve the efficiency of heath care systems, the U.S. Health Insurance Portability and Accountability Act of 1996 (HIPAA) explicitly calls out RBAC requirements [24], and the U.S. Federal Aviation Administration cites RBAC in its specifications for National Airspace System security [25]. RBAC is now being prescribed as a generalized approach to access control. For instance, RBAC was found to be "the most attractive solution for providing security features in multidomain digital government infrastructure" [26] and has shown its great relevance in meeting the complex security needs of Web-based applications [27].

Although RBAC can be justified squarely on economics, something else was going on over the last decade. During this period, hundreds of papers were published on topics revolving on the theme of RBAC. As we have discussed, RBAC is a packaging of closely related and dependent access control and management features and ideas. Although the focus of RBAC is clearly on access control, in many respects RBAC can be viewed as a model for regulation and management of user actions and activities within IT environments. Furthermore, these activities have been encapsulated into highly intuitive role structures that appear naturally within most business environments. As it turns out, role structures not only apply to resource provisioning systems and access control and policy management systems, they also fit naturally into workflow, process management, collaborative, and virtual enterprise environments. When RBAC models first appeared, these enterprise applications were not envisioned. However, once published, and thoroughly examined, other researchers quickly began expanding and elaborating on RBAC concepts and structures.

The pervasiveness of RBAC's application within modern day IT infrastructures is significant. Today, RBAC features are included at all levels of enterprise computing, including operating system, database management system, network, and enterprise management levels. RBAC is being incorporated and integrated within infrastructure technologies such as public key infrastructure (PKI), workflow management systems, and directory and Web services. In addition, RBAC is being proposed as an enabling technology in formulating metapolicies within collaborative and virtual enterprise systems.

1.3 Comparing RBAC to DAC and MAC

The principle motivations behind RBAC are the ability to specify and enforce enterprise-specific access control policies and to streamline the typically burdensome process of authorization management. RBAC represents a major advancement in flexibility and detail of control from the existing standards of DAC and MAC.

1.3 Comparing RBAC to DAC and MAC

As defined in the TCSEC and commonly implemented, DAC is an access control policy and mechanism that permits system users to allow or disallow other users access to the objects under their control. The TCSEC DAC policy is defined as follows:

> A means of restricting access to objects based on the identity of subjects or groups, or both, to which they belong. The controls are discretionary in the sense that a subject with a certain access permission is capable of passing that permission (perhaps indirectly) on to any other subject (unless restricted by MAC) [1].

DAC, as the name implies, permits the granting and revocation of access permissions to be left to the discretion of the individual users. A DAC mechanism allows users to grant or revoke access to any of the objects under their control without the intercession of a system administrator.

For many enterprises within industry and civilian government, end users do not "own" the information to which they are allowed access as is assumed by DAC policies. For these organizations, the corporation or agency is the actual "owner" of system objects, and it may not be appropriate to allow users to give away access rights to the objects. With RBAC, access decisions are based on the roles individual users have as part of an organization. This includes the specification of duties, responsibilities, and qualifications. For example, the roles an individual associated with a hospital can assume include doctor, nurse, clinician, and pharmacist. Roles in a bank include teller, loan officer, and accountant. Roles can also apply to military systems; for example, target analyst, situation analyst, and traffic analyst are common roles in tactical systems. An RBAC policy is based on the functions or the actions that a user is allowed to perform within the context of an organization (referred to as either *privileges* or *permissions*). The users cannot normally pass their permissions on to other users at their discretion. For example, a doctor who may posses the permission to prescribe medication should not be able to pass that permission onto a clinician.

Security policy often supports higher level organizational objectives, such as maintaining and enforcing ethics pertaining to a judge's chambers, or the laws and respect for privacy associated with the diagnosis of ailments, treatment of disease, and the administering of medication within a hospital. To support such policies, a capability to centrally control and maintain access rights is required. The security administrator, not the users for which the policies apply, must diligently represent the organization in specifying the access policy over organizational resources.

As such, RBAC is sometimes described as a form of MAC in the sense that users are unavoidably constrained by and have no influence over the enforcement of the organization's protection policies. However, RBAC is different from TCSEC MAC. MAC is defined in the TCSEC as follows:

> A means of restricting access to objects based on the sensitivity (as represented by a label) of the information contained in the objects and the formal authorization (i.e., clearance) of subjects to information of such sensitivity [1].

As rationalized in the TCSEC, MAC supports DoD requirements and regulations pertaining to unauthorized access to classified information, and in particular to the protection of the confidentiality (reading or observing) of sensitive information. Systems that support MAC policies are concerned with the unlawful flow of information from a high level to a low level. As such, policy support is with respect to controlling reading and writing. However, control over write operations is only concerned with preventing the indirect unlawful observation of sensitive information, and not with its integrity (unauthorized modification or destruction).

With regard to RBAC controls, policies may pertain to issues of confidentiality or integrity, or both: "Who can perform what actions?"

To distinguish RBAC from the policy specifics of MAC, RBAC is often characterized as nondiscretionary access control. RBAC allows for the nondiscretionary enforcement of a variety of protection policies that can be tailored on an enterprise-by-enterprise basis. The policies enforced within a stand-alone or distributed system are the net result of the administrative configuration of various components of RBAC.

1.4 RBAC and the enterprise

RBAC has emerged as the primary alternative to MAC and DAC because it is much better suited to the needs of commercial users than these earlier models. This section introduces a simple economic model that demonstrates RBAC's cost effectiveness and then discusses how RBAC fits into a large organization.

1.4.1 Economics of RBAC

From a business perspective RBAC has the potential to offer several benefits. This includes greater administrative productivity in performing common authorization management functions. These administrative functions

1.4 RBAC and the enterprise

pertain to assigning permissions for new user access to resources (both new users and new resources), reviewing and selectively removing accesses that are no longer necessary (and potentially harmful) with respect to a user's change of job assignment, and the completeness and immediacy of the removal of permissions in the event of a user's separation from the enterprise. These same features have demonstrated their ability to increase user productivity by reducing the downtime between administrative events, where the enterprise would be deprived of productivity during the period when the user is unable to access system resources. There is usually a direct relationship between the cost of administration and the number of associations that must be managed in order to administer an access control policy: The larger the number of associations, the costlier and more error-prone access control administration. In most organizations, the use of RBAC reduces the number of associations that must be managed.

A simple economic model can be used to approximate the savings that results from using a role-based approach [28]. Job positions typically are occupied by more than one individual, and most positions require more than one permission in order for an individual in a job position to carry out the responsibilities of that position. One can describe the associations authorizing permissions to individuals who perform the responsibilities of a job position as an ordered pair consisting of a set of individuals and a set of permissions (U, P) where:

U = the set of individuals in a job position;
P = the set of permissions required to perform that job position.

The number of associations required to directly relate the individuals to those permissions is $|U| \cdot |P|$, where

$|U|$ = the number of individuals in the set U;
$|P|$ = the number of permissions in the set P.

In other words, for each individual in U, there is an association for each permission in P.

A role can be described as a set of permissions. Thus, the set P can refer to a role, or a job position whose user-role and role-permission associations are represented by the ordered pair (U, P). The number of user-role and role-permission associations required to authorize each user in the set U for each of the permissions in the set P where P represents a role is $|U| + |P|$ (i.e., an association with the role P for each individual in U and an association with the role P for each permission in P).

For a job position, if $|U| + |P| < |U| \cdot |P|$, then the administrative advantage of RBAC over relating users directly with permissions is realized for that job position. A sufficient condition for $|U|+|P|<|U|\cdot|P|$ is $|U|,|P|>2$, which is typically the case for most job positions in most organizations.

If n is the number of job positions within an organization, then the administrative advantage of RBAC is realized organizationwide when

$$\sum_{i}^{n}(|U_i|+|P_i|) < \sum_{i}^{n}(|U_i|\cdot|P_i|)$$

(Note that this is only an approximation, as users may frequently fill more than one role in an organization, and roles may be hierarchically related.)

In addition to cost savings due to greater administrative and user productivity, RBAC has the advantage of avoiding future expenses incurred through breaches of security or privacy policies. Because RBAC can map naturally to organizational and business structures, is more configurable then conventional identity-based access control mechanisms, and can be managed at an abstraction above and across the systems and applications for which it controls access, RBAC can enforce a greater number and type of access control policies. Depending on the type of RBAC deployment these policies can include the enforcement of *least privilege* (the time-honored administrative practice of assigning privileges to users' that are minimally necessary for the performance of duty), and separation-of-duty policies (thus avoiding situations that can lead to a conflict of interest). RBAC can also increase user productivity by allowing users greater access to more resources and the ability to better delegate administrative responsibility to customers and partners where possible.

1.4.2 Authorization management and resource provisioning

At the lowest level, administrators control user access rights through the creation and maintenance of ACLs on a system-by-system basis. ACLs specify, for each protected resource, a list of individual users, or groups composed of individual users, with their respective modes of access (e.g., read or write) to the resource. This use of ACLs has proved problematic for a variety of reasons. ACLs are tied to particular resources. ACLs further complicate matters because they are managed on a system-by-system basis. A large number of users, each with many privileges, imply a very large number of user-privilege associations that are spread over potentially large numbers of independently managed platforms and applications. Thus, when a user takes on different responsibilities within the enterprise, administering these changes entails a thorough review, resulting in the selective addition or deletion of the user's privileges, typically within numerous systems.

1.4 RBAC and the enterprise

Authorization management and resource provisioning tools, which typically incorporate RBAC, have been developed to assist administrators in dealing with these challenges.

Security administrators who manage users, resources, and privileges on more than one platform must perform many similar tasks on different systems. Because each system has its own proprietary administrative interface, even routine tasks require security administrators to have detailed knowledge of each type of security system. They spend valuable time logging on and off different security systems while performing each task locally.

As organizations grow, users typically require access to more and more systems, including one or more applications that the user interacts with on a daily basis, an e-mail server, systems used for occasional transactions such as entering travel reimbursements or managing retirement accounts, and possibly print servers, Web sites, and a host of other systems that require authorization. All of these systems require some form of authentication and access control, and they may be changed and updated independently of one another, making it difficult for users to keep their passwords consistent across all systems. Some organizations may explicitly require that users not use the same passwords for different systems, particularly if the systems vary in sensitivity. Managing authentication and access control across multiple systems is the key problem in authorization management.

Maintaining user IDs, role memberships, permissions, and the associations between roles and permissions are all tasks included in authorization management. In most cases, system administrators must deal with these problems on a daily basis, as organizations gain and lose employees, and jobs and permissions change within the organization. Managing permissions for a large number of applications is thus not only a problem for users; it represents an enormous challenge for enterprise system administrators.

Although there are many authorization management solutions to this challenge, they all provide a means of centralizing authorization information on a server. Broadly speaking, there are two common ways of dealing with the problem of centralizing authorization, as shown in Figures 1.7 and 1.8.

In the first approach, which has been termed *user pull* [29], the user is authenticated by the authorization server, obtains some sort of credential to access applications, and then presents the credentials as authorization to the applications. The second approach, termed *server pull* [29], requires applications to authenticate users, but centralizes information about user privileges on an authorization server. When a user attempts to invoke an application, the application queries the authorization server to determine the user's permissions.

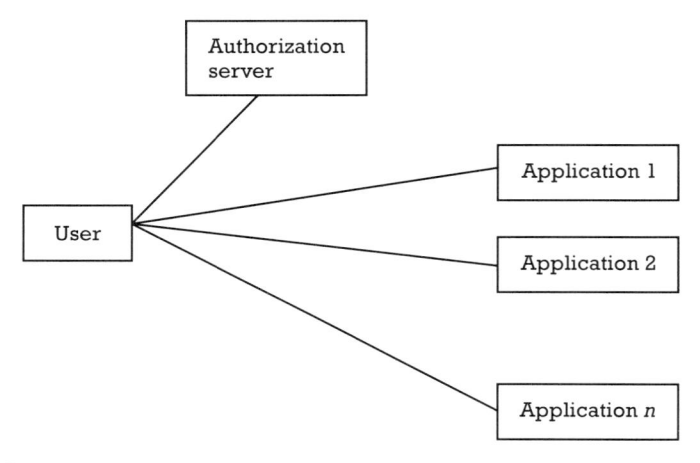

Figure 1.7 User-pull authorization architecture.

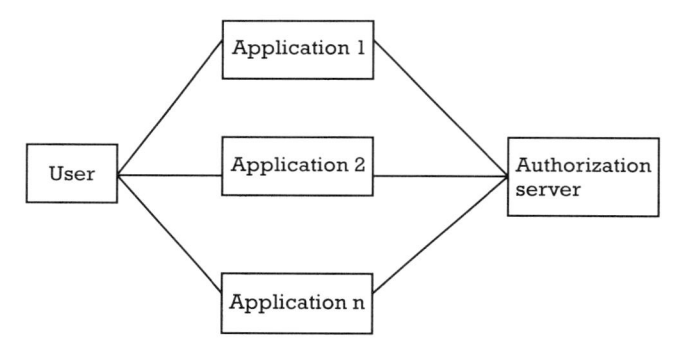

Figure 1.8 Server-pull authorization architecture.

Before users can begin accessing the applications they need to do their jobs, the organization must set up access permissions for them throughout the network. This is the problem of *resource provisioning.* In addition to thousands of employees, the company may need to establish permissions for contractors, business partners, and customers who access corporate data on the Internet. Equally important is the task of decommissioning permissions held by employees leaving the company. Surveys of corporations have found that current and prior employees are the top two sources of security breaches. Past employees are cited as a security problem nearly as often as current employees, because of the problem of deleting permissions after employees leave [30]. Creating and maintaining proper access permissions in a fast-changing business environment is a complex problem, which has led to the development of sophisticated tools typically costing from $600,000 to $800,000 [31]. Resource provisioning typically requires cooperation among computer systems from the corporate human resources, information systems, and a broad collection of other corporate departments depending on the user's job. If "Bob Smith" is hired, he must be given permissions for all the resources needed in his job. With conventional access control systems, this would mean assigning his user ID to every resource he will access. The direct linking of user with permission is not only time-consuming; it invariably leads to errors as user assignments change, resulting in users having permissions they should not have.

RBAC does not permit users to be directly associated with permissions. With RBAC, permissions are authorized for roles, and roles are authorized for users. The permissions that are authorized for a role may span multiple platforms and applications. Thus, when administering RBAC two different types of associations must be managed (i.e., associations between users and roles and associations between roles and permissions). When a user's job position changes, only the user-role associations change. If the job position is represented by a single role, then when a user's job position changes, there are only two user-role associations to change: To implement these changes, it is necessary to remove the association between the user and the user's current role and to add an association between the user and the user's new role. Complexities introduced by organizational hierarchies and constraints such as separation-of-duty requirements are hidden by the access control software. This conceptually simple approach is what gives RBAC its power and flexibility.

References

[1] DoD, *Trusted Computer System Evaluation Criteria* (TCSEC), DoD 5200.28-STD.

[2] Lampson, B. W., "Dynamic Protection Structures," *AFIPS Conference Proceedings*, 35, 1969, pp. 27–38.

[3] Ware, W. H., *Security Controls for Computer Systems (U): Report of Defense Science Board Task Force on Computer Security*, Santa Monica, CA: The RAND Corporation, February 1970.

[4] Anderson, J. P., *Computer Security Technology Planning Study Volume II*, ESD-TR-73-51, Electronic Systems Division, Air Force Systems Command, Hanscom Field, Bedford, MA, 01730, October 1972.

[5] Bell, D. E., and L. J. LaPadula, *Secure Computer Systems: Mathematical Foundations and Model*, Bedford, MA: The Mitre Corporation, 1973. *See also* D. E. Bell and

L. J. LaPadula, *Secure Computer System: Unified Exposition and MULTICS Interpretation*, MTR-2997 Rev. 1, Bedford, MA: The MITRE Corporation, March 1976, and ESD-TR-75-306, rev. 1, Electronic Systems Division, Air Force Systems Command, Hanscom Field, Bedford, MA 01731.

[6] Harrison, M., W. Ruzzo, and J. Ullman, *Protection in Operating Systems*, CACM 19, No. 8, August 1976, pp. 461–471.

[7] Clark, D. D., and D. R. Wilson, "A Comparison of Commercial and Military Computer Security Policies," *IEEE Symposium of Security and Privacy*, 1987, pp. 184–194.

[8] Dobson, J. E., and J. A. McDermid, "Security Models and Enterprise Models," in *Database Security II: Status & Prospects*, C. E. Landwehr (ed.), North Holland, 1989, pp. 1–39.

[9] Baldwin, R. W., "Naming and Grouping Privileges To Simplify Security Management in Large Database," in *Proceedings IEEE Computer Society Symposium on Research in Security and Privacy*, April 1990, pp. 184–194.

[10] Thomsen, D. J., "Role-Based Application Design and Enforcement," in *Database Security, IV: Status and Prospects*, S. Jajodia and C. E. Landwehr (eds.), North Holland, 1991, pp. 151–168.

[11] Brewer, D. F. C., and M. J. Nash, "The Chinese Wall Security Policy," *Proceedings IEEE Computer Society Symposium on Research in Security and Privacy*, April 1989, pp. 215–228.

[12] Nash, M., and K. Poland, "Some Conundrums Concerning Separation of Duty," presented at the *IEEE Symposium on Security and Privacy*, Oakland, CA, 1990.

[13] Ferraiolo, D., D. Gilbert, and N. Lynch, "An Examination of Federal and Commercial Access Control Policy Needs," in *Proceedings of the NIST-NSA National (USA) Computer Security Conference*, 1993, pp. 107–116.

[14] Ferraiolo, D., and D. R. Kuhn, "Role-Based Access Control," in *Proceedings of the NIST-NSA National (USA) Computer Security Conference*, 1992, pp. 554–563.

[15] Ferraiolo, D. F., J. Cugini, and D. R. Kuhn, "Role-Based Access Control (RBAC): Features and Motivations," in *Proceedings of the 11th Annual Computer Security Application Conference*, New Orleans, LA, December 11–15 1995, pp. 241–248.

[16] Sandhu, R. S., et al., "Role-Based Access Control: A Multidimensional View," *Proceedings of the 10th Annual Computer Security Applications Conference*, December 1994, pp. 54–62.

[17] Nyanchama, M., and S. L. Osborn, "Access Rights Administration in Role-Based Security Systems," *Proceedings of the IFIP WG11.3 Working Conference on Database Security*, 1994. See also M. Nyanchama and S. L. Osborn, "The Role Graph Model and Conflict of Interest," *ACM Transactions on Information and System* Security (TISSEC), Vol. 2, No. 1, February 1999, pp. 3–33.

1.4 RBAC and the enterprise

[18] Deinhart, K., et al., "Method and System for Advanced Role-Based Access Control in Distributed and Centralized Computer Systems," *U.S. Patent 5,911,143,* June 8, 1999.

[19] Sandhu, R., et. al., "Role-Based Access Control Models," IEEE COmputer, Vol. 29, No. 2, February 1996.

[20] Barkley, J. F., "Application Engineering in Health Care," *Second Annual CHIN Summit,* June 9, 1995.

[21] Barkley, J. F., and A. V. Cincotta. "Implementation of Role/Group Permission Association Using Object Access Type," *U.S. Patent 6,202,066,* 2002.

[22] Bertino, E., E. Ferrari, and V. Atluri, "A Flexible Model for the Specification and Enforcement of Authorizations in Workflow Management Systems," *2nd ACM Workshop on Role-Based Access Control,* November 1997.

[23] Sandhu, R., D. Ferraiolo, and R. Kuhn, "The NIST Model for Role-Based Access Control: Towards a Unified Standard," *Proc. 5th ACM Workshop on Role-Based Access Control,* July 26–27, 2000.

[24] U.S. Health Insurance Portability and Accountability Act of 1996 (HIPAA) at http://cms.hhs.gov/hipaa.

[25] Federal Aviation Administration, National Airspace System (NAS) Protection Profile Template Supplement, Version 1.0. http://www.faa.gov/aio/common/documents/NAS_PP_Supp_v1.pdf.

[26] Joshi, J., et al., "Digital Government Security Infrastructure Design Challenges," *IEEE Computer,* 33(2), February 2001, pp. 66–72.

[27] Joshi, J. B. D., et al., "Security Models for Web-Based Applications," *Communications of the ACM,* 44(2), February 2001, pp. 38–44.

[28] Ferraiolo, D. F., J. F. Barkley , and D. R. Kuhn, "A Role-Based Access Control Model and Reference Implementation Within a Corporate Intranet," *ACM Transactions on Information and System Security (TISSEC),* Vol. 2, No. 1, February 1999, pp. 34–64.

[29] Park, J. S., and R. Sandhu, "RBAC on the Web by Smart Certificates," *Proc. ACM Workshop on Role-Based Access Control 1999: 1–9,* New York: ACM Press.

[30] Daniels, J., "This is Not a Game: The Weakest Link," SANS Institute, August 9, 2001.

[31] Messmer, E., "Role-Based Access Control on a Roll," *Network World,* July 30, 2001 at http://www.nwfusion.com/news/2001/0727burton.html.

CHAPTER 2

Access Control Policy, Models, and Mechanisms—Concepts and Examples

Contents

2.1 Policy, models, and mechanisms

2.2 Subjects and objects

2.3 Reference monitor and security kernel

2.4 DAC policies

2.5 Access control matrix

2.6 MAC policies and models

2.7 Biba's integrity model

2.8 Clark-Wilson model

2.9 The Chinese wall policy

2.10 The Brewer-Nash model

2.11 Domain-type enforcement model

References

A knowledge of access control models, mechanisms, and concepts is essential in understanding how RBAC fits into the field of computer security. This chapter introduces these important concepts.

2.1 Policy, models, and mechanisms

While authentication mechanisms ensure that system users are who they claim to be, these mechanisms say nothing about what operations users should or should not perform within the system. To afford protection to that effect, it is necessary to use access control.

Access control is concerned with determining the allowed activities of legitimate users, mediating every attempt by a user to access a resource in the system. A given IT infrastructure can implement access control systems in many places and at different levels. Operating systems use access control to protect files and directories. Database management systems (DBMSs) apply access control to regulate access to tables and views. Most commercially available application systems implement access control, often independent of the operating system or DBMS, or both, on which they may be installed.

The objectives of an access control system are often described in terms of protecting system resources against inappropriate or undesired user access. From a business perspective, this objective could just as well be described in terms of the optimal sharing of information. After all, the greater objective of IT is to make information available to users and applications. A greater degree of sharing gives rise to increased productivity. Although on the surface, access control appears to get in the way of this objective, in reality, a well-managed and effective access control system actually facilitates sharing. A sufficiently fine-grained access control mechanism can enable selective sharing of information where in its absence, sharing may be considered too risky altogether.

When considering any access control system one considers three abstractions of control: access control policies, access control models, and access control mechanisms. Policies are high-level requirements that specify how access is managed and who, under what circumstances, may access what information. While access control policies may be application-specific and thus taken into consideration by the application vendor, policies are just as likely to pertain to user actions within the context of an organizational unit or across organizational boundaries. For instance, specific policies may pertain to the resources that can be accessed by consultancies, or other business partners. Such policies may span multiple computing platforms and applications. Policies may pertain to resource usage within or across organizational units or may be based on need-to-know, competence, authority, obligation, or conflict-of-interest factors. Although there are several well-known access control policies, generating such a list is of limited value, since business objectives, tolerance for risk, corporate culture, and the regulatory responsibilities that influence policy differ from enterprise to enterprise, and even from organizational unit to organizational unit. The access control policies within a hospital may pertain to privacy and competency (e.g., only doctors and nurse practitioners may prescribe medication), and hospital policies will differ greatly from those of a military system, or a financial institution. Even within a specific business domain, policy will differ from institution to institution. Furthermore, access control policies are dynamic in nature, in that they are likely to change over time in reflection of ever evolving business factors, government regulations, and environmental conditions. However, because policy requirements can rarely be completely determined in advance, access control systems are best designed to flexibly accommodate a wide variety of changing policies.

At a high level, access control policies are enforced through a mechanism that translates a user's access request often in terms of a simple table lookup—to grant or deny access. Access control mechanisms come in a wide variety of forms, each with distinct policy advantages and disadvantages. Although no well-accepted standard yet exists for determining their policy support, access control mechanisms can be characterized in a number of different ways, each bearing policy implications. In general, access control mechanisms require that security attributes be kept about users and resources. User security attributes consist of things like user identifiers, groups, and roles to which users belong, or they can include security labels reflecting the level of trust bestowed on the user. Resource attributes can take on a wide variety of forms. For example, they can consist of sensitivity labels, types, or access control lists. In determining the user's ability to perform operations on resources, access control mechanisms compare the user's security attributes to those of the resource. Access control checks can be determined (evaluated) based on a previously determined set of rules. For example, the security label of the user must be greater than or equal to the security label of the resource for the user to read the contents of the resource. Access control checks can also be determined based on an attribute-matching algorithm. The user may perform a read operation on a resource if the user's identity, and read operation pair is included in the access control list of the resource. Other characteristics of access control mechanisms include attribute review and management capabilities. For example, can the access control system determine the permissions that are associated with a user or the users that can access a resource, or better yet both? Who can specify permissions? Can permission specification be delegated, and if so, does delegation infer further delegation?

From a consumer's perspective, determining the policy implications of a given access control mechanism is a formidable task. The fact that most enterprises need to deal with a wide variety of access control mechanisms only compounds this problem.

To provide greater policy support and control, a number of enterprise management and resource-provisioning vendors offer administrative capabilities over the native access control mechanisms of file management, database management, applications, and host and network operating systems. The result is an access control management system, on top of an access control management system, on top of potentially still another access control system. What are the policy implications of this arrangement?

Rather than attempting to evaluate and analyze access control systems exclusively at the mechanism level, security models are usually written to describe the security properties of an access control system. Access control models are written at a level of abstraction to accommodate a wide variety of implementation choices and computing environments, while providing a conceptual framework for reasoning about the policies they support. Access control models are of general interest to both users and vendors. They bridge the rather wide gap in abstraction between policy and mechanism.

Models can be promoted for their support of policy, and mechanisms can be designed for their adherence to the properties of the model. Users see an access control model as an unambiguous and precise expression of requirements. Vendors and system developers see access control models as design and implementation requirements.

Access control models and mechanisms are often characterized in terms of their policy support. On one extreme an access control model may be rigid in its implementation of a single policy. On the other extreme, a security model will allow for the expression and enforcement of a wide variety of policies and policy classes. From the 1990s to the present, security researchers have sought to develop access control mechanisms and models that are largely independent of the policy for which they can be used. This is a generally considered to be a desirable objective in that it allows the use of a common mechanism for a wide variety of purposes.

2.2 Subjects and objects

There are many access control models and mechanisms, most of which are defined in terms of subjects and objects. A *subject* is a computer system entity that can initiate requests to perform an operation or series of operations on objects. The subjects may be users, processes, or domains: A domain is a protection environment in which a process executes. At some level of discourse, a subject is considered to be a process or task that operates on behalf of the user within a computing environment. An *object* is a system entity on which an operation can be performed. Within the context of an operating system, an object might represent a file, while within the context of a DBMS, an object might represent a table or a view. An executable image of a program residing in memory or stored on disk is considered to be an object; however, during its execution it becomes part of a process and, as such, is treated as part of the subject. Access to an object usually implies access to the information it contains, but it may pertain to an exhaustible system resource, such as a device. Other examples of objects include buffers, registers, blocks, pages, segments, file directories, programs, processors, and printers.

An object is an abstract concept that is useful for purposes of generically modeling access control approaches and describing access control mechanisms. However, from an enterprises' perspective, there are two types of objects: resource objects and system objects. *Resource objects* are the objects of general interest to the system's users and as such justify the very existence of the system. *System objects* are those objects that serve the system and that are merely necessary for its correct operation. It is because of the sensitivity of resource objects that system objects need to be protected.

In many situations a subject can be thought of as a user, but within a computer system, a subject is more precisely defined as a process or a collection of processes that act on a user's behalf. Although users can typically be considered human beings, users can also represent other requesting entities such as machines or devices. It is imperative that all subjects have unique identifiers. For instance, subjects acting on behalf of human users may inherit the user's ID obtained through the identification and authentication process. However, a user may sign onto the system as different subjects depending on which resources and applications the user wishes to access. For instance, a user may have a need to invoke multiple applications. Under these circumstances, two or more subjects would correspond to the same user. Because a subject can invoke or create other subjects, subjects can be represented as objects where the children subjects may be executed across platforms or applications, or both.

2.3 Reference monitor and security kernel

Since its introduction in the "Anderson Report" [1], the *Reference Monitor* concept has served the security community in two ways. First, it provides an abstract model of the necessary properties in achieving a high-assurance access control mechanism. Second, it has been used as guidance in the design, development, and implementation and subsequent analyses of secure IT systems.

The reference monitor (see Figure 2.1) is an abstract concept, whereby all accesses that subjects make to objects are authorized based on the information contained in an access control database. Conceptually, the reference monitor represents the hardware and software portion of an operating system that is responsible for the enforcement of the security policy of the system. The access control database is the embodiment of this policy in terms of subject and object attributes and access rights. When a subject attempts to perform an operation (e.g., read or write) on an object, the reference monitor must perform a check, comparing the attributes of the subject with that of the object. In addition, the reference monitor, with respect to some security policy, must control the specific checks that are made and all modifications to the access control database.

As an abstraction, the reference monitor does not dictate any specific policy to be enforced by the system, nor does it address any particular implementation. Rather, the reference monitor defines an assurance framework

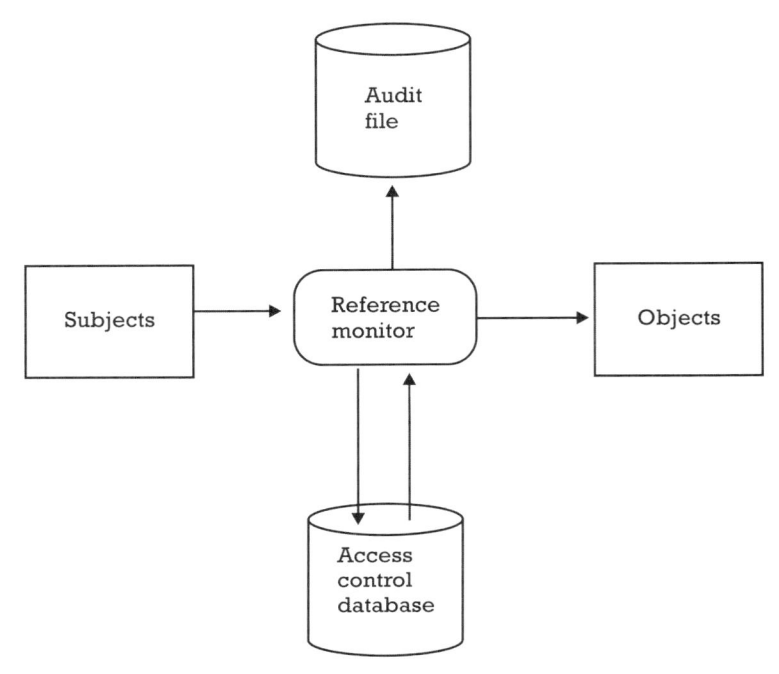

Figure 2.1 Reference monitor: All attempts by a subject to access an object are controlled by the reference monitor in accordance with a security policy embodied in the access control database. Security-relevant events are stored in the audit file.

that has been used for over 3 decades in the design, development, and implementation of highly secure IT systems, and it has served as the foundation in evaluation of the relative degrees of trust that can be assigned to a multiuser computing system.

The abstract requirements of a reference monitor are comprised of three fundamental implementation principles, described as follows:

- *Completeness:* It must be always invoked and impossible to bypass.
- *Isolation:* It must be tamper-proof.
- *Verifiability:* It must be shown to be properly implemented.

These principles provide architectural guidance pertaining to the design and development process of an access control system. The degree to which a system complies with these design principles has served as a metric for measuring the level of confidence in the correctness of the system's security controls.

2.3 Reference monitor and security kernel

2.3.1 Completeness

The completeness principle requires that a subject can reference an object only by invoking the reference monitor. Although this principle may seem intuitive—and although it might be expected that any reasonable operating system would meet this requirement—few if any mainstream operating systems completely adhere to this principle. The difficulty in meeting the absolute meaning of this principle stems from two issues. The first issue is what are considered to be the objects in the system. In general, objects are interpreted to be any system entities that can store information. Obvious places where information may be stored include files, directories, memory, and buffers. Most operating systems make reasonable attempts at controlling access to these resources. However, there is a wide variety of not so obvious places where information such as file names, segments, processors, and status and error messages and registers are stored. The completeness principle requires that all objects must be protected—not just the obvious ones.

The second architectural challenge pertaining to the completeness principle is the prevention of access to objects through methods (documented or otherwise) other than through the invocation of the policy-preserving access checker. For example, a subject could bypass a file system and issue a read request directly to the physical location of a file on disk. Access control is a basic function of not only operating systems; it is included within DBMSs and other large application programs. How does the DBMS prevent its objects (e.g., table and views) from being accessed through the underlying operating system? How do operating systems prevent objects that are under the control of the file management system from being accessed through lower-level kernel functions?

2.3.2 Isolation

The isolation principle states that the access mediation function is tamper-proof. It must be impossible for a penetrator to attack the access mediation mechanism in a manner that affects the proper performance of access checks. Even though most resource management systems are designed to protect themselves against accidental and overt break-in attempts, meeting the absolute requirements of the isolation principle of the reference monitor usually requires a security architecture consisting of both hardware and software features.

The implementation of a security kernel (Figure 2.2) is one way to achieve this isolation. The security kernel is a minimal implementation of the security-relevant features of the system. The security kernel is implemented as a primitive operating system function responsible for the

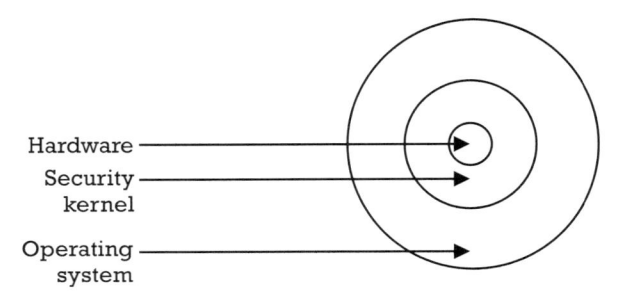

Figure 2.2 Multidomain architecture: The security kernel is an interface layer on top of hardware and controls operating system and user code and date.

enforcement of security policy. It is implemented on top of the hardware base and beneath non-security-relevant operating system functions in a domain of its own execution. Systems typically achieve this isolation using the same hardware features that are commonly used to prevent user programs from corrupting operating system code and data. The security kernel runs in the most privileged domain and has access to all memory and instructions, while the less privileged domains have access to only a portion of memory and a subset of system instructions. The important security feature is that the kernel executes in the most privileged domain and is thus protected from the code that is executed in the outer two rings. Although a process may run in any one of these domains at any moment in time, when the process is running in a given domain, that process is protected from corruption by other processes through process isolation mechanisms.

Since human programmers create process isolation features as well as all other security-relevant software, kernel code is subject to flaws and thus must be verified to be correct. This brings us to the third principle of the reference monitor.

2.3.3 Verifiability

The principle of verifiability is met through software engineering practices and design criteria. The idea is that the security kernel is made as small and simple as possible, by excluding any functionality for which the security of the system is not dependent, and by reducing the kernel to a small set of clean kernel interfaces. This is made possible through the use of sound software engineering practices. For instance, the security kernel should make use of modularity, abstract specification, and information hiding. Since the ultimate goal is to demonstrate the correctness of the kernel, thorough code inspections and positive and negative testing are critical. In extreme cases, formal mathematical modeling, formal specification, and verification techniques are applied in an attempt to prove the correctness of the kernel's implementation.

2.3.4 The reference monitor—necessary, but not sufficient

The reference monitor concept does not charge a system with enforcing any particular access control policy. It is the job of enterprises to articulate these requirements for their computer systems. From an assurance perspective, the design principles of the reference monitor should be viewed as a necessary prelude to assurance, but the reference monitor is not sufficient. Even if all vendors were to rigorously adhere to the design principles of the reference monitor, most enterprises have little control over what policies are supported by the products they buy. Essentially, consumers are forced to make do with the policy and access control management decisions of their vendors. This book introduces three additional design principles that are viewed by its authors as critical components of any access control system. These principles are described as follows:

- *Flexibility:* The system should be able to enforce the access control policies of the host enterprise.
- *Manageability:* The system should be intuitive and easy to manage.
- *Scalability:* The system's management and enforcement functions should scale to the number of users and the number of resources that are scattered across the computing platforms of the host enterprise.

By inserting these additional principles, we acknowledge that an access control system consists of more than a robust access mediation function, and includes the properties of policy configuration, ease of use, and, to some extent, interoperability.

2.4 DAC policies

DAC is a means of restricting access to objects based on the identity of users or the groups to which they belong, or both. The controls are discretionary in the sense that a user or subject given discretionary access to a resource is capable of passing that information along to another subject. To provide this discretionary control, DAC mechanisms usually include a concept of object ownership, where the object's "owner" has control permission to grant access permission to the object for other subjects. This definition of DAC has its origins with the TCSEC [2] and is rationalized based on the DoD's regulatory requirements for need-to-know access to classified or sensitive information: "... no person may have access to classified information unless ... access is necessary for the performance of official duties." By far the most common mechanism for implementing DAC policies is through the use of ACLs.

DAC mechanisms tend to be very flexible and are widely used in commercial and government sectors. Throughout the mid 1980s and 1990s, many organizations considered DAC mechanisms to be the standard of due care. During this period virtually every computer vendor demonstrated DAC compliance by undergoing a C2 TCSEC (discretionary protection) evaluation.

Even though DAC mechanisms are in wide commercial use today, they are known to be inherently weak for two reasons: First, granting read access is transitive. For example, when Chris grants Frank read access to a file, nothing stops Frank from copying the contents of Chris's file to an object that Frank controls. Frank may now grant any other user access to the copy of Chris's file unbeknownst to Chris. Second, DAC mechanisms are vulnerable to "Trojan horse" attacks. Because programs inherit the identity of the invoking user, Frank may, for example, write a program for Chris that, on the surface, performs some useful function, while at the same time reads the contents of Chris's files and writes the contents of the files to a location that is accessible by both Chris and Frank. Frank may then move the contents of the files to a location not accessible to Chris. Note that Frank's Trojan horse program could have destroyed the contents of Chris's files. When investigating the problem, the audit files would indicate that Chris destroyed his own files. What a dope!

2.5 Access control matrix

Many systems use Lampson's access control matrix [3] to represent and interpret the particular security policy. From a theoretical perspective, the access control matrix has traditionally been used to represent the secure state of an access control system. The access matrix is an array containing one row per subject in the system and one column per object. Table 2.1 illustrates a simple access control matrix. The entries in the matrix specify the operations of, or the type of access that each subject has to, each object. The basic function of an access control system is to ensure that only the operations specified by the matrix can be executed.

2.5 Access control matrix

Table 2.1 Example Access Control Matrix

Subject/Object	File_1	File_2	File_3	Process_1
Chris	Read, write	—	Write	—
Janet	—	Execute	—	Suspend
Barbara	—	Read	Read	—
Frank	Read	—	—	—

Although an access control matrix is an interesting construct from a theoretical perspective, for a system with a large number of users and objects, the matrix will become very large and will be sparsely populated. As such, an access control system is rarely implemented as a matrix but is almost always implemented as a representation of the matrix. There are two primary representations of the access control matrix as implemented in computer systems today: ACLs and capability lists.

2.5.1 ACLs and capability lists

In a capability system, access to an object is allowed if the subject that is requesting access possesses a capability for the object. A capability is a protected identifier that both identifies the object and specifies the access rights to be allowed to the accessor who possesses the capability. In a capability-based system, access to protected objects is granted to the would-be accessor possesses a capability for the object. This approach corresponds to storing the matrix by rows. Table 2.2 presents the capability lists corresponding to the access control matrix. Each subject is associated with a capability list, which stores its approved operations to all concerned objects. A subject possessing a capability is proof of the subject having the access privileges. The principle advantage of capabilities is that it is easy to review all accesses that are authorized for a given subject. On the other hand, it is difficult to review

Table 2.2 Capability List

Subject		
Chris	File_1: Read, Write	File_3: Write
Janet	File_2: Execute	Process_1: Suspend
Barbara	File_2: Read	File_3: Read
Frank	File_1: Read	

the subjects that can access a particular object. To do so would entail an examination of each and every capability list. It is also difficult to revoke access to an object given the need for a similar examination. For this reason, capability lists have been criticized in their support of DAC policies and therefore not commercially popular.

ACLs implement the access control matrix by representing the columns as lists of users attached to a protected object. Each object is associated with an ACL that stores the subjects and the subject's approved operations for the object. The list is checked by the access control system to determine if access is granted or denied. Table 2.3 presents the ACLs corresponding to the access control matrix in Table 2.1.

The principal advantage of ACLs is that they make it easy to review the users that have access to an object as well as the operations that users can apply to the object. In addition, it is easy to revoke access to an object by simply deleting an ACL entry. These advantages make ACLs ideal for implementing DAC policies that are object-oriented. Another advantage is that the lists need not be excessively long, if groups of users with common accesses to the object are attached to the object instead of the group's individual members. Although the use of groups adds the need for additional administrative functions for managing membership within groups, the availability of groups generally makes the administration of ACLs more efficient. Generally speaking, the creation and management of groups should be strictly controlled, since becoming a member of a group can change the objects accessible to any member.

2.5.2 Protection bits

A DAC mechanism familiar to most users is the implementation of protection bits that are commonly included in UNIX operating systems. Protection bit mechanisms are similar to ACLs; however, instead of associating users

Table 2.3 ACL

Object		
File_1	Chris: Read, write	Frank: Read
File_2	Janet: Execute	Barbara: Read
File_3	Chris: Write	Barbara: Read
Process_1	Janet: Suspend	

and operation entries, bits are associated with an object. Protection bits divide users into three categories, described as follows:

- *Self:* The owner of a file;
- *Group:* A collection of users sharing common access to a file;
- *Other:* Everyone else besides the owner or the group members.

The access control system regulates access to a file by associating read (r), write (w), or execute (x) operations with each of these categories of users. For example, assume that a file has the following protection bits:

```
(rwx) (r-x) (--x)
```

This string of bits indicates that self (the owner) has read, write, and execute permission to the file; the members of the group that is associated with the object have read and execute permission to the file; and all other system users have execute permission to the file. Note that the "–" marking indicates that the corresponding operation indicator is not present, thereby effectively denying the associated categories of users that particular operation on the file.

The user who created the file, by default, becomes the owner of the file. The owner of the file is typically the only one besides the superuser who can modify the protection bits.

Also note that there is only one group that is available for each file. The system administrator controls group memberships, so that as membership within these groups changes so will the capabilities of users to access files.

One problem with the protection bits method is that it is an access control mechanism that does not completely correspond to the access control matrix—thus, the system cannot accurately grant access to an object on an individual basis. For this reason many newer versions of UNIX and UNIX-like operating systems include ACL mechanisms.

2.6 MAC policies and models

In addition to DAC policies, the TCSEC defines MAC policies that are known to prevent the Trojan horse problem. With regard to this policy, security levels are assigned to users, with subjects acting on behalf of users and objects. Security levels have a hierarchical and a nonhierarchical component. For instance the hierarchical components might include unclassified (U), confidential (C), secret (S), and top-secret (TS) while the nonhierarchical components may include NATO and NUCLEAR. The security levels are partially ordered under a dominance relation, often written as "≥". For example, `TS ≥ S ≥ C ≥ U` and `S (NATO, NUCLEAR) ≥ S (NUCLEAR) ≥ S`. The security level of the user, often referred to as the user's clearance level, reflects the level of trust bestowed to the user and must always dominate the security levels that are assigned to the user's subjects. For example, Chris who is cleared to the `S (NUCLEAR)` level may initiate sessions at the `S (NUCLEAR), S, C, or U` levels. The security levels that are assigned to objects reflect the sensitivity of the contents of the objects.

Bell-Lapadula model With respect to the security level of a subject and the security level of an object, the Bell-LaPadula model [4] defines access control decisions in accordance with two properties:

- *Simple security property:* A subject is permitted read access to an object if the subject's security level dominates the security level of the object.
- *Star property:* A subject is permitted write access to an object if the object's security level dominates the security level of the subject.

Satisfaction of these properties prevents users from being able to read information that dominates (i.e., is above) their clearance level. The simple security property directly supports this policy, never allowing a subject to read information that dominates the invoking user's clearance level. The star property supports the MAC policy indirectly, by disallowing subjects from writing information of level x into a container (contents of an object) that could be subsequently read by a subject with a security level that is dominated by x. Intuitively, the star property prevents high information from ending up in a low container where a low user could read it.

With respect to the Bell-LaPadula model it is important to distinguish a user from her or his subjects. To illustrate this point consider a user Ralph, who is cleared to the top-secret level. Ralph's *range of capabilities* includes the ability to read and write all objects for which his clearance level dominates. Ralph's subjects, on the other hand, do not enjoy this same freedom. Although we can trust Ralph not to leak top-secret information, we are not able to levy such trust on Ralph's subjects because subjects are typically computer programs, which may be compromised. Therefore, for Ralph to successfully write to an object at, for example, the secret level, Ralph must adjust his session to a level that is dominated by the secret security level of the object (see Figure 2.3).

Now consider the case where Frank, who is cleared at the confidential level, wishes to steal secret nuclear instructions using the same Trojan horse

2.7 Biba's integrity model

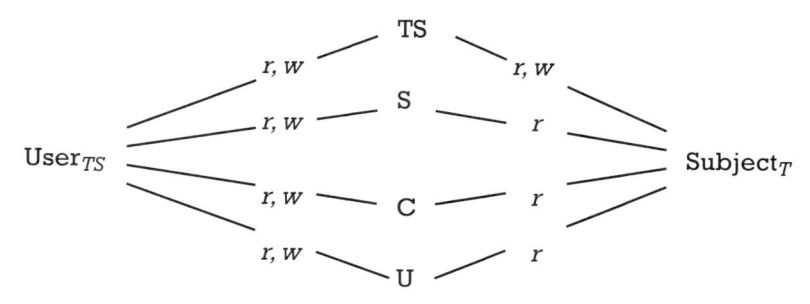

Figure 2.3 User's range of capabilities versus subject's permitted accesses.

program that he used to steal Chris's files. Frank once again tricks Chris [who is cleared S, (NUCLEAR)], into invoking his malicious software, this time while invoking a S (NUCLEAR) session. Although Frank's Trojan horse will be able to successfully read the S(NUCLEAR) instructions, under the simple security property, the Trojan horse will fail in its attempt to write the instructions to a location that is accessible to Frank. Note, however, that Frank's malicious program may still destroy any of Chris's files that are labeled at Chris's session level or above. If Chris invokes Frank's software during an unclassified session, Frank, or more accurately speaking, Frank's program, is able to destroy all of Chris's files.

2.7 Biba's integrity model

Even though the Bell-LaPadula security model controls the writing of information, its policy is to protect confidentiality (read protection). The multi-level security policy does nothing to prevent unauthorized modification of information. Soon after the Bell-LaPadula security model was introduced, users quickly recognized that there was a need for a model with a property similar to the star property to prevent a process at a higher security level from reading lower-level objects without being negatively affected by information at the lower security level.

The Biba integrity model [5] was introduced in 1977 not as an alternative but as an adjunct to the Bell-LaPadula model. As the Bell-LaPadula model pertains exclusively to confidentiality issues while ignoring integrity issues, the Biba model (a dual of the Bell-LaPadula model) addresses integrity issues while sacrificing confidentiality. Under Biba, read and write restrictions are based on integrity levels (consisting of a hierarchical and categorical component) assigned to subjects and objects. The integrity level associated with a user indicates the user's level of trust regarding modification of information at that level, and the integrity level associated with an object reflects the object's sensitivity regarding its modification. For example, these may include critical (C), important (I), and ordinary (O). The properties of the Biba model are similar to the Bell-LaPadula model except that the dominance relations controlling read and write are reversed. These relations are described as follows:

- *Simple integrity property:* A subject is permitted read access to an object if the object's security level dominates the security level of the subject.
- *Integrity star property:* A subject is permitted write access to an object if the subject's security level dominates the security level of the object.

In compliance with the properties of this model, writes from lower levels are prohibited, as are reads from higher levels to lower levels.

2.8 Clark-Wilson model

While the TCSEC did a great deal to spur research and development of computer security products, most of the commercial world recognized that it was of limited benefit for their operations. Clark and Wilson documented the differences between commercial and military security requirements in detail in 1987 [6], arguing that the primary concern for most commercial applications is integrity, rather than secrecy. For example, the 600-year-old principle of double-entry bookkeeping helps to ensure the accuracy and integrity of accounts by requiring that every credit entry be matched by a debit entry to ensure a balance between the source and destination of funds. Integrity in the computer security context refers to the accuracy and authenticity of information, as well as the need to ensure that objects are modified only in authorized ways by authorized personnel.

Clark and Wilson documented a generalized view of commercial security policies, showing how they differed from the military-oriented policies that are the focus of the TCSEC. They proposed two principles as most important in ensuring information integrity: well-formed transactions and SoD. Well-formed transactions constrain the ways in which users can modify data, thus ensuring that all data that starts in a valid state will remain so after the execution of a transaction. The basic unit of access control in the Clark-Wilson model is the "access control triple," composed of *user, transformation procedure,* and *constrained data item* (see Figure 2.4).

2.8 Clark-Wilson model

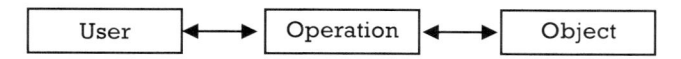

Figure 2.4 Clark-Wilson access control triple.

A transformation procedure (TP) is a transaction, and a constrained data item (CDI) is one for which integrity must be preserved. Unconstrained data items (UDIs) are those that are not protected by the integrity model. Integrity verification procedures (IVPs) ensure that a data item is in a valid state. Clark and Wilson proposed nine rules to ensure the integrity of data. They are described as follows:

1. For any CDI, there must also be an IVP that ensures that the data item is in a valid state.
2. Every TP that modifies a CDI must be certified to modify CDIs only in valid ways.
3. A CDI can only be modified by a certified TP.
4. Every TP must be certified to log its changes to CDIs.
5. Every TP that takes input from a UDI must be certified to ensure that it will transform UDIs to CDIs only in valid ways.
6. Only certified TPs can modify UDIs.
7. A user can access CDIs only through TPs for which the user is authorized.
8. Every user must be authenticated by the system before executing a TP.
9. Only a security administrator can authorize users for TPs.

Unlike the Bell-LaPadula security model, which relies on access mediation in the operating system kernel, Clark and Wilson's approach relies on application-level controls. This difference in design results from the goals of the two models. The military multilevel security model seeks to control information flow, which can be defined in terms of low-level read and write operations. The commercial integrity model, as defined by Clark and Wilson, must ensure that information is modified only in authorized ways by authorized people, a requirement that is impossible to meet using only control over kernel-level operations. The importance of control over transactions, as opposed to simple read and write access, can be seen by considering typical banking transactions. Tellers may execute a savings deposit transaction, requiring read and write access to specific fields within a savings file and a transaction log file. An accounting supervisor may be able to execute correction transactions, requiring exactly the same read-and-write access to the same files as the teller. The difference is the process executed and the values written to the transaction log file.

SoD is another major component of the Clark and Wilson model that contributes to integrity, preventing authorized users from making improper modifications. This goal is achieved indirectly by separating all operations into multiple subparts and requiring that a different person perform each subpart. The process of purchasing and paying for some item, for example, might involve authorizing a purchase order, recording the arrival of the item, recording the arrival of the invoice, and authorizing payment. The last step should not be performed unless the previous three have occurred. If a different person performs each step, improper modification should be detected and reported, unless some of these people conspire. If one person can execute all of these steps, then fraud is possible—an order is placed and payment made to a fictitious company without any actual delivery of an item. In such a case, the books appear to balance; the error is in the correspondence between real and recorded inventory.

2.9 The Chinese wall policy

The Chinese wall policy is simple and easy to describe; however, as we will see, its implementation and deployment is less straightforward. Brewer and Nash [7] identified the policy to address conflict-of-interest issues related to the consulting activities within banking and other financial disciplines. Like Clark-Wilson, the Chinese wall policy is application-specific in that it applies to a narrow set of activities that are tied to specific business transactions. The stated objective of the Chinese wall policy is to prevent illicit flows of information that can result in a conflict of interest. Consultants naturally are given access to proprietary information to provide a service for their clients. When a consultant gains access, for example, to the competitive practices of two banks, the consultant gains knowledge—amounting to insider information—that can undermine the competitive advantage of one or both institutions or that can be used for personal profit. The objective of the Chinese wall policy is to identify and prevent the possibility for the flow of information that can give rise to such conflicts.

Company-sensitive information is categorized into mutually disjoint conflict-of-interest categories (COIs). Each company belongs to only one COI, and each COI has two or more member companies. The membership within a COI includes like companies, whereby a consultant obtaining sensitive information regarding one company would risk a conflict of interest if he or she were to obtain sensitive information in regard to another. Several COIs may coexist. For example, COI_1 may pertain to banks, while COI_2 may pertain to energy companies. The Chinese wall policy aims to prevent a consultant from reading information for more than one company in any given COI.

There are several observations that we can make regarding this policy with respect to read operations: First, as long as a consultant has not read information belonging to any institution, the consultant is not yet bound by the policy and is free to read any sensitive information of any institution. Note that although a consultant may be free to read sensitive information under the Chinese wall policy, she or he may be restricted from reading sensitive information with respect to another policy—say a DAC policy. Second, once a consultant has read sensitive information of say, bank *A*, the consultant is prohibited from reading sensitive information belonging to any other bank included in the COI of which bank *A* is a member. Third, all consultants are free to read all the public information of all institutions.

As is evident, the Chinese wall policy is relatively straightforward regarding read operations. We now consider the implications of write operations with respect to this policy as defined in the Brewer-Nash model.

2.10 The Brewer-Nash model

This model views data as objects, each belonging to a company dataset. The company datasets are further categorized into COIs.

Similar to Bell-LaPadula, Brewer-Nash defines two rules, one for reading and one for writing. Under the read rule, subject *S* can read object *O* only if one of the following is true:

- *O* is in the same company dataset as some object previously read by *S*.
- *O* belongs to a COI class for which *S* has yet to read an object.

Under the write rule, subject *S* can write object *O* only if the following are true:

- S can read O under the read rule.
- No object can be read within a different company dataset than the one for which write access is requested.

Note that the Brewer-Nash rules do not make a distinction between users and subjects, as does the Bell-LaPadula model, but instead recognizes subjects to include both users and the processes that are acting on behalf of the user. However, similar to Bell-LaPadula, the Brewer-Nash rule for writing takes into consideration the possibility of a Trojan horse.

In illustrating the need for the write rule, consider the case in which Chris has read access to energy company *A* objects and read and write access to bank *A* objects, and Frank has read access to energy company *A* and bank *B* objects. A Trojan horse program running with Chris's privileges may read bank *A* objects and write to energy company *B* objects, giving Frank read access to both bank *A* and bank *B* objects.

It is also interesting to note the temporal differences between these two models. With respect to Bell-LaPadula, the policies regarding reading and writing are applied within the life span of a subject-user session. With respect to the Brewer-Nash model, the policy regarding reading applies for the life of the user. Once a user reads an object from a company data set, the user is forever precluded from reading an object from the data set of another company belonging to the same COI.

2.11 Domain-type enforcement model

The domain-type enforcement (DTE) model is an abstraction of the concepts involved in the DTE mechanism. The DTE mechanism [8], in turn, is an enhanced type enforcement (TE) mechanism, which is a table-oriented access control mechanism, developed by Boebert and Kain in the 1980s [9] in support of the Bell-LaPadula MAC model. In particular the DTE mechanism has been used in firewalls [10] and operating systems [11] and has been shown to support a variety of security policies expressible through RBAC models [12].

The DTE model, like many other access control models, divides the computerized system into two logical entities: subjects and objects. Subjects are active entities (usually processes). Objects are passive entities (e.g., files, directories, devices, and memory segments). A domain is associated with a subject. A type is associated with an object. The assignment of a "domain" label for a subject generally depends upon its function (e.g., a business process transaction). An object is assigned a type based on its integrity

2.11 Domain-type enforcement model

requirements. Access control permissions are associated with both domains and types. This gives rise to two groups of permissions: domain-domain permissions and domain-type permissions. Each of these two groups of permissions is represented using corresponding table types. The domain-domain access control table (DDAT) is a two-dimensional table with an entry for each ordered pair of domains. Similarly, the domain-type access control table (DTAT) is a two-dimensional table with an entry for each (domain, type) pair. Since there can be more than one permission associated with a domain-domain pair or domain-type pair, each entry in these tables contains a set of the permissions. All the entries in these two types of tables together constitute the DTE database for an environment.

Examples of domain-domain permissions (in the context of a UNIX operating system) are create (C) and kill (K). Examples of domain-type permissions are read (R), write (W), execute (E), and browse directory (T). The semantics of domain-type permissions should be self-evident. The domain-domain permissions are created to express allowed interactions between subjects. For example, a subject *A* (process *A*) can create an instance of another process (process B) only if there exists a create entry between subject A's domain and subject B's domain.

The DDAT and DTAT tables in DTE are conceptually similar to the access control matrix described in Section 2.5. However, DTE considerably reduces table entries by grouping subjects into domains and objects into types before specifying access control permissions.

Several comparisons can be made between the concepts of the DTE model and the RBAC model. RBAC ties users to roles and describes how a role limits the operations available to a user. DTE ties subjects to domains and describes how a domain limits the operations available to a subject. It is these similarities in concepts that have been utilized by Hoffman [12] to implement RBAC-expressible policies in the DTE-based secure operating system LOCK. Specifically RBAC model entities have been mapped to DTE model entities and the underlying DTE mechanism then facilitates implementation of the RBAC policy. Hoffman's implementation takes a set of roles, a set of users, and user-role assignments and links them to DTE model entities like subjects and domains. Each subject is assigned a role, and users are associated with a subject. For every subject, the role of the subject must be an authorized role for the subject's user. Similarly, a set of domains is associated with a role. Since a subject is already associated with a role, the domain of a subject should be in the set of domains authorized for the role. Thus, by constraining subject-role association and user-subject association using the user-role assignments of the RBAC model and by constraining the subject-domain association using the role-domain assignment, a DTE model can be made to implement the policies represented by an RBAC model. Furthermore, the abstract set of permissions associated with a role takes a concrete form when roles are assigned to domains, since the domains in a DTE model encapsulate the processes relevant to a platform (e.g., daemons, file systems, and system utilities in an operating system). Since domains are associated with other domains and object types through DDAT and DTAT table entries, the specification of permissions associated with a role becomes complete.

References

[1] Anderson, J. P., *Computer Security Technology Planning Study*, Volume II, ESD-TR-73-51, Electronic Systems Division, Air Force Systems Command, Hanscom Field, Bedford, MA, 01730 (October 1972).

[2] DoD National Computer Security Center, *Department of Defense Trusted Computer Systems Evaluation Criteria*, December 1985, DoD 5200.28-STD.

[3] Lampson, B., "Protection," *ACM Operating Sys. Reviews*, 8(1), 1974, pp. 18–24.

[4] Bell, D. E., and L. J. LaPadula, *Secure Computer Systems: Mathematical Foundations and Model*, Bedford, MA: The Mitre Corporation, 1973. *See also* D. E. Bell and L. J. LaPadula, *Secure Computer System: Unified Exposition and MULTICS Interpretation*, MTR-2997 Rev. 1, Bedford, MA: The MITRE Corporation, March 1976; also ESD-TR-75-306, rev. 1, Electronic Systems Division, Air Force Systems Command, Hanscom Field, Bedford, MA, 01731.

[5] Biba, K. J., *Integrity Considerations for Secure Computer Systems*, Bedford, MA: The MITRE Corporation, 1977.

[6] Clark, D. D., and D. R. Wilson "A Comparison of Commercial and Military Computer Security Policies," *IEEE Symposium of Security and Privacy*, 1987, pp. 184–194.

[7] Brewer, D., and M. Nash, "The Chinese Wall Security Policy," *Proc. IEEE Computer Society Symposium on Research in Security and Privacy*, April 1989, pp. 215–228.

[8] Badger, L., et al., "A Domain and Type Enforcement Prototype," *Usenix Computing Systems*, Volume 9, Cambridge, MA, 1996.

[9] Boebert, W., and R. Kain, "A Practical Alternative to Hierarchical Integrity Policies," *Proceedings of the 8th National Computer Security Conference*, October 1985.

[10] Ostendorp, K. A., et al., "Domain and Type Enforcement Firewalls," *DARPA Information Survivability Conference and Exposition*, 2000, DISCEX '00, Vol. 1, 1999, pp. 351–361.

2.11 Domain-type enforcement model

[11] Tidswell, J., and J. Potter, *An Approach to Dynamic Domain and Type Enforcement,* Microsoft Research Institute, Department of Computing, Macquarie University, NSW, Australia, 2000.

[12] Hoffman, J., "Implementing RBAC on a Type-Enforced system," *Proceedings of the 13th Annual Computer Security Applications Conference,* December 1997.

CHAPTER 3

Core RBAC Features

Contents

3.1 Roles versus ACL groups

3.2 Core RBAC

3.3 Mapping the enterprise view to the system view

The RBAC security model is both abstract and general. It is abstract, because properties that are not relevant to security are not included, and it is general because many designs could be considered valid interpretations of the model. Thus, the model is usable as a basis for the design of a variety of IT systems.

The RBAC model described here and in the next two chapters is sufficient to support a variety of security policies. In particular, an argument is made for least privilege and SoD. Least privilege is the time-honored administrative practice of selectively assigning privileges to users such that the user is given no more privilege than is necessary to perform his or her job function. The principle of least privilege avoids the problem of an individual having the ability to perform unnecessary and potentially harmful actions merely as a side effect of gaining the ability to perform desired functions. Permissions (or privileges) are rights granted to an individual, or subject acting on behalf of a user, that enable the holder of those rights to act in the system within the bounds of those rights. The question then becomes how to assign the set of system privileges to the aggregates of functions or duties that correspond to a role of a user. Least privilege provides a rationale for installing the separation boundaries that are to be provided by RBAC protection and management mechanisms. Ensuring adherence to the principle of least privilege is largely an administrative challenge that requires the identification of job functions, the specification of the set of privileges required to perform each function, and the restriction of the user to a domain with those privileges and nothing more.

SoD refers to the partitioning of tasks and associated privileges among different roles associated with a single user to prevent users from colluding with one another. These separation concepts include multiplexing shared resources, naming distinctive sets of permissions to include functional decomposition, categorically classifying users, and granting hierarchical decomposition privileges.

The major purpose of RBAC is to facilitate authorization management and review. Administration RBAC features range from the simple to the complex. Because of the wide range of possible RBAC deployments, different RBAC features apply to different environments based on their scope of control and risk profile. Even identifying the bounds of RBAC is a point of dispute. Research continues to this day to extend the RBAC model in attempts to increase its functionality in support of new policies and to integrate RBAC into a greater range of IT infrastructures and enterprise processes. For instance, work is being conducted to include RBAC as a core technology within workflow management systems (see Section 10.1) and to extend RBAC policy to include temporal issues (see Section 5.3). However, there are several basic RBAC features that are well accepted and that are being widely implemented as a major component of government and commercial IT infrastructures. To avoid diluting RBAC's essential features and motivations and distorting its basic properties, a taxonomy has been developed to distinguish the features incorporated in several RBAC models proposed in the literature.

The RBAC model taxonomy consists of four models—core RBAC, hierarchical RBAC, static constrained RBAC, and dynamic constrained RBAC. This chapter discusses the concepts of the core RBAC model as well as approaches used for mapping the abstract concepts of core RBAC onto the concrete structures of host operating systems and applications. Core RBAC covers the basic set of features that are included in all RBAC systems. It is the inclusion of this set of features that distinguishes RBAC from other forms of authorization management systems. Chapter 4 details hierarchical RBAC. Hierarchical RBAC adds the concept of a role hierarchy, defined as a partial ordering on roles, using an inheritance relation. Chapter 5 covers constrained RBAC in terms of the static and dynamic SoD properties. Statically constrained RBAC adds constraint relations imposed on role assignment relations. Dynamic constrained RBAC imposes constraints on the activation of sets of roles that may be included as an attribute of a user's subjects.

Before reviewing the core RBAC model's features, we first describe the similarities and differences between roles and groups.

3.1 Roles versus ACL groups

An ACL is a lower-level mechanism that contains the names of subjects that are authorized to access the object to which it refers, as well as specific permissions that are granted to each authorized subject. Thus, when a subject wants to access an object, the system searches for an entry of the subject in the appropriate ACL. If an entry exists, and if the requested operation is part of that entry, then the system permits access. The privilege to create and modify ACLs is restricted to the owners of the objects for which the ACLs protect. To support discretionary policies, ownership or control typically resides with the creators of the objects. In an attempt to support nondiscretionary policies, which are typical of many organizations, ownership is assumed by the enterprise, with security administrators centrally controlling ACL entries on behalf of the enterprise. For administrative efficiency reasons, a group is often used as an entry on the ACL as a shorthand notation for describing a collection of individual subjects. For purposes of access control calculations, the subject's identity is compared to the identities maintained in the group. If a match is found, the subject is allowed to perform the operation corresponding to the group entry.

At a basic level, roles can be considered to be equivalent to groups. A role can represent a collection of users, and a user can be a member of multiple roles. Similarly, a single privilege can be associated with one or more groups or roles and a single group or role with one or more privileges. As such, assigning a user to a group or role provides the user with the ability to execute those privileges that are associated with the group or role. At this level of discourse a role is not unlike that of a group within the context of an ACL. However, roles and groups have different semantics in access control models and different usage in their implementation.

Groups are implementation-specific. Therefore, the characteristics of a group may change from one implementation to another. For example, within some UNIX environments, only one group can be associated with a particular file; other operating system environments allow multiple groups to coexist among the access control entries of a file, while still other access control systems prevent a user from being a member of more than one group at a time. Commensurate with restrictions on group membership, or group usage, are restrictions on administrators or object owners' specificity and granularity of control.

As a central element of the RBAC model, a role is defined in terms of a set of properties (with fixed characteristics). Regardless of its implementation, a role will always exhibit the properties defined by the RBAC model. A group may or may not exhibit these properties. For example, the properties of an RBAC role allow for the naming of many-to-many relations among users and permissions. For a group to meet this same property, the group structure as implemented must not place any practical restrictions on the number of the following:

- Groups that could be created;
- Users that could become a member of any group;
- Groups to which a user can have simultaneous membership;
- Individual groups that can be included within access control entries of a single access control list.

Many, but not all, application and operating system group or ACL mechanisms meet this requirement and thus may be considered equivalent to a role according to the RBAC model. Because of their compliance to the RBAC model they are known to provide the administrative benefits associated with a simple RBAC role within their scope of control.

Because RBAC is a model and not a mechanism, it may be implemented within many types of systems to include network and enterprise management systems with a scope of control that is far more expansive than a single operating system or application. Regardless of its embodiment, users and roles are treated as global entities under the RBAC model. By implementing RBAC within an enterprise management system, the system administrator treats and manages the users and roles as abstractions of system- and application-specific permission. For instance, assigning a user to a role may grant the user a set of permissions within and across multiple operating systems and applications. From the enterprise perspective, it may be far more efficient to manage user permissions through global roles than through the individual groups of potentially many operating systems and applications.

Central to RBAC is the concept of role relations. By taking advantage of the fixed properties of a role, RBAC serves as a semantic construct around which an access control policy is formulated. In addition to user and permission assignment relations, the RBAC model includes user and permission inheritance relations and a variety of static and dynamic constraint relations. Although it is plausible that a group structure could be extended to provide a semantically equivalent set of relations, in general, groups are product-specific with differing characteristics and therefore are better viewed as serving rather then competing with the RBAC model roles.

3.2 Core RBAC

Core RBAC recognizes five administrative elements: (1) users, (2) roles, and (3) permissions, where permissions are composed of (4) operations applied to (5) objects. Central to RBAC is the concept of role, where a role is a semantic construct around which access policy is formulated. The most basic of these relations are user and permission assignments. In RBAC, permissions are associated with roles, and users are made members of roles, thereby acquiring the roles' permissions. Figure 3.1 shows the relationship between users, roles, and permissions. Figure 3.1's use of double-headed arrows indicates a many-to-many relationship. For example, a single user can be associated with one or more roles, and a single role can have one or more user members.

This arrangement provides great flexibility and granularity of assignment of permissions to roles and users to roles. Any increase in flexibility in controlling access to resources also strengthens the application of the principle of least privilege.

3.2.1 Administrative support

One of RBAC's greatest virtues is the administrative capability that it supports. The administration of authorization data is widely acknowledged as an onerous process with a large and recurring expense. Under the core RBAC model, users are assigned to roles based on their competencies, authority, and responsibilities. User assignments can be easily revoked, and new assignments established as job assignments dictate. With RBAC, users are not granted permissions to perform operations on an individual basis; instead, permissions are assigned to their roles. Role associations with new permissions can be established, while old permissions can be deleted as

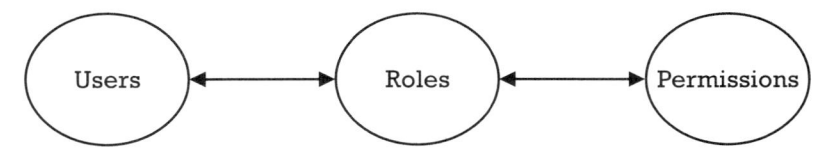

Figure 3.1 User, role, and permission relationships.

organizational functions change and evolve. This basic concept has the advantage of simplifying the understanding and management of permissions: System administrators can update roles without updating the permissions for every user on an individual basis.

As an alternative to providing these conveniences, it is often the practice to establish user permissions based on a concept of "cloning." Cloning is the practice of assigning permissions to a user based on the duplication of permissions of a second user who performs a similar function to that of the first user. Cloning is usually performed without regard to the details of the permissions that are assigned to users. Although cloning may be a quick and efficient method for the establishment of permissions, due to the coarse nature of permission assignment, cloning is generally considered to be a dangerous practice.

Another advantage of RBAC is that system administrators specify access requirements to resources at the same level of abstration as typical business processes in an enterprise. Under the RBAC model, system managers administratively create roles for various job positions in the organization. For example, a role can include teller or loan officer in a bank, or doctor, nurse, or clinician in a hospital. The permissions that are assigned to a role constrain members of the role to a specific set of actions. For example, within a hospital system, the role of a doctor can include permissions to perform diagnosis, prescribe medication, and order laboratory tests; the role of researcher can be limited to gathering anonymous clinical information for studies; the role of social worker may be reviewing patient profiles to flag possible suicidal patients or to determine possible abuse cases.

3.2.2 Permissions

In modeling an access control system, system administrators may treat permission as an abstract concept that refers to the arbitrary binding of computer operations and resource objects, and, in the case of a transaction-based system, the system administrator may take processes and values into consideration. Because of this implied action, one can consider permissions to represent an atomic unit of work exercised within a computing environment. The collection of permissions assigned to a role confers the potential to perform duties, tasks, functions, or any other abstraction of a work-related activity. Assigning a user to a role gives the user the ability to perform these activities.

Permissions that are assigned to roles reflect policy decisions on the part of the host organization. These permission assignments can be detailed in terms of both granularity of method and granularity of access. To

3.2 Core RBAC

understand the importance of granularity of method, consider the differences between the access needs of a teller and an accounting supervisor in a bank. An enterprise defines a teller role as being able to perform a savings deposit operation. This requires read and write access to specific fields within a savings file. An enterprise may also define an accounting supervisor role that is allowed to perform correction operations. These operations require read and write access to the same fields of the savings file as the teller needs. However, the accounting supervisor may not be allowed to initiate deposits or withdrawals but only perform corrections after the fact. Likewise, the teller is not allowed to perform any corrections once the transaction has been completed. These two roles are distinguished by the operations that can be executed and the values that are written to the transaction log file.

To understand the importance of the granularity of access, consider the needs of a pharmacist to access a patient's record to check for interactions between medications and to add notes to the medication section of the patient record. Although such operations may be necessary, the pharmacist should not be able to read or alter other parts of the patient record.

The assignment of permissions to roles can comply with rules that are self-imposed. For example, a health care provider may decide to constrain the role of clinician to posting only the results of certain tests, rather than distributing them where routing and human errors can result in a violation of a patient's right to privacy. Permission assignments may pertain to the enforcement of laws or regulations. For example, a system could constrain a nurse to adding a new entry to a patient's history of treatments, rather than being able to generally modify a patent record. A pharmacist can be provided with permissions to dispense, but not prescribe, medication.

The type of operations and the objects that RBAC controls are dependent on the type of system in which it will be implemented. For example, within an operating system, operations might include read, write, and execute; within a DBMS, operations might include insert, delete, append, and update; and within a transaction management system, operations would take on the form of and exhibit all the properties of a transaction. The set of objects covered by the RBAC system includes all of the objects accessible by the RBAC operations. However, system objects need not be included in an RBAC scheme. For instance, access to system-level objects such as synchronization objects (e.g., semaphores, pipes, and message segments) and temporary objects (e.g., temporary files and buffers) may not necessarily be controlled within the RBAC protection set. It is the job of the resource management system of the underlying operating system to protect these objects to support process isolation and to prevent security bypass attacks, as pointed out in Section 2.3. RBAC objects need not be limited to information containers. RBAC objects can represent exhaustible system resources, such as printers, disk space, and CPU cycles.

As an illustration of the relations described above, Figure 3.2 shows a pair of binary relations: one between operation and object, referred to as a permission, and the other between role and permission.

3.2.3 Role activation

Consistent with many other types of models, RBAC includes the concepts of subjects and objects. In general, the properties and mappings defined by the RBAC model can be divided into two separate but dependent static and dynamic components. The static component that has been discussed thus far is defined in terms of RBAC relations that do not involve the notion of a subject (in practical terms of ten equivalent to session). In applying a dynamic security policy to a computing system, we speak of subjects, which are active entities whose access to roles, operations, and objects must be controlled. A subject acting on the user's behalf carries out all the requests of a user. Each subject is uniquely referenced by an identifier, which is used to determine whether the subject is authorized for a role and can become active in the role. A user may be associated with multiple subjects at any moment in time. Each subject may have a different combination of active roles. This feature supports the principle of least privilege in that a user that is assigned to multiple roles may activate any subset of these roles to suit his or her tasks. Limiting the roles that can be activated by a subject restricts the subject to the space of accesses that are defined by the permissions that are assigned to the roles in activation. Chapter 5 defines constraint relations that can be applied to role activation in support of SoD policies and enhanced least privilege features.

The dynamic component of core RBAC includes role activation and subject access. Properties of core RBAC ensure that the active roles of a subject are a subset of the roles that are assigned to the subject's user and that the active roles of a subject are applied in the performance of object access checks. In addition to these properties, the dynamic component of the core

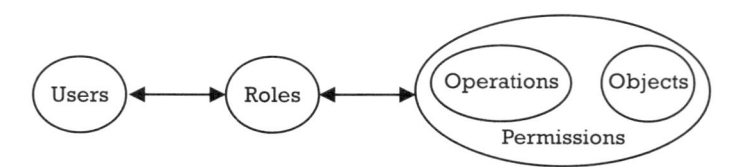

Figure 3.2 Core RBAC static element.

RBAC model defines two mapping functions. The first maps a subject back to a single user, and the second maps each subject to an active role set. Definition 3.1 formally defines core RBAC.

Figure 3.3 illustrates the set of dynamic mappings and static relations that are necessary for a user to access an object. The dotted arrows depict dynamic mappings, and the solid arrows depict static relations.

3.3 Mapping the enterprise view to the system view

In our terminology, privileges are system-specific, and permissions are mapped into privileges. Each system supports its own class of operations and has its own class of resources. The *scope of a role* pertains to the class of privileges that can be expressed by the operations and resources of the systems for which RBAC controls access. Although privileges are system-specific, users and roles can take on a common meaning across multiple systems.

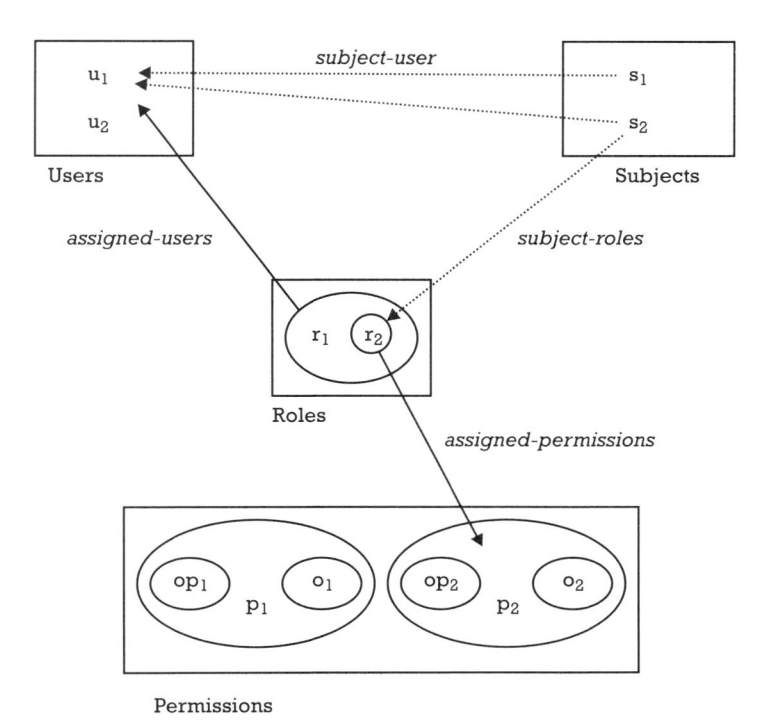

Figure 3.3 User u_1 can perform operation op_2 on object o_2 because $p_2 \in assigned\_permissions(r_2) \land u_1 \in assigned\_users(r_2) \land u_1 \in subject\_user(s_2) \land r_2 \in subject\_roles(s_2)$.

Definition 3.1 The Core RBAC model is defined as follows:

- *USERS, ROLES, OPS,* and *OBS* (users, roles, operations, and objects, repectively).
- $UA \subseteq USERS \times ROLES$, a many-to-many mapping between users and roles (user-to-role assignment relation).
- $assigned\_users: (r:ROLES) \rightarrow 2^{USERS}$, the mapping of role r onto a set of users. Formally: $assigned\_users(r) = \{u \in USERS \mid (u,r) \in UA\}$
- $PRMS = 2^{(OPS \times OBS)}$, the set of permissions.
- $PA \subseteq PRMS \times ROLES$, a many-to-many mapping between permissions and roles (role-permission assignment relation).
- $assigned\_permissions(r: ROLES) \rightarrow 2^{PRMS}$, the mapping of role r onto a set of permissions. Formally: $assigned\_permissions(r) = \{p \in PRMS \mid (p,r) \in PA\}$.
- *SUBJECTS*, the set of subjects.
- $subject\_user(s: SUBJECTS) \rightarrow USERS$, the mapping of subject s onto the subject's associated user.
- $subject\_roles(s:SUBJECTS) \rightarrow 2^{ROLES}$, the mapping of subject s onto a set of roles. Formally: $subject\_roles(s_i) \subseteq \{r \in ROLES \mid (subject\_user(s_i),r) \in UA\}$

Property 3.1 Role authorization. A subject can never have an active role that is not authorized for its user.

$\forall s:SUBJECTS, u : USERS, r :ROLES$
$r \in subject\_roles(s) \land u \in subject\_user(s) \Rightarrow u \in assigned\_users(r)$

- $access: SUBJECTS \times OPS \times OBS \rightarrow BOOLEAN;$
- $access(s, op, o) = 1$ if subject s can access object o using operation op, 0 otherwise.

Property 3.2 Object access authorization. A subject s can perform an operation op on object o only if there exists a role r that is included in the subject's active role set and there exists an permission that is assigned to r such that the permission authorizes the performance of op on o.

$s:SUBJECTS, op:OPS, o:OBS$
$access(s, op, o) \Rightarrow$
$\exists r: ROLES, p:PRMS \; r \in subject\_role \land p \in assigned\_permissions(r) \land (op, o) \in p$

3.3 Mapping the enterprise view to the system view

User "John Smith" may possess a number of system accounts and may be able to access resources within a variety of systems. Similarly, the role accounts receivable clerk may be assigned privileges that span a number of different systems and applications. In general, users, roles, and permissions can be treated as global entities, while privileges that are ultimately assigned to a role are specific to local computing environments.

In Figure 3.4, Tom and John are loan officers. They use their role permissions to read account data, write loan data, and execute transactions *A*, *B*, and *C*. The role permissions authorize the users assigned to the role to access the protected resources to perform their work. To put the role permissions into effect, access rights must be set up in the servers and applications affected—in other words, the permissions must be mapped into system-specific privileges.

The question remains, how are these role permissions reflected in real systems? This depends greatly on the type of environment and the scope of control for which RBAC is implemented. For example, when system administrators implement RBAC within an operating system, DBMS, or application environment, RBAC can be directly designed into the native resource management and access control system. In these environments, the RBAC system could directly manage the users, roles, operations, and resources that are included within these environments. With respect to a distributed heterogeneous computing environment, no single or overarching resource management or access control system exists. To further complicate the issue, the privilege names and semantics vary from system to system. For example, the read operation to access a protected file is called "r" within most UNIX systems or "READ" in RACF. A write operation could include a

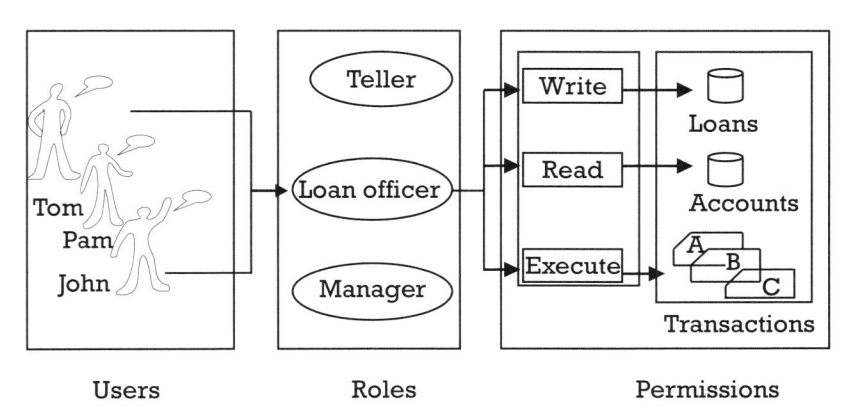

Figure 3.4 User-roles and role-privilege associations.

read operation in some systems but not in others. To deal with system-dependent permissions, a number of different approaches have been proposed and, in fact, are being implemented within enterprise management and resource-provisioning systems.

Regardless of the approach, to deliver the prescribed benefits of RBAC, core RBAC requires vendors to provide a method for mapping and maintaining role-permission relations. It is important to emphasize that the RBAC model does not dictate how these mappings are to be implemented but rather specifies that user-role and role-permission relations must be in place.

Because the RBAC model does not specify requirements for techniques in mapping an enterprise view of RBAC to the system level view, IT consumers must evaluate and compare competing products with respect to their specific needs and applications. The following sections discuss two generic approaches to providing this mapping. See Section 12.2 for RBAC model concepts implemented in commercially available enterprise security software.

3.3.1 Global users and roles and indirect role privileges

The first approach to mapping an enterprise-level RBAC view onto a system-level view involves creating and maintaining direct associations between RBAC users and local user IDs and between RBAC roles and local groups. The local administrative interface can then be used to protect local resources in terms of the RBAC system's created user IDs and groups.

Under this approach, the RBAC system links the user IDs of user accounts on various systems to one user at the enterprise level. This makes it possible to manage all the user IDs of one user (person) from a single point. User IDs on a particular system are often organized into user groups. Accordingly, a security administrator can authorize a group to access a resource instead of having to authorize each individual user. Groups and user IDs are central to mapping RBAC entities on the enterprise level to privileges at the system level.

At the enterprise level, users are organized into roles based on their role assignments. A role is responsible for the execution of a portion of the overall work performed by the enterprise. The work is performed through the invocation of permissions that are assigned to roles. To create a mapping of an enterprise view onto a system-level group, the RBAC system populates the group with the users who are assigned to its corresponding role. For the RBAC system to grant a user membership into a local group, the user must possess an account on the system. As a consequence, for each user who is included within any group on the local system, the RBAC system must first create a local user account. The RBAC system may perform this user and role-to-user ID and group mapping over any number of local systems where there exists a single user and single role that would be mapped onto multiple systems. Thus, deleting a user's role assignment at the enterprise level would result in the deletion of the user's membership within multiple groups in multiple systems. Assigning a user to a role at the enterprise level would result in the creation of user IDs and the granting of group memberships within any system for which the role has been previously mapped. Using this scheme, the RBAC system can manage user IDs and groups across its scope of control through manipulating user-role assignments at the enterprise level. The mapping relations could be stored in any central database or directory for convenient access and retrieval.

Once the RBAC system has created the user IDs, groups, and group memberships at the system level, local administrators are free to protect local resources by employing user IDs and groups in expressions of local privileges. For example, a native ACL mechanism can be used in this expression of privilege. Once these local privileges are established, the users assigned to those roles mapped to those groups used as an expression of privilege in protecting a resource on a local system can log on to that system and access the resource.

In Figure 3.5, the users Tom and John are assigned to the role loan officer at the enterprise level. Tom and John's role is mapped onto system 1 at the system level by creating corresponding user IDs and a corresponding group that includes Tom and John as group members. At the system level, a local administrative interface is used to create an ACL that gives the group loan officer read access to the files contained in the loan_data directory.

3.3.2 Mapping permissions into privileges

To allow for the definition of system-independent permissions, the RBAC system provides abstract operations and abstract resources at the enterprise level. Each abstract operation may map one-to-many onto the real operations of real systems at the system level. Through this mapping process, system-specific interpretations of the generic operations are resolved by the creation of equivalent but system-specific operations. Similarly, abstract resources can be mapped one-to-many onto real resources on real systems. The RBAC administrator may centrally grant role permissions in terms of these abstract operations and abstract resources, resulting in the creation of ACLs (i.e., privileges) on real resources across one or more systems. Once mappings are established, any changes to permissions would result in

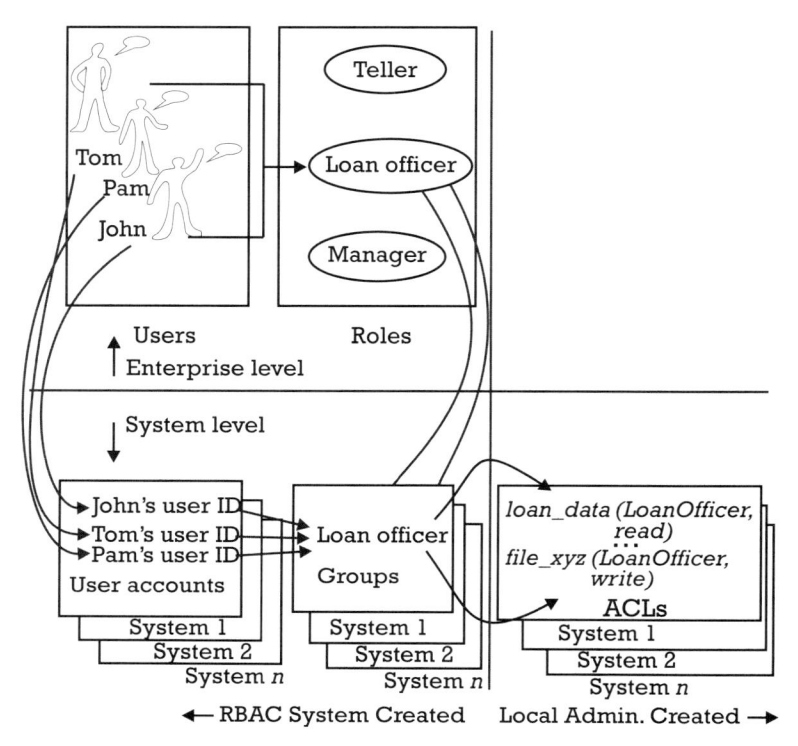

Figure 3.5 Mapping global users and roles to local user accounts, groups, and privileges.

corresponding changes to these ACLs (privileges). In Figure 3.6, because loan officers are assigned the permission to perform write operations on loans, wherever the abstract loans resource is instantiated (mapped), there would result the automatic formulation of an ACL in terms of the local system's interpretation of the abstract operation "write." In Figure 3.6, the abstract resource "loans" is mapped to the real resource "loan_data" on system 1 and to two other real resources on other systems at the system level. The abstract operation "write" corresponds to the "w" operation on system 1.

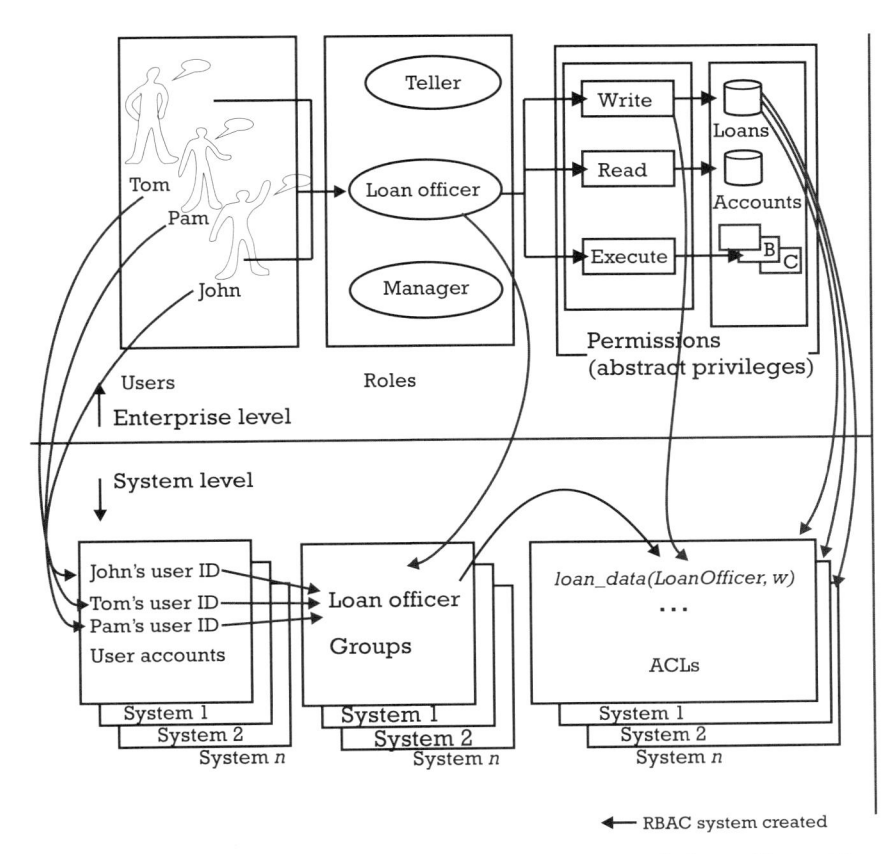

3.3 Mapping the enterprise view to the system view

Figure 3.6 Mapping abstract permissions assigned to the role loan officer at the enterprise level to real ACLs at the system level.

CHAPTER 4

Role Hierarchies

Contents

4.1 Building role hierarchies from flat roles

4.2 Inheritance schemes

4.3 Hierarchy structures and inheritance forms

4.4 Accounting for role types

4.5 General and limited role hierarchies

4.6 Accounting for the Stanford model

References

As a major component of an RBAC system, role hierarchies go beyond the basic core RBAC structures described in Chapter 3 in their ability to depict and manage user privileges. These enhanced capabilities are a consequence of the inheritance or containment relationships that are used to define role hierarchies. Simply by virtue of a role's relative position in a role hierarchy, the permissions that are assigned to the role are known to contain, or be contained by, other roles in the hierarchy.

In addition to the user and permission role assignments that are characteristic of flat role structures, the role inheritance relation creates a third kind of authorization in addition to user-role and role-permission authorizations. If a role A inherits role B, it means that all of B's permissions are available via role A. In other words, B's permissions are a proper subset of the permissions of A. System, organizational, and enterprise role hierarchies are created through the strategic establishment of role inheritance relationships that exist among roles. Through the creation of relations, administrators are better able to formulate access policies in terms of organization-specific functions and business structures. For instance the permissions that are authorized for a role can be decomposed into lower-level roles representing the functions, duties, and tasks that comprise the role. Once these lower-level roles are created, they may be reused in the creation of higher-level roles.

Although the required effort involved in the planning and construction of a role hierarchy is no doubt significant, the benefits of such an effort are immediate and long-lasting. These benefits include increased administrative productivity in the distribution, review, and revocation of permissions as well as the ability to better specify and analyze access control policies.

This chapter investigates the technical aspects of role hierarchies that have been included within various RBAC models [1–3], permission management schemes [4, 5], and product offerings. In addition, we discuss the practical uses of role inheritance relations in building organizational functions and business structures [6] for the formulation and management of privilege distribution policies.

4.1 Building role hierarchies from flat roles

The motivation for role hierarchies is the observation that individual roles within an organization often have overlapping functions; that is, users belonging to different roles may be authorized for common permissions. In extreme circumstances, there are general functions performed by all or most users within a department or enterprise. For example, general permissions may relate to the ability to download e-mail, access an internal Web site, or fill out and submit a travel voucher. In the absence of role hierarchies, it is inefficient and administratively cumbersome to specify these general permissions repeatedly for a large number of roles, or to assign large numbers of users to general roles. In the presence of a role hierarchy, the collection of permissions that comprise a job function can be defined by multiple subordinate roles, each of which may be reused in the sharing of common permissions and formulation of other roles.

To illustrate the potential for overlapping permissions and functions consider five typical roles within a hospital—resident, physician, cardiologist, oncologist, and accounts receivable clerk. Because the cardiologist and oncologist are both physicians, it is reasonable to assume that all of the permissions that are assigned to the physician would also be assigned to the cardiologist and oncologist roles. From an authorization management perspective, each permission assigned to the physician role would also have to be assigned to the cardiologist and oncologist roles. In addition, because a resident performs many of the duties of a physician, the permissions that are assigned to the resident role would also need to be assigned to the physician role, while the physician role may be assigned additional permissions that are not assigned to the resident role. Although the cardiologist and oncologist roles may be assigned a common set of permissions, each of these roles would also include a unique and disjoint set of permissions for the respective specialty. Finally, because the duties that pertain to the accounts receivable clerk would be completely disjointed from those of any of the other roles, it is reasonable to expect that there would be no permission overlap with respect to the permissions that are assigned to the accounts receivable clerk role and the permissions that are assigned to any of the other four roles of this example.

Now consider the role graph of Figure 4.1, which illustrates the five roles and the overlapping permission relations described above. In this example, the roles cardiologist and oncologist inherit the roles physician and resident. Since the inheritance of permissions and role memberships is reflexive and transitive, for the example in Figure 4.1, any user that is assigned to the cardiologist role is *authorized* for the permissions that are assigned to the role cardiologist and authorized for the permissions that are assigned to the roles physician and resident. Not all roles have to be hierarchically related. The roles cardiologist, oncologist, and accounts receivable clerk are not hierarchically related, but they can inherit some or all of the same roles, as is the case of cardiologist and oncologist.

4.2 Inheritance schemes

Researchers have proposed several inheritance schemes. Although all role hierarchy schemes are similar in their support of a basic inheritance relation to characterize permission set inclusion among roles, the specific role definitions and supporting authorization structures that define these schemes can differ considerably.

4.2.1 Direct privilege inheritance

Some role inheritance schemes use the term role to refer simply to a named collection of privileges. Under this approach, role inheritance refers to

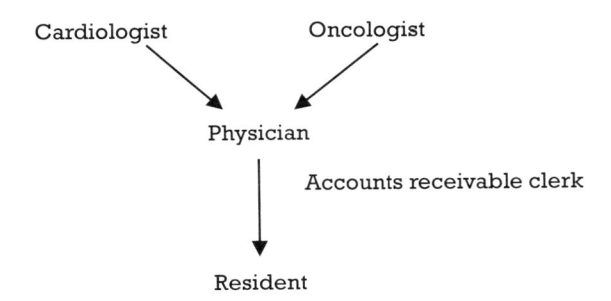

Figure 4.1 Example of the functional role hierarchy.

permission subsetting [3, 4] (i.e., r_1 "inherits" role r_2 if all permissions of r_2 are also permissions of r_1). Note that a role exists as an entity separate from and independent of the role holder. As such, users and groups of users are free to be administered separately. Assigning users or groups to roles grants the users or members of the groups authorization to the permissions defined by the role. For example, Baldwin's approach [4] makes use of a permission graph (Figure 4.2) that includes function, role, and user-group nodes. Any path from a user-group node to a functional node implies that the user is authorized to perform the privileges encapsulated by the functional node. Because users must be assigned to groups, the user-group node in Figure 4.2 includes the subnodes user and group, where users may be assigned to groups, or users may be assigned directly to roles. Although roles may be globally defined within an enterprise or organization, permissions are system-specific. For this reason, direct permission inheritance schemes are often implemented as part of a *closed management system* such as that of a DBMS. Within these systems, the resources and operations that are used in the formulation of permissions and assigned to roles all belong to a single class of operations and resources.

4.2.2 Permission and user membership inheritance

Another inheritance scheme uses the term role to refer to a structure that includes both users and permissions [5]. Under this scheme, a role in the role hierarchy serves both as a collection of permissions on one side and a collection of users on the other side (Figure 4.3). The roles toward the top of the hierarchy or role graph represent the more powerful roles (i.e., those

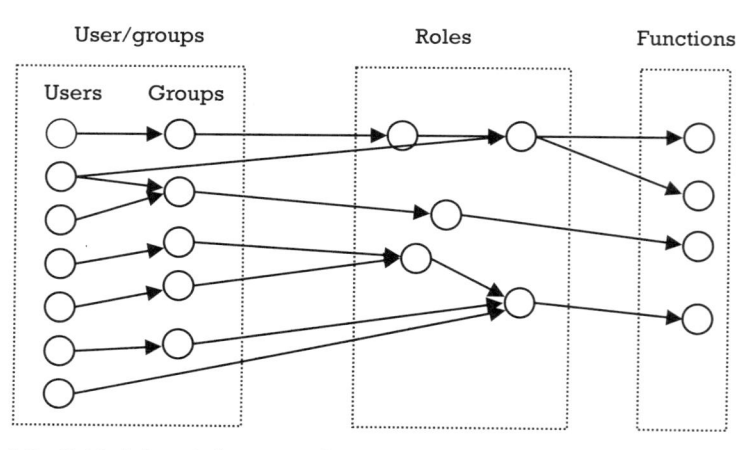

Figure 4.2 Baldwin's privilege graph.

4.2 Inheritance schemes

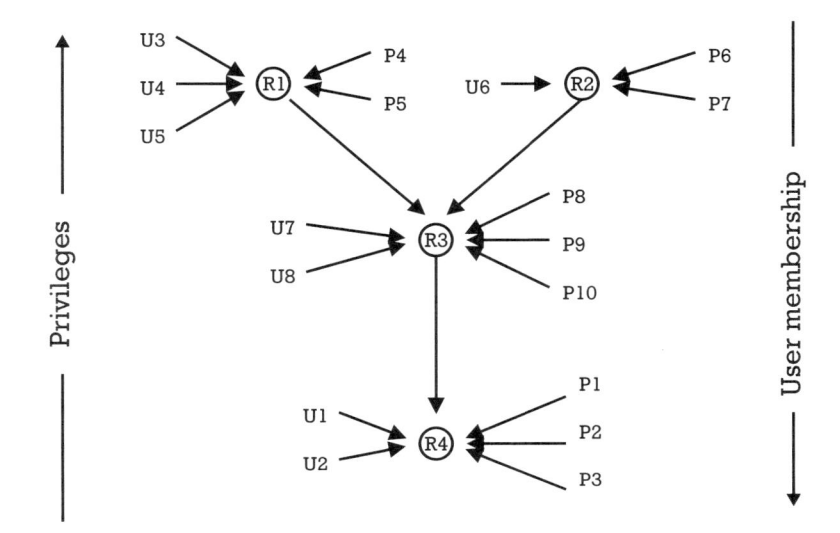

Figure 4.3 Combined user and privilege inheritance.

roles containing a greater number of authorized permissions and fewer authorized users), and the roles toward the bottom of the graph represent the more general roles (i.e., those roles containing fewer authorized permissions and a greater number of authorized users). Assigning a user to a role has the effect of authorizing the user for the permissions assigned to the role and to all the permissions that are assigned to the roles inherited by that role. For example, the authorized permissions for $U3$, $U4$, and $U5$ that are assigned to $R1$ include $P4$ and $P5$ by permission assignment, and $P8$, $P9$, $P10$, $P1$, $P2$, and $P3$ by inheritance. Similarly, assigning a permission to a role has the effect of authorizing the permission to the users who are assigned to the role and to all users who are assigned to the roles that inherit that role.

Notice that under Baldwin's permission graph, greater opportunities for the redundant authorization of permissions to a user exist, because a user may be assigned directly to a role, or to one or more groups, or both. Because these groups are administered separately from the role hierarchy, the system has no way to determine the users that are actually being assigned to its roles via the role hierarchy. This is an important distinction between the permission graph approach and more recent role-based security models. Determining the users who are assigned to a role and their membership relation with respect to other roles for which the role has an inheritance relation is a natural consequence of the scheme depicted in Figure 4.3.

4.2.3 User containment and indirect privilege inheritance

For some distributed RBAC implementations, role permission assignments are not managed directly, while role hierarchies are. Under this scheme, permissions are assigned to groups, and groups are mapped to roles that are organized into a role hierarchy. For these systems, role hierarchies are managed in terms of user containment relations: Role r_1 "contains" role r_2 if all users authorized for r_1 are also authorized for r_2. Assigning a user to a role r in a user containment hierarchy assigns the user to the groups that are mapped to r, and to the groups that are mapped to the roles that are contained by r. Note, that user containment implies that a user assigned to r_1 has (at least) all the permissions of a second role r_2 that is contained by r_1, while the permission inheritance for r_1 and r_2 does not imply anything about user assignment.

Role hierarchies are intended to help administrators to set up access control information based on a user's function in an enterprise. The permissions that make up these functions may be scattered across numerous platforms and applications. To manage access to these permissions, a role hierarchy uses the notions of abstract users, roles, and permissions that are global to the enterprise. However, many operating systems and applications do not recognize roles; they perform access checks by using actual user accounts, groups, and ACLs on target systems. User containment hierarchies can be used to create and automatically maintain a mapping between roles, users, and abstract privileges on one hand, and groups, user accounts and actual privileges on the target systems it controls, on the other hand (Figure 4.4).

Because the permissions defined within a specific target system may not apply to all roles within the hierarchy, mapping users, roles, and role memberships to user accounts and groups on a target system must be based on the concept of a *subgraph* within the RBAC model graph. For example, a subgraph maybe defined by one or more base role(s) within the role hierarchy and all the roles and users that inherit or contain the base role(s). For example, a subgraph may define all the users and roles within the payroll department. The mapping process is straightforward, with the only rule being that the entire subgraph has to be mapped onto the target system. Each user in the subgraph is mapped to a user account on the target system. For each role in the subgraph, a group of the same name is created on the target system and is populated with user accounts according to the role membership defined by the inheritance relations (user containment) of the subgraph.

For example, the subgraph defined by $R4$ of Figure 4.4 is mapped onto target system 1. Mapping the subgraph onto target system 1 creates corresponding user accounts $u1$, $u2$, $u3$, and $u4$ for the abstract users $U1$, $U2$, $U3$,

4.2 Inheritance schemes

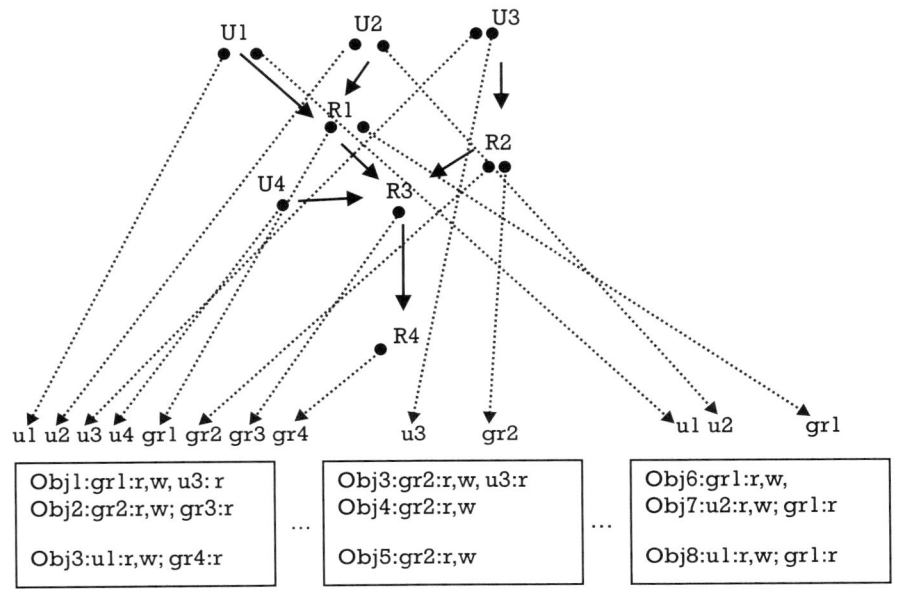

[Figure: diagram showing users U1, U2, U3, U4 mapped to roles R1, R2, R3, R4, which map down to user accounts u1, u2, u3, u4 and groups gr1, gr2, gr3, gr4 across target systems]

```
Obj1:gr1:r,w, u3:r          Obj3:gr2:r,w, u3:r          Obj6:gr1:r,w,
Obj2:gr2:r,w; gr3:r         Obj4:gr2:r,w                Obj7:u2:r,w; gr1:r

Obj3:u1:r,w; gr4:r          Obj5:gr2:r,w                Obj8:u1:r,w; gr1:r
```

Target system 1, Subgraph R4   Target system n, Subgraph R1

Target system 2, Subgraph R2

Figure 4.4 User containment hierarchy.

and $U4$ of the subgraph. Groups $gr1$, $gr2$, $gr3$, and $gr4$ corresponding to roles $R1$, $R2$, $R3$, and $R4$ are also created on target system 1 and are populated as follows:

- $gr1$ has $u1$ and $u2$ as members;
- $gr2$ has $u2$ as a member;
- $gr3$ and $gr4$ has $u1$, $u2$, $u3$, and $u4$ as members.

By selecting an appropriate subgraph an administrator of a target system may automatically create a mapping of users, roles, and role relations onto local groups and user accounts. Subsequent changes to the portion of the role hierarchy that corresponds to the mapped subgraph results in corresponding changes to groups and user accounts. For example, deleting user $U1$'s assignment to role $R1$ will automatically delete the user's corresponding assignment to user account $u1$ and delete the user's membership within groups $g1$, $g3$, and $g4$ on target system 1. Because user $U1$ is also included within a subgraph ($R1$) that has been mapped onto target system n, the deletion of *U*1's assignment to *R*1 will also result in the deletion of *U*1's account and *U*1's membership within group *gr*1 on target system *n*.

Taking advantage of the intermediate mappings of users and roles onto local user accounts and groups, role/permission management is provided through the use of these user accounts and groups as expressions of permission within the local target system. As illustrated in Figure 4.4, these permissions may be in the form of ACL entries. Here it is the specification of a role, or more accurately speaking, a group corresponding to a role in the role hierarchy, in conjunction with an operation that comprises an indirect role-permission relationship.

As illustrated in Tables 4.1 and 4.2, although a user containment hierarchy does not directly support permission inheritance, effectively it is equivalent to the permission and user membership inheritance of Section 4.2.2.

Table 4.1 Role Assignments and Authorizations

	*R*1	*R*2	*R*3	*R*4
Assigned users	*U*1, *U*2	*U*3	*U*4	
Authorized users	*U*1, *U*2	*U*3	*U*1, *U*2, *U*3, *U*4	*U*1, *U*2, *U*3, *U*4
Assigned privileges	*r,w*, (*obj*1), *r,w* (*obj*6), *r*(*obj*7), *r*(*obj*8)	*r,w*(*obj*2), *r,w*(*obj*3), *r,w*(*obj*4), *r,w*(*obj*5)	*r*(*obj*2)	*r,w*(*obj*3)
Authorized privileges	*r,w*, (*obj*1), *r,w* (*obj*6), *r*(*obj*7), *r*(*obj*8), *r*(*obj*2), *r,w*(*obj*3)	*r,w*(*obj*2), *r,w*(*obj*3), *r,w*(*obj*4), *r,w*(*obj*5), *r*(*obj*2), *r,w*(*obj*3)	*r*(*obj*2), *r,w*(*obj*3)	*r,w*(*obj*3)

Table 4.2 User Assignments and Authorizations

	*U*1	*U*2	*U*3	*U*4
Role assignments	*R*1	*R*1	*R*2	*R*3
Authorized roles	*R*1, *R*3, *R*4	*R*1, *R*3, *R*4	*R*2, *R*3, *R*4	*R*3
Assigned privileges	*r,w*(*obj*3), *r,w*(*obj*8)	*r,w*(*obj*7)	r(*obj*1), *r*(*obj*3)	
Authorized privileges	*r,w*(*obj*3), *r,w*(*obj*8), *r,w*, (*obj*1), *r,w* (*obj*6), *r*(*obj*7), *r*(*obj*8), *r*(*obj*2), *r,w*(*obj*3)	*r,w*(*obj*7), *r,w*, (*obj*1), *r,w* (*obj*6), *r*(*obj*7), *r*(*obj*8), *r*(*obj*2), *r,w*(*obj*3)	r(*obj*1), *r*(*obj*3), *r,w*(*obj*2), *r,w*(*obj*3), *r,w*(*obj*4), *r,w*(*obj*5), *r*(*obj*2), *r,w*(*obj*3)	*r,w*(*obj*3), *r*(*obj*2), *r,w*(*obj*3)

4.3 Hierarchy structures and inheritance forms

Regardless of the scheme, role hierarchies can be used to support several organizational structures such as line of authority, functional delineation, and geographic responsibilities. Before discussing role hierarchical representations of these business structures, we first describe inheritance properties.

A binary relation between roles, called *immediate inheritance*, defines a role hierarchy. The reflexive-transitive closure (i.e., both immediate and indirect inheritance) of the immediate inheritance is called simply *inheritance*. Intuitively, a first role inherits a second role if all permissions of the second role are also permissions of the first role and all users of the first role are also users of the second role. Accordingly, the role hierarchy helps define new roles in terms of existing roles, providing the advantage of being able to visualize and reason about the distribution of permissions while avoiding role permission and membership redundancy.

The inheritance relation, shown as →, defines both permission inheritance and user membership inheritance. Because we represent the graph with the arcs corresponding to the inheritance relation oriented top-down, we say that role *membership* is inherited top-down and that role permissions are inherited bottom-up. Under this scheme, the roles toward the top of the hierarchy represent more powerful roles while roles toward the bottom represent the more general roles.

Given that user and role permissions can be highly diverse and fine-grained, role hierarchies offer a means of visualizing and managing the distribution of permissions. User access rights can be managed as a result of creating or revoking a user-role assignment, creating or revoking a role-permission assignment or by creating or deleting a role inheritance relation. Since inheritance properties dictate that higher-order roles can execute the permissions of lower-order roles within a role hierarchy, we can minimize the role-permission assignments required to facilitate a desirable distribution by assigning permission at the lowest point in a role hierarchy where it is appropriate. Similarly, we assign users to one or more roles in the hierarchy to allow authorization to the greatest set of permissions that is minimally necessary for the performance of duties. Role hierarchies also offer increased administrative efficiency. Assigning a user to the cardiologist role of Figure 4.1 has the effect of authorizing the user to the permissions that are assigned to the cardiologist role and—by virtue of inheritance—to the permissions that are assigned to the physician and resident roles.

4.3.1 Connector roles

Although organizing flat roles into a role hierarchy offers increased visualization and administrative efficiency, by including *connector roles* within the hierarchy we can further enhance these advantages. Intuitively, connector roles exist within a role hierarchy for the convenience of defining collections of permissions to be inherited by higher-order roles within the hierarchy. Generally speaking it would not be meaningful for users to be directly assigned to a connector role, so connector roles would not exist in the absence of a role hierarchy. In Figure 4.5, specialist and general hospital are connector roles: Specialist captures the commonality between cardiologist and oncologist as well as any other specialist role that may be created; while general hospital captures the commonality among all roles within the hospital. Regarding specialist, permissions can be assigned that are not appropriate for a physician but that are shared by all roles that inherit specialist. Regarding general hospital, permissions can be assigned to include access to a hospital-wide calendar application or an internal Web site. Although the use of connector roles will obviously lead to an increased number of roles that need to be managed, the number of role-permission assignments will be further minimized. For most applications this is a positive trade-off.

In general, connector roles can encapsulate arbitrary collections of permissions as an abstraction of, for example, functions, duties, tasks, or

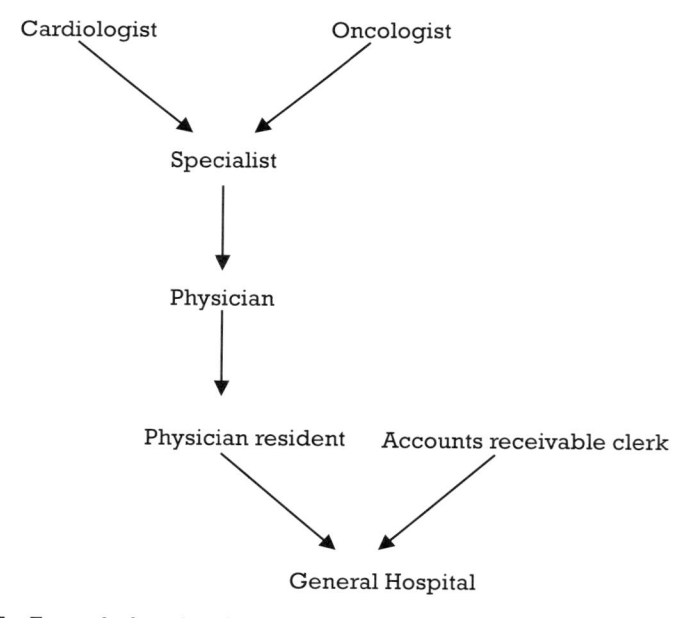

Figure 4.5 Example functional role hierarchy with connector roles.

4.3 Hierarchy structures and inheritance forms

Formal definitions: Formally we define the set of all roles by ROLE, the immediate inheritance relation by $\rightarrow$. The pair (Role, $\rightarrow$) is a directed acyclic graph, whose nodes represent the roles, and whose arcs represent the relationships $q \rightarrow r$. Usually we draw the graph with the arcs oriented in the general direction top-to-bottom. In this way we say that q is an immediate ascendant of r and that r is an immediate descendant of q, if and only if $q \rightarrow r$.

The inheritance relation $\rightarrow$ defines both the permission inheritance and user membership inheritance (i.e., $r_1 \rightarrow r_2$) if and only if all permissions of r_2 are also permissions of r_1, and all users of r_1 are also users of r_2. We denote by $\rightarrow^*$ the reflexive-transitive closure of the inheritance relation (i.e., $r_1 \rightarrow^* r_2$ iff $r_1 = q_1 \ldots q_n = r_2$) where $n \geq 1$. Note that this definition allows for r_1 and r_2 to coincide. Also, the same relation can be used to denote the user assignment to roles, as well as permission inheritance from a role to its assigned users. Regarding the terminology, a user u is said to be assigned to role r if $u \rightarrow r$, while u is said to be authorized for role r if $u \rightarrow^+ r$, where $\rightarrow^+$ is the transitive closure of the $\rightarrow$ relation.

Other properties of the inheritance relation include reflexivity and antisymmetry. Given roles r_1 and r_2, we have $r_1 \rightarrow r_1$ (reflexivity) since assigned_permissions(r_1) $\subseteq$ assigned_permissions(r_1) and assigned_users(r_1) $\subseteq$ assigned_users(r_1). Also, $r_1 \rightarrow r_2 \wedge r_2 \rightarrow r_1 \Rightarrow r_1 = r_2$.

From the ordering, we define a chain of authorizations that are linear orders of roles according to increased authority, connected by the inheritance relation $\rightarrow$. In the graph thus defined, $r_x \succeq r_y$ if and only if there is a directed path (sequence of arrows) from r_x to r_y. Also, there are no (directed) cycles in the graph since the order relation is antisymmetric and transitive.

We can now formally define general hierarchies.

Definition 4.1 General role hierarchies:

- $RH \subseteq ROLES \times ROLES$ is a partial order on ROLES called the inheritance relation, written as $\succeq$, where $r_1 \succeq r_2$ only if all privileges of r_2 are also permissions of r_1, and all users of r_1 are also users of r_2. Formally: $r_1 \succeq r_2 \Rightarrow$ authorized_permissions(r_2) $\subseteq$ authorized_permissions(r_1) $\wedge$ authorized_users(r_1) $\subseteq$ authorized_users(r_2).

- authorized_users(r: ROLES)$\rightarrow 2^{USERS}$, the mapping of role r onto a set of users in the presence of a role hierarchy. Formally, authorized_users(r) = $\{u \in USERS \mid r' \succeq r, \wedge (u, r') \in UA\}$.

- authorized_permissions(r: ROLES)$\rightarrow 2^{PRMS}$, the mapping of role r onto a set of permissions in the presence of a role hierarchy. Formally, authorized_permissions(r) = $\{p \in PRMS \mid r' \succeq r, (p, r') \in PA\}$.

activities. In doing so, system administrators are free to use and reuse these abstractions in the formulation of any other higher-order role, to include other connector roles.

It is important to note that in the absence of a role hierarchy, each role would be forced to completely encapsulate, as a single collection of permissions, all lower-level permission abstractions. Also, note that although higher-order permission abstractions are composed from lower-level abstractions, there are no hard and fast rules that dictate any sequence of composition with respect to these levels of abstraction. For example, a role that is assigned to a user may be composed of a collection of duties, and these duties may bypass tasks and activities and be defined directly as collections of permissions. In this same respect, although users are typically not directly assigned to connector roles, there are no hard rules that would prevent such an assignment if it were deemed appropriate.

In addition to adding structure and providing convenience in grouping permissions, a connector role can be used for *limiting permission inheritance* within a role hierarchy. It is often the case that a role may merely share a large subset of permissions with a second role, where the total inheritance of permission by the first role would be inappropriate. For example, although a cardiologist may be trained and well-qualified to perform the functions of a general physician, there are still certain functions that are performed on a routine basis by the general physician that the specialist could not appropriately perform. In situations such as these, the cardiologist may retain the permissions of the general physician but not participate in situations where these functions would be performed. In other situations, there might be a large portion of permissions common between roles, but nevertheless, regulatory or institutional requirements would forbid a complete inheritance of permission. Such a relationship may exist between a teller in a bank, and the teller supervisor. In situations such as these, connector roles may be used to limit some portion of permission inheritance within the hierarchy while retaining the convenience of inheriting the complement of permissions, as illustrated in Figure 4.6. While both the teller and teller supervisor inherit select common permissions from the teller functions role, both the teller and teller supervisor roles retain permissions that are unique

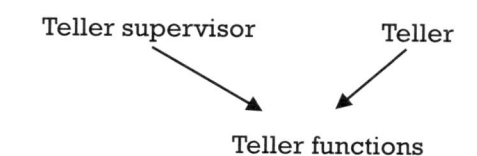

Figure 4.6 Connector role used as a means of blocking permission inheritance.

4.3 Hierarchy structures and inheritance forms

to their specific functions. As is the case of using connector roles for other structural situations, the added burden of role proliferation may be justified by the reduction in the number of redundant role permission assignments.

For example, if there is an 80% or greater permission overlap between roles, an organization may choose to create a connector role as a means of expressing and managing the permissions that correspond to the overlapping functions. Keeping in mind that roles can be thought of as an abstract collection of functions and permissions, the addition of connector roles within a role hierarchy may help make it easier to visualize the distribution of permissions among roles.

So far this chapter has discussed functional roles and their inheritance relations. However, role hierarchies can be used to capture other organization structure characteristics. Sections 4.3.2 and 4.3.3 explore organizational units and geographic locations as a means of contributing to the structure of role hierarchies.

4.3.2 Organization chart hierarchies

Most enterprises are structured and managed along organizational boundaries such as departments, divisions, groups, and teams. Although the naming convention used to describe these OUs may differ from enterprise to enterprise, the concept of OUs in one form or another exists across almost all enterprises as a means of delineating lines of authority, resource ownership, and areas of responsibility.

With respect to authority and responsibility, OUs are often used to describe an enterprise hierarchy where one OU is managed or subsumed by another. Hierarchical relations are often depicted in the form of an organizational chart, where each named OU includes an individual responsible for

---

Formal definitions: Connector roles define a form of relationship between two roles where there is a form of permission sharing in which the roles have a nonempty intersection of their permission sets but where neither of the permission sets are a subset nor superset of the other. If there exists a role whose authorized permission set is some or all of this intersection, then we say such a role is a connector role.

Definition 4.2 Connector roles: $\forall\, r, r_1, r_2 : ROLES$, r is a connector role of r_1 and r_2 if $r_1 \succeq r \wedge r_2 \succeq r \,\wedge\,$ authorized_permissions$(r) \subseteq$ (authorized_permissions$(r_1) \cap$ authorized_permissions(r_2))

where $r_1 \neq r$ and $r_2 \neq r$.

its management. Figure 4.7 depicts a portion of a sample organizational chart detailing the organizational structure of a hospital that includes a chief operations officer, four divisions, and the financial, administrative, legal, medicine, and admissions departments. Each organizational unit (OU) pertains to a set of functions that are performed within the enterprise. The managing authority of each OU may be given a budget for maintaining a professional staff, performing IT functions, and purchasing equipment and other supplies by a higher authority. In each case, the OU is responsible for running the organization in an efficient manner while providing a core set of functions and services. During periods of reduced revenue the managing authority may be asked to provide the same functions and services with a reduced budget. To be accountable for these budgetary and functional responsibilities, a managing authority must assume ownership and managing authority over the OU. To meet regulatory requirements, share the burden of managing the OU, or introduce base competencies, an OU is organized into subfunctional disciplines. For example, Figure 4.7 shows the finance department broken into accounting and forecasting departments. The specialties department is organized using professional activities—neurology, cardiology, and anesthesiology.

Clearly, organizational charts alone are not intended to define complete sets of job positions or roles within an OU, nor do they prescribe privilege inheritance relations within or among the OUs. The chief operations officer position within the organizational chart of Figure 4.7, for example, is not

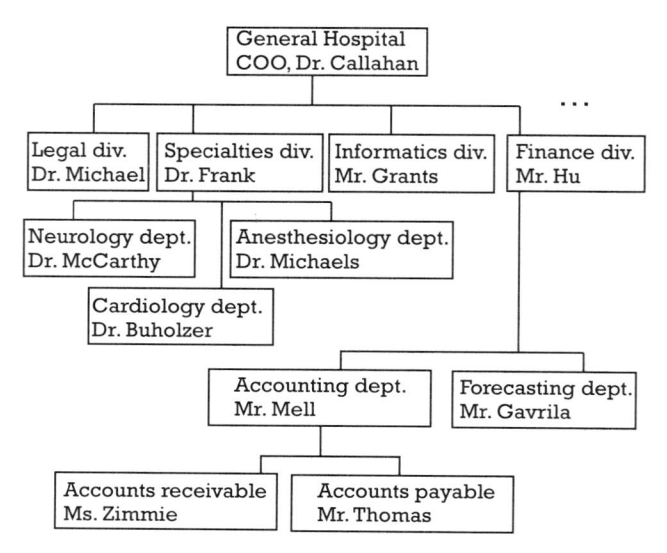

Figure 4.7 Example organizational chart.

meant to infer the ability to perform all enterprise functions and access to all enterprise resources [6]. However, OUs can assist in defining roles and represent collections of functions and users; as such, they are valuable structures in contributing to the overall strategy of distributing and managing of privileges within the enterprise. For instance, OUs often assume ownership of resources to include servers, databases, and devices. Most users within an enterprise belong to or are guests within a specific OU and as such are selectively given access to the resources that are owned by the unit. It is the local administrators—closer to the day-to-day operations of an OU—who are best suited for making these access control decisions.

Furthermore, OUs help in defining the business processes and work flows that RBAC helps in creating. For instance, travel orders that are requested within an OU may need to be approved by the managing authority within the business unit. A purchase request under $2,500 may be approved by a department manager, while requests for purchases at or over $2,500 may need approval at the division level.

OUs can be viewed as containers of users, roles, and resources. Thus, they can be used for defining specific roles or role types within the context of the OU. The cardiology department may include a number of cardiology specialists including physicians, cardiologists, and various types of nurses. When these functional roles are placed within the cardiology department they gain access to the resources that are owned and managed by the department. Their specific accesses are governed and are often regulated by the competencies and duties that are inferred from the roles. For example, a nurse practitioner (NP) may have the capability to perform a diagnosis and prescribe medicine as a consequence of being an NP; an NP within the cardiology department may be provided the additional capability to access patient records and add entries to the treatment history of patents that are being treated within the department.

Systems administrators can also create specific types of security administrative roles. For example, a security administrative role may be created and given permission to assign users to the collection of roles that are contained within the cardiology department. Application or system administrators may assign privileges to the cardiology department roles by selectively specifying access rights to the resources that they are responsible for managing.

4.3.3 Geographical regions

Many enterprises are organized and locally managed with respect to geographical regions. While they are usually required to adhere to specific standards, in many cases, a regional operation can be independently responsible for such functions as manufacturing, help desk operation, quality assurance, marketing, sales, and profit. However, in almost all cases, regional operations must report to a central authority and in many cases benefit from globalized activities such as research and development or product marketing. From a resource access perspective, regional operations will have a significant impact on the structure of a role hierarchy.

Let us return to our hospital example, where the hospital offers pediatric and chemotherapy services at two regional clinics, along with core health care operations at its downtown hospital. Each clinic requires access to the hospital patient records while maintaining local records pertaining to patient treatment, accounts receivable, and cashier functions. Figure 4.8 illustrates the roles pertaining to clinics respectively offering pediatric and chemotherapy services.

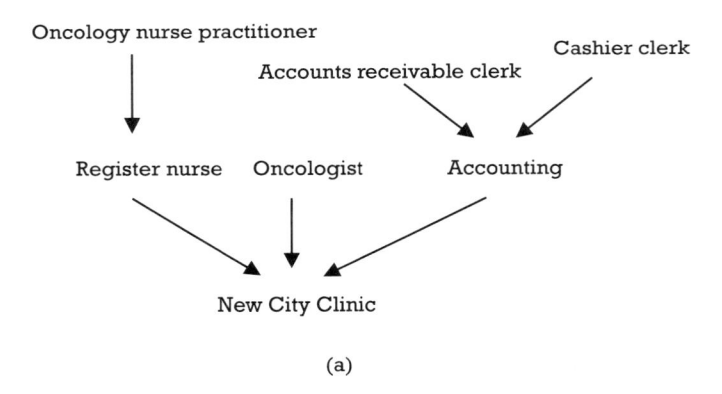

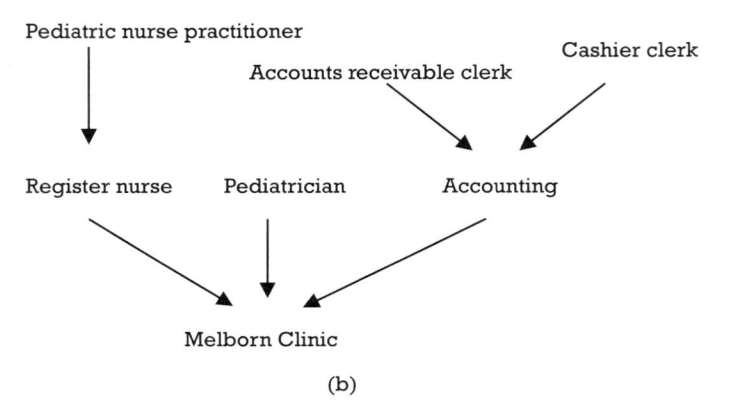

Figure 4.8 (a) New City Clinic roles, and (b) Melborn Clinic roles.

4.4 Accounting for role types

For many distributed enterprises each location or OU may have employees whose roles are identical, but the resources that each employee accesses pertain at least in part to the location. Examples include tellers, supervisors, and financial advisors across branches of a bank, or secretaries across departments. For these roles, there may be hardware resources like file servers or printers, or customer records tied to a specific office location for which employees in the office should have access. When a generic role (common across locations) is incorporated within a specific location, the result is what is often referred to as a *role type*.

To avoid having many separate and unrelated role permissions for tellers, for example, roles can include *qualifiers*. Common qualifiers are the location, the name of a branch, the OU, or the region where the particular functions of the role are fulfilled. This mechanism provides a way of customizing the permissions assigned to a role so that they are specific to some characteristic of the user. It should be noted that this mechanism need only apply to some permissions assigned to the roles, since there may also be enterprisewide permissions that apply to all roles of a specific type.

Figure 4.9 shows three types of loan officer roles—northeast, southeast, and west. For each role type, permissions are uniquely assigned depending on the region qualifier. Tom and John are assigned to the role loan officer east, have the permissions to read northeast accounts and execute northeast transactions *A*, *B*, and *C*. All users that are assigned to a loan officer role, regardless of its type, have the permission to write to national loans. When assigning permissions to role types only those permissions that are unique to the role type (defined by the qualifier) need to be assigned. Permissions that are generic to all role types can be assigned directly to the generic role.

Although the concept of a role type can be implemented using role qualifiers as illustrated in Figure 4.9, in reality, a role type is a simple form of

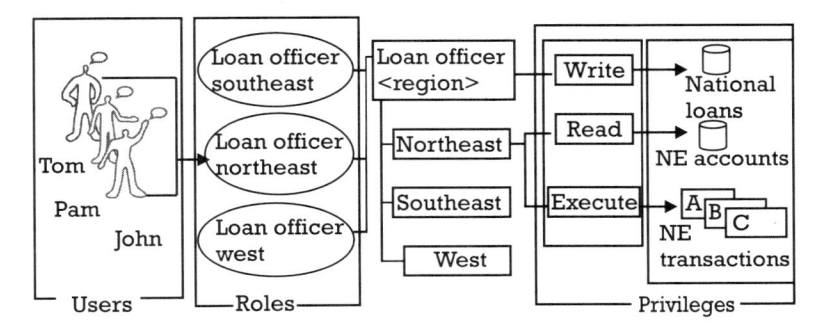

Figure 4.9 Roles and role qualifiers.

role hierarchy. Figure 4.10 is a role hierarchy equivalent to that of Figure 4.9. The generic permission to write to national loans could be assigned to the national loan officers' role, and the specialized (local) permission to read northeast accounts and execute northeast transactions A, B, and C could be assigned to the northeast loan officer functions role. Assigning Tom and John to loan officer northeast achieves the same access control policy as that depicted in Figure 4.9.

4.5 General and limited role hierarchies

In practice, role hierarchies are of two types—general role hierarchies and limited role hierarchies. General role hierarchies provide support for an arbitrary partial order to serve as the role hierarchy to include the concept of multiple inheritances of permissions and user membership among roles. General role hierarchies allow a role to have more than one immediate ascendant (potentially inheriting user membership from multiple sources) and at the same time one or more immediate descendents (potentially inheriting permissions from multiple sources). Limited role hierarchies

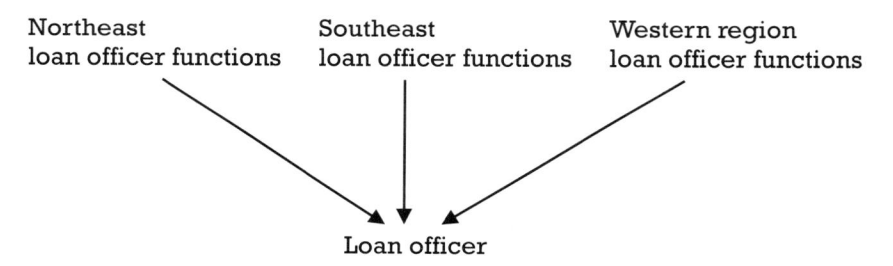

Figure 4.10 A role hierarchy that is equivalent to a role type using location as a qualifier.

Formal Definitions: We represent r_1 as an immediate descendent of r_2 by $r_1 \rightarrow r_2$, if $r_1 \succeq r_2$, but no role in the role hierarchy lies between r_1 and r_2. That is, there exists no role r_3 in the role hierarchy such that $r_1 \succeq r_3 \succeq r_2$, where $r_1 \neq r_2$ and $r_2 \neq r_3$.

We now define limited role hierarchies as a restriction on the immediate descendents of the general role hierarchy.

Definition 4.3 *Limited role hierarchies:*
Definition 4.1 with the following limitation:
$$\forall r, r_1, r_2 \in ROLES, r \succeq r_1 \wedge r \succeq r_2 \Rightarrow r_1 = r_2$$

4.5 General and limited role hierarchies

impose restrictions resulting in a simpler tree structure (e.g., a role may have one or more immediate ascendants but is restricted to a single immediate descendent, or vice versa).

Roles in a limited role hierarchy are restricted to a single *immediate descendent*. Although limited role hierarchies do not support multiple inheritances, they nonetheless provide clear administrative advantages over flat role structures.

Thus far in this chapter our examples and role graphs have been restricted to simple tree structures. The functional, organizational, and geographical graphs described above are characterized as limited inheritance role hierarchies. Each graph includes a common root node with two or more subnodes accurately depicting the union of user membership. In the case of OUs, illustrated as an organization chart, permission containment with respect to the definition of role inheritance could not be justified, although it is accurate with respect to resource ownership and lines of authority.

To date, the implementation of limited role hierarchies remains the norm within most popular commercial authorization management products, although general role hierarchies offer greater flexibility in defining the complex role structures that are common to many user enterprises. This state of commercial implementation is due to a variety of circumstances.

Traditionally, commercially available products lag behind the research community. It is always easier to create a new security model or write a paper than to implement and market a new feature. This situation has been especially true with respect to new security features because security features are typically considered by vendors to diminish performance and detract from other high value services. Also, as suggested earlier, the current state of authorization management is so dismal that any technological advancement has the potential to be successfully marketed and would be welcomed by the user community. Finally, tree structures have become the industry norm for visualizing and managing system resources. Vast numbers of users have become accustomed to the use of trees to perform mundane tasks such as managing directories, files, and domains, and even the more recently available directory storage structures are organized according to tree structures. General hierarchies, therefore, represent a departure from the past and thus will require some adjustment on the part of users. However, any fear that users will reject general hierarchies is probably unfounded. This is because general hierarchies are, in reality, just as intuitive, more natural, and more powerful in articulating enterprise structures than the simple tree structures to which we have all become accustomed. Figure 4.11 shows an example of a general role hierarchy.

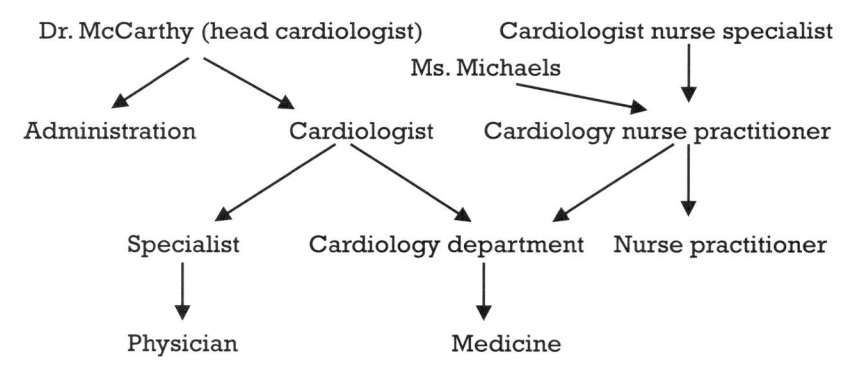

Figure 4.11 General hierarchy with functional and organizational roles.

Figure 4.11 combines organizational and functional roles into one role inheritance graph. General role hierarchies support the concept of *multiple inheritance*, which provides the ability to inherit permissions from two or more role sources and to inherit user membership from two or more role sources. Multiple inheritances provide the ability to compose a role from multiple subordinate roles (with fewer permissions) in defining roles and relations that are characteristic of the organizational and business structures, which these roles are intended to represent. Because general hierarchies place no restrictions on the number of immediate role inheritance relations, the cardiologist role is able to inherit permissions from the functional role specialist and the organizational role cardiology department. Head cardiologist Dr. McCarthy is assigned to the cardiologist role and accordingly is authorized for the privileges that are assigned to the cardiologist role. Definition 4.1 also authorizes Dr. McCarthy for the permissions that are assigned to any role that is inherited by the cardiologist role. Because the graph that is depicted in Figure 4.11 represents a general role hierarchy, any node in the graph may inherit permissions from multiple role sources. Thus, the cardiologist role is able to inherit permissions from

Formal definitions: Combiner roles define a form of relationship in which a role inherits permissions from disjointed immediate descendent roles, combining their authorized permissions into a single, higher-level role. Notice that the definition of combiner roles is the dual of that for connector roles.

Definition 4.4 Combiner roles: $\forall r, r_1, r_2 : ROLES$, r is a combiner of roles r_1 and r_2 if $r_1 \preceq r \wedge r_2 \preceq r \wedge$ *authorized_permissions*$(r') \supseteq$ (*authorized_permissions*$(r_1) \cup$ *authorized_permissions*(r_2)), where $r_1 \neq r$ and $r_2 \neq r$

both the specialist role and the cardiology department role, and by virtue of transitivity, the permissions that are assigned to the physician and medicine roles. As such, the cardiologist role is neither a functional nor an organizational role, but rather a hybrid. Similarly, cardiologist NP is also a hybrid role, and by virtue of role inheritance, so is cardiologist nurse specialist. The cardiologist role is referred to as a *combiner* role, since it combines the authorized permissions of the roles that it inherits.

Another interesting characteristic of multiple inheritance is the ability to accurately represent users and their role assignments within the role hierarchy through the uniform treatment of user/role assignments and the immediate role inheritance relations. By virtue of role assignment, the user is authorized for the permissions that are assigned to the user or inherited by the role, and the user's membership is inherited by the role and any other role that is inherited by the role.

Although within a limited role hierarchy, a single user assignment may also be represented through the immediate role inheritance relation, a user can be assigned to multiple roles. Therefore, representing all of a user's role assignments would require multiple user instances.

Within a general hierarchy, all user role assignments can be represented as a single user instance. Dr. McCarthy's role assignments in Figure 4.11 are represented as two immediate inheritance relations. Deleting Dr. McCarthy from the role graph has the effect of deleting all of Dr. McCarthy's permissions that are managed by RBAC. This is the behavior that would be expected intuitively.

4.6 Accounting for the Stanford model

General hierarchies also allow for an object-oriented approach to managing an enterprise's distribution of permissions, consistent with that prescribed by the Stanford model [7]. The Stanford model (see Figure 4.12) recognizes several layers of abstractions at the enterprise level. Under this model, permissions are recorded as non-system-specific *entitlements,* which can be grouped together into *tasks,* and then further managed as groups of tasks that describe job *functions.* Finally, job functions can be assigned to organizational *roles* rather than to individuals to facilitate the assignment of authority as people move in and out of a specific role. Although the Stanford model does not directly recognize permissions, entitlements are mapped one-to-many onto permissions that may exist across systems. Also, the Stanford model allows a user to be assigned to more than one role.

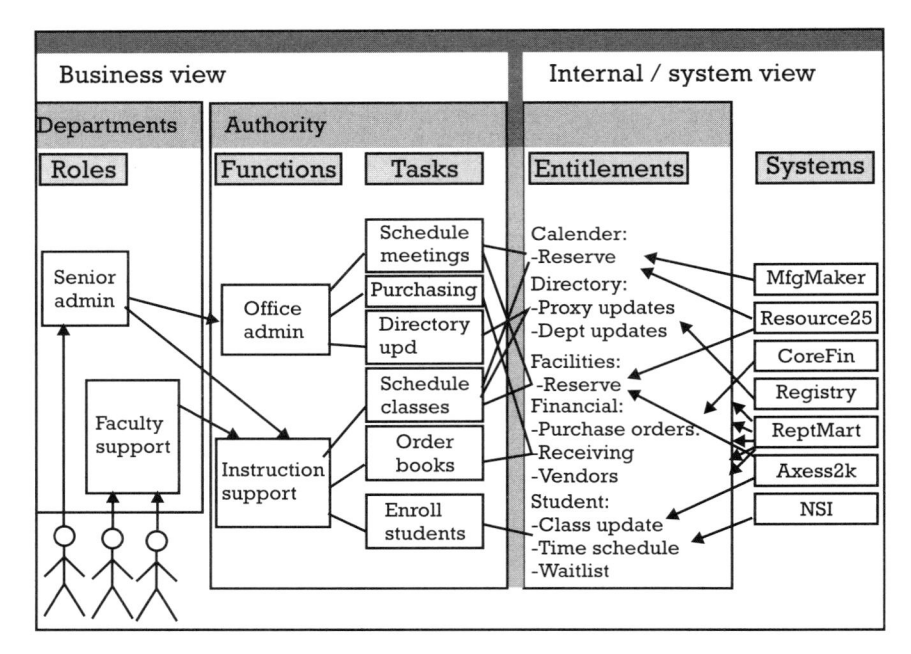

Figure 4.12 Stanford model enterprise and system abstractions.

Although RBAC does not specifically call out the various abstractions defined in the Stanford model, these same abstractions could be constructed using general hierarchies. Under the RBAC model, a user can be assigned to one or more roles, and one or more permissions can be assigned to a role. However, in the context of a role hierarchy, neither users nor permissions need to be directly assigned to a role (see Figure 4.13). Therefore, roles are free to be created to represent functions and tasks where the functions are exclusively inherited by roles, and tasks are exclusively inherited by functions. Also, under the RBAC model, roles can be created to represent entitlements so that each of the roles is exclusively inherited by roles that represent tasks and is composed of a collection of permissions that spans one or more systems.

Although the Stanford model does not stipulate multiple inheritance relations between adjacent abstractions, Figure 4.12 clearly illustrates such a relationship. As such in order for a system to meet these requirements would require the use of a general role hierarchy.

4.6 Accounting for the Stanford model

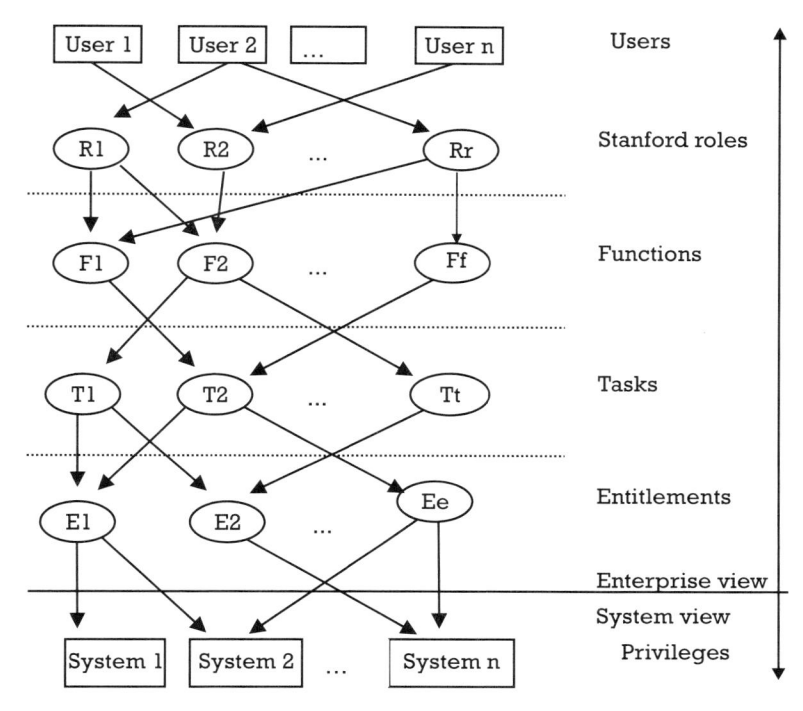

Figure 4.13 Representing the Stanford model's abstractions using roles and inheritance relations.

References

[1] Ferraiolo, D., and R. Kuhn, "Role-Based Access Control," *Proc. of the NIST-NSA Nat. (USA) Comp. Security Conf.,* 1992, pp. 554–563.

[2] Ferraiolo, D., J. Cugini, and R. Kuhn. "Role-Based Access Control: Features and Motivations," *Proc. of the Annual Computer Security Applications Conf.,* New Orleans: IEEE Press, 1995.

[3] Sandhu, R., et al., "Role-Based Access Control Models," *IEEE Computer,* 29(2), February 1996.

[4] Baldwin, R. W., "Naming and Grouping Privileges To Simplify Security Management in Large Databases," *Proceedings of the IEEE Computer Society Symposium on Research in Security and Privacy,* April 1990, pp. 184–194.

[5] Nyanchama, M., and S. L. Osborn, "Access Rights Administration in Role-Based Security Systems," *Proceedings of the IFIP WG11.3 Working Conference on Database Security,* 1994. *See also* Nyanchama, M., and S. L. Osborn, "The

Role Graph Model and Conflict of Interest," *ACM Transactions on Information and System Security* (TISSEC), Vol. 2, No. 1, February 1999, pp. 3–33.

[6] Moffett, J. D., and E. C. Lupu, "The Uses of Role Hierarchies in Access Control," *Proc. of the 4th ACM Workshop on Role-Based Access Control,*" 1999, pp. 153–160.

[7] McRae, R., *The Stanford Model for Access Control Administration,* Stanford University, 2000 (unpublished).

CHAPTER 5

Contents

5.1 Types of SoD

5.2 Using SoD in real systems

5.3 Temporal constraints in RBAC

References

SoD and Constraints in RBAC Systems

SoD is a fundamental principle in security systems, both automated and manual. Although there are many variations, SoD is fundamentally a requirement that *critical operations are divided among two or more people, so that no single individual can compromise security*. Banks require that two employees be present when opening and processing deposits from an ATM or night deposit box. In the military, SoD is known as the "two-man rule" and is required for operations involving nuclear weapons. In both cases, the goal is the same: to ensure that no one person has the ability to control all the steps involved in a high-risk operation. When SoD rules are properly implemented, collusion of two or more employees is required to commit a damaging action; the risk of damage to the organization is therefore reduced. In addition to reducing the risk of fraud, SoD increases the opportunity for detecting errors, since two or more parties are involved in completing a transaction.

Accounting and financial management offices often have particularly elaborate SoD requirements to deter fraud. Figure 5.1 shows a section of an accounting manual detailing the requirements for disbursement and deposit of funds. When humans perform the tasks involved, complex requirements like those in Figure 5.1 are not difficult to implement. However, most computer security mechanisms do not easily accommodate SoD rules. One banking industry analyst notes that "the use of technology has eroded many traditional SoD controls and has provided individual employees access to greater

> **Separation of Duties**
>
> I. Disbursement of Funds
>
> The following minimum separation of duties applies to individuals in departments and accounting offices who are responsible for the disbursement of funds.
>
> > The following duties shall be performed by different individuals:
> >
> > 1. Check request reviewer—evaluates requests with respect to business purpose, applicable policy, backup documentation, and authorized signature.
> > 2. Check preparer—prepares checks and ledger entries.
> > 3. Check issuer— has checks signed and approves ledger entry.
> > 4. Check deliverer—distributes checks or sends to payees.
> > 5. Ledger reviewer—reconciles bank statement with general ledger cash account.
>
> II. Depository Funds
>
> The following minimum separation of duties applies to individuals in departments and accounting offices who are responsible for depository funds.
>
> > The following duties shall be performed by different individuals:
> >
> > 1. Mail handler—opens mail, reviews, and endorses checks.
> > 2. Cashier—processes cash, determines account coding, and deposits in bank account or delivers to another cashier.
> > 3. Auditor—ensures that all checks received are deposited and accounts coded correctly; also receives checks returned to the office.
> > 4. Ledger reviewer—reconciles department accounting records with accounting office records.

Figure 5.1 Example accounting system SoDs.

amounts of money in a single transaction" [1]. Part of the problem today is that traditional computer security software makes it difficult to build SoD constraints into computerized operations.

> **SoD definitions:**
>
> **American National Standards Institute:** "Dividing responsibility for sensitive information so that no individual acting alone can compromise the security of the data processing system." (*Telecom Glossary 2000*, American National Standard for Telecommunications, American National Standards Institute)
>
> The U.S. Office of Management and Budget's Circular A-123 (revised June 21, 1995): "Key duties and responsibilities in authorizing, processing, recording, and reviewing official agency transactions should be separated among individuals."

When controls are not implemented properly, automated systems make it easy for large amounts of money to be lost in a short time. A spectacular example of this occurred in 1995 when one of Britain's oldest merchant banks collapsed as a result of high-risk trading. The bank's Singapore office chief, Nicholas Leeson, was allowed to run both the financial derivatives trading operation in Singapore as well as back-office functions where trades were settled. This is a mix of roles that can be—and in this case was—disastrous. An SoD between making and settling trades would have prevented this disaster.

Two 1999 cases described by the inspector general of the U.S. Department of Veterans Affairs (VA) illustrate how vulnerable automated systems can be with inadequate SoD controls. In one case, a supervisor at a VA regional office stole $615,451 in less than 2 years by establishing a fraudulent disability award for her fiancé, a Gulf War veteran. A second embezzlement scheme had been going on for 12 years when it was discovered in 1999. In this case, a former VA employee had created a fraudulent disability award for himself using another person's social security number, which made it possible to avoid detection by computer-matching DoD and Social Security Administration records. The VA inspector general testified that "SoD controls intended to prevent fraud had been abandoned or circumvented" [2]. Management officials had abandoned SoD requirements in order to speed up processing:

> At some VBA[1] regions, employees were authorized for duplicative computer command authorities, in violation of VA policy, apparently to increase overall production capability. This gave the employees the ability to circumvent SoD controls and computer edits to create a benefit account and approve payment, without the need to refer the case to another employee for authorization. Employees with these extraordinary authorities could also create a fictitious benefit payment account and generate payments, or fraudulently upgrade the benefit payments of otherwise entitled beneficiaries, without the knowledge of other VBA employees. We also found other significant computer access vulnerabilities that could be exploited to perpetrate a fraud, such as by acquiring and using the computer access authorities of others to conceal the perpetrator's involvement [2].

The VA experience illustrates both the difficulty of implementing SoD controls in computer systems and the potential for loss when they are not present. Inevitably, when computer security controls are cumbersome and

---

1. Veterans Benefits Administration.

inefficient, users circumvent or disable them. One of RBAC's great advantages is that SoD rules can be implemented in a natural and efficient way. In fact, SoD has been studied more in the context of RBAC than in any other field of computer security.

5.1 Types of SoD

Researchers have proposed a great variety of SoD models, only some of which are implemented in real products. This section focuses on the most significant categories of SoD that are likely to be important in practice. A comprehensive survey by Simon and Zurko [3] found two broad categories of SoD methods: static and dynamic. A simple way to distinguish between these two forms is to consider the time at which the role constraints are applied. Static SoD places constraints on roles at the time users are authorized for roles. For example, a policy may require that if a user is authorized for role *A*, then the same user cannot be authorized for role *B*. In dynamic SoD (DSD), constraints are invoked when users are actively using the system. This is a weaker form of SoD, since, for example, it may allow a user to be authorized for both roles *A* and *B*, but not allow the user to hold these roles simultaneously in a single session. Depending on an organization's security needs and resources, either static or dynamic rules may be appropriate.

5.1.1 Static SoD

SoD relations are often used to enforce conflict-of-interest policies, which should be analyzed organizationwide, across distributed systems [4]. Conflict of interest in a role-based system may arise as a result of a user gaining authorization for permissions associated with conflicting roles. One means of preventing this form of conflict of interest is though *static SoD*—that is, to enforce constraints on the assignment of users to roles. This means that if a user is assigned to one role, the user is prohibited from being a member of a second role. For example, Figure 5.2 shows a role hierarchy with SoD constraints.

A user who is assigned to the role billing clerk may not be assigned to the role accounts receivable clerk. That is, the role billing clerk and accounts receivable clerk are mutually exclusive. A static SoD policy can be centrally specified and then uniformly imposed on specific roles. From a policy perspective, static constraint relations provide a powerful means of enforcing conflict-of-interest and other separation rules over sets of RBAC elements.

5.1 Types of SoD

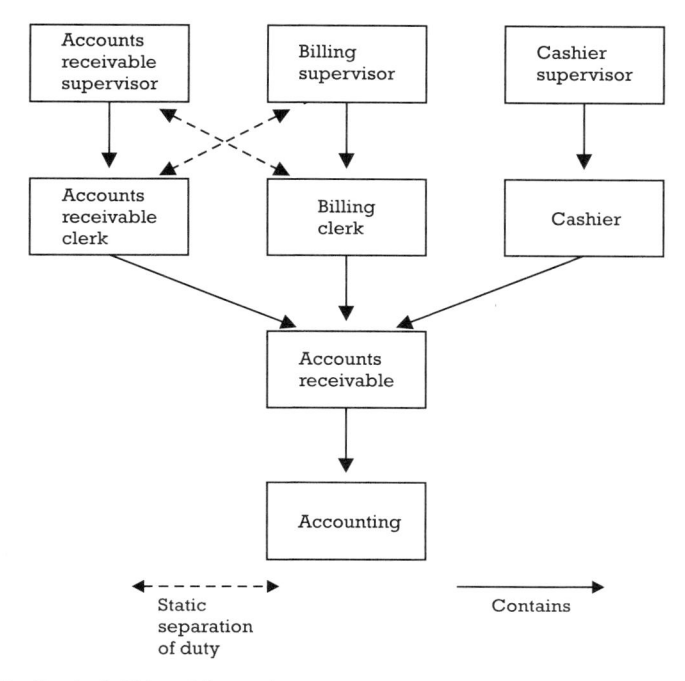

Figure 5.2 Static SoD in a hierarchy.

The static SoD policy can be centrally specified and then uniformly imposed on specific roles. Because of the potential for inconsistencies between static SoD relations and inheritance relations of a role hierarchy, we define static SoD requirements both in the presence and absence of role hierarchies:

- *Static SoD:* Static SoD relations place constraints on the assignments of users to roles. Membership in one role may prevent the user from being a member of one or more other roles, depending on the static SoD rules enforced.
- *Static SoD in the presence of a hierarchy:* This type of static SoD relation works in the same way as basic static SoD except that both inherited roles as well as directly assigned roles are considered when enforcing the constraints.

Figure 5.3 illustrates how static SoD fits into the RBAC framework. With respect to the constraints placed on the user-role assignments for defined sets of roles, we can define static SoD as a pair (*role set, n*) where no user is

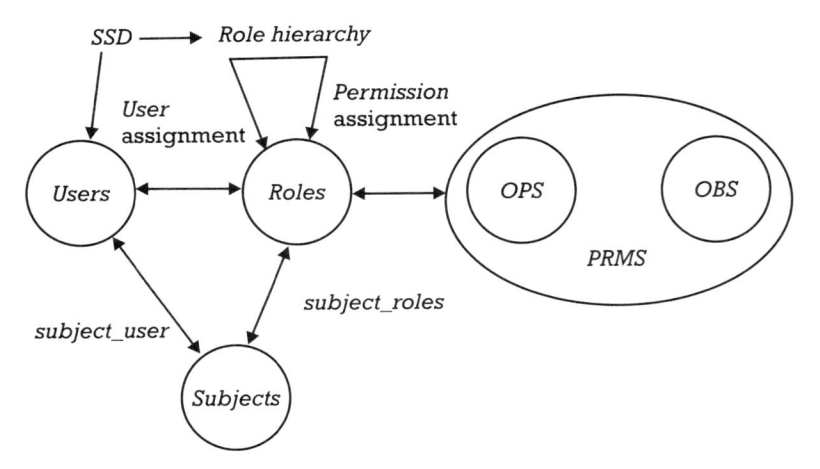

Figure 5.3 Static SoD.

assigned to *n* or more roles from the role set (in most real applications, *n* = 2). Thus, we recognize a variety of static SoD policies. For example, a user may not be assignable to every role in a specified role set, while a strong deployment of the same feature may restrict a user from being assigned to any combination of two or more roles in the role set.

Static constraints can take on a wide variety of forms. A common example is mutually disjoint user assignments with respect to sets of roles [5, 6]. However, static constraints have been shown to be a powerful means of implementing a number of other important SoD policies. For example, Simon and Zurko [3], Gligor et al. [7], and Ahn and Sandhu [8] have identified static SoD relations to include constraints on users, operations, and objects as well as combinations thereof. Some authors [8–12] have studied other forms of constraints recently, but so far consensus has not been developed.

Although static SoD appears to be overly restrictive and may not work for smaller organizations, it is often used in practice because it is easy to implement and simple to verify. Unless an organization is very small, the job titles involved in requesting or approving an expenditure (e.g., a manager), recording the expenditure (e.g., account clerk), and releasing funds (e.g., cashier) are likely to be mutually exclusive. This form of SoD policy arises naturally in organizations and is highly effective.

Static SoD is also particularly easy to implement with RBAC. Consider this discussion of SoD rules in a case study used by the American Institute of

5.1 Types of SoD

> **Formal definition: Static SoD** If static separation is required for any pair of roles r_1 and r_2, then r_1 and r_2 can have no common assigned users.
>
> $SSD \subseteq (2^{ROLES} \times N)$ is collection of pairs (rs, n) in static SoD, where each rs is a role set and n is a natural number ≥ 2, with the property that no user is assigned to n or more roles from the set rs in each
>
> $(rs, n) \in SSD$
>
> Formally:
>
> $$\forall (rs,n) \in SSD, \forall s \subseteq rs : |s| \geq n \Rightarrow \bigcap_{r \in s} assigned\_users(r) = \emptyset$$
>
> **Static SoD in the presence of a hierarchy:** In the presence of a role hierarchy static SoD is redefined based on authorized users rather than assigned users as follows:
>
> $$\forall (rs,n) \in SSD, \forall s \subseteq rs : |s| \geq n \Rightarrow \bigcap_{r \in s} authorized\_users(r) = \emptyset$$

Certified Public Accountants describing a database application that processes payroll [13]:

> For example, a payroll clerk who has been granted "update" and "add" privileges to the payroll register table should not be able to generate paychecks. If this were to happen, the payroll clerk could then produce erroneous paychecks (e.g., by modifying his or her hours worked, adding a new timecard for a friend, or adding a fictitious employee with a post office box address to which the payroll clerk possesses the key). This type of security represents a *logical* SoD. *Manual* SoD is also important; it includes restricting the payroll clerk from possessing blank payroll checks.

A conventional ACL approach is described in this case study. The clerk's user ID is attached to the ACL for the payroll register table, with "add" and "update" privileges. An audit program must then be used to ensure that the clerk's user ID is not also attached to the paycheck-generating application. Additional reviews must be made to ensure that this particular clerk does not have another user ID that violates these constraints. When an enterprise employs thousands of people, privilege audits such as these become extraordinarily complex and time-consuming.

In an RBAC system, the SoD requirements for this example can be handled by assigning the ability to update the payroll register to one role and the ability to generate payroll checks to another role. These roles are then made mutually exclusive; from this point on, the RBAC system will ensure that no individual can be assigned to both roles.

5.1.2 Dynamic SoD

Dynamic SoD (DSD) (Figure 5.4) is the second broad category of SoD. With dynamic separation, users may be authorized for roles that may conflict, but limitations are imposed while the user is actively logged onto the system. For example, consider the problem of processing expenditures in a small business. With limited personnel, it is not possible to have each of the tasks shown in Figure 5.1 performed by separate individuals. An alternative is to require that no person can be active in both roles at the same time. All employees in the firm may have privileges to request expenditures or approve them, but a DSD rule prevents them from applying both privileges to expenditures in the same session. Note the hidden assumption that a user does not terminate a session and log in with the other role. Auditing or some other mechanism is required to ensure that this loophole is not exploited when DSD is used.

Dynamic SoD relations, like static SoD relations, limit the permissions that are available to a user. However DSD relations differ from static SoD relations by the context in which these limitations are imposed. DSD requirements limit the availability of the permissions by placing constraints on the roles that can be activated within or across a user's sessions.

Similar to static SoD relations, DSD relations define constraints as a pair (*role set, n*) where *n* is a natural number ≥ 2, with the property that no user session may simultaneously activate *n* or more roles from the role set.

DSD properties provide extended support for the principle of least privilege in that each user has different levels of permission at different times, depending on the task being performed. This ensures that permissions do

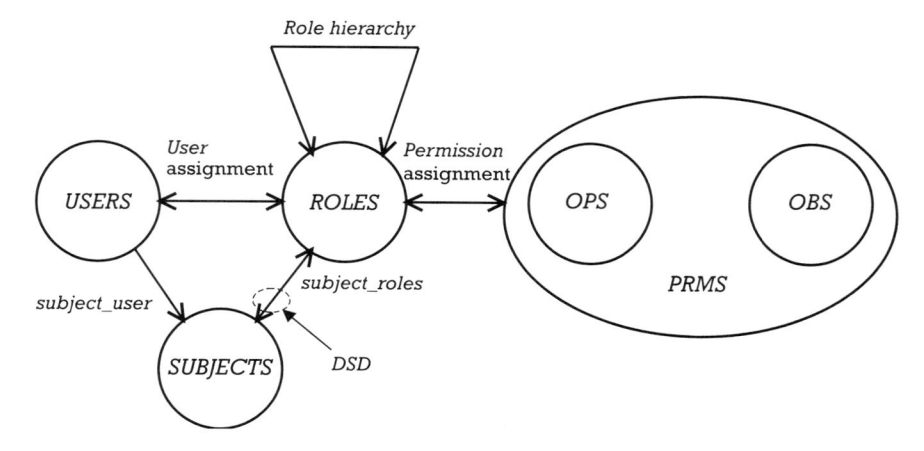

Figure 5.4 DSD.

> **Formal definition: DSD** If dynamic separation is required for any pair of roles r_1 and r_2, then r_1 and r_2 can have no common authorized users.
> $DSD \subseteq (2^{ROLES} \times N)$ is collection of pairs (rs, n) in DSD, where each rs is a role set and n is a natural number ≥ 2, with the property that no subject may activate n or more roles from the set rs in each $dsd \in DSD$. Formally:
> $\forall rs \in 2^{ROLES}$, $n \in N$, $(rs, n) \in DSD \Rightarrow n \geq 2 \wedge |rs| \geq n$, and
> $\forall s \in SUBJECTS$, $\forall rs \in 2^{ROLES}$, $role\_subset \in 2^{ROLES}$, $\forall n \in N$, $(rs, n) \in DSD$, $role\_subset \subseteq rs$, $role\_subset \subseteq subject\_roles(s) \Rightarrow |role\_subset| < n$.

not persist beyond the time that they are required for performance of duty. This aspect of least privilege is often referred to as *timely revocation of trust.* Dynamic revocation of permissions can be a complex issue without the facilities of dynamic SoD and thus has been generally ignored in the past for reasons of expediency.

Static SoD relations provide the capability to address potential conflict-of-interest issues at the time a user is assigned to a role. DSD allows a user to be authorized for two or more roles that do not create a conflict of interest when acted in independently but produce policy concerns when activated simultaneously. For example, a user may be authorized for both the roles of cashier and cashier supervisor, where the supervisor is allowed to acknowledge corrections to a cashier's open cash drawer. If the individual acting in the role cashier attempted to switch to the role cashier supervisor, RBAC would require the user to drop the cashier role, and thereby force the closure of the cash drawer before assuming the role cashier supervisor. As long as the same user is not allowed to assume both of these roles at the same time, a conflict of interest situation will not arise. Although this effect could be achieved through the establishment of a static SoD relationship, DSD relations generally provide the enterprise with greater operational flexibility.

5.1.3 Operational SoD

RBAC can be used to enforce a policy of operational SoD [14], defined as follows: No single user can be allowed to perform all operations required to perform a critical function. Implicit in this definition is a requirement that at least two roles are required for any critical function. Therefore, the failure of one role to perform as expected can be detected by the organization. In RBAC terms, the operational SoD policy can be enforced when roles are authorized for individual users and when operations are assigned to roles.

Note that this means that operational SoD can be implemented either as a static or dynamic form of separation.

5.1.4 History and object-based SoD

One form of SoD discussed in research literature, although not widely implemented, takes into account the history access to system objects. For example, it may be acceptable for one person to do both request and approval of expenditures, provided no one individual can both request and approve the same item. Small firms in particular may need this arrangement. It may be too expensive to have a single person dedicated full-time to order processing, or temporary absence may require one person to fill several roles that would be mutually exclusive in a large organization.

An early model for a flexible form of SoD was offered by Sandhu [15], who proposed the use of "transaction control expressions" that represent the potential history of access to an object. SoD rules could be enforced by maintaining a complete history on transient system objects, such as an expenditure transaction, and an abbreviated history on persistent objects, such as a general ledger. A commercial security product using "object-based" separation was described by Nash and Poland [16], who also showed that transaction control expressions could be used to define this policy. This approach allowed a user to simultaneously be authorized for mutually exclusive roles but not to act upon an object that she or he has previously acted upon. For example, a user might both prepare checks and cash them but could not cash a check that he or she had prepared. This approach is simple, but it limits users to handling only one part of a business process. If multiple steps are involved in a process, SoD could be maintained when users handle more than one step, provided that no single individual handles all steps.

A variety of recent proposals have highlighted history- and context-sensitive controls, in which a user's current task is included in the access control decision [17–19]. A recent example of such a policy, designated as "history-based," was proposed by Papenfus and Botha [20]. History-based SoD can be thought of as a dynamic form of operational SoD policy. A user can have all the privileges required for a critical task, but cannot perform all the parts of a task on the same object.

Including history in SoD controls provides the most flexible approach, but at the cost of greater complexity in the access control system. The system must keep track of the ID of each user who processes objects in a business process. This may be relatively efficient when all parts of a process are managed by a single application. For example, a database system may contain all the records required in a payroll application and provide the transactions needed to process payroll records. The DBMS transactions can pass user ID information between transactions related to a particular payroll record to provide the information needed to ensure that a single individual does not handle all parts of the business process.

With larger, more complex processes, however, this may be more difficult. Records must be passed securely between multiple computer applications, with mechanisms to ensure that the records have not been tampered with and that all records were properly originated. These requirements can generally be handled in two ways: (1) by having the access control system keep track of all objects and their current state, the users interacting with them, and their progress through applications, and (2) by attaching information to objects and records showing who has handled the object and what applications have been used. Both approaches have their own sets of advantages and problems.

History-based SoD mechanisms introduce considerable additional complexity, because they require systems to keep records of all user actions on system objects. This added complexity is one reason why general-purpose commercial access control systems (such as for DBMSs) so far have not implemented history-based approaches. Although a number of researchers have proposed sophisticated history-based mechanisms, it will likely be several years before this work makes its way from the laboratory to the marketplace. This situation results in an ironic conundrum: History-based approaches will most likely require special application development, but the small businesses that require the flexibility of history-based mechanisms are not likely to be able to afford customized software. Users, therefore, need ways to obtain the flexibility of history-based mechanisms using only the basic features that are common to most RBAC systems. Today, the most practical approach is to use a conventional static SoD mechanism but to allow overrides that can be audited to ensure compliance with SoD rules.

5.2 Using SoD in real systems

RBAC systems available on the market provide many sophisticated features, including the ability to create complex role hierarchies, but very few have strong support for SoD. Some provide mechanisms that can be used to implement SoD constraints to a limited degree. Developers and system integrators need to look closely at features provided by operating systems and DBMSs that support RBAC, because SoD is the area in which features are most often limited. This section discusses the current state of SoD features in commercial systems, how these features affect the design of systems enforcing SoD rules, and trade-offs that can be made in system design. In general, automated role engineering tools will be needed to create and check SoD rules in an RBAC system. This section aims to provide an understanding of the important concepts that are implemented in role engineering tools.

5.2.1 SoD in role hierarchies

Most RBAC systems available today support role hierarchies in some form, and SoD constraints have important implications for role hierarchies that can affect the administration of SoD rules. When roles inherit other roles, the system must ensure that the inheritance structure cannot result in a violation of separation constraints. The properties given below by Kuhn [5] are important in understanding the interaction between SoD rules and role inheritance. The first three properties are obvious from definitions:

- *Property 1:* Two roles R_i and R_j can be mutually exclusive only if neither one inherits the other, either directly or indirectly. Clearly, if a user inherits one of the roles, SoD is not maintained if he or she can also invoke the other role. Role administration is affected by this rule. To be useful, role management tools must alert the administrator to SoD violations created by inheritance.

- *Property 2:* If there are two roles R_i and R_j that are mutually exclusive, then there can be no third role that inherits both of them. As with property 1, this property must be handled properly by role management tools to allow administrators to set up role hierarchies that do not violate SoD constraints.

- *Property 3:* If static SoD holds, then DSD is maintained. Clearly, if a user is only authorized for one of two roles, then he or she can never be active in both. The practical importance of this rule is that SoD policies can be simplified if the organization has sufficient resources to permanently limit the roles that a user may activate. In Figure 5.2, for example, if a user in the role "accounts receivable clerk" will never need to have access to the role "billing clerk," static separation can be established for these roles. Since the SoD constraint is established when roles are authorized, the system never needs to check these constraints during a user session, which will improve performance and reduce the risk of vulnerabilities introduced by bugs in the software.

- *Property 4:* If there are any two roles R_i and R_j that are mutually exclusive, then there can be no "root" or "superuser" (a role that has all

5.2 Using SoD in real systems

system privileges) role active on the system. This occurs because no role can inherit two others that are mutually exclusive, and a "root" role would inherit all other roles. Note that this holds even if DSD is used. Under DSD, a single user could be authorized for all roles, but the roles could not be active simultaneously. However, because the "root" role inherits all other roles, "root" could never be activated with all its inherited roles.

Constraints, including SoD, are inherited in the opposite direction from role membership. If the role hierarchy is represented as a tree with the most general role at the root, then role membership is inherited "down." For example, consider the accounting department hierarchy in Figure 5.2, which includes the membership chain Accts Receivable Supervisor > Accts Receivable Clerk > Accounts Receivable > Accounting. An employee designated as "Accts Receivable Clerk" inherits membership down the tree, to include accounts receivable and accounting.

Constraints are inherited in the opposite direction. In Figure 5.2, since the roles accounts receivable clerk and billing clerk have a static SoD relationship, then accounts receivable supervisor also has a static SoD relationship with billing clerk. Another way of thinking of this is that any instance of accounts receivable supervisor can be treated as an instance of accounts receivable clerk. Therefore, the static SoD constraint billing clerk has with accounts receivable clerk must also apply to accounts receivable supervisor. In other words, constraints are inherited in an "up" direction in the hierarchy, toward the more specialized roles.

5.2.2 Static and dynamic constraints

The simplest way to provide SoD is to give administrators the ability to specify two roles as mutually exclusive: A user authorized for one role may not be authorized for the other role. This provides static SoD. DSD requires that users not be active in two mutually exclusive roles at the same time, although they may be authorized for both. Surprisingly, some commercial systems provide support (in a sense) for DSD without providing static SoD. Some systems allow a user to be active in only a single role at a time or give the ability to restrict the number of roles that a user can activate simultaneously. An example of this functionality is the Informix DBMS system [21], which allows the creation of roles and role hierarchies. Only one role can be activated at a time. It is not possible to specify mutual exclusion or other constraints on roles. Since only one role can be activated at a time, Informix does provide a basic form of DSD. A byproduct of preventing a user from activating more than one role at a time is thus a form of DSD. Without the ability to establish constraints on role authorization, though, these systems cannot ensure static SoD. In addition, DSD can only be ensured through the careful administration of roles. An additional tool will be needed to audit complex role sets to ensure that user-role assignments meet policy constraints.

Full support for both static SoD and DSD is available in few products. Sybase's DBMS is one example of a product that features both static SoD and DSD. Static SoD is provided by allowing administrators to specify two roles as mutually exclusive. Mutual exclusion is a simple and effective way to establish basic static and dynamic SoD. SoD policies that require keeping track of an object's history require more than the ability to set up roles as mutually exclusive, but the Sybase feature provides the necessary basis to build more sophisticated policies into applications.

5.2.3 Mutual exclusion

Existing systems, and those likely to be available in the near future, typically rely on mutual exclusion of roles to enforce SoD policies. However, mutual exclusion rules may be provided in more than one way, and the design of this feature can affect ease of use significantly. Consider again the accounting rules shown in Figure 5.1. As indicated, different individuals must fill the five different roles. How should this SoD policy be implemented? There are a number of possibilities, depending on the features of the RBAC system and on how strictly the policy is interpreted. The policy in Figure 5.1 requires that if an individual has one of the roles, she or he must be excluded from all others. If the system provides the capability, this policy might be implemented using mutual exclusion rules in one of two ways:

- *Exclusion specified by sets:* It may be possible to declare a set of roles that are mutually exclusive (i.e., membership in any one role of the set precludes membership in another). This feature is particularly desirable if the application requires elaborate SoD requirements such as in Figure 5.1. A related design by Crampton and Loizou uses lattices to provide greater flexibility in policy representation [22].
- *Exclusion specified by role pairs:* If the system provides only the capability to specify *pairs* of roles that are mutually exclusive, the problem becomes more complex. For n roles, the number of pairs is $\frac{n(n-1)}{2}$. For five roles, then, there are 10 mutual exclusion pairs that must be

specified (see Figure 5.5). For the example application, this feature is clearly much less desirable than a system that provides the ability to specify a set of roles as mutually exclusive.

If the system offers only the option of specifying pairs of mutually exclusive roles, implementation of this policy will be cumbersome, since the number of pairs increases quadratically with the number of mutually exclusive roles. An alternative to specifying 10 pairs of mutually exclusive roles would be to adopt a less strict policy that still meets the objectives of SoD. If the objective is to ensure that no individual has access to all five roles, it is sufficient to specify only one mutual-exclusion pair. For example, if "check request reviewer" and "check preparer" are mutually exclusive, then any user who is authorized for one will be excluded from the other, and thus cannot have access to all five roles.

5.2.4 Effects of privilege assignment

The discussion so far has introduced concepts that seem natural and intuitive. In systems that are fully or partially manual, SoD is relatively easy to implement. Even in elaborate accounting SoD systems, such as depicted in Figure 5.1, it is easy to see that multiple individuals will be involved with any transactions. However, fully automated systems make it much more difficult to determine whether SoD is adequate. It is not enough to ensure

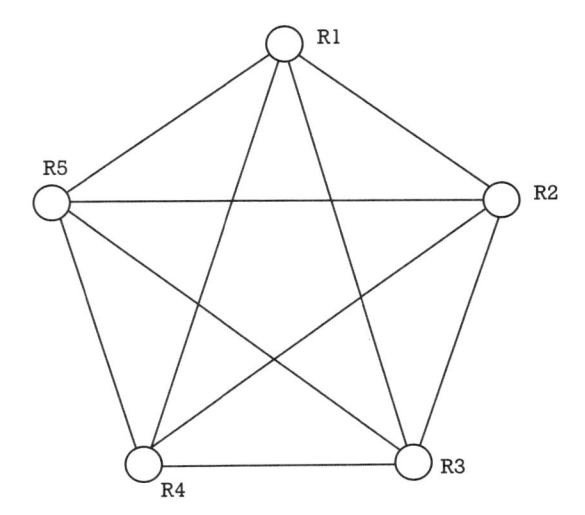

Figure 5.5 Mutual exclusion possibilities for five roles.

that people in different roles are involved with all transactions, because what are critical are the privileges available to a single individual. If all interactions are through a computerized system, there may be little human oversight of activities. If a single individual has access to all privileges needed to accomplish some critical function, then the system can be compromised regardless of the role structure. In a manual, or even semiautomated system, SoD mechanisms are easy to implement. However, there is a serious potential for violation of SoD rules when roles and privileges are assigned in a paperless office system. The assignment of privileges to roles is as critical as the establishment of SoD relationships between roles.

Complications arise if privileges are made available to other roles that may not be designated as mutually exclusive. Care must be taken to avoid a situation in which some combination of roles would allow a user to have access to privileges that should be mutually exclusive. For example, suppose there are two roles, P and Q, that are mutually exclusive, and that role Q has access to privileges b and c. Assume that role R has privilege b and that role S has privilege c. Then, a user in role P could gain access to the same capability provided by role Q through roles R and S.

For a more concrete example, consider the payroll example described in Section 5.1.1, in which a payroll clerk who has been granted "update" and "add" privileges to the payroll register table should not be able to generate paychecks. A static SoD relationship is established between the role "payroll clerk" and another role "payroll processor," which has privileges to execute the payroll program. If there is a third role, say "computer operator," whose privileges include executing the payroll program, then clearly anyone authorized for "payroll clerk" must not also be authorized for "computer operator." This example illustrates a critical point: SoD policies must be analyzed by first considering what privileges are required by particular tasks and then evaluating the distribution of privileges among roles.

As discussed in the introduction, the purpose of SoD rules is to prevent one person from doing all parts of a task to reduce the risk of malicious activity. The examples discussed above can accomplish this, but depending on how privileges are assigned, the breakdown of roles between individuals may be more restrictive than necessary, or errors may be made that allow one person all privileges required for a task. The payroll clerk example described above is an example of the latter problem. As an example of the first problem, consider the distribution of roles in Figure 5.1. Clearly this five-way separation of roles will accomplish SoD requirements, but it may be more restrictive than necessary.

In automated systems, with large numbers of privileges spread among many employees, relationships between privileges become difficult to review and manage. To help in analyzing the assignment of privileges in automated systems, we can define a *safety condition* as the condition that must be met to ensure that SoD requirements are not violated [5]. The safety condition is simply a formal restatement of the goal of SoD: *No single individual will have the ability to execute a critical task.*

If there are only two privileges needed for a task, then each privilege can be assigned to separate roles, and the roles can be made mutually exclusive. If more than two privileges are involved, then they can be split among two or more roles. While intuitively simple, the assignment of privileges to roles in a safe manner may be more difficult than it at first appears. Section 5.2.5 discusses some considerations regarding safe privilege assignments.

5.2.5 Assigning privileges to roles

Assignment of privileges to roles in a SoD environment can become complex. To accomplish this task safely, an administrator must first ensure that no single role has all privileges needed to accomplish a critical task and then ensure that roles are assigned to individuals in such a way that no individual will have all of these privileges through some combination of roles. Note that inheritance of privileges and roles through hierarchies must be considered as well.

The first problem is the following: Given a set of tasks where each task T_i requires a set of privileges P, assign privileges to roles such that no single role has access to all privileges required by any task. This appears simple, and in most cases it will be. However, in some cases it may not be possible. Consider the following case: There are three critical tasks, $T1$, $T2$, and $T3$, requiring combinations of privileges $P1$, $P2$, and $P3$, as shown in Table 5.1.

Suppose we want to allocate privileges to two roles $R1$ and $R2$, in such a way that no task is compromised with respect to SoD requirements (i.e., neither role has all the privileges needed to perform one of the critical tasks). Unfortunately, this is not possible for this example. To see this, note

---

Formal definition: Static SoD safety condition:
Given $T = \{\text{critical tasks requiring SoD}\}$
$TP_i = \{\text{privileges required for task } i\}$
$$\forall u \in USERS, TP_i \not\subset \bigcup_{r \in user\_role^*(u)} authorized\_permissions(r)$$
Alternatively,
$$\forall u \in USERS, \exists p \in PRMS, p \in TP_i \wedge p \notin \bigcup_{r \in user\_role^*(u)} authorized\_permissions(r)$$
(An analogous definition for dynamic separation would use session privileges.)

Table 5.1 Mapping of Privileges to Tasks

	P1	P2	P3
T1	X	X	—
T2	—	X	X
T3	X	—	X

that all privileges must be assigned to some role. If there are two roles, then two or more privileges must be assigned to at least one of the roles. There are $\binom{3}{2} = 3$ possible ways to choose two privileges out of three: {P1,P2}, {P1,P3}, and {P2,P3}. Because there are three tasks, each requiring a different combination of two privileges, at least one task will be compromised. The only way to ensure safe SoD in this example is to establish a third role and to ensure that no individual has access to a combination of roles that would compromise a task. In most applications this problem will not occur, because tasks normally require several privileges, and privileges are allocated among several roles. However, this example illustrates the important point that it is sometimes necessary to create an additional role that was not in the original organizational structure to ensure SoD.

5.2.6 Assigning roles to users

To maintain SoD, roles must be assigned to users in such a way that no user can violate SoD rules through a combination of roles. This requires that no single user possess all the privileges needed to accomplish a task that is controlled under SoD. In the payroll clerk example of Section 5.1.1, we noted that SoD requirements could be met by assigning the ability to update the payroll register to one role and the ability to generate payroll checks to another role (e.g., payroll clerk and payroll department computer operator). These roles could be made mutually exclusive so that the RBAC system could ensure that no individual could be assigned to both roles. There is, of course, a hidden assumption in this example that if a user is assigned to "payroll clerk," the same user could not acquire the privileges needed to generate payroll checks through a third role, even though "payroll clerk" and "payroll department computer operator" are mutually exclusive.

Given a set of roles and mutual exclusion relationships, how many separate users are required to ensure that roles can be assigned without violating SoD requirements? Consider the example in Table 5.2, which depicts the

5.2 Using SoD in real systems

Table 5.2 Example of a Mutual Exclusion Relationship

	R1	R2	R3	R4	R5
R1	—	X	X	—	—
R2	X	—	X	—	X
R3	X	X	—	X	—
R4	—	—	X	—	X
R5	—	X	—	X	—

mutual exclusion relationship between five roles, $R1$ through $R5$. [An X in cell i,j indicates that role R_i is mutually exclusive to R_j (e.g., that $R1$ and $R2$ are mutually exclusive).] It is not immediately obvious how to assign roles to users to ensure that this mutual exclusion relationship is maintained. We could, of course, assign one role to each of five users, but is it essential to have five, or could fewer users suffice?

Using graph theory, there is an easy way to determine this number, within at most one greater than the minimum. The *chromatic number*, $\chi(G)$, of a graph is the minimum number of colors that are required to color vertices so that no two adjacent vertices are the same color. We can model the mutual exclusion relationship with a graph, shown in Figure 5.6. The graph is constructed directly from Table 5.2, so that two roles are connected in the graph whenever they are designated as mutually exclusive.

Only three colors are needed to ensure that no edge in this graph connects two vertices of the same color; therefore, SoD requirements can be

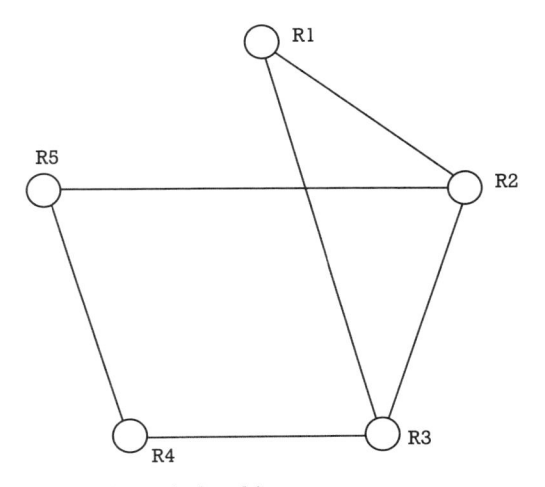

Figure 5.6 Mutual exclusion relationships.

maintained by assigning roles $R1$ through $R5$ to three different users, corresponding to the three colors. For example, if $R1$ = red, $R2$ = green, $R3$ = blue, $R4$ = green, and $R5$ = red, $\chi(G) = 3$ for this graph. It is a theorem of graph theory that the chromatic number of any graph G is equal to the largest complete graph that is a subgraph of G. A *complete* graph is one in which every node is connected to every other node. (See Figure 5.7.)

The graph in Figure 5.6 is not complete, but the five-node graph in Figure 5.7 is. It is easy to recognize a complete subgraph using an adjacency matrix like that above—a complete graph appears as a filled triangle of Xs, as highlighted in Table 5.3.

To quickly determine the size of the largest complete subgraph, we can use another theorem, which states that for any graph G, $\chi(G) \leq \Delta(G) + 1$, where $\Delta(G)$ is the *degree* of the graph. The degree is simply the largest number of edges connected to any vertex, which can be determined by counting the Xs in rows of the matrix (Table 5.3). In Table 5.3, no row has more than three Xs, so we know that no more than four users are needed to maintain the SoD relationship. If the graph is not completely connected, we can do better using a result known as Brooks' theorem, which states that $\chi(G) \leq \Delta(G)$ if G is not complete. Since our example graph is not complete, we

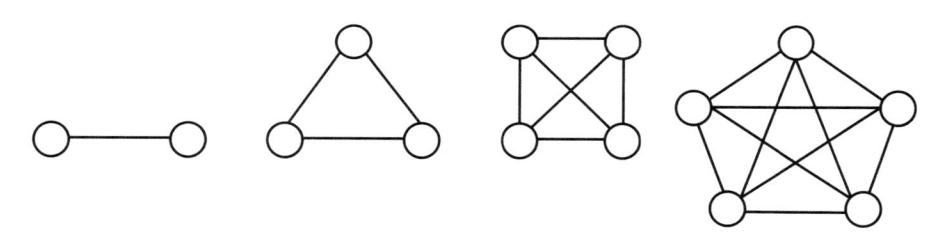

Figure 5.7 The first four complete graphs.

Table 5.3 Complete Subgraph in Example from Table 5.2

	R1	R2	R3	R4	R5
R1	—	X	X	—	—
R2	X	—	X	—	X
R3	X	X	—	X	—
R4	—	—	X	—	X
R5	—	X	—	X	—

5.2 Using SoD in real systems

can tell that no more than three users are needed simply by looking at the number of Xs in each row of the mutual exclusion table.

To better understand the complexities involved in assigning privileges, roles, and users in a SoD environment, we can consider the necessary and sufficient conditions for safe privilege assignment. A necessary condition, as the name implies, is a condition that is essential; without it, all bets are off. A sufficient condition, on the other hand, is one that guarantees the relationship we seek. It may be overkill, though, in that it may be more than needed to ensure the relationship. In most cases, some condition in between necessary and sufficient conditions will be established in real systems. For SoD, necessary and sufficient conditions are described as follows by Kuhn [5]:

- *Necessary:* For any pair of roles that are mutually exclusive, each role must contain one privilege of a critical task not available to the other role in the mutual exclusion relationship. To see why this is a necessary condition, note that if it did not hold, then the privileges of one role, $R1$, could be a subset of another, $R2$. Then mutual exclusion between $R1$ and $R2$ would be irrelevant for a user with access to role $R2$. Note that this condition is *necessary,* but not *sufficient* [i.e., maintaining this condition does not ensure the safety of role assignments, but if it is not maintained, then we cannot use mutual exclusion (alone) to ensure that a role assignment is safe].

- *Sufficient:* For any role $R1$ in a mutual exclusion relationship, no privileges in $R1$ are available to any other role $R2$. This condition is fairly obvious; if two roles $R1$ and $R2$ each have a privilege that is needed to accomplish a particular task, then making them mutually exclusive guarantees that two individuals will be needed to accomplish the task, thus ensuring SoD. This condition, though *sufficient,* is not *necessary.* In most cases it will be a stronger condition than needed to ensure SoD.

These conditions underscore a fundamental point about SoD: If privileges are accessible by more than one role, then we need to pay attention to privilege assignment when setting up mutual exclusion rules for roles. Otherwise, establishing mutual exclusion between roles may only appear to ensure SoD, while leaving a loophole that makes a system vulnerable to fraud.

5.3 Temporal constraints in RBAC

Sections 5.1 and 5.2 deal with the definition and specification of various types of SoD constraints for the RBAC model and the issues involved in their enforcement. This section examines another important class of constraints—the temporal constraints. The temporal (time-based) constraints incorporate the notion of time in specifying access control requirements. Unlike the SoD constraints, the issues relating to the support of temporal constraints in RBAC have not been studied extensively.

The incorporation of time-dependent access control requirements into the RBAC model (through specification of temporal constraints) was first proposed by Bertino et al. [23]. The resultant RBAC model was called the temporal RBAC (TRBAC) model. The TRBAC model was later extended by Joshi et al. [24] into what they called the generalized TRBAC (GTRBAC) model.

Our discussion of temporal constraints in RBAC is organized as follows: First, we briefly look at the need for supporting temporal constraints in an access control model. Next, we look at the taxonomy of the temporal constraints that it may be necessary to support in the RBAC model and illustrate how they can be specified using the specification language of the GTRBAC model. Finally, we discuss other constraint-related and implementation-related features that are required in the RBAC model for supporting temporal constraints.

5.3.1 Need for temporal constraints

Temporal constraints are formal statements of access policies that involve time-based restrictions on access to resources; they are required in several application scenarios. In some applications, temporal constraints may be required to limit resource use. In other types of applications, they may be required for controlling time-sensitive activities such as those found in workflow management systems (WFMSs). It is these time-based constraints (in addition to other constraints like workflow precedence relationships) that must be evaluated for generating dynamic authorizations during workflow execution time (refer to Section 10.1.5). Temporal constraints are also required in nonworkflow environments as well. For example, in a commercial banking enterprise, a user should be able to assume the role of a teller (to perform transactions on customer accounts) only during designated banking hours (say 9 A.M. to 2 P.M., Monday through Friday, and 9 A.M. to 12 P.M. on Saturday). To meet this requirement, it is necessary to specify

5.3 Temporal constraints in RBAC

temporal constraints that limit role availability and activation capability only to those designated banking hours.

5.3.2 Taxonomy of temporal constraints

Depending upon the application needs, an RBAC model should be able to support one or more of the following categories of temporal constraints:

- Temporal constraints on roles;
- Temporal constraints on user-role assignments;
- Temporal constraints on role-permission assignments.

Out of these three categories, the temporal constraints on user-role assignments and role-permission assignments may need to be enforced considerably less frequently than the temporal constraints on roles. Whatever the category of temporal constraint, symbols are required for the representation of time-related concepts, and a generic form is required for representation of temporal constraints. Here, we discuss the symbols developed for representing time-related concepts and the generic constraint form in the GTRBAC model. We then proceed to discuss the above three categories of temporal constraints. We also provide examples of each these categories of constraints as applicable to a specification of access control requirements for a hospital database application.

Representation of time-related concepts The two time-related concepts considered in the GTRBAC model are periodicity and duration. These two concepts are used to represent periodicity-type temporal constraints and duration-type temporal constraints, respectively. The symbols for representation of the periodicity and duration concepts are discussed as follows:

- *Periodicity:* A periodic time is represented by the pairs ([Begin,End],P), where P is the periodic expression denoting a set (possibly infinite) of periodic time instants, and [Begin,End] is a time interval denoting the lower and upper bounds that are imposed on instants in P. For example, the periodic time representation ([1/1/2002, 12/31/2002], Mondays) denotes all the Mondays of 2002.
- *Duration:* A duration is simply represented by a symbol D, which stands for either an expression or a numeral.

Generic form of temporal constraint Temporal constraints in GTRBAC have the generic form (X, E) where X is either a periodic time or duration, and E is an event expression. An example of an event expression is activate r (the event that activates role r).

Temporal constraints on roles Temporal constraints on roles are specified in GTRBAC by making a clear distinction between the concepts—role *enabling* and role *activation*. A role is enabled if a user can acquire the permission assigned to it. An enabled role is said to be *activated* when a user acquires the permissions assigned to the role in a session. The distinction between role enabling and role activation in turn leads to the notion of *role states*. A *disabled* state of a role indicates that the role cannot be used in any user session (i.e., a user cannot acquire the permissions associated with the role). A role in the disabled state can be enabled. The *enabled* state indicates that users who are authorized to use the role (because they have been assigned that role) at the time of request may activate the role, but no one has yet done so. If a user now activates that role, the state of the role becomes active. When a role is in active state, it indicates that there is at least one user who has activated that role. Once in the active state, upon subsequent activation by the same or other users, the role remains in the active state. A role in the active state can go back to the enabled state if all users deactivate that role. A role in either the enabled or active state can transition to the disabled state if a disabling event occurs.

The above discussion should give the reader an idea of the type of temporal constraints that can be specified on roles: role-enabling and -disabling constraints and role-activation and -deactivation constraints. A brief discussion of these constraints follows.

Role-enabling and -disabling constraints These constraints allow one to specify the time interval (periodicity) during which a role is enabled or disabled. It is also possible to denote the length of time (duration) for which a role can remain enabled or disabled. Thus, the role-enabling and role-disabling constraints can be of either the periodicity type or the duration type. For a duration-type constraint to become applicable, a role-enabling or -disabling event should have taken place.

A representation of a periodicity-type constraint that states that the *doctor-on-call* role can be enabled only between 10 P.M. and 6 A.M. during the period November 1, 2002, to March 31, 2003, follows:

```
(([1-Nov-2002,31-March-2003], 22-06), enable
   doctor-on-call)
```

The duration-type constraint that states that a *NurseInTraining* role can remain enabled only for 3 hours follows:

    (2 Hours, enable NurseInTraining)

This constraint can become applicable only when an event had already enabled the *NurseInTraining* role.

Role-activation and -deactivation constraints   These constraints specify how a user should be restricted in activating a role. There is no periodicity-type restriction for a role-activation or -deactivation constraint since a role can be activated or deactivated at the discretion of the user. However a duration-type restriction can be specified for a role-activation or -deactivation constraint.

Suppose a hospital periodically puts up special health reports (SHRs) on some high-incidence diseases and that it allows public health workers to download those reports by assuming the *download-SHR* role. To limit the duration time for which a public health worker remains active in that role (so as not to increase the load on the FTP server), a duration-type constraint for role activation can be specified as follows:

    (45 Min, active download-SHR)

Temporal constraints on user-role assignments   These are constructs to express either a specific interval or duration in which a user is assigned to a role. Very often hospitals hire and make use of the services of outside doctors. These doctors are given the *consulting-physician* role to enable them to access certain patient-related information like clinical tests. A periodicity-type constraint that states that a specialist Dr. Ken is assigned the consulting-physician role from November 1, 2002, to December 31, 2002, can be expressed as follows:

    ([1-Nov-2002,31-Dec-2002], assign Dr.Ken to
      consulting-physician

Temporal constraints on role-permission assignments   These are constructs to express either a specific interval or duration in which a permission is assigned to a role. Suppose a hospital offers several health insurance plans for its employees and that it provides a window of time at the close of the year for employees to change their subscribed health insurance plan. The periodicity-type constraint that states that the permission to change the health insurance plan for an employee (accessing the system with an *employee* role) is only available between December 1, 2002, and December 31, 2002, is expressed as follows:

```
([1-Dec-2002, 31-Dec-2002], assign change-
   health-plan to employee)
```

5.3.3 Associated requirements for supporting temporal constraints

In RBAC models, the constraint enforcement results in an event. Examples of events include the enabling of a role and the activation of a role. In many application domains, there is a requirement for some related events to occur when an event occurs. For example, in the hospital environment, when an attending-physician role is enabled, there is the requirement to enable a nurse-on-duty role as well. In the GTRBAC model, the notion of a role trigger is defined to support such event dependencies. An example of a role trigger to support the dependencies we stated earlier follows:

```
Enable attending-physician    enable Nurse-on-Duty
```

In addition to the automatically enforced temporal constraints (which cause events), there may be practical situations where a security administrator may have to intervene and dynamically initiate certain events. For example, a security administrator may need to enable or disable certain roles and assign or de-assign users or permissions to roles at run time. The GTRBAC model provides constructs to express these run-time requests. In our hospital setting, an intern may be required to take care of some post-surgical patient care tasks. The request to activate an intern role for a specific intern by name Susan is expressed as:

```
Activate intern for Susan after 1 hour
```

In addition to supporting some related event requests (like role triggers and run-time requests), a complete implementation of an RBAC model that supports temporal constraints requires several supporting data stores and functional modules. For example, data stores are required for storing role triggers, occurred events, active roles, and pending actions. Functional modules (called action handlers) are required for executing various types of actions that are a consequence of periodicity and duration constraints, role triggers, and run-time requests. A detailed description of the architecture of the GTRBAC model is given in [24].

Supporting temporal constraints on the RBAC model affects the semantics of the role hierarchies specified in the model. The default semantics of the role hierarchy in the absence of temporal constraints (or for that matter in the hierarchical RBAC model) is that since a senior role inherits the permissions of all its junior roles, activation of a senior role by a user allows that user to acquire all the permissions of all of its junior roles. The presence of various timing constraints relating to role-enabling or role-activation and role-permission assignments results in dynamic hierarchies called *temporal hierarchies*. These temporal hierarchies do not possess the complete permission inheritance properties found in the role hierarchies of RBAC models without the associated temporal constraints. Readers interested in the analysis of the implication of temporal constraints on role hierarchies may refer to [25].

References

[1] Proctor, K., "Why All Banks Should Practice Risk Management," *Hoosier Banker,* April 2001.

[2] Griffin, R. J., *Statement of the Honorable Richard J. Griffin, Inspector General, Department of Veterans Affairs, Before the United States House of Representatives Committee on Veterans Affairs, Subcommittee on Oversight and Investigations Hearing on Fraud and Mismanagement in VA,* September 23, 1999.

[3] Simon, R. T., and M. E. Zurko, "Separation of Duty in Role Based Environments," *Proc. Computer Security Foundations Workshop X,* Rockport, MA, June 1997.

[4] Moffett, J., and M. Sloman, "Policy Conflict Analysis in Distributed Systems Management," *Journal of Organizational Computing*, Vol. 4, No. 1, (1994), pp. 1–22.

[5] Kuhn, D. R., "Mutual Exclusion of Roles as a Means of Implementing Separation of Duty in Role-Based Access Control Systems," *Proceedings 2nd ACM Workshop on Role-Based Access Control,* Fairfax, VA, 1997. pp. 23–30.

[6] Giuri, L., and P. Iglio, "A Formal Model for Role-Based Access Control with Constraints," *Proc. of the Computer Security Foundations Workshop,* Piscataway, NJ: IEEE Press, 1996, pp. 136–145.

[7] Gligor, V., S. I. Gavrilla, and D. F. Ferraiolo, "On the Formal Definition of Separation of Duty Policies and Their Composition," *Proceedings IEEE Symposium on Security and Privacy,* May 1998, pp. 172–183.

[8] Ahn, G. J., and R. Sandhu, "The RSL99 Language for Role-Based Separation of Duty Constraints," *Proceedings of the Fourth ACM Workshop on Role-Based Access Control*, October 28–29, 1999, Fairfax, Virginia, pp. 43–54.

[9] Ahn, G. J., and R. Sandhu, "Role-Based Authorization Constraints Specification," *ACM Transactions on Information and System Security* (TISSEC), Vol. 3, No. 4, November 2000.

[10] Tidswell, J. E., and T. Jaeger, "Integrated Constraints and Inheritance in DTAC," *Proceedings of the Fifth ACM Workshop on Role-Based Access Control,* July 26–28, 2000, Berlin, Germany, pp. 93–102.

[11] Schaad, A., and J. D. Moffett, "The Incorporation of Control Policies into Access Control Policies," Policy 2001: *Workshop on Policies for Distributed Systems and Networks,* Bristol, United Kingdom.

[12] Botha, R. A., and J. H. P. Eloff, "Separation of Duties for Access Control Enforcement in Workflow Environments," *IBM Systems Journal,* Vol. 40, No. 3, 2001.

[13] Hunton, J. E., and T. L. Jones, "Recreation, Inc., An Information Technology Risk Assessment Case Study of Enterprise Resource Planning (ERP) Systems," *AICPA Case Development Program, Case No. 2000-02,* American Institute of Certified Public Accountants, 2000.

[14] Ferraiolo, D., J. Cugini, and R. Kuhn, "Role-Based Access Control: Features and Motivations," *Proc. of the Annual Computer Security Applications Conf.,* Piscataway, NJ: IEEE Press, 1995.

[15] Sandhu, R., "Transaction Control Expressions For Separation Of Duties," *Proc. 4th Aerospace Computer Security Applications Conference,* Orlando, FL, December 1988, pp. 282–286.

[16] Nash, M. J., and K. R. Poland, "Some Conundrums Concerning Separation of Duty," *Proceedings 1990 IEEE Symposium on Security and Privacy,* May 1990, pp. 201–207.

[17] Cholewka, D. G., R. H. Botha, and J. H. P. Eloff, "A Context-Sensitive Access Control Model and Prototype Implementation," *Proceedings of the IFIP TC11 15th International Conference on Information Security,* Beijing, China (2000), pp. 341–350, 2000.

[18] Georgiadis, C. K., et al., Flexible "Team-Based Access Control Using Contexts," *Proceedings of ACM RBAC97,* 1997.

[19] Kumar, A., N. Karnik, and G. Chafle, "Context Sensitivity in Role-Based Access," *ACM SIGOPS Operating Systems Review,* Vol. 36, Issue 3 (July 2002), pp. 53–66, http://portal.acm.org/citation.cfm?id=567331.567336&coll=portal&dl=ACM&idx=J597&part=newsletter&WantType=Newsletters&title=Operating%20Systems&CFID=5328156&CFTOKEN=18503687-FullText.

[20] Papenfus, C., and R. Botha, "An XML-Based Approach to Enforcing History Based Separation of Duty Policies in Heterogeneous Workflow Environments," *SACJ/SART,* No. 26, 2000, pp. 60–68.

[21] Chandramouli, R., and R. Sandhu, "Role-Based Access Control Features in Commercial Database Management Systems," *21st National Information Systems Security Conference,* October 6–9, 1998, Crystal City, Virginia.

[22] Crampton, J., and G. Loizou, "Authorization and Antichains," *Operating Systems Review,* 35(3), 6–15, 2001.

[23] Bertino, E., A. Bonatti, and E. Ferrari, "TRBAC: A Temporal Role-Based Access Control Model," *ACM Transactions on Information and System Security,* 4(4), pp. 65–104, September 2001.

[24] Joshi, J. B. D., A. Bertino, and A. Ghafoor, "Temporal Hierarchies and Inheritance Semantics for GTRBAC," *Seventh ACM Symposium on Access Control Models and Technologies,* Monterey, CA, 2002.

[25] Joshi, J. B., D. Bertino, and A. Ghafoor, "Temporal Hierarchies and Inheritance Semantics for GTRBAC," *Seventh ACM Symposium on Access Control Models and Technologies,* Monterey, CA, 2002.

CHAPTER 6

RBAC, MAC, and DAC

Contents

6.1 Enforcing DAC using RBAC

6.2 Enforcing MAC on RBAC systems

6.3 Implementing RBAC on MLS systems

6.4 Running RBAC and MAC simultaneously

References

Before RBAC, the most widely implemented forms of access control were conventional DAC and MAC. The availability of RBAC does not obviate the need for MAC and DAC policies, however. Whenever secrecy and information flow are primary concerns, these conventional access control systems may be needed, particularly for military and government systems that require multilevel secure (MLS) MAC controls for classified information. Thus, it is important to understand the relationship between RBAC, MAC, and DAC approaches to access control.

RBAC is more general than either MAC or DAC. Unlike MAC, which was designed to prevent unauthorized information flow, RBAC is policy-independent, meaning that it can support a variety of policies. Accordingly, we would expect RBAC to be able to implement an information flow policy in addition to integrity-oriented constraints such as SoD. As it turns out, this is indeed the case. Nyanchama and Osborn [1]; Sandhu [2]; Osborn, Sandhu, and Munawer [3]; and Ferraiolo and Hu [4] presented methods for simulating lattice-based MLS systems in RBAC. A simple construction allows RBAC to be configured for MAC information flow policies. Similarly, Sandhu and Munawer [5] have shown that DAC can be implemented by the appropriate configuration of RBAC systems, although it is much more complex to implement than MAC. Surprisingly, given RBAC's greater generality, it is also possible to configure a MAC-based system to support most of the RBAC model. A construction due to Kuhn [6] makes it possible to implement RBAC by configuring security categories on an MLS system, with the restriction that the RBAC system supports

121

only a tree hierarchy, rather than a fully general partial order structure for roles. Since nearly all RBAC systems implement only simple tree hierarchies, this may not be a serious restriction in practice. This chapter reviews these methods for implementing traditional MAC and DAC policies on RBAC, or RBAC policies on MAC, and then discusses considerations for operating RBAC and multilevel secure MAC systems simultaneously.

6.1 Enforcing DAC using RBAC

Although RBAC is nondiscretionary in nature, Sandhu and Munawer [5] have shown that it is possible to implement DAC in RBAC by using roles associated with each object. Several variations of DAC can be supported in RBAC using this method. The approach is more of a theoretical than a practical interest, because it consumes an enormous number of resources. However, it could be used to provide DAC within RBAC on small collections of objects rather than across the RBAC system. This result also confirms that RBAC is policy neutral and more general than DAC because, while RBAC can simulate DAC, the reverse is not true.

DAC provides for owner-controlled administration of access rights to objects (i.e., access is granted at the owner's discretion). Researchers have proposed an extensive variety of DAC models, including the following:

1. *Strict DAC,* in which only the owner has the authority to grant access to an object. Ownership cannot be transferred to another user.

2. *Liberal DAC,* which allows the owner to delegate authority to grant access to other users. Subcategories of liberal DAC are defined by the extent to which access authority can be delegated:

   - *One-level grant:* The owner can give access granting authority to another user, but the authority cannot be passed on.

   - *Two-level grant:* A user who has received access granting authority from the object owner can give access granting authority to a third user, but the authority cannot be passed on by that third user.

   - *Multilevel grant:* As its name implies, any user who has received access-granting authority can pass it on with no restrictions on further grants.

3. *DAC with change of ownership,* which allows the object owner to pass on ownership to another user.

6.1 Enforcing DAC using RBAC

In addition to access-granting authority, we must consider the revocation of access rights in any definition of DAC. Two types of revocation are important:

1. *Grant-dependent revocation,* which is the more intuitive form, allows only the party who originally granted access to revoke the access rights of another user.

2. *Grant-independent revocation,* which allows a third party, rather than the original granter, to revoke access rights.

6.1.1 Configuring RBAC for DAC

The Sandhu-Munawer construction can be used to simulate the variations of DAC described above and has enough flexibility to implement more specialized forms of DAC. The method requires, for each object in the system, the creation of four roles and eight permissions. The roles required are listed as follows:

- *Three administrative roles:* OWN_O, PARENT_O, and PARENTwithGRANT_O;
- *One ordinary role:* READ_O.

Table 6.1 lists the permissions and the roles to which they are assigned.

Table 6.1 Permission Assignments

Permission	Role Assigned to	Function
CanRead_O	READ_O	Authorizes read operation on object O
DestroyObject_O	OWN_O	Authorizes deletion of the object
AddReadUser_O	PARENT_O	Adds users to role READ_O
DeleteReadUser_O	PARENT_O	Removes users from role READ_O
AddParent_O	PARENTwithGRANT_O	Adds users to role PARENT_O
DeleteParent_O	PARENTwithGRANT_O	Deletes users from role PARENT_O
AddParentWithGrant_O	OWN_O	Adds users to role PARENT_O
DeleteParentWithGrant_O	OWN_O	Deletes users from role PARENT_O

Object deletion is handled by removing the roles OWN_O, PARENT_O, PARENTwithGRANT_O, and READ_O, along with the eight permissions in Table 6.1. As shown in Table 6.1, only the owner can delete objects, through the DestroyObject_O permission.

6.1.2 DAC with grant-independent revocation

With this set of roles and permissions, it is possible to simulate the varieties of DAC described earlier by changing cardinality constraints on the specialized roles OWN_O, PARENT_O, and PARENTwithGRANT_O and then allowing authorized users to assign other users to READ_O as appropriate. The configurations described in the following sections support *grant-independent* revocation. Grant-dependent revocation is more complex, as will be explained in Section 6.1.3.

Strict DAC Because OWN_O has a cardinality constraint of 1, only the owner can grant or revoke read access to objects:

Role	Constraint
OWN_O	cardinality = 1
PARENT_O	cardinality = 0
PARENTwithGRANT_O	cardinality = 0

Liberal DAC—one-level grant In this variety of DAC, the owner can assign any number of users to PARENT_O, who can in turn assign other users to READ_O, enabling others to have read access to the object, but the constraint on PARENTwithGRANT_O prevents this authority from being passed on:

Role	Constraint
OWN_O	cardinality = 1
PARENT_O	none
PARENTwithGRANT_O	cardinality = 0

Liberal DAC—two-level grant For two-level grant, the constraint on PARENTwithGRANT_O is removed, allowing authorized users to assign other users to PARENT_O:

6.2 Enforcing MAC on RBAC systems

Role	Constraint
OWN_O	cardinality = 1
PARENT_O	none
PARENTwithGRANT_O	none

Liberal DAC—multilevel grant To support multilevel grants, we add permission to the role PARENTwithGRANT_O to assign others to the PARENTwithGRANT_O role. The additional permission, AddParentWithGrant_O, is added when the object is created, along with the DeleteParentWithGrant_O permission. An alternative for this configuration is to keep DeleteParentWithGrant_O only in the OWN_O role:

Role	Constraint	Additional Permissions
OWN_O	cardinality = 1	—
PARENT_O	none	—
PARENTwithGRANT_O	none	AddParentWithGrant_O, DeleteParentWithGrant_O

6.1.3 Additional considerations for grant-dependent revocation

To simulate grant-dependent revocation, it is necessary to follow the procedures for grant-independent revocation, with the added complication that additional roles must be established for every user authorized to do a grant by the object owner. Specifically, the roles OWN_O, PARENT_O, and PARENTwithGRANT_O are replaced by roles U_iOWN_O, U_iPARENT_O, and U_iPARENTwithGRANT_O for every user U_i authorized to do a grant. These roles must be created by the system whenever an object owner authorizes user U_i. In addition to new per-user roles, user-specific administrative permissions must also be created at the same time. For example, in simulating one-level grant, permissions addU_i_ReadUser_O and deleteU_i_ReadUser_O are assigned to U_iPARENT_O, to permit adding users to U_i_ReadUser_O and deleting users from U_i_ReadUser_O. Other roles must be similarly established for each user.

6.2 Enforcing MAC on RBAC systems

Simulating DAC on RBAC is not a straightforward process, despite DAC's apparent simplicity. Part of the difficulty is that RBAC is by nature a nondiscretionary approach to access control. Perhaps because of its nondiscretionary nature, RBAC can be configured to implement MAC much more easily than DAC. This problem has been studied by a number of authors, including Nyanchama and Osborn [1], Sandhu [2], and Osborn [7]. A compilation of results by Osborn, Sandhu, and Munawer [3] shows how to configure RBAC to support lattice-based access control policies, including several varieties of MAC.

As with DAC, a number of different rules have been proposed for MAC. These rules have been introduced in Chapters 1 and 3, but are reviewed here. Recall that a security label combines both a level (e.g., secret, topsecret) and a set of security categories. One rule common to all multilevel secure MAC systems is the simple security property, for subjects and objects with security levels given by $L(s)$ and $L(o)$, respectively.

Simple security property   A subject s can read an object o only if $L(s) \geq L(o)$. The simple security property is the familiar "no read up" property introduced in Chapter 1. It prevents users from reading information for which they are not cleared. Rules for writing information can vary, depending on the organization's requirements. The most important forms of write rules are the liberal and strict *-property rules, which enforce a "no write down" policy.

Liberal *-property   A subject s can write object o only if $L(s) \leq L(o)$. Because this rule could allow malicious users (or, more likely, a compromised user session) to overwrite and destroy information above their clearance level, a second form of *-property is defined in the following.

Strict *-property   A subject s can write object o only if $L(s) = L(o)$. The strict *-property enforces a "write equal" policy, which, of course, implies "no write down" as well.

6.2.1 Configuring RBAC for MAC using static constraints

Unlike DAC, MAC rules are relatively easy to enforce on an RBAC system. A construction developed by Sandhu [2] shows that by appropriately combining role hierarchies and constraints, a variety of policies can be implemented. This section explains MAC for liberal and strict *-properties. This discussion presumes a set of security labels $\{L_1, L_2, \ldots L_n\}$ that combine clearance level and categories.

Liberal *-property   For each security label, read (L_iR) and write (L_iW) roles are defined:

1. Two disjoint role hierarchies are used, one for read and the other for write. The basic idea is to place high security levels on the top of the read hierarchy and at the bottom of the write hierarchy (see Figure 6.1). This allows users to read objects at or below their level and write objects at or above their level, exactly as required by the liberal *-property.

2. Permissions (o, r) and (o, w) are established for each object o in the system.

3. Each user is assigned roles xR and LW, where x is the user's security label and LW is the write role for the lowermost security level.

4. Each user session has two roles, yR and yW.

5. Permissions are assigned to roles as follows:

   - (o, r) is assigned to xR if and only if (o, w) is assigned to xW.
   - (o, r) is assigned to exactly one role xR, where x is the label of o.

Strict *-property This construction uses the same rules as those for liberal *-property, with the exception that no hierarchical relationship is established for the write roles (see Figure 6.2). In this way, users are prevented from writing above their levels.

6.2.2 Configuring RBAC for MAC using dynamic constraints

It is also possible to use dynamic constraints, in particular dynamic SoD (see Chapter 5), to implement multilevel security on an RBAC system [4]. To implement the multilevel secure MLS policy in RBAC, assume that we have users cleared to the levels of high (H), medium (M), and low (L) and objects

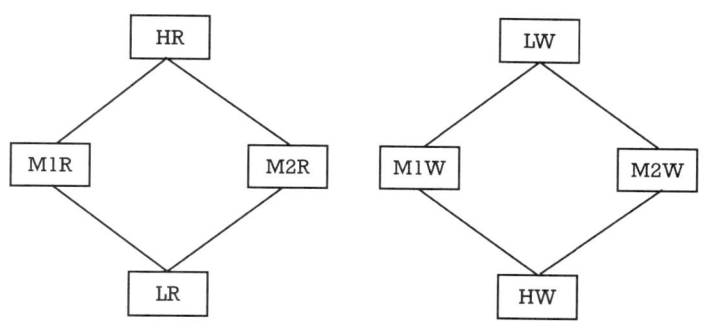

Figure 6.1 Configuration of RBAC for liberal *-property.

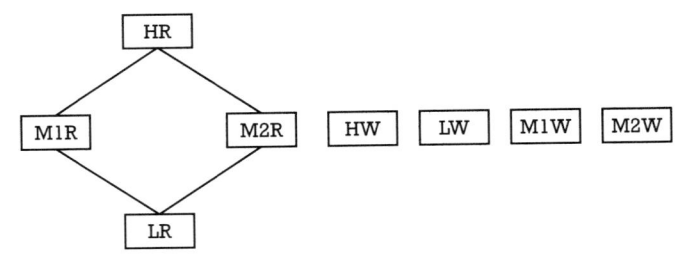

Figure 6.2 Configuration of RBAC for strict *-property.

that are classified at the high, medium, and low levels. We are able to define the range of capabilities for H, M, and L users using the PE permission relations depicted in Figure 6.3(a). Table 6.2 is an access matrix presentation of the same range of accesses that are depicted in Figure 6.3(a). Note that the access control policy defined thus far preserves the simple security property but is in violation of the *-property.

To accommodate the *-property, we impose the following dynamic constraints on the active user sets of all subjects: $dsd(H, H^c)$, $dsd(M, M^c)$, $dsd(L, L^c)$DSD, where H^c, M^c, and L^c, are the complements of H, M, and L respectively. As such the subjects of H users will be constrained to activation, H, M,

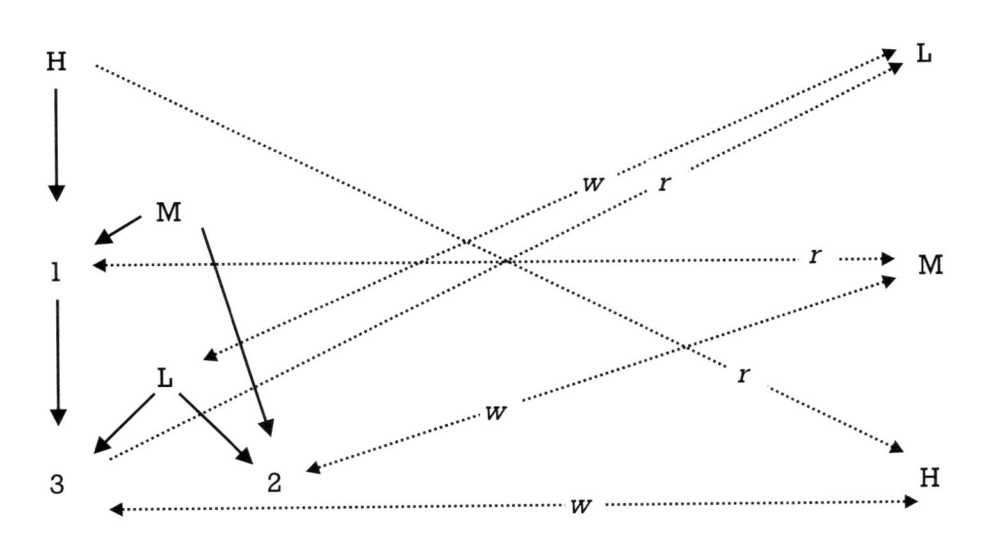

Figure 6.3 H, M, L user's range of capabilities.

6.2 Enforcing MAC on RBAC systems

or L role sets, and M users will be constrained to the activation of M or L role sets. Because L users are only authorized for L role sets, their subjects are by default restricted to the activation of only the L role set. All subjects are restricted to the activation of H, M, or L role sets.

As a consequence of the permission relations depicted in Figure 6.3 and the DC relations defined above, results in the access policy depicted by the access matrix of Table 6.2. The access matrix of Table 6.2 defines the set of subject and object set accesses with respect to the H, M, and L active role set (ARS) subject attributes. Note that the policy depicted in Table 6.2 preserves both the simple security and *-property of the multilevel security model.

The constructions shown in Table 6.2 offer new opportunities to developers of RBAC systems, because they allow the same trusted computing system to address the needs of both commercial (primarily RBAC) and MLS users with the same product. One of the primary reasons for RBAC's success is its ability to address the needs of the commercial marketplace. Developers of MLS systems had long hoped that MLS systems providing MAC and DAC would be sufficient for commercial users. An early view of computer security was that commercial users needed the same type of security as military users, only less of it. Had this vision been correct, MLS systems would have found a much broader market, making it possible to reduce their cost. However, the inability of MLS systems to meet the needs of most commercial users led to the recognition of a need for a different approach to security, embodied by RBAC and related designs. Yet there is still a need for MLS systems within some organizations. The methods described in this section allow these organizations to take advantage of RBAC's flexibility while providing traditional MAC rules. However, government policies may require that the system provide MLS controls at the kernel level, rather than layered on top of an RBAC system. Section 6.3 shows that it is possible to take the opposite approach to combining RBAC and MLS controls by layering RBAC on a traditional MLS platform.

Table 6.2 The Effective Access Matrix for Subjects (ARS) Constrained Under DSD Relations

subject(ARS)\os	H	M	L	1	2	3
subject(H)	r, w	r	r	r	r	—
subject(M)	w	r, w	r	r	—	w
subject(L)	w	w	r, w	w	w	—

6.3 Implementing RBAC on MLS systems

Sections 6.1 and 6.2 demonstrate that RBAC can be used to implement the traditional DAC and MAC rules. This section does the reverse, configuring a system that supports MAC to implement RBAC. A construction defined by Kuhn [6] allows RBAC to be implemented directly on MLS systems that support the traditional lattice-based controls. This is significant because it means that the enormous investment in MLS systems can be applied to implementing RBAC systems. In addition, this method allows simultaneous support of RBAC and MLS access rules, with MLS controls remaining at the kernel level.

A role can be thought of as a set of permissions or privileges. RBAC can then be implemented on an MLS system by establishing a relationship between privilege sets within the RBAC system and category sets within the MLS system. To implement RBAC, a trusted interface function is developed to ensure that the assignment of levels and categories to users is controlled according to the RBAC rules. No modifications to the MLS system are necessary. Roles and their associated privilege sets must be mapped by the interface function to sets of categories. Each time a user establishes a session, the interface presents the user's role options and then checks to ensure that the user is authorized for the requested role. The trusted interface then sets the subject's categories according to a mapping function that determines a unique combination of categories based on the privileges associated with requsted role (see Figure 6.4.).

A problem arises in the choice of the mapping function. One possibility is the one-to-one assignment of MLS categories to RBAC privileges. This approach is used in the Data General DG/UX B2 secure system [8], for example. For small numbers of privileges, this is an efficient solution. DG/UX supports up to 128 separate roles. Users can be assigned a set of categories that correspond to the privileges of their roles; then, access is handled by the MLS system.

Unfortunately, most MLS systems support a relatively small number of categories and levels, typically 64 to 128 of each. Obviously, if the MLS system were testing that $L(s) \geq L(o)$ and $C(o) = C(s)$, rather than $L(s) \geq L(o)$ and $C(o) \subseteq C(s)$, then we could simply use subsets of categories to map to privileges, giving a total of 2^c mappings. However, since we want to be able to control access to RBAC privileges simultaneously with MLS access control without changing the MLS system, we need a method that can uniquely represent a large number of privileges using MLS categories and levels.

One alternative is to establish a mapping between RBAC privileges and pairs of MLS categories. This approach would support a total of $(n^2-n)/2$ privilege mappings. If 64 categories are available on the MLS system, then

6.3 Implementing RBAC on MLS systems

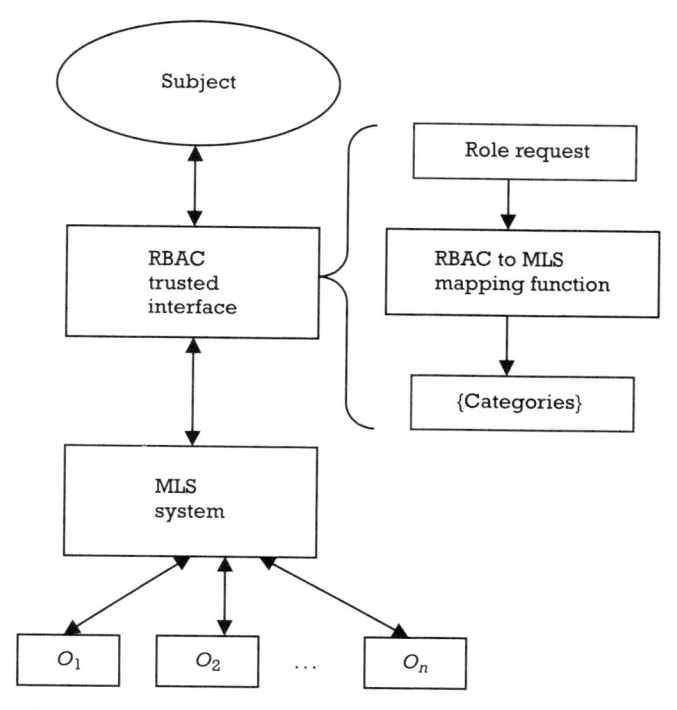

Figure 6.4 RBAC/MLS interface.

2,016 privileges could be mapped to MLS categories. This is a more reasonable number, but large organizations may require many more individual privileges to be controlled. Also, in some applications only a very small number of categories may be available (for example, if there is a need to reserve a large number of categories for MAC use). If only 10 categories were available, then only 45 privileges could be controlled in this manner. A more generalized approach is to use combinations of categories.

This section describes a method of implementing RBAC by mapping from roles to categories at system initialization time. Only category sets are used; security levels are not needed to control access to RBAC-protected objects. This makes it possible to use RBAC simultaneously with the MAC policies supported on MLS systems. One possible limitation of this construction is that the role to category mapping must be regenerated if changes are made in the role structure. In practice, however, role structures change relatively slowly, and the mapping can be regenerated automatically without impacting users. Another potential problem is that the hierarchy created by the algorithm must be a tree, rather than a lattice or partial order.

Fortunately, this should not be a serious limitation, because existing role-based systems use tree hierarchies.

Note that the data objects controlled by MAC rules can still be organized into a lattice. The MAC system will use both levels and categories, while the RBAC system uses only a set of categories with all processes labeled at system-low (if appropriate). This architecture may be particularly advantageous in a military system that must support both roles and MAC security. For example, a system for satellite photo analysts could provide a role structure to control access to photos that are classified into different clearance levels and categories. Because the Kuhn construction is limited to tree hierarchies, it does not invalidate the claim that RBAC is more general than MLS MAC, since this method does not allow simulation of the full RBAC model on an MLS system. (Please note that the construction described in this section is the subject of a patent owned by the U.S. government. Licensing requirements, if any, are established by the U.S. Department of Commerce.)

6.3.1 Roles and privilege sets

Let R be a tree of roles and associated privileges, where the root R_0 represents one or more privileges that are available to all roles in the system. Child nodes represent more specialized privilege sets. A child node R_j can access all privileges associated with role R_j and any associated with roles R_i, where R_i are any ancestor nodes of R_j. The privilege sets are assumed to be disjoint. If roles exist with overlapping privilege sets, then new roles can be created with the common privileges, and existing roles can inherit from them. For example, if R_i and R_j have privilege sets $P(R_i)$ and $P(R_j)$ that overlap, then the following steps are necessary:

1. Create a new role R_k with privilege set $P(R_i) \cap P(R_j)$;
2. Remove privileges in $P(R_i) \cap P(R_j)$ from R_i and R_j;
3. Modify the role hierarchy so that role R_i and R_j inherit from R_k, and R_k inherits from the role that R_i and R_j previously inherited from.

Let
C = total number of categories on the MLS system to be used to implement RBAC;
d = maximum depth of child nodes from the root, where the root is level 0. This is equivalent to the maximum level of the leaf nodes.

6.3 Implementing RBAC on MLS systems

The categories from C will be assigned to roles and privilege sets. If the tree is relatively balanced, then C/d categories are available at each level for representing privilege sets. To distinguish between privilege sets, combinations of categories are used. At each level in the tree, where n is the number of categories available for representing roles at that level, the number of privilege sets that can be distinguished is $\binom{n}{n/2}$. Using C/d categories at each of d levels, the total number of privilege sets in the tree is therefore (depending on how well balanced the tree is) approximately $\binom{C/d}{C/2d}^d$

6.3.2 Assignment of categories to privilege sets

Privilege sets are associated with categories as follows:

1. A role at the root of the tree, with privileges available to all users, is associated with a randomly selected category. This category is removed from the set of categories available to designate roles.

2. Roles at level l of the tree, where N_l indicates the number of nodes at level l, are associated with unique sets of categories drawn from the set of remaining categories.

    The number of categories needed for level l is the smallest number c such that $N_l \leq \binom{c}{c/2}$. Choose c categories from the remaining set of categories. Remove these c categories from the set of categories available to designate roles.

3. From the set of c categories chosen in step 2, assign a unique set of categories to each privilege set at level l. Step 2 ensures that there are enough categories to make all the sets different.

    One way of implementing this step is to generate a list L_1 of numbers from 1 to $2^c - 1$, then extract from this list a second list L_2 containing all numbers whose binary representation contains $c/2$ bits. Each bit is associated with a category. Assign to each privilege set at level l a different number from L_2. Then label each privilege in a privilege set with category i if and only if bit i in the binary representation is a 1. For example, the mapping from bits to categories in Table 6.3 shows how the procedure works for $c = 3$ categories. Extracting all sets of two categories from the list gives $\{c_2, c_1\}$, $\{c_3, c_1\}$, $\{c_3,$

c_2}. (These are highlighted with brackets in Table 6.3. It would also be possible to have three distinct sets of one category each; two are used simply to demonstrate the procedure.) Because all of the numbers associated with privilege sets have $c/2$ bits, each privilege set will be labeled with a different set of categories.

4. Repeat steps 2 and 3 until all privilege sets have been assigned a set of categories.

6.3.3 Assignment of categories to roles

Each role must be able to access all privileges associated with its privilege set and all privilege sets associated with roles that it inherits (i.e., roles that are represented by ancestor nodes in the role hierarchy). Categories are assigned to roles as follows:

1. Assign to role R_i the set of categories assigned to its privilege set.
2. For each ancestor role R_j from which role R_i inherits privileges, add to the labels for role R_i the categories associated with the privilege set for R_j.

6.3.4 Example of MLS to RBAC mapping

Figure 6.5 shows an example of category labeling for a hierarchical privilege set defining 36 roles. The tree has a depth of 2 and a maximum branching factor of 6. A total of nine categories is needed. The privilege sets assigned to a role are those labeling the role's node in the tree, plus the labels of any

Table 6.3 Mapping of Privileges to Categories

L_1	L_2:binary $x_3 x_2 x_1$	Categories $Cp = \bigcup_{j\mid xj=1} c_j$
1	001	c_1
2	010	c_2
3	{011}	{c_2, c_1}
4	100	c_3
5	{101}	{c_3, c_1}
6	{110}	{c_3, c_2}
7	111	c_3, c_2, c_1

6.3 Implementing RBAC on MLS systems

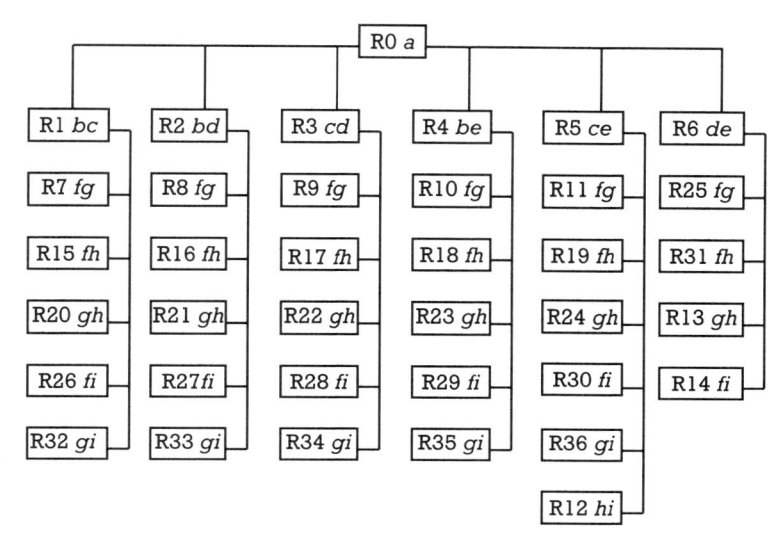

```
                              ┌──────┐
                              │ R0 a │
                              └──────┘
┌──────┬──────┬──────┬──────┬──────┬──────┐
│R1 bc │R2 bd │R3 cd │R4 be │R5 ce │R6 de │
├──────┼──────┼──────┼──────┼──────┼──────┤
│R7 fg │R8 fg │R9 fg │R10 fg│R11 fg│R25 fg│
├──────┼──────┼──────┼──────┼──────┼──────┤
│R15 fh│R16 fh│R17 fh│R18 fh│R19 fh│R31 fh│
├──────┼──────┼──────┼──────┼──────┼──────┤
│R20 gh│R21 gh│R22 gh│R23 gh│R24 gh│R13 gh│
├──────┼──────┼──────┼──────┼──────┼──────┤
│R26 fi│R27 fi│R28 fi│R29 fi│R30 fi│R14 fi│
├──────┼──────┼──────┼──────┼──────┤
│R32 gi│R33 gi│R34 gi│R35 gi│R36 gi│
                        ├──────┤
                        │R12 hi│
```

Figure 6.5 Example of hierarchical privilege mapping.

ancestor nodes. For example, role R_{33} has categories a, b, d, g, and i. Consider roles R_0, R_1, and R_{20}. Privileges authorized for role R_0 are assigned category a. Privileges authorized for role R_1 are assigned categories a, b, and c (a from role R_0 and b and c from role R_1). Privileges authorized for role R_{20} are assigned categories a, b, c, g, and h (a from role R_0; b and c from role R_1 and g and h from role R_{20}). A user who establishes a session at role R_1 will be assigned categories a, b, and c. Note that this user can access the privileges assigned to role R_0, because the user has category a. A user who establishes a session at role R_{20} will be assigned categories a, b, c, g, and h. This user can access all inherited privileges, but not any other privilege sets because all others have at least one category not assigned to role R_{20}. Figure 6.6 shows a portion of Figure 6.5 with privilege sets associated with various roles. Each of the privileges, P_1 and P_2, associated with role R_0 is labeled with category a. Therefore, any user authorized for role R_0, or any role that inherits privileges from R_0 (e.g., R_1 and R_7) can access privileges P_1 or P_2. Note that a user authorized only for R_0 cannot access privileges such as P_5; P_6; P_7, because these are labeled with categories a, b, and c, but R_0 has only category a. A user authorized for role R_1, or any role that inherits from R_1 can access P_5; P_6; P_7, because R_1 has categories a, b, and c.

The construction described in this section provides an alternative approach to implementing RBAC jointly with MLS. It presents a number of advantages. Many firms have spent millions of dollars building, testing, and

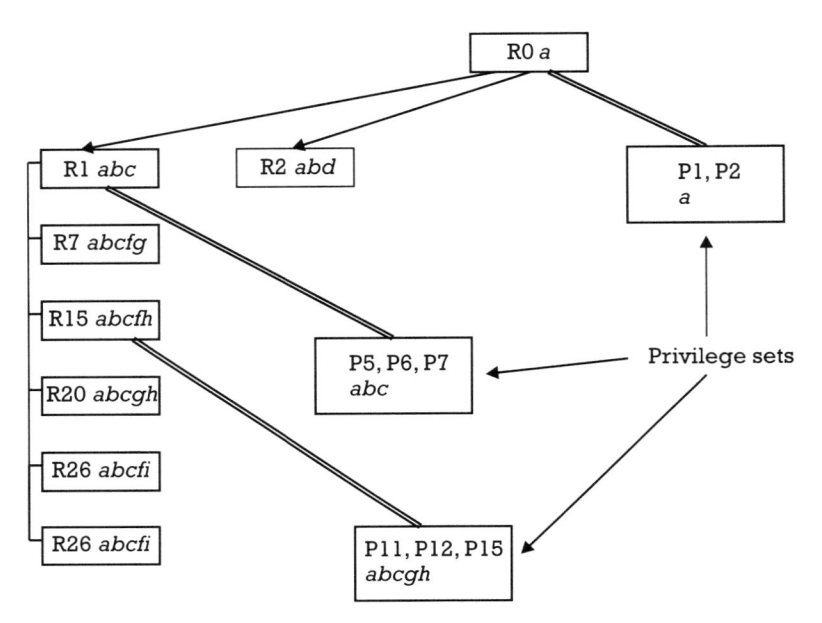

Figure 6.6 Roles and privilege sets with category labels.

maintaining MLS systems. By implementing RBAC using a single trusted process, this investment can be leveraged to produce new systems that have great commercial value without requiring a similarly large investment to build entirely new RBAC systems. In addition to the initial design cost, the assurance process for trusted systems is lengthy and expensive. By confining RBAC to a single trusted process that sits above the MLS kernel, the assurance process should be much less expensive than that required for an entirely new system. Since RBAC is implemented through configuration options, a system can provide RBAC while retaining the same high assurance level.

6.4 Running RBAC and MAC simultaneously

Sections 6.1 to 6.3 have shown ways to use conventional systems and RBAC to implement each other, but there are important considerations when operating RBAC simultaneously with a MLS system. RBAC's utility has made it attractive not only for commercial systems, but for a wide variety of systems that process classified information (see, for example, [9, 10]). The U.S. DoD's Global Command and Control System incorporates RBAC [11], as do some cryptographic key management systems. These systems, and

6.4 Running RBAC and MAC simultaneously

many others, may have requirements to incorporate MAC rules in a role-based security environment.

Researchers have investigated the interrelationship between multilevel security and RBAC. Osborn [7] showed that significant constraints exist on the ability to assign roles to subjects without violating MAC rules. To analyze the assignment of roles, it is necessary to consider all objects that can be read or written by users with a role. The collection of read-and-write privileges for a particular role, termed the *modified privilege set,* is the set of pairs (*object, operation*) that are accessible to the role either directly or indirectly, where *operation* is either read or write. Then the *r-level* is defined as the *maximum* security level of any object for which (o, *read*) is in the modified privilege set of the role. Similarly, the *w-level* is the *minimum* security level of any object for which (o, *write*) is in the modified privilege set of the role.

Once *r-level*(R) and *w-level*(R) for a role R have been determined, it is possible to analyze the assignment of users to the role. Clearly, users must not be allowed to read objects above their clearance levels. This requirement leads us to the first constraint, which ensures the "no read up" property:

- *Constraint 1:* Any subject s assigned to a role R must have $L(s) \geq$ *r-level*(R). The "no write down" property must also be maintained, so for the liberal *-property we also have the following.

- *Constraint 2:* Any subject s assigned to a role R must have $L(s) \leq$ *w-level*(R). Combining these two constraints, we can see that the third property, termed the "role lemma" [7], must hold for any role.

- *Constraint 3:* *w-level*(R) $\geq$ *r-level*(R). For the strict *-property, the constraints become even tighter. This version of the *-property requires that $L(s)$ = *w-level*(R), so every object that can be written to by a user in role R must be at the same security level.

Since a role might require read and write access to objects at a broad range of security levels, these constraints could theoretically present a problem in implementing RBAC with MAC. However, practical applications provide a way around this limitation. In practice, the traditional *-property may be relaxed to allow write access if the data written does not depend on the data read, reducing constraints on role assignment depending on the degree to which there is independence between read-and-write data in "typical" applications. Of course, the constraints above must hold for any data where there are dependencies between read-and-write operations.

To date, systems supporting both MAC and RBAC have not been produced, but the approaches discussed in this chapter show that such a system is possible. Deciding whether to use a MAC on RBAC (Section 6.2) or RBAC on MAC approach (Section 6.3), or some hybrid design, will depend on organizational requirements and available resources. In either case, the constraints described above must be observed.

References

[1] Nyanchama, M., and S. L. Osborn, "Information Flow Analysis in Role-Based Systems," *Journal of Computing and Information*, 1(1), May 1994, Special Issue: *Proc. of the 6th International Conference on Computing and Information (ICCI)*, Peterborough, Ontario, Canada.

[2] Sandhu, R., "Role Hierarchies and Constraints for Lattice-Based Access Controls," *Proc. of the Fourth European Symposium on Research in Computer Security*, Rome, Italy, September 25–27, 1996.

[3] Osborn, S., R. Sandhu, and Q. Munawer, "Configuring Role-Based Access Control To Enforce Mandatory and Discretionary Access Control Policies," *ACM Transactions on Information and System Security*, Vol. 3, No. 2, May 2002, pp. 85–106.

[4] Ferraiolo, D. F., and V. Hu, *The Policy Machine: A Policy Engine and Language for Generalized Attribute-Based Access Control*, (unpublished) 2002.

[5] Sandhu, R., and Q. Munawer, "How To Do Discretionary Access Control Using Roles," *Proc. of the 3rd ACM Workshop on Role-Based Access Control (RBAC-98)*, Fairfax, VA, October 1998, ACM Press.

[6] Kuhn, D. R., "Role-Based Access Control on MLS Systems Without Kernel Changes," *Proceedings ACM Workshop on Role-Based Access Control*, 1998, pp. 25–32.

[7] Osborn, S. L., "Mandatory Access Control and Role-Based Access Control Revisited," *Proceedings of the Second ACM Workshop on Role-Based Access Control*, November 1997.

[8] Meyers, W. J., "RBAC Emulation on Trusted DG/UX," *Proceedings Second ACM Workshop on Role-Based Access Control*, 1997.

[9] Phillips, Jr., C. E., S. A. Demurjian, and T. C. Ting, "Towards Information Assurance for Dynamic Coalitions," *Proceedings 2002 IEEE Workshop in Information Assurance*, United States Military Academy, West Point, New York, June 2002.

[10] Khair M., I. Mavridis, and G. Pangalos, "Design of Secure Distributed Medical Database System," in *Database and Expert Systems Applications (DEXA '98)*, August 1998.

6.4 Running RBAC and MAC simultaneously

[11] Phillips, Jr., C. E., T. C. Ting, and S. A. Demurjian, "Mobile and Cooperative Systems: Information Sharing and Security in Dynamic Coalitions," *Seventh ACM Symposium on Access Control Models and Technologies,* June 2002. Also "Information Sharing and Security in Dynamic Coalitions," University of Connecticut, Technical Report CSE-TR-02-1, 2002.

CHAPTER 7

NIST's Proposed RBAC Standard

Contents

7.1 Overview

7.2 Functional specification packages

7.3 The RBAC reference model

7.4 Functional specification overview

7.5 Functional specification for core RBAC

7.6 Functional specification for hierarchical RBAC

7.7 Functional specification for SSD relation

7.8 Functional specification for a DSD relation

Reference

NIST has proposed a U.S. national standard for RBAC [1]. This chapter provides an overview of the structure and contents of the standard. All the terms and features of the standard will be familiar to those who have read the first chapters of this book, but it is important to understand which RBAC features have been included in the proposed standard. The chapter also summarizes the major components of application program interfaces (APIs) for RBAC systems that implement the standard. Readers should consult the final version of the standard for definitions of specific features.

7.1 Overview

Standardization over a stable set of RBAC features would provide a number of benefits. These benefits include a common set of benchmarks for vendors, who are already developing RBAC mechanisms, to use in their product specifications. In addition, it will give IT consumers, who constitute the principle beneficiary of RBAC technology, a basis for the creation of uniform acquisition specifications. Moreover, an RBAC standard will allow for the subsequent development of a standard RBAC API that would in turn promote the development of innovative authorization management tools by guaranteeing interoperability and portability.

Large organizations are beginning to expect RBAC, and the number of vendors that offer RBAC features is growing rapidly. This development has continued without general agreement on RBAC features. The standard is designed to provide an authoritative definition of well-accepted RBAC features for use in authorization management systems. RBAC features included in the proposed standard represent a stable and well-accepted set of features and are known to be included within a wide range of commercial products and reference implementations.

Standard structure   The proposed standard is in two parts, described as follows:

- A *reference model*, defined as a collection of four model components: core RBAC, hierarchical RBAC, static SoD relations, and DSD relations. The model components exist to provide a standard vocabulary of relevant terms for defining a broad range of RBAC features.
- A *functional specification* that casts the reference model into a congruent set of functional components, where each component defines specific requirements for administrative operations to create and maintain RBAC sets and relations, review functions, and system features pertaining to the corresponding model component.

Options and packaging   Not all RBAC features are appropriate for all environments, nor do vendors necessarily implement all RBAC features. Accordingly, the standard provides a method of packaging features through the selection of functional components and feature options within a component, beginning with a core set of RBAC features that must be included in all packages. Other components that may be selected in arriving at a relevant package of features pertain to role hierarchies, static constraints (static SoD), and dynamic constraints (DSD). An RBAC system conforms to this international technical specification if it complies with all the requirements for a specified component and feature option.

Standards conformance   A conformity assessment would be done through a supplier's declaration, with the cost of assessing conformity borne by suppliers. The common criteria protection profile for RBAC provides means for assessing conformance with some parts of the proposed standard and could be expanded to encompass other parts of the standard.

7.2 Functional specification packages

The standard defines a family of four functional components that include core RBAC, hierarchical RBAC, static SoD relations, and dynamic SoD

7.2 Functional specification packages

relations. Each functional component includes three sections—administrative operations for the creation and maintenance of RBAC sets and relations, administrative review functions, and system-level functions for the binding of roles to a user's session and making access control decisions.

The standard describes a logical approach for defining packages of functional components, where each package may pertain to a different threat environment or market segment. The basic concept is that each component can optionally be selected for inclusion into a package with one exception—core RBAC must be included as a part of all packages. See Figure 7.1 for an overview of the methodology for composing functional packages.

In defining functional packages Core RBAC is unique in that it is fundamental and must be included in all packages. Thus, any package must begin with the selection of core RBAC. Core RBAC includes an advanced review feature that may be optionally selected. For some environments, the selection of the single core RBAC component may be sufficient.

Hierarchical RBAC includes two subcomponents—general role hierarchies and limited role hierarchies. System managers who select hierarchical RBAC for inclusion in a package must choose which of these subcomponents to include. Like core RBAC, hierarchical RBAC includes an advanced review feature that may be optionally selected.

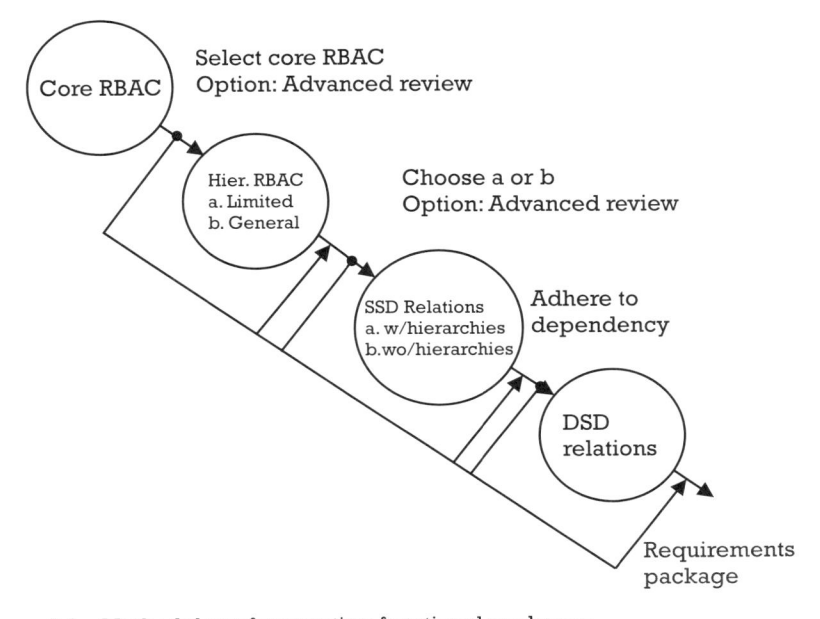

Figure 7.1 Methodology for creating functional packages.

The static SoD relations component also includes two subcomponents—static SoD relations and Static SoD relations in the presence of a hierarchy. If this component is selected for inclusion in a package then a dependency relation must be recognized. That is, if the package includes a hierarchical RBAC component then static SoD relations in the presence of a hierarchy must be included in the package; otherwise it is necessary to select the static SoD relations subcomponent.

The final component is dynamic SoD relations. This component does not include any options or dependency relations other than core RBAC.

7.3 The RBAC reference model

The RBAC model is defined in terms of four *model components*—core RBAC, hierarchical RBAC, static SoD relations, and dynamic SoD relations. Core RBAC defines a minimum collection of RBAC elements, element sets, and relations to completely achieve a RBAC system. This includes user-role assignment and permission-role assignment relations, considered fundamental in any RBAC system. In addition, core RBAC introduces the concept of role activation as part of a user's session within a computer system. (Note: a *session* is effectively equivalent to a *subject* as described in previous chapters. Session is a term more readily understood by users.) Core RBAC is required in any RBAC system, but the other components are independent of each other and may be implemented separately.

The hierarchical RBAC component adds relations for supporting role hierarchies. Hierarchical RBAC goes beyond simple user and permission role assignment by introducing the concept of a role's set of authorized users and authorized permissions. A third model component, static SoD relations, adds exclusivity relations among roles with respect to user assignments. Because of the potential for inconsistencies with respect to static SoD relations and the inheritance relations of a role hierarchy, the SSD relations model component defines relations in both the presence and absence of role hierarchies. The fourth model component, dynamic SoD relations, defines exclusivity relations with respect to roles that are activated as part of a user's session.

Each model component is defined by the following subcomponents:

- A set of basic element sets;
- A set of RBAC relations involving those element sets (containing subsets of Cartesian products denoting valid assignments);

- A set of mapping functions that yield instances of members from one element set for a given instance from another element set.

It is important to note that the RBAC reference model defines a taxonomy of RBAC features that can be composed into a number of feature packages. Rather than attempting to define a complete set of RBAC features, this model focuses on providing a standard set of terms for defining the most salient features as represented in existing models and implemented in commercial products.

7.4 Functional specification overview

This section provides an overview of the functionality involved in meeting the requirements for each of the components defined in Section 7.3. Section 7.3 defined RBAC as four model components in terms of an abstract set of element sets, relations, and administrative queries. This section casts the abstract model concepts into functional requirements for administrative operations, session management, and administrative review. The RBAC functional specification outlines the semantics of the various functions that are required for the creation and maintenance of the RBAC model components (element sets and relations), as well as supporting system functions.

The three categories of functions in the RBAC functional specification and their purpose are described as follows:

1. *Administrative functions:* Creation and maintenance of elements sets and relations for building the various component RBAC models;

2. *Supporting system functions:* Functions that are required by the RBAC implementation to support the RBAC model constructs (e.g., RBAC session attributes and access decision logic) during user interaction with an IT system;

3. *Review functions:* Functions that review the results of the actions created by the administrative functions.

Appendix A of the standard provides a complete specification of these functions using the Z notation. The functional descriptions in Appendix A are intended to provide a level of detail sufficient for evaluating RBAC implementations for conformance with the RBAC reference model.

7.5 Functional specification for core RBAC

7.5.1 Administrative functions

The administrative functions are described as follows:

- *Creation and maintenance of element sets:* The basic element sets in core RBAC are USERS, ROLES, OPS, and OBS. Of these element sets, OPS and OBS are considered predefined by the underlying information system for which RBAC is deployed. For example, a banking system may have predefined transactions (OPS) for savings deposits, for example, and predefined data sets (OBS) such as savings files and address files. Administrators create and delete USERS and ROLES and establish relationships between roles and existing operations and objects. Required administrative functions for USERS are AddUser and DeleteUser and for ROLES, AddRole and DeleteRole.

- *Creation and maintenance of relations:* The two main relations of core RBAC are (1) user-to-role assignment (UA) relation and (2) permission-to-role assignment (PA) relation. Functions to create and delete instances of UA relations are AssignUser and DeassignUser. For PA, the required functions are GrantPermission and RevokePermission.

7.5.2 Supporting system functions

Supporting system functions are required for session management and for making access control decisions. An active role is necessary for regulating access control for a user in a session. The function that creates a session establishes a default set of active roles for the user at the start of the session. The user can then alter the composition of this default set during the session by adding or deleting roles. Functions relating to the addition and dropping of active roles and other auxiliary functions are listed as follows:

- *CreateSession:* Creates a user session and provides the user with a default set of active roles;
- *AddActiveRole:* Adds a role as an active role for the current session;
- *DropActiveRole:* Deletes a role from the active role set for the current session;
- *CheckAccess:* Determines if the session subject has permission to perform the requested operation on an object.

7.5.3 Review functions

When UA and PA relation instances have been created, it should be possible to view the contents of those relations from both the user and role perspectives. For example, from the UA relation, the administrator should have the facility to view all the users assigned to a given role as well to view all the roles assigned to a given user. In addition, it should be possible to view the results of the supporting system functions to determine some session attributes—like the active roles in a given session and the total permission domain for a given session. Since not all RBAC implementations provide facilities for viewing role, user, and session permissions or active roles for a session, these functions have been designated as optional or advance functions in our requirement specification. Mandatory (M) and optional (O) review functions are described as follows:

- *AssignedUsers (M):* returns the set of users assigned to a given role;
- *AssignedRoles (M):* returns the set of roles assigned to a given user;
- *RolePermissions (O):* returns the set of permissions granted to a given role;
- *UserPermissions (O):* returns the set of permissions a given user gets through his or her assigned roles;
- *SessionRoles(O):* returns the set of active roles associated with a session;
- *SessionPermissions (O):* returns the set of permissions available in the session (i.e., the union of all the permissions assigned to a session's active roles);
- *RoleOperationsOnObject (O):* returns the set of operations a given role may perform on a given object;
- *UserOperationsOnObject (O):* returns the set of operations a given user may perform on a given object (obtained either directly or through his or her assigned roles).

7.6 Functional specification for hierarchical RBAC

7.6.1 Hierarchical administrative functions

The administrative functions required for hierarchical RBAC include all the administrative functions that were required for core RBAC. However, the semantics for DeassignUser must be redefined because the presence of role hierarchies gives rise to the concept of authorized roles for a user. In other words, a user may inherit authorization for a role even if he or she is not directly assigned to the role. The hierarchy allows users to inherit permissions from roles that are junior to their assigned roles. An important issue is whether a user can only be deassigned from a role that was directly assigned to the user or can be deassigned from one of the (indirectly) authorized roles. The appropriate course of action is left as an implementation issue and is not prescribed in this specification.

The additional administrative functions required for the hierarchical RBAC model pertain to the creation and maintenance of the partial order relation (RH) among roles. The operations for a partial order involve either (1) creating (or deleting) an inheritance relationship among two existing roles in a role set, or (2) adding a newly created role at an appropriate position in the hierarchy by making it the ascendant or descendant role of an another role in the existing hierarchy. The name and purpose of these functions are summarized as follows:

- *AddInheritance:* establishes a new immediate inheritance relationship between two existing roles;
- *DeleteInheritance:* deletes an existing immediate inheritance relationship between two roles;
- *AddAscendant:* creates a new role and adds it as an immediate ascendant of an existing role;
- *AddDescendant:* creates a new role and adds it as an immediate descendant of an existing role.

The model provides for both general and limited hierarchies. A general hierarchy allows multiple inheritances, while a limited hierarchy is essentially a tree (or inverted tree) structure. For a limited hierarchy, the AddInheritance function is constrained to a single ascendant (or descendent) role.

The outcome of the DeleteInheritance function may result in multiple scenarios. When DeleteInheritance is invoked with two given roles—for example, role *A* and role *B*—the implementation system is required to do one of two things:

1. The system may preserve the implicit inheritance relationships that roles *A* and *B* have with other roles in the hierarchy. That is, if role *A* inherits other roles—say *C* and *D*—through role *B*, role *A* will maintain permissions for *C* and *D* after the relationship with role *B* is deleted.

2. A second option is to break those relationships because an inheritance relationship no longer exists between role *A* and role *B*.

The question of which semantics the DeleteInheritance should carry is left as an implementation issue and is not prescribed in our specification.

7.6.2 Supporting system functions

The supporting system functions for hierarchical RBAC are the same as those for core RBAC and provide the same functionality. However because of the presence of a role hierarchy, the functions *CreateSession* and *AddActiveRole* have to be redefined. In a role hierarchy, a given role may inherit one or more of the other roles. When a user activates that given role, the question of whether the inherited roles are automatically activated or must be explicitly activated is left as an implementation issue, and no one course of action is prescribed as part of this specification. However, when the latter scenario is implemented (i.e., explicit activation), the corresponding supporting functionality shall be provided in the supporting system functions. For example, in the case of CreateSession function, the active role set created as a result of the new session shall include not only roles directly assigned to a user but also some or all of the roles inherited by those "directly assigned roles" (that were previously included in the default active role set) as well. Similarly, in the AddActiveRole function, a user can activate a directly assigned role or one or more of the roles inherited by the "directly assigned role."

7.6.3 Review functions

All the review functions specified for core RBAC remain valid for hierarchical RBAC as well. In addition, the user membership set for a given role includes not only users directly assigned to that *given role*, but also those users assigned to *roles that inherit the given role*. Analogously, the role membership set for a given user includes not only roles *directly assigned to the given user* but also those *roles inherited by the directly assigned roles*. To capture this expanded "User Memberships for Roles" and "Role Memberships for a User" the following functions are defined:

- *AuthorizedUsers:* returns the set of users directly assigned to a given role as well as those who were members of those "roles that inherited the given role";
- *AuthorizedRoles:* returns the set of roles directly assigned to a given user as well as those "roles that were inherited by the directly assigned roles."

Because of the presence of partial order among the roles, the permission set for a given role includes not only the permissions directly assigned to a given role but also permissions obtained from the roles that the given role inherited. Consequently, the permission set for a user who is assigned that given role becomes expanded as well. These "permissions review" functions are listed below. As already alluded to, since not all RBAC implementations provide this facility, these are treated as advanced/optional functions:

- *RolePermissions:* returns the set of all permissions either directly granted to or inherited by a given role;
- *UserPermissions:* returns the set of permissions of a given user through his or her authorized roles (sum of directly assigned roles and roles inherited by those roles);
- *RoleOperationsOnObject:* returns the set of operations a given role may perform on a given object (obtained either directly or by inheritance);
- *UserOperationsOnObject:* returns the set of operations a given user may perform on a given object (obtained directly or through his or her assigned roles or through roles inherited by those roles).

7.7 Functional specification for SSD relation

7.7.1 Administrative functions

The administrative functions for an SSD RBAC model without hierarchies shall include all the administrative functions for core RBAC. However since the SSD property relates to the membership of users in conflicting roles, the AssignUser function shall incorporate functionality to verify and ensure that a given user assignment does not violate the constraints associated with any instance of an SSD relation.

As already described under the SSD RBAC reference model, an SSD relation consists of a triplet—(SSD_Set_Name, role_set, SSD_Card). The SSD_Set_Name indicates the transaction or business process in which common user membership must be restricted to enforce a COI policy. The role_set is a set containing the constituent roles for the named SSD relation (and is referred to as the named SSD role set). The SSD_Card designates the cardinality of the subset within the role_set to which common user memberships must be restricted. Hence, administrative functions relating to the creation and maintenance of an SSD relation are operations that create and delete an instance of an SSD relation, add and delete role members to the

7.7 Functional specification for SSD relation 151

role-set parameter of the SSD relation, and change or set the SSD_Card parameter for the SSD relation. These functions are summarized as follows:

- *CreateSSDSet:* creates a named instance of an SSD relation;
- *DeleteSSDSet:* deletes an existing SSD relation;
- *AddSSDRoleMember:* adds a role to a named SSD role set;
- *DeleteSSDRoleMember:* deletes a role from a named SSD role set;
- *SetSSDCardinality:* sets the cardinality of the subset of roles from a named SSD role set for which common user membership restriction applies.

For the case of SSD RBAC models with role hierarchies (both general role hierarchies and limited role hierarchies), the above functions produce the same end result with one exception: Constraints governing the combination of role hierarchies and SSD relations shall be enforced when these functions are invoked. For example, roles within a hierarchical chain cannot be made members of a role set in an SSD relation.

7.7.2 Supporting system functions

The supporting system functions for an SSD RBAC model are the same as those for the core RBAC Model.

7.7.3 Review functions

All the review functions for the core RBAC model are needed for the implementation of the SSD RABC model. These include (1) a function to reveal the set of named SSD relations created, (2) a function that returns the set of roles associated with a named SSD role set, and (3) a function that gives the cardinality of the subset within the named SSD role set for which common user membership restriction applies. These functions are summarized as follows:

- *SSDRoleSets:* returns the set of named SSD relations created for the SSD RBAC model;
- *SSDRoleSetRoles:* returns the set of roles associated with a named SSD role set;

- *SSDRoleSetCardinality:* returns the cardinality of the subset within the named SSD role set for which common user membership restriction applies.

7.8 Functional specification for a DSD relation

7.8.1 Administrative functions

The semantics of creating an instance of DSD relation are identical to that of an SSD relation. While constraints associated with an SSD relation are enforced during user assignments (as well as while creating role hierarchies), the constraints associated with DSD are enforced only at the time of role activation within a user session. The list of administrative functions that shall be provided for a DSD RBAC model and their purposes are listed as follows:

- *CreateDSDSet:* creates a named instance of a DSD relation;
- *DeleteDSDSet:* deletes an existing DSD relation;
- *AddDSDRoleMember:* adds a role to a named DSD role set;
- *DeleteDSDRoleMember:* deletes a role from a named DSD role set;
- *SetDSDCardinality:* sets the cardinality of the subset of roles from a named DSD role set for which user activation restriction within the same session applies.

7.8.2 Supporting system functions

Recall that the supporting system functions for core RBAC are (1) CreateSession, (2) AddActiveRole, and (3) DeleteActiveRole. These system functions shall be available for a *DSD RBAC model implementation without role hierarchies* as well. However, the additional functionality required of these functions in the DSD RBAC model context is that they should enforce the DSD constraints. For example during the invocation of the CreateSession function, the default active role set that is made available to the user should not violate any of the DSD constraints. Similarly, the AddActiveRole function shall check and prevent the addition of any active role to the session's active role set that violates any of the DSD constraints.

The semantics of the supporting system functions for a DSD RBAC model with role hierarchies (both general role hierarchy and limited role hierarchy) are the same as those for corresponding functions for hierarchical RBAC:

7.8 Functional specification for a DSD relation 153

- *CreateSession:* creates a user session and provides the user with a default set of active roles;
- *AddActiveRole:* adds a role as an active role for the current session;
- *DropActiveRole:* deletes a role from the active role set for the current session.

7.8.3 Review functions

All the review functions for the core RBAC model are needed for the implementation of the DSD RABC model. These include (1) a function to reveal the set of named DSD relations created, (2) a function that returns the set of roles associated with a named DSD role set ,and (3) a function that gives the cardinality of the subset within the named DSD role set for which common user membership restriction applies. They are described as follows:

- *DSDRoleSets:* returns the set of named SSD relations created for the DSD RBAC model;
- *DSDRoleSetRoles:* returns the set of roles associated with a named DSD role set;
- *DSDRoleSetCardinality:* returns the cardinality of the subset within the named DSD role set for which user activation restriction within the same session applies.

Reference

[1] National Institute of Standards and Technology, *Proposed Standard for Role-Based Access Control,* http://csrc.nist.gov/rbac/rbacSTD-ACM.pdf.

CHAPTER 8

Role-Based Administration of RBAC

Contents

8.1 Background and terminology

8.2 URA02 and PRA02

8.3 Crampton-Loizou administrative model

8.4 Role control center

References

One of the principal purposes of RBAC is to provide a cost-effective and more accurate approach to the management of access control data. However, the deployment of RBAC can potentially result in the creation of a large number of user roles, which in turn need to be administered. In a large enterprise the number of roles can be in the hundreds or thousands; the number of users can be in the tens, hundreds of thousands, or in extreme circumstances over a million; and the number of objects can easily exceed a million. In other words, the deployment of RBAC replaces the very difficult and intractable problem of managing authorization data, scattered over numerous platforms and administrative domains, with a less difficult but significant problem of managing roles. An appealing concept is to administer RBAC relations through the use of RBAC. One can consider role administration to be just another application of RBAC.

8.1 Background and terminology

In administering RBAC with RBAC we need to make a distinction between administrative roles and user roles, between administrative objects and user objects, and between administrative operations and user operations. This distinction is clearly defined by Sandhu et al. in their popular RBAC model commonly referred to as RBAC96 [1]. Figure 8.1 illustrates

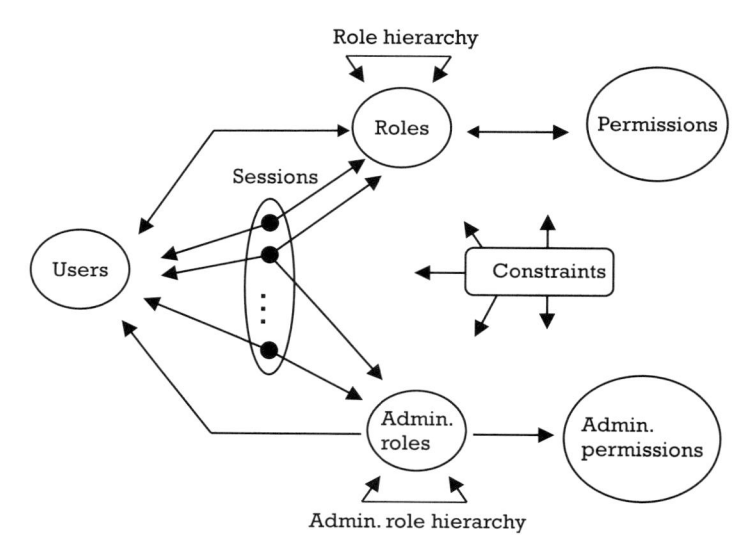

Figure 8.1 Summary of RBAC96 model.

RBAC96. The top half of Figure 8.1 shows users, roles, and permissions that control or protect access to data and resources; the bottom half shows administrative roles and permissions. Note that arbitrary constraints may be placed on user and administrator roles and relations.

Administrative roles are used to administer *user roles*. Example administrative roles include that of a payroll administrator, who may be responsible for administering the user roles and relations within the payroll department, or that of project 1 administrator, who may be responsible for managing the roles and relations pertaining to project 1. The set of administrative objects that are accessible by a particular administrative role is referred to as the *administrative scope of control*.

A role administrator performs the role management functions through the execution of administrative permissions (administrative operations on RBAC elements and relations) that are assigned to administrative roles. These permissions are comprised of the management operations that are required to create and maintain user roles and role relations. Examples of role administrative operations include creating and deleting roles, creating and deleting user role assignments, and creating and deleting role inheritance relations.

The operations and resources that are assigned to the payroll administrator may, for example, include the administrative operations for creating and deleting user assignments to the roles in the payroll department.

8.1 Background and terminology

The use of RBAC principles for managing RBAC systems have not been studied to the extent of that of RBAC models in general. Nonetheless, significant advances have been made. The NIST model and Web implementation of RBAC incorporates an administrative tool that provides rudimentary support for an RBAC database that stores information about user and permission role assignments and role hierarchies [2]. Nyanchama and Osborn [3] defined a role graph model that rigorously specified operational semantics for manipulating role relations in the contexts of a role hierarchy. ARBAC97 built on these previous attempts to construct administrative models [4] over all aspects of the RBAC model. ARBAC97 has three components: URA97 (user-role assignment '97), PRA97 (permission-role assignment '97), and RRA97 (role-role assignment '97), incorporating the functionality provided by the NIST implementation and the administrative operations defined by the role graph model. Fundamental to ARBAC97 and to all subsequent efforts to develop role-based models for RBAC administration are the principles of *decentralization of administrative authority, administrative autonomy,* and control over *anomalous side effects.* Although ARBAC97 can be credited with identifying these essential administrative principles, each of its components has been systematically updated and improved upon in attempts to alleviate identified erroneous conditions and to provide greater administrative flexibility and control.

Central to RRA97 is the notion of an *encapsulated range* for defining the administrative scope of control. An encapsulated range is a self-contained subhierarchy defining a set of roles and relations over which an administrative role may perform administrative operations. The idea is that administrative operations cannot cause side effects to occur outside of the range. The Crampton-Loizou model [5] provides a simpler yet more flexible means of defining the administrative scope of control than that of RRA97 while preserving many of its intended properties (e.g., support for decentralization and autonomy and prevention of anomalous changes to the hierarchy). Both ARBAC97 and the Crampton-Loizou models are defined in the context of RBAC96.

URA97 and PRA97 authorize administrative roles by means of *role ranges* and *prerequisite conditions* in terms of an existing role hierarchy. For example, before a user may be assigned to a role, the user must exist as a member of some other role lower (<) in the hierarchy, or before a permission can be assigned to a role, the permission must be currently assigned to a role higher (>) in the hierarchy. Acknowledging this dependency's unacceptable impact on role hierarchies, Oh and Sandhu [6] have redefined prerequisite conditions in terms of external organizational structures and thereby alleviated their dependence and erroneous impact on a role hierarchy. In keeping with a consistent nomenclature to that of ARBAC97, Oh and Sandhu called their new administrative components URA02 and PRA02.

On a completely different research track than that of ARBAC97 is the role control center [7, 8], an RBAC administrative tool for managing (creating and deleting) and mapping abstract users, roles, and permissions relations onto concrete system-level user accounts, groups, and ACLs. The role control center supports still a third approach to supporting administrative authority and autonomy through its ability to define administrative views, encompassing roles, inheritance relations, and user and permission role assignments in terms of a connected role graph and a fine-grained delegation feature.

The remainder of this chapter examines the Sejong and Sandhu administrative components (ARA02 and PRA02), the Crampton-Loizou alternative model component to that of RRA97, and the role control center implementation.

8.2 URA02 and PRA02

URA02 and PRA02 are two of three components in ARBAC02 that are required in administering RBAC relations through the use of administrative roles. The development of these model components was driven by support of decentralized administration, autonomy of control, and the prevention of anomalous changes with regard to user-role and role-permission assignments in the presence of a role hierarchy.

We explain these components with an example, using the end-user role hierarchy and administrative role hierarchy of Figure 8.2. Sejong and Sandhu and others have traditionally used these examples, which first appeared in an earlier paper by Sandhu, to illustrate administrative concepts. Figure 8.2(a) models the roles within an engineering department (ED). PE1 and PE2 are production engineers; QE1 and QE2 are quality engineers; PL1 and PL2 are project leader roles for engineers E1 and E2, respectively. E represents the employee role, and DIR is the director of the engineering department.

User-role assignment is managed under a *can-assign* relation that includes three parameters: *can-assign*(x, y, z), where a is an administrative role, y is a prerequisite condition, and z is a role range consisting of a set of roles.

The administrative roles belong to any role included in the role hierarchy. The prerequisite condition is a Boolean expression that indicates the user's positive membership within an organizational unit (indicated by the

8.2 URA02 and PRA02

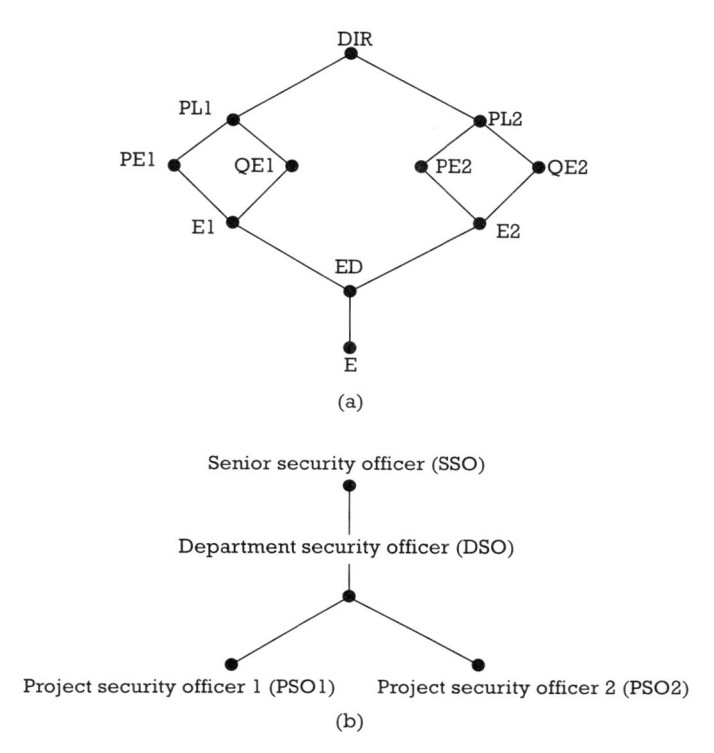

Figure 8.2 (a) Example end-user role hierarchy, and (b) administrative role hierarchy.

@ symbol to distinguish organizational units from roles) or a condition regarding the user's nonmembership within an existing role of the end-user hierarchy, or both. For example, *can-assign* (PSO1, @ED ∧ ¬ E2, [E1, PL1]) indicates that any user who is authorized for the administrative role PSO1 can assign any user who is currently a member of the @ED organizational unit and is not assigned to the E2 role to any of the roles included in the range between and including E1 and PL1 (i.e., {E1, PE1, QE1, PL1}). Membership within an organization is treated outside the scope of the URA02 model and, thus, is not regulated by the model. Intuitively, prerequisite conditions can afford a level of safety. For example, before a user can be assigned to the role PE1, the user must be known to possess a competency, officially recognized by the enterprise. This competency may be implied, for example, by the human resource department granting the user membership within the organizational unit engineering department. The use of the @ symbol signifies reference to an organizational unit.

Organizational units are typically organized as a simple tree structure as depicted by Figure 8.3. A user—or for that matter any employee not intended to be a system user—is given membership into an organizational unit, which may imply implicit membership in higher-order organizational units. By virtue of the human resource department granting an employee membership within the quality control organizational unit, for example, the user also becomes a member of the manufacturing department and the production department.

Regarding the role range, left or right brackets or parentheses may be used in defining a range. A bracket indicates the inclusion of an end point, and a parenthesis indicates the exclusion of an end point. For example, [E2, PL2) defines the roles included in the set {E2, PE2, QE2}.

User revocation is managed under a *can-revoke* relation that includes two parameters: *can-revoke(x, z)*, where x is an administrative role, and z is a role range. Note that under the URA02 model component, the revoke relation does not include a prerequisite condition and thus is much simpler. Although not explicitly included in URA02, a practical implementation of ARBAC02 might require the revocation of user-role assignments in the event that a user's membership within an organizational unit is revoked. Tables 8.1 and 8.2 show example *can-assign* and *can-revoke* administrative policies under URA02.

PRA02 is similar to URA02. PRA02 has two subcomponents, one for assigning permissions to roles and one for revoking permissions from roles. Permission assignment is managed under a *can-assignp* relation that includes three parameters: *can-assignp(x, ,y, z)*, where x is an administrative role, y is a prerequisite condition, and z is a role range. Similar to the can-assign relation of the URA02, for the can-assignp relation the administrative roles may belong to any role included within the role hierarchy. The prerequisite condition is a Boolean expression that indicates the permission's positive membership within a unit of an organizational structure (indicated by the @

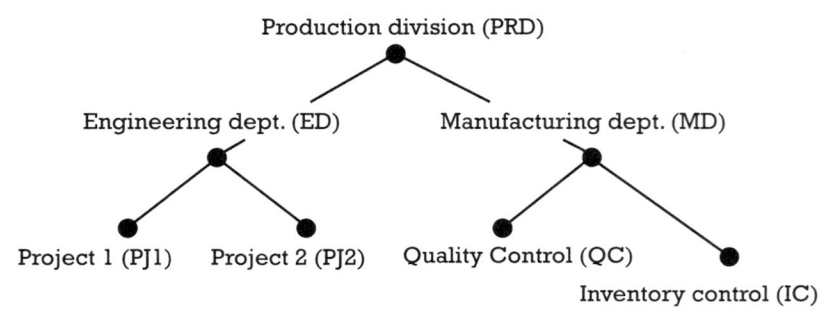

Figure 8.3 Example organization units.

8.2 URA02 and PRA02

Table 8.1 Example *can-assign* in URA02

Administrative Role	Prerequisite Condition	Role Range
PSO1	@PJ1 ∧ ¬QE1	[PE1, PE1]
PSO2	@PJ2 ∧ ¬PE2	[PE2, PE2]
DSO	@ED	(ED, DIR)

Table 8.2 Example *can-revoke* in URA02

Administrative Role	Role Range
PSO1	[PE1, PL1)
PSO2	[PE2, PL2)
DSO	(ED, DIR)

symbol to distinguish the organizational unit from that of a role) or a condition regarding the permission's exclusivity among the existing permissions that are currently assigned to a role within the end-user hierarchy.

Opposite that of the organizational user structure, the organizational unit permission structure is organized as an inverted tree. For example, consider the permission structure depicted in Figure 8.4. Common permissions are included in the lower units of the organizational structure, and the more specialized permissions are included in the higher units of the organization structure. Thus, permission containment is inherited up the tree. For example, all units would contain the permissions that are assigned to the production division unit, while the project 1 unit would contain the permissions assigned to the project 1 unit as well as the permissions that would be assigned to the engineering department and production division units. Unlike organizational user structures that are likely to be managed by the human resource department, permission assignments within permission

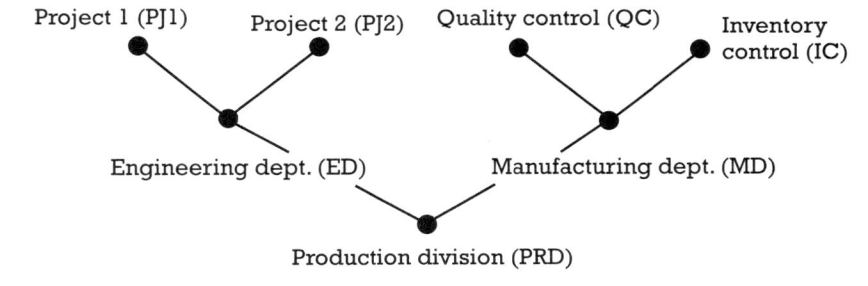

Figure 8.4 A sample permission organization.

units are likely to be managed by the IT department, affording safety policies. For example, before a transaction may be assigned to the engineering department role, the IT department may need to test and certify its correct operation. Once testing and certification is completed, the IT department may only then publish the transaction by assigning it to the engineering department organizational unit. This has the effect of preventing the arbitrary assignment of permissions to sensitive roles. Table 8.3 includes sample *can-assignp* relations.

Similar to the *can-revoke* relation of the of the URA02 subcomponent, the *can-revokep* relation of the PRA02 subcomponent consists of two parameters of the form can-*revokep*(x, z) where x is an administrative role, and z is a role range. Although not explicitly included in PRA02, a practical implementation of ARBAC02 might require the revocation of *permission-role* assignments in the event that a permission entry is deleted from an associated organizational permission unit.

8.3 Crampton-Loizou administrative model

Central to the Crampton-Loizou model is the concept of administrative scope and its use in controlling hierarchical operations.

Crampton-Loizou recognizes the following operations: *AddRole*(r, ▲r, ▼r), *DeleteRole*(r), *AddEdge*(c, p), and *DeleteEdge*(c, p), where ▲r is the set of immediate children of r, ▼r is the set of immediate parents of r, c the child role, and p the parent role.

Administrative scope is defined in terms of what we refer to as up-roles and down-roles respectively written as ↑r and ↓r.

As an example, consider the role hierarchy depicted in Figure 8.2(a): ↑$E1$ = {E1, PE1, QE1, PL1, DIR} and ↓$QE1$ = {QE1, E1, ED, E}.

Table 8.3 Example *can-assignp* in PRA02

Administrative Role	Prerequisite Condition	Role Range
PSO1	@PJ ∧¬ QE1	[PE1, PE1]
PSO2	@PJ2 ∧¬ QE2	[PE2, PE2]
DSO	@ED	[ED, DIR)

Let $S \subseteq R$; define ↑S = {r∈ R: r ≥ s for some s∈ S} and ↓S = {r∈ R: r ≤ s for some s∈ S}

Definition of up-role and down-role

8.3 Crampton-Loizou administrative model

Informally speaking role *s* is an element of $A(r)$, the administrative scope of *r*, if and only if *s* is a down-role of *r* such that each up-role of *s* is either an up-role of *r* or a down role of *r*.

Consider the following examples depicted in Figure 8.5. The down-roles of PL1 = {PL1, PE1, QE1, E1, ED, E}. The up-roles that subsume the down-roles of PL1 = $A(PL1)$ = {PL1, PE1, QE1, E1}. Note that ED and E are not included in $A(PL1)$ because their up-roles include {E2, PE2, QE2, PL2, DIR}, which are not included in the down-roles of PL1.

Crampton and Loizou formally define administrative scope as follows:

$A(r) = \{s \in R : s \leq r, \uparrow s \setminus \uparrow r \leq \downarrow r\}$
Crampton-Loizou formal definition of administrative scope

8.3.1 Flexibility of administrative scope

The administrative scope of a role is dependent on the current inheritance relations of the role hierarchy and therefore changes dynamically as the hierarchy changes. For example, as Figure 8.6 shows, the operation AddRole(*X*, {QE1}, DIR}), removes {E1, QE1} from $A(PL1)$ because their up-roles now include *X*, which is not included in the down-roles of PL1.

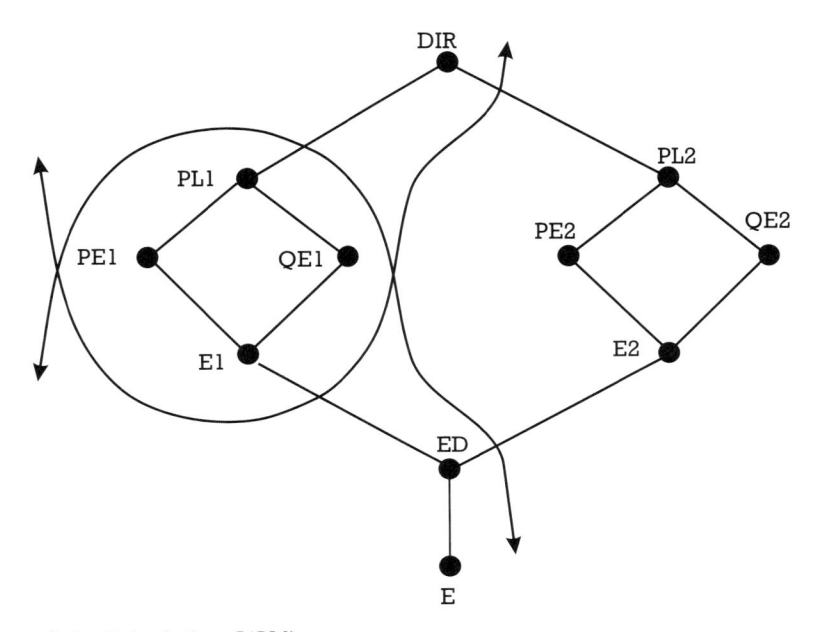

Figure 8.5 Calculating $A(PL1)$.

8.3.2 Decentralization and autonomy

As noted above, RBAC96 makes a distinction between administrative and end-user roles. The Crampton-Loizou RBAC administrative model does not assume the existence of disjoint administrative roles. In other words, administrative roles may exist within the same role graph as end-user roles. According to the definition of administrative scope, for all roles r in the role hierarchy, r is included in $A(r)$. Under many circumstances, an administrator role should not be in its own administrative scope. Accordingly, Crampton and Loizou define the concept of *strict* administrative scope. The strict administrative scope of r is $A(r)$ minus $\{r\}$, denoted as $A_s(r)$. If s is included as an element of $A_s(r)$, r is said to be the administrator of s. Although s may be an element of both $A_s(x)$ and $A_s(y)$, where $x \neq y$, either $x > y$ or $y > x$. From a practical perspective, any two administrative roles of s are always comparable, and thus, s will always have a minimum administrative role, which is referred to by Crampton and Loizou as the *line manager* of s.

8.3.3 A family of models for hierarchical administration

This section describes the four subcomponents of Crampton-Loizou—RHA$_1$ thru RHA$_4$, where RHA1 is considered the base model, and each sequential model subcomponent adds increased rigor.

8.3.3.1 RHA$_1$

RHA$_1$ is the most basic subcomponent of the Crampton-Loizou model. It is defined in terms of administrative scope and the circumstances under which a hierarchical operation may be permitted.

A role a is permitted to perform a hierarchical operation as follows:

- *AddRole*(r, ▲r, ▼r) provided r has at least one parent or child, ▲r $A_s(a)$, ▼r $A(a)$;
- *DeleteRole*(r) provided $r \in A_s(a)$;
- *AddEdge*(c, p) provided c, $p \in A(a)$;
- *DeleteEdge*(c, p) provided c, $p \in A(a)$.

RHA$_1$ allows an existing role within the role hierarchy to assume administrative authority over a designated portion of the hierarchy defined by administrative scope. For example, the project leader PL2 may perform the administrative operations defined above on the set of roles and relations included in project 1.

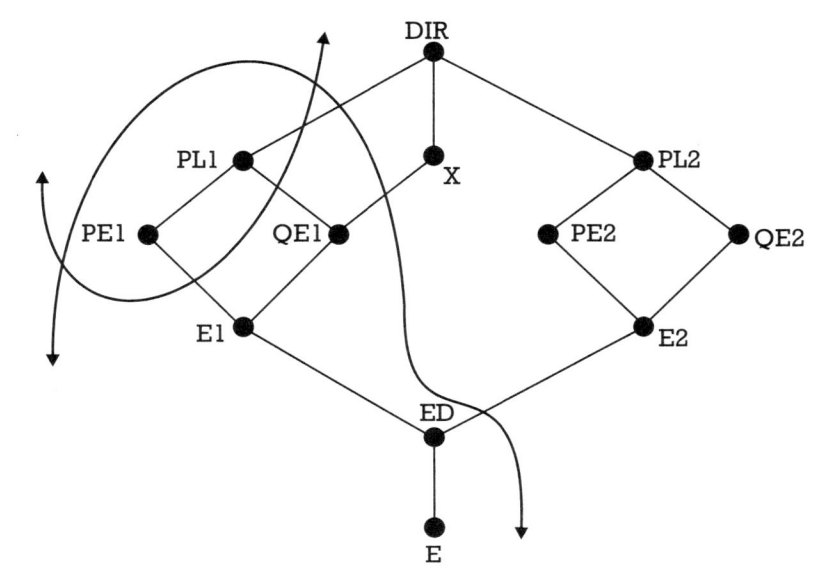

Figure 8.6 Recalculating A(PL1) after adding role X.

8.3.3.2 RHA$_2$

RHA$_2$ extends RHA$_1$ by requiring that in addition to satisfying the administrative scope condition that the administrative role a must be assigned the appropriate administrative privileges. As such RHA$_2$ adds a finer granularity of specificity regarding administrative operations that may be applied over the roles and relations defined by administrative scope.

8.3.3.3 RHA$_3$

RHA$_3$ extends RHA$_2$ by introducing an *administrative authority* binary relation. If $(a, r) \in$ *admin-authority* then role a is said to be the administrative role and is the controller of r. The set of roles that are controlled by role a is denoted by $C(a)$.

Imposing the *admin-authority* relation effectively extends the hierarchy. Consider the effect of the following *admin-authority* relations on the example role hierarchy depicted in Figure 8.7 where the elements are represented by broken lines:

- *Admin-authority (PSO1, PL1);*
- *Admin-authority (DSO, DIR);*
- *Admin-authority (DSO, PSO1).*

> $A(a) = \{r \in R: \uparrow r \setminus \uparrow C(a) \subseteq \downarrow C(a)\}$
> $A_s(a) = A(a) \setminus C(a)$
> Extended definition of administrative scope

Note that $C(PSO1) = \{PL1\}$ and $C(DSO) = \{DIR, PSO1\}$.

In addition, RHA_3 requires that the second field of the admin-authority relation must be unique. This ensures that each role r is controlled by, at most, one administrative role. This constraint is introduced to underscore the concept of a line manager.

Crampton and Loizou extend the definition of administrative scope, by including administrative control (see Figure 8.7):

For example, $A(PSO1) = \{PL1, PE1, QE1, ED1\}$. Note also that $A(DSO)$ includes $PSO1$ and $A(PSO1)$.

8.3.3.4 RHA$_4$

RHA_4 extends RHA_3 to allow the administration of the *admin-authority* relation. This type of administration can be conducted in one of two ways. The first is through adding or deleting *admin-authority* relations to the extended

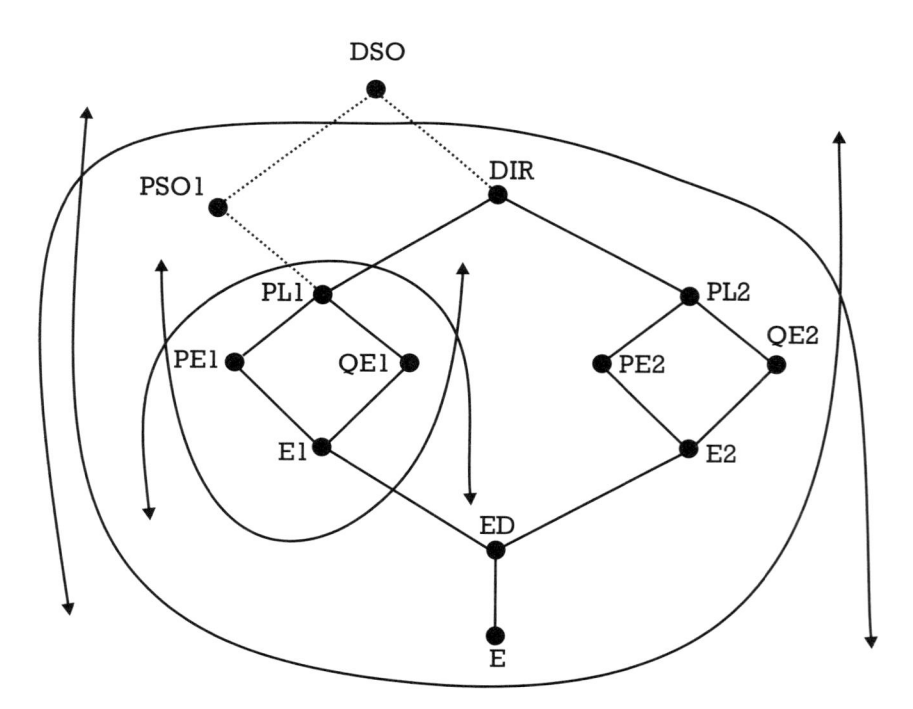

Figure 8.7 Extended hierarchy that includes administrative roles.

8.3 Crampton-Loizou administrative model

hierarchy. The second is by performing hierarchy administrative operations on the nodes and relations of the extended hierarchy.

Adding or deleting an *admin-authority* relation is equivalent to adding or deleting a corresponding edge to or from the extended hierarchy. The ordered pair (a, r) can only be removed from the set of *admin-authority* relations by an administrative role a' provided that $a \in A(a')$ and $r \in A_s(a')$. In the event that r was removed from $A(a')$ as a result of the deletion of an edge then it would follow that a new edge $(a'\ r)$ would be added to preserve the administrative scope of a'. The rule for adding a relation is similar to deleting a relation. The relation (a, r) can only be added by a' provided that $a \in A(a')$ and $r \in A_s(a')$.

As a consequence of performing an administrative operation on the hierarchy, it may be necessary to update the set of *admin-authority* relations to preserve the administrative scope or to remove any redundancies that result from the application of the operation.

In the event of performing an AddRole operation to the extended hierarchy where there is no parent role, the new role would have no administrators and thus would require that (a, r) be added to the existing set of *admin-authority* relations. For example, assume the need to create a new role QE2' for the establishment of an independent quality engineering function as indicated in Figure 8.8. The new role QE2' is added as a parent of QE2, were QE2' has no parent of its own. As a consequence of this operation, QE2' has no administrators. To elevate this situation (DSO, QE2') is added to the *admin-authority* relation.

In the event that a role r is deleted from the hierarchy, where $(a, r) \in$ *admin-authority*, there is the possibility that administrator a may lose administrative control. However this is not necessarily always the case. In Figure 8.8, if QE2' were deleted, DSO would not lose any administrative control over any of the remaining roles included in $A(DSO)$. On the other hand, if PL1 were deleted, as indicated in Figure 8.9, PSO1 would lose administrative control over PE1, QE1, and E1. Accordingly, we add (PSO1, PE1) and (PSO, QE1) in order to reestablish PSO1's appropriate administrative control. Note that PE1 and QE1 were child roles of PE1 that were included in the original $A(PSO1)$.

Adding an edge to the role hierarchy makes it possible to introduce redundancies in administrative control. Although such redundancies do not undermine administrative control, they add clutter and, therefore, the opportunity for confusion and error. As an example, consider the invocation of the operation AddEdge(QE2', DIR), as indicated in Figure 8.10. As a consequence of the AddEdge operation, QE2' is redundantly included in $A(DSO)$. Therefore, we remove (DSO, QE2').

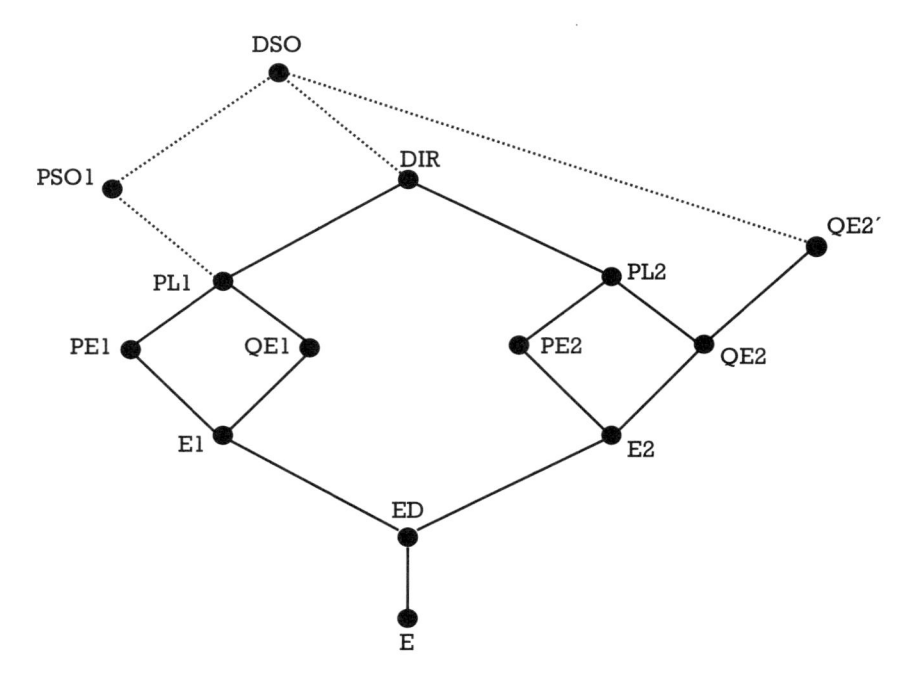

Figure 8.8 AddRole(QE2′, {QE2}).

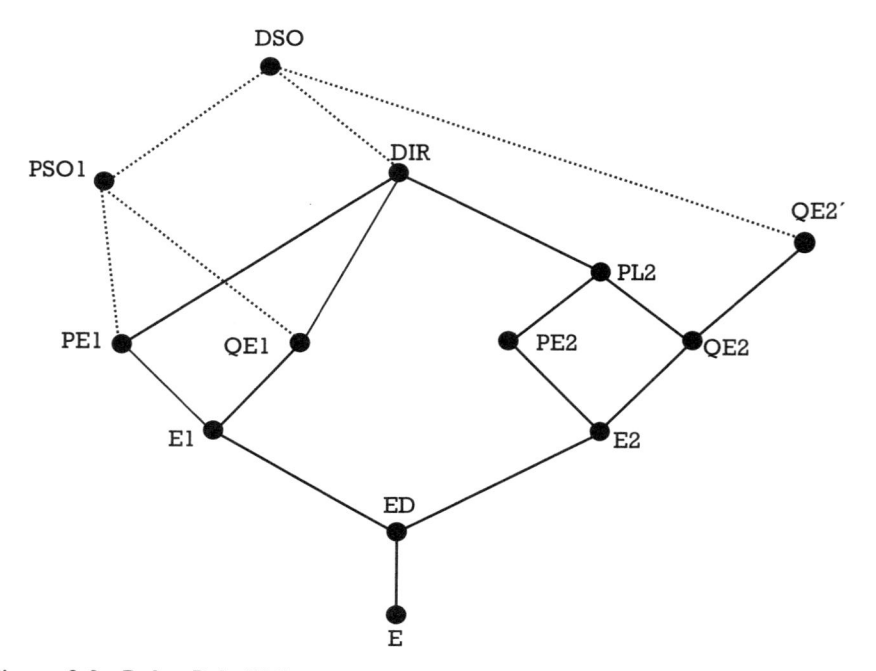

Figure 8.9 DeleteRole(PL1).

8.4 Role control center

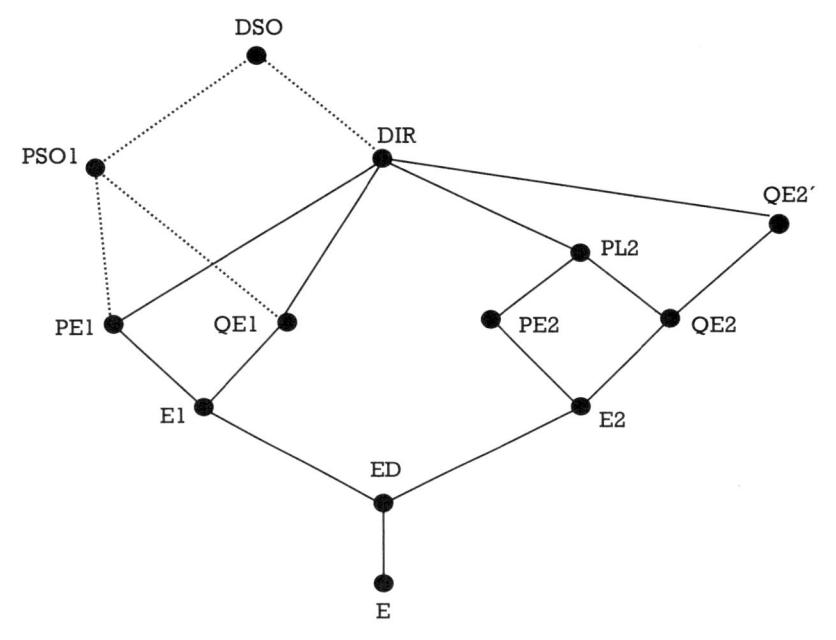

Figure 8.10 AddEdge(QE2′, DIR).

Deleting an edge (c, p) from the role hierarchy presents the possibility for the loss of administrative control. For example, deleting (PL2, DIR) results in DSO's loss of control over PL2 and PE2. Accordingly, we add (PL2, DSO) as indicated in Figure 8.11.

8.4 Role control center

Role control center (RCC) is a role graph–centric implementation of the RBAC model, providing support for the management of user-role assignments, role-privilege assignments, and role-role inheritance relations to include exclusivity relations of user membership among roles [7, 8]. RCC—like the models for the administration of RBAC relations described above—provides support for the principles of decentralization of administrative authority, administrative autonomy, and control over anomalous side effects. To support these principles, RCC provides support for authority through use of an RCC structure referred to as a *view*. Each view is defined as a subset of the nodes that are included within the overall role graph. The concept of a view supports a coordinated and logical approach to carving up

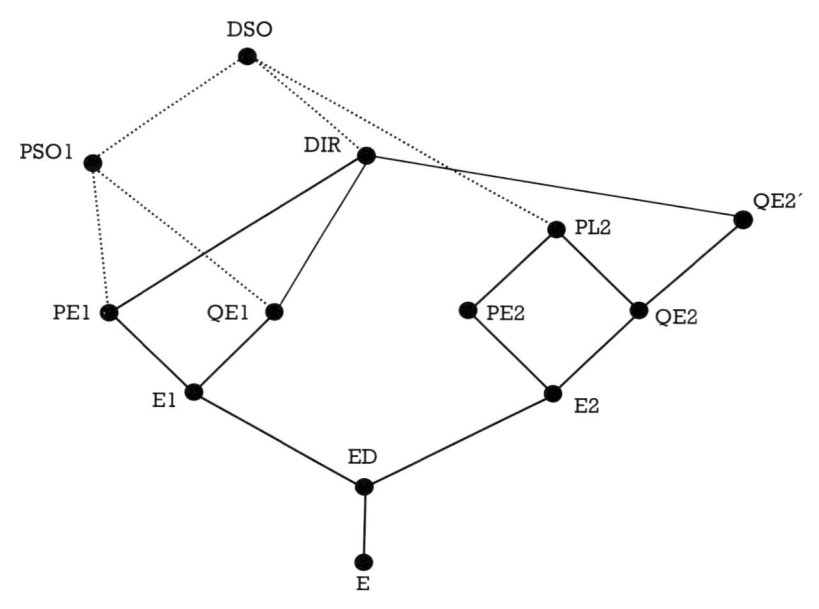

Figure 8.11 DeleteEdge(PL2, DIR).

the overall administrative responsibility of managing the role relations defined by the role graph into local administrative interests, while supporting the administration of global policies over collections of administrative interests (i.e., a view may contain a view). Consistent with Crampton-Loizou, RCC does not assume the existence of disjoint administrative roles. The administrative roles exist within the same role graph as end-user roles. Unlike the administrative models and model components described previously in this chapter, RCC provides support for the delegation of administrative operations over defined views from a more powerful administrator (one with more permissions) to a less powerful administrator. Through RCC's delegation feature, virtually any number and type of role administrator can be conveniently created, down to the granularity of a single RCC administrative operation on a single node of the role graph.

8.4.1 Inheritance and the role graph

RCC assumes that the inheritance relation $\geq$ defines both the privilege inheritance and user membership containment (i.e., $r_1 \geq r_2$ if and only if all privileges of r_2 are also privileges of r_1, and all users of r_1 are also users of r_2).

8.4 Role control center

In the role graph, nodes represent both users and roles, and the arcs drawn as "→" represent the edges of the graph. We denote by →* the reflexive-transitive closure of the inheritance relation (i.e., $r_1 \to^* r_2$ iff $r_1 = q_1 \to \ldots \to q_n = r_2$, where $n \geq 1$). (Note that the definition allows for roles r_1 and r_2 to coincide.) RCC requires the inheritance relation →* to be a partial order on the set of RBAC users and roles. Consequently, the role graph is a directed acyclic graph. We represent the graph with the arcs corresponding to the inheritance relation → oriented top-down. Thus, we can say that the role membership is inherited top-down, and the role privileges are inherited bottom-up.

RCC includes the users in the role graph, using the same relation → to denote the user assignment to roles, as well as the privilege inheritance from a role to its assigned users. Regarding the terminology, a user u is said to be *assigned* to role r if $u \to r$, while u is said to be *authorized* for role r if $u \to^+ r$, where →+ is the transitive closure of the → relation.

For example, in the role graph of Figure 8.12, where the users are represented by double ellipses and the roles by single ellipses, user David is assigned to role PayrollSuper and is authorized to roles PayrollSuper, PayrollClerk, Taxes, and Payroll. Also, the privileges of PayrollSuper are the union of the privilege sets of Payroll, Taxes, PayrollClerk, and the privileges directly granted to PayrollSuper.

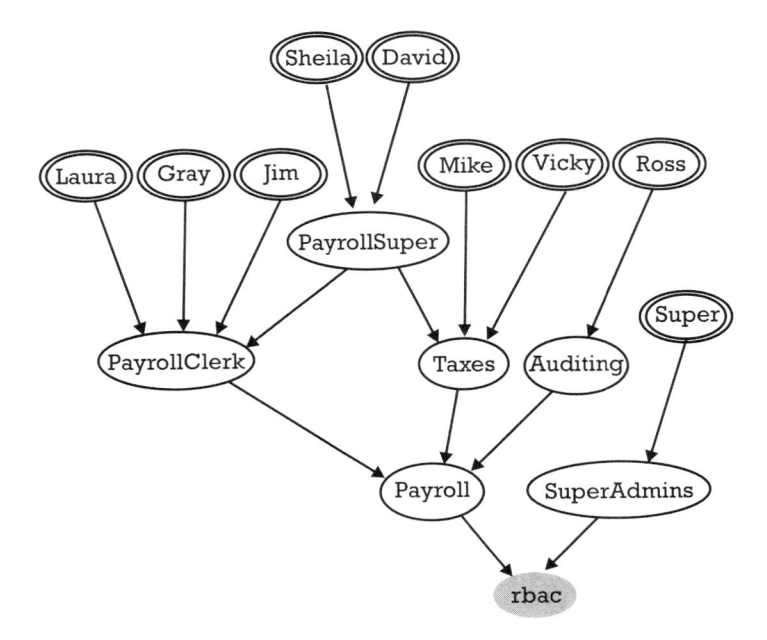

Figure 8.12 A role graph.

In Figure 8.12, the role *rbac* is the base role defined as the least common node within the role graph. The remainder of this section will use the name *rbac* to designate the base role. The base role serves several purposes. It guarantees that the graph is always connected. Implementing the base role as the smallest element of the role set requires the following actions: When a user or role is created without specifying whose ascendant it is, the new user or role is made a direct ascendant of *rbac*. When a role r is set to inherit another role r', the direct inheritance $r \to rbac$ is deleted if it exists. When an inheritance $r \to r'$ is deleted and consequently role r has no direct descendants, then the direct inheritance $r \to rbac$ is established.

8.4.2 Constraints

RCC can enforce a rule of SSD. This means that a user may be authorized as a member of a role only if that role is not designated as mutually exclusive with any of the other roles for which the user already is authorized. For example, in the graph of Figure 8.12, the role Auditing should be mutually exclusive with Taxes and PayrollClerk. This means that no user may be authorized for Auditing and PayrollClerk, or Auditing and Taxes, or Auditing and PayrollSuper.

8.4.3 Role views

RCC introduces the concept of a role view, as a means of defining users, roles, and role inheritance relationships within the role graph. Views can be defined to represent organizational units, divisions, projects, or any other ad hoc collection of relations down to the granularity of a single user.

A *role view* defined by a set of roles $\{r_1,...,r_n\}$ is defined as a subgraph of the overall role graph with the following properties:

- The view contains $r_1,...,r_n$ as nodes.
- If the view contains a role r, then it contains any user or role q such that $q \to r$.
- The view contains no other nodes except those included by rules 1, 2.
- The view contains an arc $q \to r$ if q and r are included in the view, and $q \to r$ is an arc in the original graph.

As a consequence, to define a view it suffices to indicate the "most general" roles contained in that view, which are called the *principal nodes* of the view. If the view obtained from those principals applying the above

8.4 Role control center

properties is not a connected graph, then a base role is added when displaying the view. For example (see Figure 8.13), roles *PayrollClerk* and *Auditing* define the view shown in Figure 8.14. Note that the subgraph is built from the principals, their direct and indirect ascendants, and their inheritance relationships and is augmented with the base role *rbac* as a direct descendant of the principals *PayrollClerk* and *Auditing*. Views may overlap; for example *PayrollSuper*, *Sheila*, and *David* are common to the views defined by the principals {*PayrollClerk, Auditing*} and {*Taxes*}.

RCC uses role views to define sets of relevant users and roles to delegate administrative privileges for certain portions of the role graph to administrative roles.

8.4.4 Delegation of administrative permissions

The number of roles and role relationships within a large enterprise can become overwhelming for a single administrator to maintain. In addition, administrators who are closer to the day-to-day operations of a specific organization are typically better suited to administer the roles and role relationships for that organization. To deal with this issue, RCC supports the delegation of administrative permissions (i.e., the assignment of access

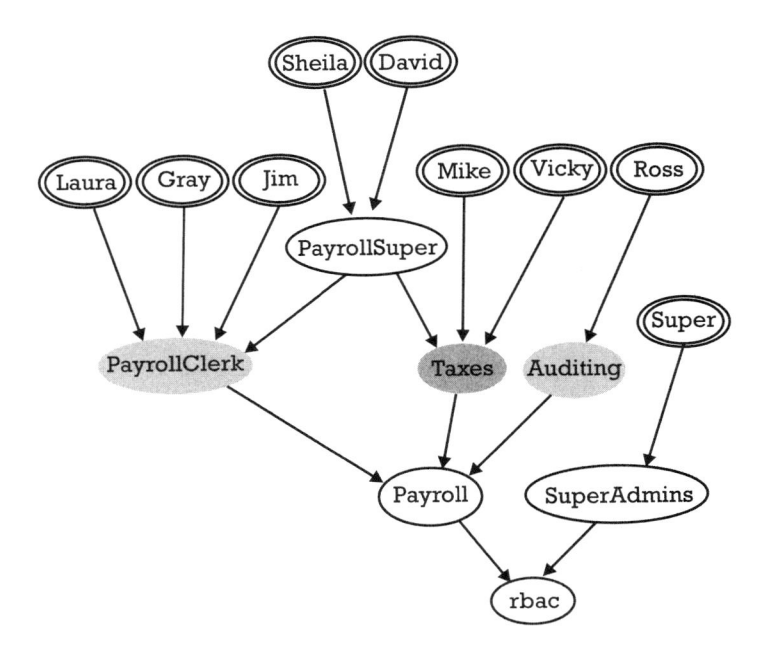

Figure 8.13 Defining a role view.

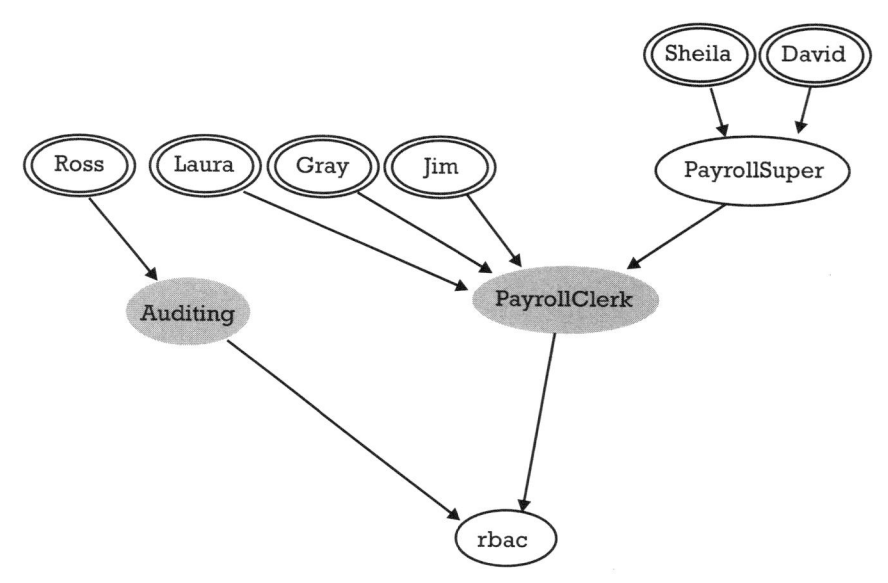

Figure 8.14 A view displayed by RCC.

rights necessary to manage the roles and role relationships from one role administrator to a second role administrator).

In the context of RCC, delegation refers to the administrative operation of transferring administrative permissions for the management of roles and role relations from one administrative role to another. Furthermore, it is often desirable to impose policy constraints across administrative boundaries. Administrative permissions are just ordinary permissions defined on (abstract) resources, which happen to be roles and role relations. An RBAC application is a good example of a role-aware application, which uses roles, their assigned users, and their permissions to control access to its data: roles, users, relationships, and permissions.

In order for one role administrator to transfer permissions to another role administrator, the first role administrator must possess (be assigned) the set of permissions that are being transferred and the permission to delegate permission. Because delegation refers to a collection of roles and relations over which delegated administrative operations are applied, role hierarchies are considered a valuable supporting feature.

The delegation process is best described by an example. Assume that the enterprise role graph is much more complex than that of Figure 8.12 but still contains the view with the principal *Payroll*. The *super* user, which may

8.4 Role control center

perform all RCC operations on all users and roles, may want to delegate the administration of the *Payroll* view to user *Ronald*. To that purpose, *super* may create a new, administrative role, called *PayrollAdmins*, grant it all permissions on the roles included in the *Payroll* view (see Figure 8.15), and assign the user *Ronald* to *PayrollAdmins*. *Ronald* will be able to perform all RCC operations, but only on roles included in the *Payroll* view. Note that the RCC user interface allows for defining permissions on all roles in a view by checking the "Apply to Entire View" box. Figure 8.16 shows the per-user review of permissions for *Ronald*. The small arrow in front of permissions indicates that the permission is inherited from an assigned role, and not directly granted to *Ronald*.

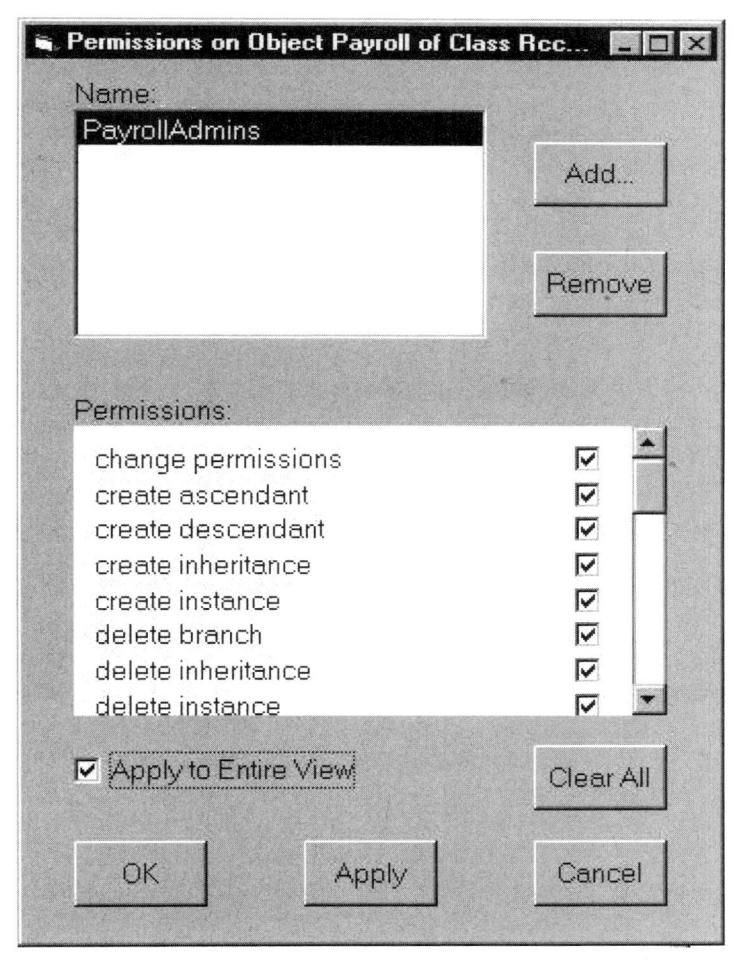

Figure 8.15 Granting permissions to PayrollAdmins.

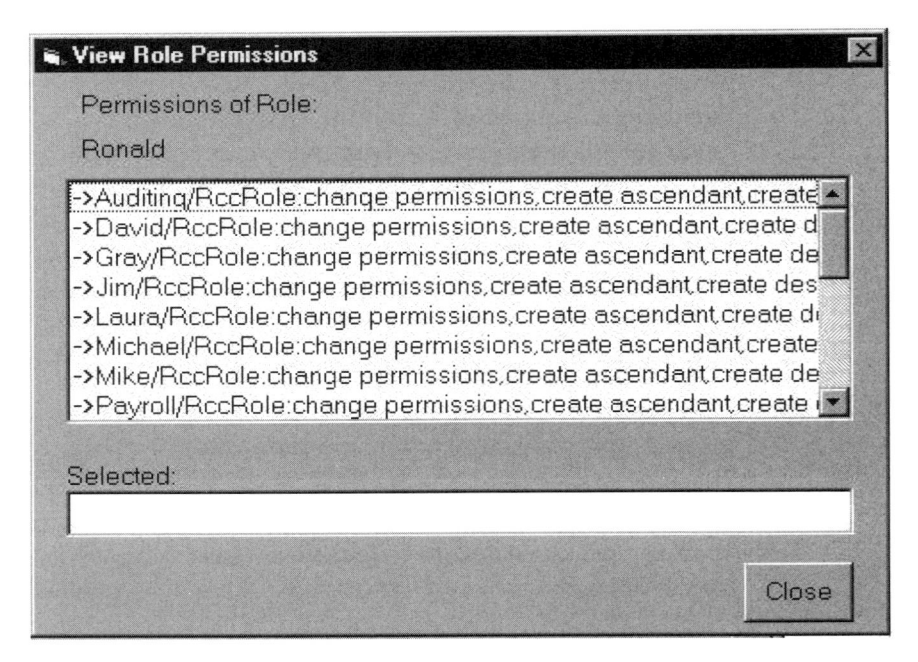

Figure 8.16 Ronald's permissions.

Administrative operations, such as *change permissions* and *create ascendant*, are just ordinary operations defined on (abstract) objects that happen to be roles (*RccRole* in Figure 8.13 denotes the class of role objects).

In turn, *Ronald* may want to delegate the administration (or at least some administrative duties) of the *Taxes* view to a third administrator, *Michael*. To this purpose, Ronald may create a new administrative role *TaxAdmins* (but as an ascendant of *Payroll*—remember that *Ronald* has no access to roles outside the *Payroll* view), grant *TaxAdmins* some administrative permissions to the *Taxes* view, and assign *Michael* to *TaxAdmins*. Ronald is allowed to grant *TaxAdmins* permissions on roles in the Taxes view if and only if *super* has granted him (through the PayrollTaxes role) the permission to *change permissions* on those roles.

8.4.5 Decentralization and autonomy

In contrast to the Crampton-Loizou model, RCC does not include an extended hierarchy to define administrative scope, but rather administrative roles are included in a separate role class as to the user roles for which they

8.4 Role control center

manage. Under this management scheme, each role may (but is not required to) have single a line manager. For example, in Figure 8.17, the Chief Admin has management authority over the entire role graph, including administrative roles. The Payroll Admin has administrative authority over the entire payroll department, including the Adjustments roles and relation. Furthermore, the Adjustment Admin only has administrative authority over the Adjustments branch. Therefore, the Adjustment Admin is considered the line manager of the adjustment branch; the Payroll Admin is the line manager of the Taxes branch. Also, if the Chief Admin granted the Payroll Admin permission to grant administrative permissions to other administrators, the Payroll Admin may have, in turn, granted this permission to the Adjustment Admin. Note that because of the Payroll Admin's position in the Administrative hierarchy, the Payroll Admin inherits the Adjustment Admin's permissions to any roles or relations that may be created by the Adjustment Admin.

The autonomy of control is less precise. Because administrative authority is based on the concept of a view, nothing prevents an administrator of view 1 from creating a parent relation to some role that is included within a second view for which the administrator has no administrative authority. Although RCC permits the creation of such a relation, RCC effectively does not extend the administrator's authority into the second view. Thus, there is no local administrative action that can be used to undermine administrative authority. However, if a more powerful administrator wishes to grant administrative permission into overlapping views that is the administrator's prerogative.

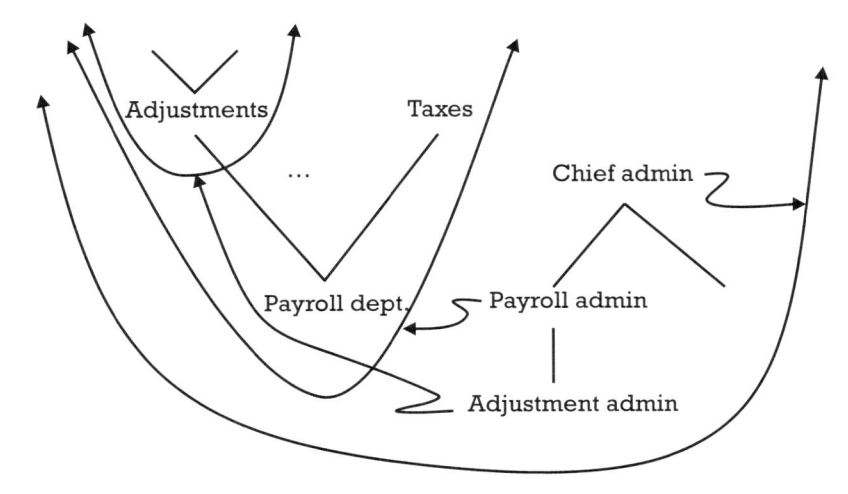

Figure 8.17 Administrative authority by view.

References

[1] Sandhu, R., et al., "Role-Based Access Control Models," *IEEE Computer,* 29(2), February 1996.

[2] Ferraiolo, D., and J. Barkley, "Specifying and Managing Role-Based Access Control Within a Corporate Intranet," *Proc. of the 2nd ACM Workshop on Role-Based Access Control,* 1997, pp 77–82.

[3] Nyanchama, M., and S. Osborn, "The Role Graph Model and Conflict of Interest," *ACM Transactions on Information and System Security,* 2(1), 1999, pp. 3–33.

[4] Sandhu, R., V. Bhamidipati, and Q. Munawer, "The ARBAC97 Model for Role-Based Administration of Roles," *ACM Transactions on Information and System Security,* 1(2), 1999, pp. 105–135.

[5] Crampton, J., and G. Loizou, "Administrative Scope and Role Hierarchy Operations," *Proc. of the 7th ACM Symposium on Access Control Models and Technologies,* 2002, pp. 145–154.

[6] Oh, S., and R. Sandhu, "A Model for Role Administration Using Organization Structure," *Proc. of the 7th ACM Symposium on Access Control Models and Technologies,* 2002, pp. 155–162.

[7] Ferraiolo, D., and S. Gavrila, "A Method for Visualizing and Managing Role-Based Policies on Identity-Based Systems," *Proceedings of the 1999 ACM INFOSECU99,* October 1999.

[8] Ferraiolo, D., G. Ahn, and S. Gavrila, "The Role Control Center: Features and Case Studies," *Proc. of the 8th ACM Symposium on Access Control Models and Technologies,* June 2003.

CHAPTER 9

Contents

9.1 Conceptual view of EAFs

9.2 Enterprise Access Central Model Requirements

9.3 EAM specification and XML schemas

9.4 Specification of the ERBAC model in the XML schema

9.5 Encoding of enterprise access control data in XML

9.6 Verification of the ERBAC model and data specifications

9.7 Limitations of XML schemas for ERBAC model constraint representation

9.8 Using XML-encoded enterprise access control data for enterprisewide access control implementation

9.9 Conclusion

References

Enterprise Access Control Frameworks Using RBAC and XML Technologies

An enterprise access control framework (EAF) refers to the infrastructure needed to administer access control on the various IT resources of the enterprise. These IT resources encompass a combination of hardware, operating systems, general-purpose software (e.g., DBMS and Web server software) and business application systems. Before we proceed to build an infrastructure for an EAF, it is first necessary to obtain a clear conceptual understanding of what constitutes such a framework.

9.1 Conceptual view of EAFs

Any access control system or module can be looked upon conceptually as having the following building blocks:

1. A policy specification component with its associated access control model;

2. An access enforcement mechanism.

The policy specification component is used to specify the access control policy. An access control policy defines authorized modes of access (e.g., read and write) for all IT resources in the enterprise for the various business processes and, by implication, for the various users who use the IT system to carry out those business processes. The access enforcement mechanism implements the policy by mediating all user accesses and ensuring that those accesses comply with the policy requirements. The policy requirements themselves are not arbitrary free-form stipulations but are specified using a formal framework called an access control model.

An access control model contains mathematical formalisms and abstractions for describing the entities involved (and their attributes) in any IT resource access. For example in the lattice-based access control model (a variant of the MAC model), the entities involved are subjects (users or their invoked programs, or both) and objects (such as files and databases). The attributes that govern the accesses of subjects on objects are the clearance levels of subjects and the classification levels of objects (also called labels). These clearance levels (or classification levels) are organized in the form of a mathematical structure called the lattice. Thus, the lattice-based access control model provides the formalism for an access control policy based on labels.

A desirable feature in an access control module would be a logical separation between its constituent entities—policy specification component (and associated access control model) and enforcement mechanism. This separation would enable different enforcement mechanisms to enforce the same policy or to have mechanisms enforce multiple policies. However, in practically all platforms (e.g., operating systems, DBMSs, and Web servers) where an access control module is present, the supported access control models and their corresponding enforcement mechanisms are geared to meet the requirements of a specify policy. This tight coupling between the policy and the enforcement mechanism forces the security administrator to state or cast the protection requirements for objects in a given application system in terms of the artifacts of the policy that is supported on the platform that is hosting the application system. Those protection requirements that cannot be cast into the supported policy framework are implemented as part of the application code itself.

In spite of living with the reality of an integrated access control policy specification and enforcement modules on all its platforms in its IT infrastructure, an enterprise would still be required to specify, represent, and maintain a business process view of access control requirements for all its IT resources. This requirement may be due to a combination of reasons: internal audit and control requirements as well as external statutory requirements like HIPAA [1]. Apart from control and legal requirements, there may be situations where an enterprise is expected to maintain separation of policy specification and enforcement components even for technical reasons. For example, let us say that an enterprise has to develop access control specifications for a distributed system. A typical distributed system consists of many application components, each hosted on different platforms with their own native access control modules. In this situation, the enterprise should definitely have a means for specifying access control policies for all the IT resources that will be under the control of the distributed system regardless of the exact platform in which the individual IT resources will be hosted.

The above discussion underscores the need for an enterprise to create and maintain a platform-independent specification of access control policies and requirements. In a platform-dependent specification, the access control requirements are stated in terms of the data structures provided by the access control modules in the various platforms. Examples of platform-dependent specifications are ACLs in Windows NT and protection bits in UNIX platforms. However, in a platform-independent specification, access control policies and requirements are stated at a higher level of abstraction than platform-dependent artifacts. In other words, the conceptual framework for a platform-independent policy specification (i.e., the access control model) should also be at a higher level of abstraction. This abstract higher-level access control model is what we call an enterprise access control model to distinguish it from an access control model, which refers to the access control policy specification framework supported in a given platform and which is dependent on the access enforcement mechanism on that platform.

A mere specification of access control requirements for all IT resources in an enterprise (which we shall refer to as enterprise access control data) in a platform-independent manner using an enterprise access control model (EAM) alone will not be practically useful. There should be a means to map the data in these specifications into the format of the native access control models in the various heterogeneous platforms in the enterprise. Such mapping is only possible if the EAM as well as its associated enterprise access control data is in machine-readable form. Hence we need tools and programs to create and maintain the EAM and its associated data as well as to map the data to artifacts of access control module in the various application-hosting platforms in the enterprise. Thus we see that a supporting infrastructure is needed for a centralized enterprise level specification and implementation of access control. This supporting structure is the EAF. The exact components required to support this EAF framework very much depend on the characteristics of the enterprise—its size and the diversity and distribution of IT resources. However, based on our discussion, we can identify a minimal set of required components for supporting an EAF. They are listed as follows:

- *EAF-COMP1* (MODEL): An enterprise access control model (EAM);
- *EAF-COMP2* (ACCESS CONTROL DATA): Enterprise access control data that corresponds to the model;
- *EAF-COMP3* (TOOL SETS): A set of administrative tools and programs to create, maintain, and validate the EAM and its data as well as to map that data to the various heterogeneous systems within the enterprise (called Target Systems).

This chapter illustrates an approach to develop an EAF using RBAC and XML technologies. In terms of the minimal components identified above, the candidate for the enterprise access control model is RBAC and the supporting tool and programming infrastructure is provided by XML technologies. This chapter is organized as follows: Section 9.2 outlines the general requirements for the EAM and describes how RBAC meets those requirements. We call the resultant RBAC model used in an enterprise context the enterprise RBAC (ERBAC) model. Section 9.3 discusses EAM specification issues and how XML-based schemas are good candidates for representing an EAM. Section 9.4 details the development of an model for a commercial bank using one of the XML schema languages called the XML schema. Section 9.5 provides the encoding of the enterprise access control data that is associated with the XML schema representation of the model for a banking enterprise in XML. Sections 9.6 to 9.8 deal with the following:

1. The verification of enterprise access control data in XML documents for conformance to the XML schema representation of the model using XML APIs and tool sets (Section 9.6);
2. The limitations of XML schemas for RBAC model constraint representation (Section 9.7);
3. The use of XML-encoded access control data for enterprisewide access control implementation (Section 9.8).

9.2 Enterprise Access Central Model Requirements

The EAM is the structure used to represent the various elements (as well as the relationships among them) involved in specifying access restrictions on the various IT resources within the enterprise. The two basic requirements for the EAM are multiple-policy support and administrative ease.

9.2 Enterprise Access Central Model Requirements

9.2.1 EAM's multiple-policy support requirement

The diverse nature of IT resources in the enterprise calls for different sets of access control policies for different resources. Hence the EAM should have the requisite structural flexibility to represent many different types of policies. In other words, the EAM should be policy-neutral.

Chapter 6 shows that RBAC is policy-neutral by illustrating that RBAC components can be used to specify traditional access policies like DAC and MAC. On examining the approach adopted in Chapter 6, we find that the RBAC modeling features that enabled support for the previously discussed access control policies are role relationships (e.g., hierarchies), user-role assignments, and role-privilege assignments. It has been shown in [2–4] that these same features can be used to support arbitrary, organization-specific policies in the form of authorization constraints. Several authorization constraints may need to be enforced in an organization to prevent fraud and information misuse. An important class of authorization constraints is SoD. This class of constraints seeks to reduce the risk of fraud by not allowing any individual to possess sufficient privileges within the system to single-handedly commit fraud. The RBAC features that can be used to enforce an SoD constraint are (1) role-privilege assignment—by not allowing the two privileges that together enable fraud commitment to be on the privilege set of the same role—and (2) user-role assignment—by disallowing the assignment of roles that together grant the fraud-enabling privileges to the same user.

9.2.2 EAM's ease of administration requirement

The second requirement for an EAM is that it should be easy to administer. Since the EAM is a structured representation of enterprise access control policies, which may be continuously evolving in light of changes in the business environment and IT infrastructure, it is imperative that the EAM should undergo changes as well. To manage these changes efficiently, the EAM should facilitate ease of administration.

Security administration on any access control model has two facets: user management and privilege management. Both these facets of administration are greatly simplified in RBAC by the use of roles to organize the privileges. Users are granted membership into roles based on their competencies, credentials, and responsibilities in the enterprise. If a user moves to a new area of responsibility, the system administrator can simply remove the user from existing roles and assign a new set of roles commensurate with the new functions. In many access control models this user migration will involve revocation of the user's old privileges individually and the granting of new privileges.

The privilege set associated with a job function may have to be updated either due to redefinition of the job function or changes in IT application system technologies. The privilege management tasks that this entails are again simplified in RBAC since the privilege set in the roles that represent that job function can be easily updated without updating the permissions for every user (who performs that job function) on an individual basis. The determination of the initial privilege set for a job function is also facilitated through the use of role hierarchies or role graphs that allow roles to implicitly include the privileges of the descendant roles in the role hierarchy or the role graph.

Furthermore, RBAC provides for the modular security administration of EAMs of very large enterprises. This is done in RBAC through the definition of special administration roles that are designated to manage other roles. These administrative roles can also be hierarchically organized to provide a well-organized security management structure, especially for enterprises with diverse IT application systems (such as legacy systems and multitier Web-based systems).

9.3 EAM specification and XML schemas

Having chosen RBAC as the EAM (which we shall henceforth refer to as the ERBAC model), the next step in our development of EAF is the specification of this model and the associated enterprise access control data in a form that can be easily manipulated and evolved. The approach commonly adopted for the specification of many access control models is the use of a policy specification language [5, 6], since every access control model has been tailored to explicitly meet the requirements of a specific policy. However, these specification languages cannot be used for the specification of our ERBAC model since our model potentially can represent any access control policy (or policies), and since each specification language by itself has limitations in the types of policies it can express. Even if a particular policy specification language is powerful enough to express an EAM for a given enterprise context, it may be lacking the capability to analyze the policy for conflicts and inconsistencies and may not be extensible enough to cater to a new type of policy. Furthermore, the access control model specification and its associated data represented in a proprietary policy specification language may not be accessible from all the different types of heterogeneous

9.3 EAM specification and XML schemas

systems in an enterprise that needs to translate the enterprise access control data into a format suitable for enforcement by its native access control mechanisms.

Many of the challenges and limitations in representing structured information (such as models and their associated data) using policy specification languages have been overcome in the language specifications provided by XML technologies [7]. Apart from the core mark-up language XML [which is a simplified version of the generalized markup language (SGML)], the XML specifications provide several meta or schema languages like DTD and XML Schema [8, 9]. A schema language is used for metadata specification—description of the structure and the data content of an XML document. For example, the XML schema language will specify the various elements found in an XML document (also called the XML tags), its structure (e.g., nesting), its occurrence constraints (number of times it can occur in a document), and its data types (both standard and user-defined).

The XML schema and XML are now being increasingly used for representation and exchange of metadata and associated data content, respectively, in a platform-independent fashion. Because of its support for structural, occurrence and data-typing constraints, the XML schema language has the necessary constructs for describing the role structures, user-role assignments, and role-privilege assignments that are the key structural relationships in an RBAC model. There have been some research approaches to specify RBAC models in terms of the other schema languages such as DTD [10] but these fall short in terms of modeling capabilities. Hence, we choose to employ the XML schema language to define a grammar (or schema) for our ERBAC model. We shall call the specification of the ERBAC model in the XML schema syntax an "ERBAC XML schema." The enterprise access control data based on the model will be encoded in XML.

Let us now take stock of where we are with respect to our goal of building the components EAF-COMP1, EAF-COMP2, and EAF-COMP3 (refer to Section 9.1) needed for the EAF. Based on our discussion in Section 9.2, we have chosen RBAC as the candidate for the EAM (EAF-COMP1) and have called the resulting model the ERBAC model. Our survey on the availability of specification languages for access control models has led us to choose the XML schema language for the specification of the ERBAC model, and we call the resulting specification the ERBAC XML schema. The choice of XML schema for the EAM automatically chooses for us the representation framework for the enterprise access control data (EAF-COMP2) [i.e., the extensible markup language (XML)].

9.4 Specification of the ERBAC model in the XML schema

Before representing the ERBAC model using the XML schema we have to choose the exact RBAC model itself from the many RBAC models proposed in the literature. We have chosen the NIST RBAC reference model [11] here because of its comprehensiveness and formal definition. In the NIST RBAC reference model, the main components are users, roles, permissions, and sessions. If we are simply to specify the NIST RBAC reference model without a specific enterprise context (e.g., a healthcare enterprise or bank enterprise), we would be specifying only the structural aspects of the various RBAC components (like users, roles, permissions, and sessions) and the various associations between the components, such as user-role assignment and role-privilege assignment. We would not be able to specify some enterprise context–related constraints like the valid names of roles and the maximum (or minimum) number of users who can be assigned to any role. An RBAC model without these types of constraints cannot be called an ERBAC model since any EAM should contain constraints related to the enterprise context. We generally refer to these types of constraints as the domain constraints to distinguish them from the category of structural constraints that are more related to the model structure than to any aspect of the enterprise.

Since our objective is to provide a specification of an ERBAC model, we have to choose a reference enterprise context and then specify the RBAC model for that enterprise context. For the purpose of our EAF framework here we will choose a commercial banking enterprise. Hence, the RBAC model we will be specifying here will be an ERBAC model for a banking enterprise and will therefore contain constraints related to the banking enterprise context. Therefore, the XML schema specification of our ERBAC model for banking enterprise context should attempt to represent constraints not only related to our ERBAC model structure but also some domain constraints related to the banking enterprise environment. Therefore, during our XML schema development process, we will be pointing out the distinction between the structural and domain constraints.

Before developing the XML schema for the ERBAC model, we view our ERBAC model as consisting of two sets of entities: *model elements* and model relations. The model elements are user, role, privilege, and session. The *model relations* are role hierarchies, user-role assignment, role-privilege assignment, user-session assignment, and privilege-session assignment. In the XML schema specification we will only be modeling user, role, and privilege components and not the session component. This is because a session is a platform-dependent artifact. For example, the definition of a

9.4 Specification of the ERBAC model in the XML schema 187

session varies from, for example, an operating system (OS) and a DBMS and even varies within different OSs and DBMSs. Hence in the specification of an enterprise-level RBAC model, the specification of a session is not relevant. The concept of privilege is also dependent on the type of resource or application objects within a platform (e.g., files in an OS and tables within a DBMS), but since a specification of an EAM does not make sense without the specification of privileges, we will use generalized resources in our XML schema specification.

Hence our overall strategy for developing the XML schema specifications for our ERBAC model for a banking enterprise will be as follows: We will first develop specifications for the RBAC model elements user, role, and privilege and then proceed to develop specifications for the RBAC model relations—role hierarchies, user-role assignments, and role-privilege assignments.

9.4.1 XML schema specifications for ERBAC model elements

An RBAC model element is represented by the concept *element* in the XML schema. A user-defined data type for that XML schema element is used to capture the internal structure of the RBAC model element. For example, the XML schema element and an associated type for representing the RBAC model element User are as follows:

```
<xs:element name= user type= userType/>
```

After having designated the data type for the user element as "userType," the definition of that type in the XML schema provides the structural representation of the RBAC element User. If our structural representation of the element User consists of two attributes: *userID* and *fullname,* then the definition for the data type "userType" will be as follows:

```
<xs:complexType name= userType>
   <xs:attribute name= userID type= xs:ID use= required/>
   <xs:attribute name= fullname  type= xs:string use= optional/>
   </xs:complexype>
```

The above XML schema syntax defines that the user-defined data type called the "userType" has two attributes userID and fullname. The type for userID is "xs:ID," which means that the value for this attribute must be unique. The type for the attribute fullname is simply a string and this attribute is optional when representing any user.

Let us now proceed to define the XML schema specification for our next RBAC model element—role. Here we must remember that what we are developing is not a generic ERBAC model but a model that is relevant in the context of a particular enterprise environment. The difference between a generic ERBAC model and an ERBAC model for a particular domain is that some domain-specific constraints must be incorporated into the RBAC model representation. The XML schema language has limitations with respect to representation of an arbitrary domain constraint. However, constraints relating to cardinality, enumeration, and nature of existence (optional and mandatory) can be expressed because of XML schema's support for complex data types. Some of these constraints are used to define the data type called the "roleType" for the element "role," which stands for the RBAC model element role.

```
<xs:element name= role  type= roleType/>
<xs:complexType name= roleType/>
  <xs:attribute name= roleID type= xs:ID
use= required/>
  <xs:attribute name= rolename  type= validRole
  use= required/>
  <xs:attribute name= cardinality type= role-
    Limit  use= optional/>
</xs:complexType>
```

The above syntax means that the structured representation of a role consists of attributes *roleID, rolename,* and *cardinality* of types xs:ID, validRole, and roleLimit, respectively. For our ERBAC model, we need the rolename to be one of the valid roles for the banking enterprise. Supposing this valid set consists of the following roles: BranchManager, Customer_Service_Rep, Loan_Officer, Accounting_Manager, Internal_Auditor, Teller, and Accountant. To represent the fact that the attribute role name can take on values only from this set of valid strings, its corresponding type (i.e., valid Role) should be an enumerated type:

```
<xs:simpleType name= validRole>
  <xs:restriction base= xs:string>
    <xs:enumeration value= BranchManager/>
    <xs:enumeration value= Customer_Service_Rep/>
    <xs:enumeration value= Loan_Officer/>
    <xs:enumeration value= Accounting_Manager/>
```

9.4 Specification of the ERBAC model in the XML schema

```
      <xs:enumeration value= Internal_Auditor/>
      <xs:enumeration value= Teller/>
      <xs:enumeration value= Accountant/>
    </xs:restriction>
  </xs:simpleType>
```

Similarly a domain-specific constraint that states that the value for the cardinality attribute of a role (which stands for the maximum number of users who can take on that role) can only take on values between 0 and 10 can be represented using the range data type definition of the XML schema as follows:

```
<xs:simpleType name= roleLimit>
  <xs:restriction base= xs:integer>
    <xs:minInclusive value= 0/>
    <xs:maxInclusive value= 10/>
  </xs:restriction>
</xs:simpleType>
```

Now the only RBAC model element we need to specify is the **Privilege**. A privilege or permission (as it is often referred to) is represented as a tuple <data_resource, operation>. It stands for a particular operation on a given data resource. There are valid sets of operations associated with a given data resource. For example, the valid set of operations on a text file is read, delete, modify, and append. The valid operations on a relational database table include read (select), update (modify), delete, and insert. However, specifying privileges relevant to a specific type of resource requires making assumptions about the platform in which that resource will be hosted. Hence, in the ERBAC model, we use the concept of a *generalized data resource*. A generalized data resource stands for assets in an enterprise that are designated from a business perspective. For example, in our banking enterprise these generalized data resources include deposit accounts (e.g., savings and checking), loan accounts, line-of-credit accounts, term deposits, and investment accounts. To specify privileges on these generalized data resources, we have to use generalized operations. These generalized operations should be consistent with the business process designations in the enterprise domain. For example, the generalized operations associated with deposit accounts are Open (create a new account for a customer), Close (close the account), Credit (withdraw money from the account), and Debit (deposit money into the account). The generalized privilege definition then becomes the tuple <generalized_data_resource, generalized_operation>.

Using the generalized privileges discussed above, the XML schema specification for the RBAC element **Privilege** is given as

```
<xs:element name= privilege type= privilegeType/>
 <xs:complexType name= privilegeType>
  <xs:attribute name= privilegeID  type= xs:ID
  use= required />
  <xs:attribute name= gen_resource
  type= xs:String  use= required/>
  <xs:attribute name= gen_oper   type= operType
  use= required/>
 </xs:complexType>
```

The data type "operType" should be used to enumerate the valid set of operations and hence is declared as an enumerated type as follows:

```
<xs:simpleType name= operType >
 <xs:restriction base= xs:string >
  <xs:enumeration value= Open/>
  <xs:enumeration value= Close/>
  <xs:enumeration value= Debit/>
  </xs:enumeration value= Credit/>
 </xs:restriction>
</xs:simpleType>
```

9.4.2 XML schema specifications for ERBAC model relations

Now that we have completed the XML schema specifications for the ERBAC model elements—user, role, and privilege—we are ready to develop similar specifications for the ERBAC model relations.

First, we will discuss the role inheritance structures. Although the organization of roles can theoretically take on any structures, the structure that very often results based on the composition of privilege sets in the roles is the hierarchy. This is not really surprising since roles represent organizational functions or domains of responsibilities, and these domains are generally organized in a hierarchical fashion. Hence our specification of the role inheritance structure is as follows:

```
<xs:element name= role_inherit type= InheritType/>
<xs:complexType name= InheritType>
 <xs:sequence>
  <xs:element name= FromRole type= validRole
minOccurs= 1 maxOccurs= 1/>
```

9.4 Specification of the ERBAC model in the XML schema

```
<xs:element
name= ToRole type= validRole minOccurs=
1 maxOccurs= 1/>
</xs:sequence>
</xs:complexType>
```

Please note that in each specification of the role inheritance relation, we can have only one instance of a parent role and child role (as the number of allowed occurrences for both "FromRole" and "ToRole" should be exactly 1).

Next we take up the specification of user-role assignment relations. In modeling the user-role assignment relations we have two choices. In each instance of a user-role assignment specification we can either specify all the roles that are associated with a single user (user-centric) or specify all the users that are associated with a single role (role-centric). In any enterprise, since the number of roles is much fewer than the number of users, choosing a role-centric representation results in economy of specification:

```
<xs:element name= UserRoleAssignment type= URAType/>
<xs:complexType name= URAType>
  <xs:sequence>
    <xs:element name= role  type= xs:IDREF/>
    <xs:element name= user  type= xs:IDREF maxOc-
curs= 10/>
  </xs:sequence>
</xs:complexType>
```

Please note that in our above specification of the user-role assignment relationship, the data type for both the elements "role" and "user" is "xs:IDREF," meaning that any instance of the UserRoleAssignment in the associated XML document should refer to a valid role and valid user, respectively. More specifically, the valid value for a string under the element tag "role" (or user) should be one of the "roleID" (or "userID") values used under the specification of RBAC model component "role" (or user).

Now the only RBAC model relations we have to model and specify is the role-privilege assignment relation. Similar to the user-role assignment relationship, we have theoretically two choices here. We can model the role-privilege assignment in either a role-centric (associating the privileges for a single role) or privilege-centric (providing the list of roles where a privilege can be found) fashion. From a practical viewpoint, we never ask the question, "What are the roles in which a privilege is found?" Rather we always ask the question, "What are the privileges associated with or assigned to a given role?" since our main objective is to ensure that a role has been assigned the most appropriate set of privileges (no more and no less) to perform the requisite enterprise functions without compromising the security of the operations of the enterprise.

Based on the above discussion, we provide here a role-centric XML schema specification of the role-privilege assignment relationship:

```
<xs:element name= RolePrivilegeAssignment
type= RPAType/>
<xs:complexType name= RPAType>
 <xs:sequence>
  <xs:element name= role  type= xs:IDREF/>
  <xs:element name= privilege  type= xs:IDREF/>
 </xs:sequence>
</xs:complexType>
```

Again to ensure referential integrity (that an instance of RolePrivilegeAssignment refers to a valid instance of a role and privilege) we have used the data type "xs:IDREF" for both these elements.

After representing the individual elements and relations of the ERBAC model for the banking enterprise, the entire model itself is represented using an element called "BANK_RBAC_Model" with elements representing all the model elements and relations as subelements.

```
<xs:element name= Bank_RBAC_Model type=
  BankRBACModelType/>
<xs:complexType name= BankRBACModelType>
 <xs:sequence>
  <xs:element ref= user maxOccurs= unbounded/>
  <xs:element ref= role maxOccurs= unbounded/>
  <xs:element ref= privilege maxOccurs= unbounded/>
  <xs:element ref= role_inherit maxOccurs= unbounded/>
  <xs:element ref= UserRoleAssignment maxOccurs= unbounded/>
  <xs:element ref= RolePrivilegeAssignment
    maxOccurs= unbounded/>
 </xs:sequence>
</xs:complexType>
```

9.5 Encoding of enterprise access control data in XML

Now that we have completed the XML schema specification of the ERBAC model, we are ready to encode the enterprise access control data in XML. The structure of the resulting XML document should conform to the XML schema specification of the ERBAC model (which we will refer to as the ERBAC XML schema).

We encode a sample set of users as follows:

```
<userid= DrayJ fullname= Jim Dray/>
<userid= GranceT fullname= Tim Grance/>
<userid= VincentH fullname= Vincent Hu/>
<userid= MiraM fullname= Mira Mouli/>
<userid= JansenW/>
<userid= TomK fullname= Tom Karygiannis/>
<userid= MellP fullname= Peter Mell/>
<userid= MorganK fullname= Kim Morgan/>
```

We see that our above encoding does not violate our XML schema definition of the "user" element. Since the "fullname" attribute is optional, it need not be present in every user instance. Also, there can be no repeating value for the userid attribute since it is of type "xs:ID."

We encode a sample set of roles in the banking enterprise as follows:

```
<roleID= BRM rolename= BranchManager
   cardinality= 1/>
<roleID= CSR rolename= Customer_Service_Rep
   cardinality= 3/>
<roleID= LNO rolename= Loan_Officer cardinality= 2/>
<roleID= ACM rolename= Accounting_Manager
   cardinality= 1/>
<roleID= AUD rolename= Internal_Auditor
   cardinality= 1/>
<roleID= TEL rolename= Teller cardinality= 6/>
<roleID= ACC cardinality= 2/>
```

Our XML representation of the set of privileges in the banking enterprise is as follows:

```
<privilege privilegeID= PV111 gen_resource=
   DepAcct gen_oper= Open />
<privilege privilegeID= PV112 gen_resource=
   DepAcct gen_oper= Debit />
```

```
<privilege  privilegeID= PV113   gen_resource=
   DepAcct   gen_oper= Credit />
<privilege  privilegeID= PV114   gen_resource=
   DepAcct   gen_oper = Close />
<privilege  privilegeID= PV211   gen_resource=
   LoanAcct  gen_oper= Open />
<privilege  privilegeID= PV212   gen_resource=
   LoanAcct  gen_oper= Debit />
<privilege  privilegeID= PV213   gen_resource=
   LoanAcct  gen_oper= Credit />
<privilege  privilegeID= PV214   gen_resource=
   LoanAcct  gen_oper = Close />
```

We have provided an XML-encoded set of data corresponding the ERBAC model elements. We now provide data corresponding to the ERBAC model relations. Again these encodings should conform to the corresponding XML schema specifications. Recall that we have three types of ERBAC model relations for which to provide data—role inheritance, user-role assignment, and role-privilege assignment.

Our sample set of data for role inheritance relations corresponds to the role structure for a hypothetical banking enterprise given in Figure 9.1.

The XML encoding of the role inheritance data for our banking enterprise (corresponding to Figure 9.1) is given below:

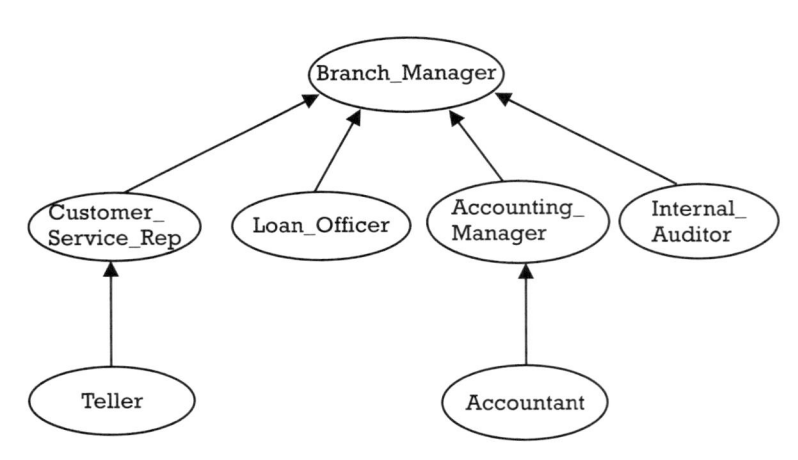

Figure 9.1 Role hierarchies in a banking enterprise.

9.5 Encoding of enterprise access control data in XML

```
/* Customer Service Representative Role inherits
   its privileges from Teller Role */
<role_inherit>
  <FromRole>Teller</FromRole>
  <ToRole>Customer_Service_Rep</ToRole>
</role_inherit>
/* Accounting Manager Role inherits its privileges
   from Accountant Role */
<role_inherit>
  <FromRole>Accountant</FromRole>
  <ToRole>Accounting_Manager</ToRole>
</role_inherit>
```

The following XML encodings represent the various inheritance relations involving the branch manager role. It represents the fact that the branch manager role inherits its privileges from the customer service representative, loan officer, accounting manager, and internal auditor roles.

```
<role_inherit>
  <FromRole>Customer_Service_Rep</FromRole>
  <ToRole>BranchManager</ToRole>
</role_inherit>
<role_inherit>
  <FromRole>Loan_Officer</FromRole>
  <ToRole>BranchManager</ToRole>
</role_inherit>
<role_inherit>
  <FromRole>Accounting_Manager</FromRole>
  <ToRole>BranchManager</ToRole>
</role_inherit>
<role_inherit>
  <FromRole>Internal_Auditor</FromRole>
  <ToRole>BranchManager</ToRole>
</role_inherit>
```

The sample set of XML-encoded data for the user-role assignment relations follows:

```
<UserRoleAssignment>
  <role>BRM</role>
  <user>GranceT</user>
  <user>JansenW</user>
</UserRoleAssignment>
<UserRole Assignment>
```

```
    <role>  CSR</role>
    <user>  TomK</user>
</UserRoleAssignment>
<UserRoleAssignment>
    <role>LNO</role>
    <user>MarksD</user>
</UserRoleAssignment>
<UserRoleAssignment>
    <role>ACM</role>
    <user>DrayJ</user>
</UserRoleAssignment>
<UserRoleAssignment>
    <role>AUD</role>
    <user>MorganK</user>
</UserRoleAssignment>
<UserRoleAssignment>
    <role>ACC</role>
    <user>VincentH</user>
</UserRoleAssignment>
```

Now the only RBAC model relation for which we are left to provide data is the role-privilege assignment relation. A sample set of data for this relation is given below:

```
<RolePrivilegeAssignment>
<role>TEL</role>
<privilege>PV112</privilege>
<privilege>PV113</privilege>
</RolePrivilegeAssignment>
<RolePrivilegeAssignment>
<role>CSR</role
<privilege>PV111</privilege>
<privilege>PV114</privilege>
</RolePrivilegeAssignment>
<RolePrivilegeAssignment>
<role>LNO</role>
<privilege>PV211</privilege>
<privilege>PV212</privilege>
<privilege>PV213</privilege>
<privilege>PV214</privilege>
</RolePrivilegeAssignment>
```

9.6 Verification of the ERBAC model and data specifications

We have now completed the encoding in XML of all enterprise access control data. So far we have talked about the XML specification of the ERBAC model and the XML encoding of the enterprise access control data without really mentioning the tools we have used to create these specifications. Merely using a text editor to create these two documents is not sufficient for the following reasons:

1. The metadata descriptions (or rather element descriptions) in the ERBAC XML schema document should conform to the syntax of the XML schema language. This verification process is called checking for *well-formedness* of the XML schema specification.

2. The XML encoding of the enterprise access control data should conform to the XML language specification. Again, verifying this property is called checking for *well-formedness* of the XML document. Stated more formally, an XML document is said to be well-formed if the physical structure of the document obeys the XML tag rules (i.e., every opening tag should have an ending tag).

3. Since the encoding syntax in the XML document containing enterprise access control data should conform to the specification rules (structural, cardinality, and data typing) in the ERBAC XML schema document, we should have a means for checking this property. This verification process is called checking for the *validity* of the XML document. More formally, an XML document is said to be valid if it conforms to the specifications in the XML schema it references.

Fortunately there are many commercial tools under the category of XML parsers or processors [12, 13] that help in the creation of well-formed XML schema and XML documents as well as valid XML documents (ones that conform to associated XML schema specifications). We have used one such tool, XML Spy [12], to create the ERBAC XML schema and the XML document containing the enterprise access control data.

In fact we have deliberately introduced some errors in our XML encoding to test the validation capabilities of our tool. For example in our encoding of the following role (refer to Section 9.5), we left out the mandatory rolename attribute:

```
<role roleID>= ACC    cardinality= 2 />
```

Our XML parser tool produced the following error message:

```
Validation Error:
Reason: Required Attribute  rolename  is missing
```

Similarly in our user-role assignment data, we used an invalid user (a user we did not specify in our list of users) in the following specification.

```
<UserRoleAssignment>
  <role>LN0</role>
  <user>MarksD</user>
</UserRoleAssignment>
```

Since this is in violation of the following referential constraint in the XML schema specification,

```
<xs:element name= UserRoleAssignment  type=
   URAType />
<xs:complexType name= URAType >
 <xs:sequence>
   <xs:element name= role   type= xs:IDREF />
   <xs:element name= user   type= xs:IDREF
     maxOccurs= 10 />
 </xs:sequence>
</xs:complexType>
```

Our XML parser tool produced the following error message:

```
Validation Error:
Reason: The ID  MarksD  is referenced but not
   defined in the document
```

9.7 Limitations of XML schemas for ERBAC model constraint representation

We can see from our XML schema specification of the ERBAC model that the XML schema language has provided us with flexibility in the syntactic representation of enterprise access control data. An example of syntactic flexibility follows:

- The attributes "roleID" and "userID" are mandatory attributes in the specification of a particular role or user, respectively. However, the

9.7 Limitations of XML schemas for ERBAC model constraint representation

attributes "fullname" and "cardinality" for the user and role specifications, respectively, are optional.

A critical reader would have noticed by this time that the XML schema is able to provide a good syntactic representation of the ERBAC model but not much semantic information pertaining to the enterprise context. Semantic information pertaining to an enterprise context can only be specified in a metadata representation using constraints that are based on the content or value of the data. These constraints are generally called the domain constraints. For example, in the ERBAC model for a banking enterprise, we would like the following domain constraints to exist:

- No more than one user can be assigned to the role of "branch manager" (role cardinality constraint).
- The roles "auditor" and "accountant" cannot be assigned to the same user (SoD constraint).

The above domain constraints will translate to following respective requirements on the XML encoding of the enterprise access control data (we will refer to the string under a particular tag as the value of the tag).

- When the value of the "role" tag under a roleAssignment tag is "BRM" (which is the roleID for branch manager), there cannot be more than one instance of a "user" tag under that roleAssignment tag.
- None of the user tag values under a roleAssignment tag (with role tag value "AUD") should match with user tag values under a roleAssignment tag (with role tag value "ACC").

From the above examples it should be clear that any practical domain constraint is content-based. However, we should point out at this juncture, that the XML schema language can be used to specify a limited class of domain constraints through its data typing and occurrence features. An example of a domain constraint that can be specified using data typing and occurrence features is described as follows:

- Constraint using data typing feature: The role name (or identifier for a role) should occur from a valid list. We have already placed this constraint in our XML schema by specifying the data type associated with a "rolename" attribute of the role element as an enumerated type.

- Constraint using occurrence feature: The total number of roles in the enterprise cannot exceed 10. We already have inserted this constraint into our XML schema by specifying the value associated with the maxOccurs attribute of the role element as 10.

The reason for the limitation of the XML schema in the specification of domain constraints is the fact that the XML schema is a grammar-based language, and a grammar-based language cannot deal with content-based constraints. Hence an XML schema is not sufficient for a complete specification of the ERBAC model for an enterprise since the latter contains content-based domain constraints.

One of the common approaches proposed in the literature to overcome the limitations of the XML schema in representing semantic information pertaining to the domain is to augment the XML schema specification with semantic information using domain modeling languages such as RDF [14] or pattern-based languages like Schematron [15]. In the following paragraphs we provide a few examples of how *content-based constraints using the Schematron language can be included in an XML schema specification* of the ERBAC model. The reader is certainly encouraged to look at approaches involving the annotation of XML schemas with RDF schemas for incorporating domain constraints in the research journals and conference proceedings.

Augmenting the XML schema specifications with Schematron constraints The Schematron language was developed for the validation of the contents of XML documents through features for expressing rules. These rules are expressed using the syntax of Xpath, which, in turn, provides expressions for locating information within an XML document. For example, to refer to a role whose text content is "TEL" within a UserRoleAssignment (i.e., locating user role assignments for the teller role), the Xpath syntax is:

```
UserRoleAssignment[role[text ( )= TEL ]]
```

Using the above content-addressing syntax provided by Xpath, a Schematron rule expression that expresses the fact that there should exists an instance of UserRoleAssignment where the role has the text "TEL" (meaning that there should be at least one user assignment for the teller role) has the form:

```
UserRoleAssignment[count(role[text ( )= TEL ])
   >= 1]
```

9.7 Limitations of XML schemas for ERBAC model constraint representation 201

In Schematron, constraint expressions can be used for generating alerts (or diagnostic messages) both for the situation where a constraint is violated as well as for a situation where it is found to be true within the XML document contents. The Schematron specification of the constraint expression in the case where a violation should trigger an alert (or diagnostic message) is specified under an <assert> tag as follows:

```
<sch:assert
  test= UserRoleAssignment[count(role[text (
)= TEL ])>= 1] >
   There should be an assignment for Teller Role
</sch:assert>
```

However, a constraint or rule expression alone does not constitute the complete Schematron specification. The context in which the rule expression must be evaluated should also be provided. For the above constraint, the context is the topmost element in the XML schema specification of the ERBAC model (i.e., ERBAC XML schema) since the "UserRoleAssignment" element is a subelement under this topmost element.

```
<sch:rule context= Bank_RBAC_Model >
```

We have so far provided an example of how a domain constraint can be expressed using a Schematron specification. The next issue that arises is where this Schematron specification is located. A Schematron specification is never provided as a standalone specification for an XML document content but is always embedded within the associated XML schema specification. In fact, the exact location for a Schematron specification is within the "annotation" tag of the XML schema specification. This feature is intended to help the software tool (called the Schematron validator [16]) to not only locate the Schematron constraints but also to establish the proper context for validating a given XML document for conformance to those constraints.

Based on the above discussion, the complete Schematron specification (including its location within the XML schema specification) of the banking domain constraint that states there should exist at least one user assignment for the teller role is as follows:

```
<xs:complexType name= BankRBACModelType >
  <xs:annotation>---(Start of Schematron constraint)
    <xs:appinfo>
      <sch:pattern name= Role Assignment Rules >
        <sch:rule context= Bank_RBAC_Model >
```

```
          <sch:assert test= UserRoleAssignment[count
            (role[text ( )= TEL ])>= 1] >
          There should be an assignment for Teller
          Role
          </sch:assert>
        </sch:rule>
      </sch:pattern>
    </xs:appinfo>
  </xs:annotation>---(End of Schematron constraint)
<xs:sequence>
<xs:element ref= user   maxOccurs= unbounded />
```

As already alluded to, the validation of our enterprise access control data in the XML document for conformance to the above domain constraints expressed through the Schematron specifications is done through a class of tool called Schematron Validator [16]. The reader could see that the Schematron Validator performs, in the context of Schematron specifications, a function identical to what the XML Parser does in the context of the XML schema specification.

The error generated by the Schematron Validator on our XML document containing enterprise access control data is illustrated here (since we deliberately did not provide an assignment for the teller role).

```
From pattern  Role Assignment Rules :
  Assertion fails:  There should be an assignment
for Teller Role  at
 /Bank_RBAC_Model[1]
    <Bank_RBAC_Model
xsi:noNamespaceSchemaLocation= A:\Bank_RBAC_model.
  xsd >...</>
```

9.8 Using XML-encoded enterprise access control data for enterprisewide access control implementation

At this stage in our EAF development effort, we have accomplished the following:

- An XML schema specification of the ERBAC model augmented with Schematron specifications (for representation of some domain constraints). Let us call this document Bank_RBAC_model.xsd.

9.8 Using XML-encoded enterprise access control data

• The XML encoding of the enterprise access control data (in a document we will call the Bank_RBAC_data.xml). We also validated the contents of the Bank_RBAC_data.xml document for the satisfaction of structural and some rudimentary domain constraints through an XML schema validator. In addition, we validated the access control data in that document for the satisfaction of some domain constraints expressed through the Schematron specification using a Schematron validator.

(The complete listing of the XML document Bank_RBAC_data.xml and the XML schema specification augmented with Schematron constraints in the document Bank_RBAC_model.xsd are given in appendixes at the end of the book.)

Now, the practical value of the enterprise access control data in Bank_RBAC_data.xml can only be realized if it can be programmatically interpreted, extracted, and mapped to define the access control information in the native format of the several application platforms in the enterprise. Consistent interpretation of the data in an XML document across all programs is only possible if a standardized API is defined for processing the contents of XML documents. Fortunately, there are two prominent APIs that have been standardized and utilized in the industry. They are (1) the DOM API [17] that was issued as a W3C recommendation in October 1998 and (2) the SAX API [18]. These APIs have been implemented in a class of tools called XML processor or parsers. In other words, an XML parser provides a library of routines or methods that have implemented either a DOM or SAX API and those in turn are then callable from a procedural language. For example, the library of methods in an XML parser for Java can be utilized by Java programs to access (and even modify) the structure and content of XML documents.

We will now illustrate the process of interpreting and extracting the enterprise access control data in Bank_RBAC_data.xml using a Java program that makes use of IBM's XML parser for Java [13] (which has implemented the DOM API). In the same Java program we will also show how the extracted data can be utilized to define access control information for a SQL relational database application platform. Before we proceed to describe our Java program (let us call it as Bank_RBAC_to_SQL.java), we have to understand the basic logic involved in the extraction of contents from XML documents using the DOM API. In DOM, an XML document is represented as a tree-structured object (an object of a type called document) whose nodes are such items as elements and texts. An XML parser parsing an XML document generates an instance of this tree (also called a DOM object) and a processing program (that is utilizing the same XML parser) is able to manipulate the nodes of the tree through the set of DOM-provided APIs.

To programmatically parse the document Bank_RBAC_data.xml for the purpose of extraction of its contents, the first task our Java program (Bank_RBAC_to_SQL.java) has to do is create a DOM object from the Bank_RBAC_data.xml document by specifying the URL of this XML document [19]. Our Java code for this task (including all the other housekeeping activities) is as follows:

```
import com.ibm.xml.parser.*;
import org.w3c.dom.*;
Try {
  URL u = new URL(http://RBAC_BOOK.org/xml/Bank_RBAC_data.xml);
  InputStream i = u.openStream ( );
  Parser ps = new Parser ( Extracting enterprise access control data for SQL DBMS application );
  Document doc = ps.readStream(i);
} catch (Exception e) { }
```

By creating the DOM object (called the document object) of our Bank_RBAC_data.xml file using the XML parser, we have prepared ourselves to extract the information contained in that XML file. The document object (created from our BANK_RBAC_Data.xml file) now contains a tree of nodes (this is the DOM's view of the XML file). There are methods available in the node interface to check the following information about each node:

- The type of the node (there are two important node types—ELEMENT_NODE and TEXT_NODE);
- The value (or string) contained in the node (this is true for nodes of type TEXT_NODE);
- Whether a node has children (this is true for nodes of type ELEMENT_NODE).

Now our enterprise access control data in Bank_RBAC_data.xml has become the document object that, in turn, is nothing but a container of nodes. We also know that there are two types of nodes—TEXT_NODE and ELEMENT_NODE. To meaningfully process the contents of the nodes in our document object, we need to know the association between these nodes and the elements in our XML schema specification. This is because of the fact that our understanding of the structure and semantics of the ERBAC

9.8 Using XML-encoded enterprise access control data

model is in terms of the elements in the XML schema specification document Bank_RBAC_model.xsd. Fortunately there exists an association between the nodes generated by the XML parser and the elements in the XML schema specification. It so happens that there is an interface called element in the DOM API that extends the node. More specifically, a node of type ELEMENT_NODE is also an element.

Now that we know that there is a node of type ELEMENT_NODE (or elements), information under the various tag names like role and user (that we encounter in our Bank_RBAC_data.xml file) can be accessed since these tag names correspond to elements in the XML schema file. However, then we find that in our XML file there is no single instance of tag names like role or user. These tag names occur several times, denoting the number of roles and number of users in the enterprise, respectively. Hence we need an interface (and a corresponding object) that can refer to a list of nodes (instead of a single node) based on common property (e.g., tag name). Fortunately, the DOM specification provides for such an interface by name NodeList interface. The NodeList objects are generated by node objects of type ELEMENT_NODE (or element objects). Since our document object (called doc in our case) is also an element object, it has a method called getElementsByTagName (string tagname) that returns a NodeList of all elements with that tag name.

To solidify the above discussion, Table 9.1 provides the association between various entities in the XML document, the XML schema specification, and the DOM API nodes.

We now have a fair idea of how to interpret the tags in an XML document and extract the values under the various tags as well as specified attributes. To illustrate how we interpret the contents of the

Table 9.1 Mapping from XML Document Tags to DOM API Interfaces

XML Document	XML Schema Spec	DOM API Interface/Method
Tag	Element	Node of type ELEMENT_NODE or Element
Text string under a tag (or tag value)		Node of type TEXT_NODE
Group of tags with the same tag name		NodeList
Value associated with a tag		Node.getNodeValue ( )
Value of a named attribute under a given tag		Node.getAttribute(named attribute)

Bank_RBAC_data.xml document, let us assume that we are interested in extracting the names of all the roles in the document for the purpose of defining these roles in the SQL DBMS application environment. To do this we have to obtain a reference to an object that contains a list of nodes whose tag name is "role." In other words, we have to create a NodeList object that contains element objects with the tag name "role" from our document object . The Java code to create this NodeList object containing a list of "role" elements is as follows:

```
NodeList listofRoles = doc.getElementsByTagName
   ( role );
```

Now that we have the NodeList object containing all the "role" elements (which are also nodes), we can iterate over the set of nodes to extract information about each individual "role" element (node). There are two methods in the NodeList interface that help us to carry out this process. They are listed as follows:

- *NodeList.getLength( ):* gives the total number of nodes that the NodeList object is pointing to;
- *NodeList.item(int index):* returns the specific node located by the index.

Specifically, within each "role" element we are interested in getting the value of the attribute "rolename." We can obtain the value associated with a named attribute on a given "role" Element (i.e., specific node) using the method: getAttribute(string name) where name is the name of the attribute.

Making use of the methods referred above, here is the code to iterate over the set of "role" elements (or nodes) and obtain the names of the roles (value associated with the attribute "rolename"):

```
int numberOfRoles = listOfRoles.getLength ( );
for (int i=0 ; i < numberOfRoles ; i ++) {
  String rolename = ((Node) listOfRoles.item(i)).
    getAttribute( rolename );
}
```

Recall that our interest in extracting the role names is to define those roles in the SQL DBMS application environment. Java programs generally connect to SQL database servers using a piece of software called a database driver (which provides the necessary communication pipe) as well as a set of libraries called a Java Database Connectivity (JDBC). In fact, the JDBC

9.8 Using XML-encoded enterprise access control data

libraries provide a class called the DriverManager into which the loaded driver must be registered. The java command to load a driver is:

```
String mydriver = weblogic.jdbc.oci.driver ;
Class.forName(myDriver);
```

Once a driver is loaded, it creates an instance of itself and automatically registers itself with the DriverManager. Once the driver has been loaded, we are in a position to open a database connection and obtain a connection object by simply calling the driver manager's static getConnection( ) method. The getConnection method requires as its parameters the following: (1) the database location specified using a URL syntax (consisting of protocol:subprotocol:server address:database name), (2) a user name, and (3) a password. The code snippet to create an instance of a connection object consists of:

```
String DB_URL= jdbc:weblogic:oracle:bankdb ;
String user= dba ;
String password= manager ;
Connection dbcon = DriverManager.getConnection
   (DB_URL, user, password);
```

Before using any SQL statement to create the required roles, a statement object needs to be obtained using the connection object. This is accomplished using:

```
Statement stmt = dbcon.createStatement ( );
```

Now the statement interface of the JDBC specification provides methods to send both queries and updates/creates to the database. Since our intention here is to send in a SQL statement to create a new role, it is an example of a create statement, and the appropriate statement interface method is executeUpdate, since this executeUpdate method returns an integer whose value should be zero if the SQL create statement is successful. Constructing a java string of the SQL create statement for the creating a role with name "rolename" and passing that string as a parameter to executeUpdate method we get:

```
SqlString =   create role   + rolename;
int count = stmt.executeUpdate(sqlString);
```

In summary, we have now illustrated the case of using the DOM API and JDBC libraries within a Java program to parse our Bank_RBAC_data.xml and extract the role names and create those roles in a target application hosted on a relational DBMS platform. In fact the above logic can be used to parse all DOM nodes (and hence all the tags and their values in the XML document that contains our enterprise access control data) and define the necessary access control information for the various target application platforms. It is needless to state that the appropriate SQL statement for creating an instance of each type of access control information should be used. The SQL command strings for creating these instances of access control information (which in the target application platform are also considered to be RBAC-based access control data) are

```
SqlString =  Create user   + username;
   (for creating a user)
SqlString =  grant role   + fromRole +   to   +
   toRole; (for creating a role hierarchy with the
   toRole as the parent and fromRole as the child).
```

9.9 Conclusion

This chapter has illustrated an approach for developing an EAF. This framework provides the infrastructure to specify the access control requirements (using the formalism of an access control model) for all the IT resources in an enterprise that embodies multiple policies in a platform-independent format and to map those specifications to the various access control modules found in the diverse application environments of the enterprise. We have shown that RBAC (more specifically ERBAC)—because of its support for multiple policies and ease of administration—is the candidate of choice for an EAM. We have described in detail how the XML language vocabularies, APIs, and tool sets can be used to specify an ERBAC model, encode the corresponding enterprise access control data, and map that data into the format required by access control modules in the heterogeneous application platforms within the enterprise.

References

[1] Department of Health and Human Services, "Security and Electronic Signature Standards; Proposed Rule," *Federal Register*, Vol. 63, No. 155, August 12, 1998.

9.9 Conclusion

[2] Ferraiolo. D., J. Cugini, and D. J. Kuhn, "Role-Based Access Control (RBAC): Features and Motivations," *Proc. 11th Annual Computer Security Applications Conference,* New Orleans, LA, December 1995.

[3] Ferraiolo, D. F., J. F. Barkley, and D. R. Kuhn, "A Role-Based Access Control Model and Reference Implementation Within a Corporate Intranet," *ACM Trans. Info. Syst. Security,* 2, 1, February 1999, pp. 34–64.

[4] Sandhu R. S., et al., "Role-Based Access Control Models," *IEEE Computer,* Vol. 29, No. 2, February 1996, pp. 38–47.

[5] Bai, Y., and V. Varadharajan, "A Logic for State Transformations in Authorization Policies," *Proceedings of the IEEE Computer Security Foundations Workshop,* June 1997.

[6] Jajodia, S., P. Samarati, and V. S. Subhramanian, "A Logical Language for Expressing Authorizations," *Proceedings of the IEEE Symposium on Security and Privacy,* May 1997.

[7] The Extensible Markup Language, Version 1.0, in http://www.w3.org/TR/REC-xml, February 1998.

[8] Guide to the W3C XML Specification ("XMLspec") DTD, Version 2.1, http://www.w3.org/XML/1998/06/xmlspec-report-v21.html.

[9] XML Schema Part 0: Primer W3C Recommendation, 2 May 2001, http://www.w3.org/TR/xmlschema-0.

[10] Vuong N. N., G. S. Smith, and Deng Yi, "Managing Security Policies in a Distributed Environment Using Extensible Markup Language (XML)," *Proceedings of the 16th ACM SAC2001 Symposium on Applied Computing,* Las Vegas, NV, March 2001

[11] Ferraiolo D. F., et al., "Proposed NIST Standard for Role-Based Access Control," *ACM Transactions on Information and Systems Security,* Vol. 4, No. 3, August 2001.

[12] http://www.xmlspy.com/download.html.

[13] XML Parser for Java, http://www.ibm.com/xml.

[14] Resource Description Framework (RDF), http://www.w3.org/RDF.

[15] Schematron—Pattern-Based Schema Language, http://www.ascc.net/xml/resource/schematron/schematron.html.

[16] Schematron Schema Validator, http://www.topologi.com.

[17] Document Object Model—Level—1 Recommendations, in http://www.w3.org/TR/REC-DOM-Level-1, October 1998.

[18] SAX—Event-Driven API for XML, http://www.megginson.com/SAX.

[19] Maruyama, H., K. Tamura, and N. Uramoto, *XML and Java—Developing Web Applications,* Reading, MA: Addison-Wesley, 1999.

CHAPTER 10

Contents

10.1 RBAC for WFMSs

10.2 RBAC integration in Web environments

10.3 RBAC for UNIX environments

10.4 RBAC in Java

10.5 RBAC for FDBSs

10.6 RBAC in autonomous security service modules

10.7 Conclusions

References

Integrating RBAC with Enterprise IT Infrastructures

This chapter discusses the research concepts and associated prototypes that have been developed to integrate RBAC model concepts into existing enterprise IT infrastructures. Our choice of technologies under the umbrella of enterprise IT infrastructures is motivated by the success achieved so far in integrating RBAC into the building blocks of these technologies. The technologies we have considered include WFMSs, Web applications, the UNIX OS, distributed file systems or network file systems (NFSs), Java, and federated database system (FDBS). The reader is reminded that this chapter deals only with research frameworks and prototypes. Chapter 12 focuses on the implementation of RBAC into commercial products.

Our discussion of the integration of RBAC with each of the above mentioned technologies is organized as follows: We first provide brief background information on each of these technologies and then refer to the research ideas that have been proposed for incorporation of role-based access enforcement (i.e., integrating a RBAC model) in the deployment of these technologies. We also discuss the salient features of the prototype tools (if any) that have been developed based on these research ideas. In the course of the discussions of each particular RBAC integration aspect, we refer readers to conference and journal articles providing more details on that topic. Section 10.1 discusses the integration of RBAC model concepts into WFMSs. Section 10.2 deals with the integration of the RBAC model into the Web applications' access control framework through cookies and X.509 digital certificates. Section 10.2 also discusses a prototype that has integrated RBAC into an e-commerce-type Web application where the user base is not known in advance. Section 10.3 describes a prototype that has integrated RBAC into the access control framework of a commercial UNIX operating System (i.e., Solaris) and illustrates how it facilitates decentralized administration. In addition, Section 10.3 discusses a prototype describing the incorporation of RBAC into a well-established distributed file system NFS (from Sun Microsystems). Section 10.4 illustrates research ideas that have been proposed to incorporate role-based access enforcement in the Java 2 Security Model (JDK 1.2) enhanced with the Java Authentication and Authorization Service (JAAS). Section 10.5 describes the architecture of a role-based authorization and access control subsystem that has been developed as part of the security system of a FDBS. Section 10.6 describes an implementation of RBAC model in an autonomous security services module.

10.1 RBAC for WFMSs

WFMSs are computerized systems used for supporting (coordinating and streamlining) business processes in various application domains like finance and banking, health care, telecommunications, and manufacturing. Examples of business processes in a manufacturing organization are order processing, goods procurement, and production scheduling.

WFMSs, as they support the definition of business processes and the enforcement of control over those processes, are called upon to support various policies including access control policies. RBAC, with its policy-support capabilities and ease of access management, becomes a natural candidate for incorporation into WFMSs.

To appreciate the usefulness of the RBAC framework for the enforcement of access control policies in WFMSs, we need a good overview of workflow concepts and the distinct access control requirements of WFMSs. These are the topics of Sections 10.1.1 and 10.1.2. Subsequently, we discuss some of the research concepts and prototypes that have used RBAC to specify and enforce access control policies within WFMSs.

10.1.1 Workflow Concepts and WFMSs

Based on the definition provided by the Workflow Management Coalition (WFMC) [1], an international organization of workflow vendors, users, and research groups, a workflow is a representation of an organizational or business process in which "... documents, information, or tasks are passed from one participant to another in a way that is governed by rules or procedures." A workflow separates the various activities of a given organizational process into a set of well-defined tasks. Hence, typically, a workflow (often synonymous with a process) is specified as a set of tasks and a set of dependencies among the tasks. The various tasks in a workflow are usually carried out by several users in accordance with organizational rules relevant to the process represented by the workflow.

A WFMS is a computerized information system that is responsible for scheduling and synchronizing the various tasks within the workflow, in accordance with specified task dependencies, and for sending each task to the respective processing entity (e.g., Web server or database server). The data resources that a task uses are called work items.

As already stated, the representation of a business process using a workflow involves a number of organizational rules or policies. An important class of organizational policies is security policies. Within the realm of security policies, access control policies play a key role, and hence defining and enforcing access control requirements becomes a key function of a WFMS.

It has been found, from the point of view of ease of security administration, that specifying access control requirements for workflows in terms of roles is preferable to specifying them in terms of individuals (e.g., only the department manager can approve a purchase order for the department). Furthermore, role-based authorization is particularly beneficial in workflow environments in facilitating dynamic load balancing when several individuals can perform a task. This is the reason that commercial WFMSs, such as Lotus Notes and Action Workflow, support role-based authorizations [2, 3].

10.1.2 WFMS components and access control requirements

WFMSs consist of two main components—design time and run time. The design-time component consists of a set of tools (called the process definition tools) that are used for defining and modeling the business processes and their constituent tasks. A process definition consists of process name (e.g., purchase order process), the definition of various tasks within the process (e.g., purchase order approval task), and a set of business rules associated with the process (e.g., task sequence or data flow among tasks). The run-time component of a WFMS (also called a workflow engine) consists of a set of servers that interpret the process definition and create and maintain process instances. Task instances associated with each process instance are also created (based on process definition). The list of instantiated tasks pending to be executed is presented to the user (for his or her action) through a worklist server. The tasks themselves are executed in task servers. Data servers act as repositories of data that is needed by tasks (referred to earlier as work items). In addition, there are monitor servers that maintain the execution history for various processes or tasks instances to facilitate run-time access control decisions. Figure 10.1 presents a schematic diagram of the overall architecture of a WFMS.

10.1.3 Access control design requirements

The overall business rules that have gone into the definition of various processes in a workflow are also the determinants for the access control design requirements for WFMSs. A characteristic feature of these access control design requirements is the incorporation of execution-context information.

To appreciate the importance of context information for access control specification in workflow environments, let us consider the workflow representation for a purchase order business process. This process involves four tasks: initiate a purchase order, approve a purchase order, authorize payment, and sign checks. Figure 10.2 provides a representation of the purchase order workflow along with role-task assignment.

From Figure 10.2, it should be clear that a role can be assigned to perform more than one task (e.g., manager role can perform tasks T1 and T2) and that a task can be performed by more than one role (e.g., T1 can be performed by the roles employee and manager). Furthermore, we see from Figure 10.2 that a certain task may have to be executed more than once (e.g., task T4) in a workflow. Each invocation of a task is called task

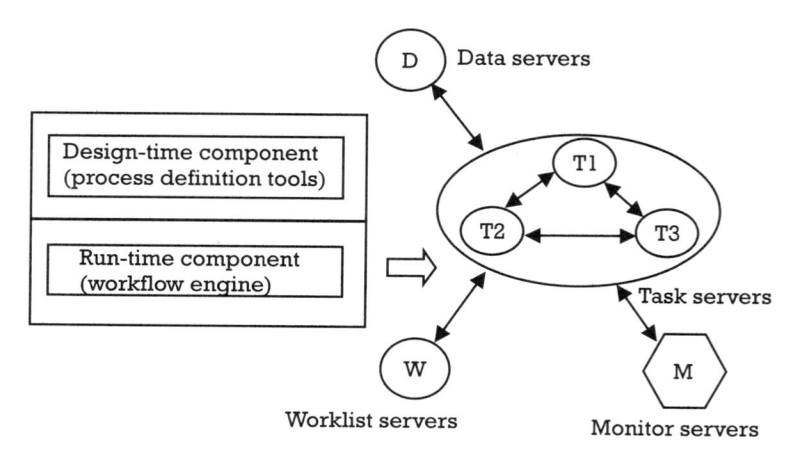

Figure 10.1 Components of the WFMS.

10.1 RBAC for WFMSs

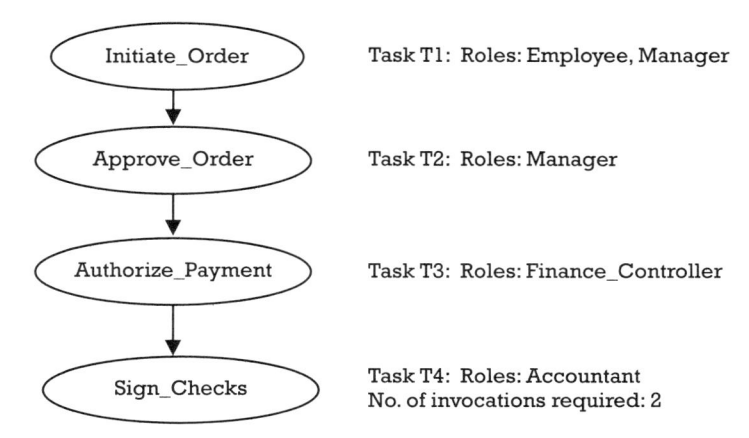

Figure 10.2 Purchase order workflow with role-task assignment.

- Initiate_Order — Task T1: Roles: Employee, Manager
- Approve_Order — Task T2: Roles: Manager
- Authorize_Payment — Task T3: Roles: Finance_Controller
- Sign_Checks — Task T4: Roles: Accountant, No. of invocations required: 2

activation. In other words, certain tasks in a workflow may have more than one activation. A particular purchase order—for example, "purchase order #1003 initiated by Jack for purchasing 100 Zip disks on 8/23/02"—is called a workflow instance.

At first glance it might appear for the above workflow specification, that the designated role-task assignments, along with a suitable role hierarchy and user-role assignments would complete the access control specification (and in our case an RBAC model specification) for the "purchase order" workflow environment. However, close examination reveals that our access control specification in its present form does not have answers to the following questions:

- *Question 1 (Q1):* Can a manager who is authorized to both initiate and approve purchase orders approve an order instance that he or she has initiated himself or herself?
- *Question 2 (Q2):* Can a manager approve a purchase order that does not carry price quotes?
- *Question 3 (Q3):* Can both activations of task $T4$ (sign checks) be done by the same user?

It should be clear from the nature of the above questions that they can only be answered if we carry information pertaining to execution history (e.g., who performed the order initiation task for the workflow instance identified by purchase order #1003) and the contents of the data resource affected by a task (e.g., purchase order table in a relational database). More specifically, execution history is required for answering queries Q1 and Q3, and the content information on a data resource is required for answering query Q2.

Having seen the necessity for context information in the access control specification for a WFMS, let us now take a look at the various access control design requirements that have been identified by researchers [4]. These requirements—strict least privilege, order of events, and SoD—are collectively called context-sensitive access control requirements:

1. *Strict least privilege:* The concept of least privilege requires that a user receive no more access permissions than those required to carry out his or her job responsibilities. Strict least privilege reinforces that concept by taking into account that some of these permissions in some specific instances may be inappropriate. For example, a manager may be authorized to both initiate and approve purchase orders. As part of the purchase order initiation activity, the manager may have permission to edit the details of an order. However, when the manager is approving a purchase order initiated by some other employee, he or she should not be allowed to make changes to (or edit) the contents of that particular order.

2. *Order of events:* This requires that certain privileges can only be granted or exercised once others have been exercised. For example, a manager cannot approve a purchase order until the initiating employee has submitted it; similarly, a purchase order cannot be submitted until quotes have been obtained and filled up against the requested items.

3. *SoD:* The primary objective of this concept is the prevention of fraud and errors, thus maintaining the semantic integrity of business information. This requirement is formulated as a set of business rules such as "a person may not approve his or her own purchase order" or "a check requires two different signatures."

10.1.4 RBAC model design and implementation requirements for WFMSs

Let us now take a look at the RBAC model design and implementation requirements based on the access control design requirements we saw in the previous section. The RBAC model design requirements for WFMSs have an impact on the following activities:

- *User-role assignment:* Certain SoD requirements (those that deal with preventing situations that should never occur) must be enforced during design or administration time. These requirements are referred to in the RBAC literature as static SoD. For example, in the purchase order process, the roles Accountant and Finance_Controller should not be assigned to the same person. This may result in a Finance_Controller approving and releasing a company check based on a phony order approved by a manager friend.

- *Role hierarchy definition:* The design of roles and role structures should be based on task responsibilities within the various workflow processes and not on the reporting structure of an organization. For example, an Accountant may report to a Finance_Controller, but the Finance_Controller role should not be made the parent role for the Accountant, making the former inherit all the latter's permissions. This would defeat the basic motive behind the process definition for the purchase order process where the Finance_Controller and Accountant are expected to have distinct nonoverlapping responsibilities.

- *Role-permission assignment:* The definition of permissions directly assigned to the roles must be abstract and tied to the semantics of the workflow processes. For example with respect to the purchase order process the following should be role-permission assignments (since tasks are the semantic entities representing the user operations):

```
<employee, initiate_order (T1)>
<manager, approve_order (T2)>
<finance_controller, authorize_payment (T3)>
<accountant, sign_check (T4)>
```

The permissions required on the underlying data sources (object-level permissions) for the successful execution of each of the tasks (stated in the role-permission assignments) should also be mapped as part of the RBAC model definition. Thus, the overall role-permission assignment is complete only when we have role-task assignments and task-permission assignments [5]. This is depicted through tables in Figure 10.3.

Having seen the RBAC model design-time requirements, let us take a look at the RBAC model implementation requirements for workflow environments. These implementation requirements are also called run-time requirements since they are to be enforced when a business process instance has been defined and its constituent tasks are being executed in a WFMS. The run-time requirements are described as follows:

Roles \ Tasks	T1	T2	T3	T4
R1	x			
R2	x	x		
R3			x	
R4				x

Role-task assignments

Tasks \ Objects	O1 M11	O1 M12	O2 M21	O2 M22	O3 M31	O3 M32	O3 M33
T1	R	W					
T2			R	W	W		
T3				R	W		
T4					R	W	W

Task–object permissions assignment

Figure 10.3 Complete role-permission assignments in WFMS.

- *Role-activation constraints:* These types of constraints must be defined and enforced during run time to ensure that certain permissions are not misused. These requirements are referred to in the RBAC literature as dynamic SoD constraints. An example of such a constraint would be "a manager may not approve his own purchase order." The enforcement of these types of constraints is possible in WFMSs due to the information provided by the worklist and monitor servers. The monitor server keeps a log of execution history (i.e., who performed task T1—say an initiation of a purchase order—in workflow (process) instance #35). The worklist presents a list of pending tasks associated with process instance #35. Suppose that a manager who has initiated the purchase order in the instance #35 wants to approve that same order by executing task *T2*. To execute the pending task *T2* (approving the purchase order with instance #35), a manger has to activate the "manager" role but he or she will be prevented from doing so, if a suitable role activation constraint is defined.

10.1.5 RBAC for workflows—research prototypes

Research in the area of applying RBAC concepts for access control in workflow systems covers the gamut of formal models [6] and research prototypes [7, 8]. Since one of the research prototypes [7] makes use of the model referenced in [6], we will confine our discussion to the research prototypes. A common feature of the two research prototypes is that the RBAC specification and enforcement modules (let us call them collectively the workflow authorization server) are layered on top of existing WFMSs. Specifically the workflow engine component of WFMSs (refer to Figure 10.1) interacts with the workflow authorization server to obtain and revoke authorizations during workflow execution time.

In the prototype by Payne et al. [7] (referred to as the Napoleon prototype), the workflow authorization server is the Napoleon tool, a multilayered role definition and enforcement tool. Each of the levels in Napoleon is used to define roles at various policy levels or levels of abstraction. The bottom-most layer is used to define application-specific roles (i.e., roles in terms of application resources and the access control mechanism of the hosting platform). Each of the higher layers contains progressively more abstract roles, while the roles at the top-most layer are assigned to the users. Figure 10.4 shows these multiple layers.

Each of the semantic layers is defined based on the particular enterprise requirements. In the Napoleon prototype, a new layer called the workflow layer, which is structurally similar to other semantic layers, is built. This layer contains roles and role constraints directly associated with workflow tasks in the various processes. The workflow engine managing a workflow (process) instance requests Napoleon to grant access to an active task. The

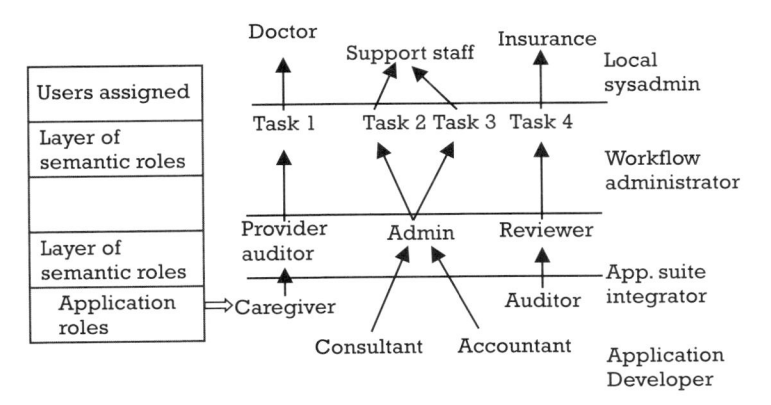

Figure 10.4 Layers of roles in the Napoleon tool.

Napoleon receives a request along with a host of other information, such as user identities. Napoleon then makes use of information such as user-role assignments, role constraints, execution history of the process instance, and role-task assignments to associate roles for the current active task. Since the subsequent lower layers in Napoleon contain more application-specific roles, eventually resource-specific permissions are generated to enable the current active task to be carried out if the dynamic role-task association is successful. Similarly, the WFMS can request Napoleon to revoke access to all inactive tasks.

Like the Napoleon prototype, the prototype by Huang et al. [8] (the SecureFlow prototype) is also designed to work with existing WFMSs. In the SecureFlow prototype, a workflow authorization server (WAS) interacts with the workflow engine (called the workflow execution server) to provide authorization support during workflow execution. The WAS consists of an authorization specification module (ASM), an authorization generation module (AGM), and an authorization repository. The ASM allows security administrators to state workflow-related access control policy specifications that, in turn, are written to the authorization repository to be enforced during the workflow execution. The various specifications are user specification, role specification, user-role assignments, authorization template (AT) specification (static role-task assignments and role-to-object permissions), object type specification, and constraint specification. The AGM generates authorizations during workflow execution time. It makes use of a constraint manager submodule to assemble all constraints relevant to the current task, executes the constraints, and generates what is called the eligible subject set (ESS). The ESS contains a subset of the original subjects assigned to the role, since some of the subjects might have been eliminated due to the imposition of the constraints. If the current subject(s) requesting authorization is in the ESS, the AGM makes use of the AT specifications to generate the required authorization. Figure 10.5 is a schematic diagram showing the contents of the WAS and its interactions with the components of the WFMS in the SecureFlow architecture.

10.2 RBAC integration in Web environments

A survey of the suitability of various access control models for Web-based applications reveals that RBAC models have the most desirable features [9]. The heterogeneous platform-based, distributed nature of Web-based applications requires an access control model that is flexible, multipolicy-supportable, and scalable, thereby providing good support for security

10.2 RBAC integration in Web environments

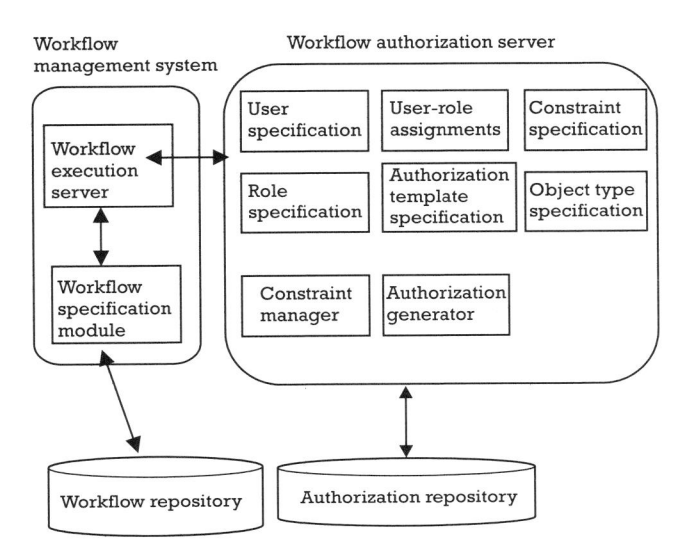

Figure 10.5 Modules in SecureFlow WAS.

management and administration. RBAC models do possess these characteristics. Consequently, several architectures have been proposed and demonstrated for providing access control services for Web-based applications using RBAC. A common thread through these several research ideas and prototypes is that most of them, if not all, rely on public key infrastructure (PKI) facilities with a major portion of RBAC model information residing on Web servers.

10.2.1 Implementing RBAC entirely on the Web server

One of the earliest implementations of RBAC on the Web server was the project initiated at NIST by Ferraiolo et al. [10]. The first step in their architecture was the definition of signatures of various function calls needed to define an RBAC model and to query the model for enforcing access control by designing what they called the RBAC/Web API. Implementing the RBAC/Web API for a given Web server environment will result in support for role-based access enforcement for all the applications on a Web server. They came up with two prototype RBAC implementations on the Web server. One type implemented the RBAC model as a CGI program on a Microsoft IIS server and did not involve any change to the Web server source code. The second type implemented the RBAC model by modifying the Apache Web server source code to implement access enforcement on its resources based on the user roles and role permissions instead of user identity. Neither implementation required any change to the client or the Web browser.

10.2.2 Implementing RBAC for Web server access using cookies

Park, Sandhu, and Ahn [11] have developed a prototype implementation of RBAC for access control on a Web server using the concept of secure cookies. Cookies were invented to maintain continuity and state information as the HTTP protocol that enables communication between a browser and Web server is stateless. When a user visits a cookie-using Web server through his or her browser, the Web server creates a string of text characters called a cookie, encoding relevant information about the user and sends them to user's machine via the browser. When the user revisits the same Web server, the Web server can obtain information about the user from the cookie instead of asking for the information all over again. (In some instances, a different Web server can recognize the cookie generated by another Web server.) However, cookies are generally transmitted in clear text and therefore cannot be used for sending sensitive information.

Park et al.'s motivation in making cookies secure is to use them as a medium for transmitting sensitive authorization information. Specifically they use cookies as the medium for clients (browsers) to present their authorized role(s) to the Web servers. The rest of the RBAC model information—role hierarchies, permission role assignment, and constraints—are all stored in the Web server and are used by the Web server to enforce access control on resources accessed by the user. In fact, the user obtains his or her authorized role(s) from a central role server that stores the user role assignment information. The set of assigned roles (let us call it the role credentials) is presented to the Web server through the medium of cookies along with the requested URL. In Park et al.'s "RBAC-using secure cookie" prototype, the role server generates a set of secure cookies (the secure cookie set) after the user logs into the role server with a user identification and password. Table 10.1 lists the names of the various cookies generated and the main information that they contain.

The role server uses the following information to generate each of the cookies in the above set. The user identification and password (needed for Name_Cookie and Pswd_Cookie, respectively) are provided by the user during login to the role server. The encryption of the password is done using the Web server's public key by making use of encryption software like the PGP. The IP address of the user's machine (needed in IP_Cookie) is directly

10.2 RBAC integration in Web environments

Table 10.1 Cookies in the Secure Cookie Set

Cookie Name	Main Information
Name_Cookie	User identification
Role_Cookie	Role(s) Assigned to the user
Life_Cookie	Expiry date for the presented cookie set
Pswd_Cookie	User Password encrypted using Web server's public key
IP_Cookie	IP address of the user's machine
Seal_Cookie	Role server's digital signature of cookie contents

retrieved by the role server. The role(s) assigned to the user (and set in the Role_Cookie) are obtained from a user-role assignment database in the role server. Finally, the role server creates a hash of the information in all the cookies and digitally signs it using its private key and sends it as the Seal_Cookie.

The above set of secure cookies generated by the role server is sent to the user's (client) machine and stored securely in the user's hard drive so that the user does not need to go back to the role server to get his or her assigned roles until the cookies expire. When the user requests access to a Web server—by typing the server URL in his browser as well as by typing a user id and password through a HTML form—the browser sends the corresponding set of secure cookies to the Web server. The Web server is provided with a special program to process the cookies. The Web server cookie program checks the authenticity of the owner of the cookie by using the relevant cookies, such as the IP_Cookie and Pswd_Cookie, by comparing the values in the cookies with the values from the user (the encrypted password is decrypted using the Web server's private key). The Web server cookie program then verifies the integrity of the cookie set by verifying the digital signature in the Seal_Cookie with the role server's public key. If all the cookies are valid and successfully verified, the Web server is in a position to trust the role information in the cookie set, and hence the Web server cookie program retrieves the user's role information from the Role_Cookie to be used by the Web server to determine the user's permissions. Figure 10.6 is a schematic diagram of the cookie set presentation and verification process.

An efficiency-related limitation of Park et al.'s secure cookie RBAC prototype is that every Web server has to go through the entire verification process for a user. Within a corporate domain, there may be many Web servers with hyperlinked Web documents, and it is clearly very inefficient if the same user has to go through the verification process for each Web server accessed within a given user browser session. Recognizing the fact that the

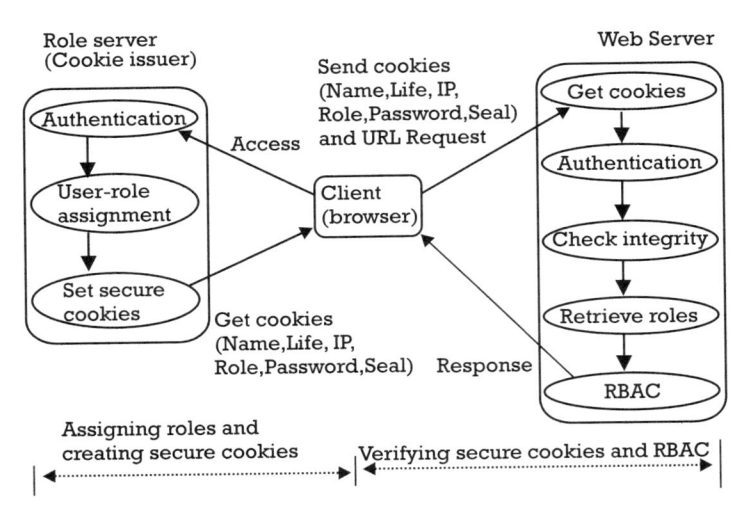

Figure 10.6 RBAC on the Web using secure cookies.

role authorization for a user is different in different Web servers, Shim and Park [10, 12] have proposed a slightly modified architecture using secure cookies. In Shim's et al.'s architecture, the user presents only authentication cookies to a Web server (say WS_A). If the authentication is successful WS_A then generates what is called a "Valid_Cookie" containing the user name and password and sends it to the user to be stored in the user's memory space (and not in the user's hard disk). In the meantime, WS_A retrieves the authorized roles for the user directly from a role server and based upon the permissions associated with retrieved roles, grants or denies the user's URL request. When the same user visits another Web server in the same domain (say WS_B), the WS_B does not go through the verification process for the user. Based on the information from the "Valid_Cookie," the WS_B lets the user access the Web server resources based on the roles and role permissions applicable for WS_B (which is obtained by WS_B from role server). In this architecture, the "Valid_Cookie" is valid only as long as the user's browser is open.

10.2.3 RBAC on the Web using attribute certificates

The concept that is gaining widespread acceptance for providing access control for Web-based applications is the use of attribute certificates (ACs). Edition 4 of X.509 [13] published by ITU-T in 2001 was the first edition to fully standardize the X.509 AC. Hence, there are now two major types of X.509

10.2 RBAC integration in Web environments

certificates: the X.509 identity certificate and the X.509 AC. While X.509 identity certificates (also called public key certificates) are used to maintain a strong binding between a user's name and his or her public key, an AC maintains a strong binding between a user's name and one or more privilege attributes. Each privilege attribute is defined using a combination of attribute type and attribute value. Just like a X.509 public key certificate forms the basis for a PKI, X.509 AC forms the basis for a privilege management infrastructure (PMI). While public key certificates are issued by a certification authority (CA), the ACs are issued by an attribute authority (AA). The root of trust in a PKI is called the root CA. Similarly, the root of trust in a PMI is called the source of authority (SOA). In short, X.509 PMI is to authorization what X.509 PKI is to authentication.

The European Commission (EC)–funded Privilege and Role Management Infrastructure Standards Validation (PERMIS) Project [14] was the first project to build an RBAC-based X.509 PMI that could be used by different Web-based applications. The PERMIS project defines several ACs to store RBAC-model information. Table 10.2 lists the names of the various ACs and the RBAC model information they contain.

Table 10.2 shows that the PERMIS project used two types of ACs. The role-assignment AC and the role-specification AC (the first two ACs) are collectively called the role ACs. The ACs numbered 3 through 9 are called policy ACs. The encoding of policy information in the policy ACs has been done using XML syntax. It is interesting to note that the role-specification AC has two attribute types: role and permission. Those ACs containing roles as attribute types associate one or more roles with the holder (which is also a role) and are thus used to carry role hierarchy information. Both the role

Table 10.2 ACs and Contents in PERMIS Project

AC Name	Certificate Holder	Privilege Attributes
1. Role-Assignment AC	User	Roles assigned to user
2. Role-Specification AC	Role	Roles and permissions
3. Subject-Policy AC	SOA or AA	Subject domains within the policy scope
4. RoleHierarchyPolicy AC	SOA or AA	Allowable role hierarchies
5. SOA-Policy AC	SOA or AA	Identifiers for trusted SOAs or AAs
6. RoleAssignmentPolicy AC	SOA or AA	Allowable role assignments
7. TargetPolicy AC	SOA or AA	Target (resource) domain within the policy scope
8. ActionPolicy AC	SOA or AA	Actions or methods supported by the targets
9. TargetAccessPolicy AC	SOA or AA	Which roles have permission to perform actions on which targets

ACs and policy ACs are issued by a SOA or AA and stored in a publicly accessible LDAP directory. Since ACs are digitally signed by the SOA or AA, they are tamper-resistant, and hence there is no modification risk.

The PERMIS project implemented a Java-based API to enable various Web applications to obtain access control decisions. It is a modification of the Open Group's AZN API [15] that, in turn, is based on ISO 10181-3 access control framework that specifies the interface between the access enforcement function (AEF) and the access decision function (ADF). The PERMIS API architecture (shown in Figure 10.7) enables a user to access resources (targets) via an application gateway. The AEF authenticates the user and then asks the ADF if the user is allowed to perform the required action on the particular target resource. The ADF accesses one or more LDAP directories to retrieve the set of policy and role ACs relevant to the user and bases its decision on these.

The AEF authenticates the user using his or her client certificates and thus obtains the user's distinguished name (DN)—the unique identifier for a user in the X.500 directory structure used in the LDAP directory. Furthermore, since the AEF is application-platform resident, it also contains the trusted SOA for the application as well as the list of the LDAP uniform resource identifiers (URIs). The AEF passes all this information to the ADF, which then retrieves the policy ACs and role ACs relevant for the user. The ADF parses the XML encodings in the policy ACs and uses the information there to validate the information in the role ACs. Invalid Role ACs are discarded, and the valid role ACs then constitute the credential information for the user. At each user access attempt, the AEF passes the target name and attempted action to the ADF that now contains the credential information. The ADF also associates a time-out period with the credential information thus preventing the user from keeping a connection open for a long time.

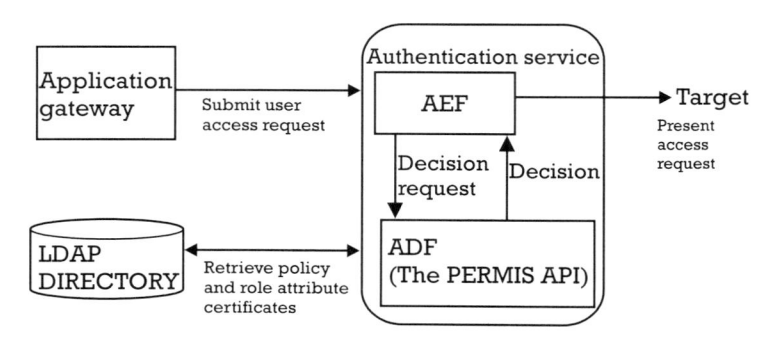

Figure 10.7 Privilege verification subsystem in PERMIS project.

10.2 RBAC integration in Web environments

There is an earlier prototype implementation of RBAC using X.509 certificates by Park, Sandhu, and Ahn [11]. In Park et al.'s prototype, the user's role information was carried in the "extensions" field of a regular X.509 identity certificate. When a user presents this certificate to a Web server, the Web server verifies the certificate, and then uses the role information there to enforce role-based access enforcement. The rest of the RBAC model information, like the role hierarchies and role-permission assignments are already defined and stored in the Web server. The user obtains the bundled X.509 identity certificate (as it contains both identity and authorization information) from a role server that contains the user-role assignment database after proper authentication.

All the RBAC implementations for the Web-based applications we have seen so far are based on the assumption that we have a pre-established and known set of users and that what is required by the Web server (or any program based on the Web server) is to authenticate them and verify the integrity of their role credentials. However in the case of sensitive (trust-requiring) Web transactions originating from users whose identity is not known in advance (which is the case in many e-commerce applications), the Web server must first establish the trust in the requesting user before finding the mapping from the user to his or her authorized roles. Herzberg, Mass, and Mihaeli [16] have presented an implementation that will enable an unknown user to establish this trust with a Web server by presenting certain attribute information (not roles) through a specially designed TE certificate and then be mapped to a set of predefined business roles. The TE and role mapping tasks are accomplished by a TE module. The rest of the RBAC model information—role hierarchies, role permission assignments, and associated constraints—are resident on the Web server itself and collectively provide the role-based access control. The TE module has been implemented in two different ways by Herzberg et al. in their two prototypes. It was implemented as a CGI program in an Apache Web server and as a servlet under the IBM WebSphere Application Server.

Let us now take a look at the specially designed TE certificate. The TE certificate has been designed by adding some attributes (or fields) to a X.509v3 certificate making use of its extension field. Since as many extensions as needed can be defined, Herzberg et al.'s TE certificate contains the mandatory attribute fields shown in Table 10.3.

The TE module maps the subject that is presenting these TE certificates to a role (or roles) based on the attribute values in these certificates using a policy set by the owner of the resource for which the subject is requesting access. (Please note that the issuer of the certificate has nothing to do with this policy). The policy can therefore be said to perform the dual task of trust

Table 10.3 Mandatory Attributes in TE Certificate

Mandatory Component	Purpose
Issuer's public key	Serves as identifier of the issuer
Subject's public key	Serves as identifier of the subject
Certificate type	Intended for supporting multiple certificate types (e.g., X.509v3, SPKI, PGP, and KeyNote); only X.509v3 implementation has been presented.
Certificate version	Self-explanatory
ProfileURL	URL that describes the certificate type, namely its structure and semantics
IssuerCertRepository	Addresses to look for more certificates for the issuer—to establish the trust in issuer as well as most recent CRL's to verify certificate validity
SubjectCertRepository	Addresses to look for more certificates for the subject—in situations the subject can only present one certificate due to client device or protocol limitations

establishment as well as access authorization. The policies in the TE module are defined using an XML-based language called trust policy language (TPL). A typical policy may involve requirements based on a combination of the affiliation of the TE certificate issuer as well as attribute values in the TE certificate. An example policy statement may run as:

> A subject (identified by its public key) can be added to the hospital role provided it presents at least two certificates issued by "Partner_Hospital_Group" and the "Level" field in each of these certificates contains the value "1."

Some policies may demand multiple TE certificates, and due to the limitation of the client machine, a subject (client) may be able to provide only one certificate. In such situations, the client may indicate through the IssuerCertRepository and SubjectCertRepository attributes in the TE certificate pointers to URL locations for extracting more certificates. A submodule of the TE module called the "certificate collector" collects certificates from certificate repositories referred to by the subject. Thus we see that the TE module is made up of a certificate collector and the policy engine along with associated databases (for storing TE certificates and policy definitions).

The sequence of steps involved in processing a user's request (through a browser) in Herzberg et al.'s RBAC-based TE architecture is as follows:

1. The user (client) requests a resource (or transaction) from the Web server through his or her browser. The resource is requested through

10.2 RBAC integration in Web environments

an SSL session, and the Web server is configured to use SSL client authentication. The Web server asks the browser for a certificate and the browser in turn displays on the user screen a list of TE certificates to choose from. The user selects a certificate and sends it to the Web server.

2. The Web server runs a CGI/servlet program and passes the client certificate to it.

3. Based on the type of resource requested, the CGI/servlet retrieves the associated policy and along with the certificate sends it to the TE module for deciding on the role(s) for the user.

4. The TE module verifies compliance to policy requirements (described using TPL) in light of the information retrieved from the certificates and, if successful, returns to the CGI/servlet program the set of role(s) for that user.

5. The CGI/servlet determines the permissions associated with the returned roles and allows or denies the user request. (Figure 10.8 shows the information exchange between CGI/servlet and the TE module.)

Herzberg et al.'s RBAC-based TE architecture based on the TE certificates described above is useful in situations where an unknown user accessing an enterprise's resources through the Web server has to be dynamically assigned to one of the enterprise-defined roles so as to regulate his or her access to resources within the enterprise. However there are other types of

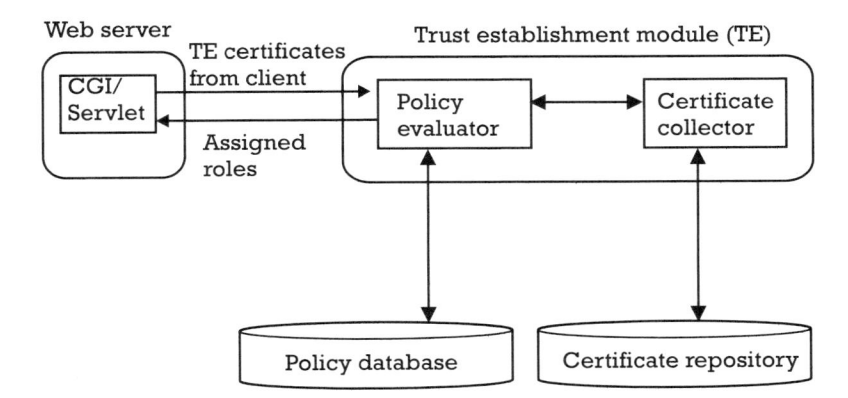

Figure 10.8 Information exchange between the CGI/servlet and TE module.

e-commerce transactions wherein it is not only required to authenticate an unknown user from another enterprise (hereafter referred to as interacting enterprise) who has initiated a transaction (e.g., sent a purchase order document) but also to ensure that the unknown user (hereafter referred to as agent) is authorized to act on behalf of the interacting enterprise and is acting in a legally binding way (i.e., the interacting enterprise can be made liable for the digital signatures its authorized agents provide). To address these issues, Opplinger, Pernul, and Strauss [17] have proposed a scheme where ACs can be used to carry the role credentials of an interacting enterprise's agent. In this scheme it is assumed that there exists a set of certificate authorities TCA = { CA1, CA2.... } for a state or country (established using a general accreditation or certification scheme) and a set of attribute authorities TAA = {AA1, AA2... } registered with an appropriate national body, such as a chamber of commerce. It is further assumed that each organization or enterprise Y has at least one attribute authority $AA(Y)$. Each $AA(Y)$ holds a public key and private key pair of which the public key is certified (and digitally signed) by an accredited CA (a member of TCA). The $AA(Y)$ issues and revokes ACs (ACs) for the authorized agents of the enterprise Y. The ACs contain the bindings between a name (that is unique within the enterprise Y) and a specific role within the corresponding enterprise. For example if John is an authorized agent for enterprise Y, he will have a certificate for his public key and an AC for the role he plays within the enterprise Y. The public key certificate is issued by a CA that is a member of the TCA, whereas the AC is issued by an attribute authority [which, in our example, is $AA(Y)$]. Whenever John has to sign a document that must be legally binding in one way or another, such as a contract (e.g., a commitment a buy an expensive custom-made piece of equipment), he uses his private key to digitally sign the document and provides his public key certificate together with the AC that certifies his role within the company Y to the intended recipients (e.g., the company that manufactures the expensive equipment). The recipient(s) in turn, use(s) the public key certificate to verify the following:

- The digital signature provided by John;
- The corresponding public key certificate presented by John (to see whether it has been issued by an accredited CA);
- The AC presented by John [issued by $AA(Y)$]—for appropriate authorization for John within enterprise Y;
- The nomination of $AA(Y)$ by an established commerce/trade entity (e.g., chamber of commerce).

10.3 RBAC for UNIX environments

We have seen that general-purpose application software like a Web server has its own implementation of RBAC regardless of the platform on which it is hosted (e.g., Windows NT, Windows 2000, or any flavor of UNIX). Hence, our study of RBAC integration in the UNIX environment will be restricted to the implementation of RBAC for access control to resources that are directly under the control of the operating system. Our first case study deals with the details of the RBAC model prototypes[1] for administration of Solaris™ and Trusted Solaris™, both of which are UNIX OS offerings by Sun Microsystems. Let us call this the RBAC-Solaris prototype. Our second case study deals with implementation of RBAC in the UNIX-based distributed file system NFS.

10.3.1 RBAC for UNIX administration

The primary motivation for the development of the RBAC-Solaris prototype is to use roles as an alternative to the traditional UNIX superuser or *root*. Traditionally, in all UNIX flavors, root access is required to perform all aspects of administration. For example, setting the system date requires root access, which in turn, provides full access to the system. This lack of granularity with respect to the assignment of privileged operations to administrators not only makes the root user powerful but also makes other users weak, thereby hampering proper distribution of administrative functions. In effect, this results in no hierarchy of privileged operations, no separation of powers, and no ability to delegate any of the powers to others—effectively preventing enforcement of all access administration policies that are required for effective decentralized administration. The RBAC model prototype for Solaris and Trusted Solaris operating systems from Sun Microsystems as described in [18] addresses these deficiencies while at the same retaining many of the core UNIX administrative concepts. The retention of the core UNIX administrative concepts resulted in a system that allowed existing applications and interfaces to work with RBAC without requiring that they be rewritten to work with new interfaces and databases.

10.3.1.1 Role semantics in the prototype

In the RBAC-Solaris prototype, RBAC has been used to partition some of the superuser's (root's) powers into a set of discrete roles. This has been done to parcel out certain capabilities to others and is not meant to restrict

---
1. These prototypes have since evolved into commercial-grade products.

the root's powers. In this prototype both roles and users are types of UNIX accounts. In this sense, a role becomes an authenticated principal. However, roles cannot be used as primary logins or be assumed without prior authorization (without being assigned to a user including the root user), and they must be formally assumed by authorized users to exercise its underlying permission set. For example, if a "root" role has been created encapsulating all superuser permissions, only an authorized user who has been assigned the "root" role and assumes that role after logging in, can exercise the root permissions. Merely logging in as root using the root password will not provide the necessary permissions. The above discussed features that enable roles to be used as special shared accounts have been implemented in the RBAC-Solaris prototype using existing mechanisms of UNIX without making changes to the kernel. Specifically, the system's pluggable authentication module (PAM) has been extended to recognize role accounts. However, it must be mentioned that a few privileged operations may still have to be directly assigned to the user instead of a role since the context here is an OS, and bootstrapping an OS has to be performed along with a login process before assuming any role.

The roles used in the prototype are not organized into any hierarchies. Hence, roles can only be assigned to users, not to other roles. The main set of attributes associated with a role is the permission sets (Section 10.3.1.2 discusses the structuring of these permission sets). In addition, roles are defined to carry other attributes. Cardinality is an attribute that specifies how many times a role can either be assigned or assumed. Mutual exclusion (denoted by mutex) specifies that a SoD relationship exists between this role and another specified role.

Assuming a role is the discrete action of activating a role that has been assigned to a user. Since roles are limited to authorized users, the identity of the user must be authenticated before the role assumption takes place. Therefore, roles cannot be used as primary login accounts. The user must first log in to the system and then use an appropriate interface to assume a role. The process of assuming a role itself involves authentication and authorization checks. An authentication check is required for assuming a role since there is a password associated with a role. Authorization checks associated with role assumption include verification that the role has been assigned to the user who is assuming it and that any dynamic restrictions, such as cardinality and mutual exclusion, are not violated.

10.3.1.2 Structuring of permissions
The last section discussed the semantics of the role in the RBAC-Solaris prototype as well as the dynamics involved in the user assuming a role. Let us

10.3 RBAC for UNIX environments

now see how the permissions are structured and assigned to the various defined roles. In most of the literature on access control, the terms *permission, privilege and authorization* are frequently used interchangeably. However in the context of the RBAC-Solaris prototype (or for that matter within the general UNIX environment itself in some cases), each of these terms carries different semantics. A *permission* is a generic term that is used to describe a transaction that a user is permitted to do through the execution of one or more programs. Since the term permission is used in an abstract sense in the UNIX content, what is of practical relevance with respect to access control on the resources of a UNIX system are the terms privileges and authorizations. The term *file* is frequently encountered in the UNIX literature. This is due to the fact that the files are used as an abstraction for most of the system resources in UNIX. Hence files may just contain data (data files), or they may be executable. Executable files are also called programs.

Associated with an executable file or program is a set of attributes called privileges (also called process attributes). The most important of these process attributes or privileges are described as follows:

- The read, write, and execute attributes associated with levels user, group, and other, totally giving rise to nine attributes or privileges.
- The effective user id (euid) and effective group id (egid) attributes that allow a program to run with the same privileges as the owner's userid and group, respectively. Usually these attributes are set only in trusted programs. One category of trusted programs are the set-userid-to-root programs that are owned by the root and are assigned these attributes. This will enable any user to run these programs with root privileges.

Having discussed the concept of privileges (which are process attributes), we turn our attention to the concept of authorizations. An *authorization* is a right assigned to a user or a role that is used to grant access to an otherwise restricted function. Authorizations, like privileges, are also fine-grained but not directly associated with programs (or processes). Instead they are associated with a user or a role and stored in a database indexed using roles or users. Authorization checks are done by applications as opposed to privilege checks, which are done in the UNIX kernel. Authorizations are expressed using a hierarchical naming convention as in Java™. The first component refers to the organization or enterprise name, the second to the class of authorizations, and the third component refers to the specific function within a class or organization. For example, the authorization to create new roles, modify their attributes, and delete them is

```
Solaris.role.write
```

where Solaris refers to the enterprise name; role refers to the authorization class; and write refers to the write function [create, delete, edit (modify attributes)]. Table 10.4 lists authorizations pertaining to the "role" authorization class and the rights associated with each of them.

In addition to associating authorizations with a user or role directly, it would be good if the ability to run certain trusted programs with root privileges (by suitably setting the process attributes discussed earlier) were restricted to only certain users or roles (since setuid-to-root programs can be run by any user). It would be still better from the point of view of distributing administrative responsibilities, if these sets of trusted programs could be run with different privileges by different users. To enable this, different sets of process attributes must be defined and dynamically associated with these trusted or privileged programs during execution time. To facilitate the implementation of these concepts, the concept of *execution profile* has been defined in RBAC-Solaris prototype. An execution profile is a collection of permissions that has the following components:

- A list of authorizations;
- A list of trusted executables and associated process attributes.

A user or role is assigned one or more execution profiles. The set of permissions available to a user or role is the cumulative set of authorizations and executables found in all the assigned execution profiles.

Now it is not sufficient if execution profiles are merely associated with a user or roles. When the trusted executables in the execution profile are

Table 10.4 Authorizations and Rights in the RBAC-Solaris Prototype

Authorization Name	Associated Rights
Solaris.role.write	Create new roles; modify their rights and delete them
Solaris.usermgr.passwd	Create role's password (here the authorization class used is usermgr since roles share some semantics with the "user"—both are UNIX accounts)
Solaris.role.assign	The right to assign (revoke) any role to (from) a user
Solaris.role.delegate	The right to delegate one's own assigned roles to other users
Solaris.role.*	Wild card authorization—covers all authorizations under the class "role"

10.3 RBAC for UNIX environments

executed, the interpreter for each executable type should be able to associate the set of attributes specified in the profile and then execute those programs. To achieve this, the RBAC-Solaris prototype made use of a profile execution program called pfexec. The standard UNIX shells, sh, csh, and ksh were modified to invoke pfexec for profile-based execution. Examples of executables are UNIX commands and executable objects in the common desktop environment (CDE) (called CDE actions).

Based on the implementation details we have discussed so far, we are now ready to summarize the layout of the RBAC database and the role-based access enforcement process in the RBAC-Solaris prototype. Table 10.5 presents the layout of the RBAC database.

Examples are listed as follows:

- User_Name= Fred Roles=SysAdmin, Profiles= All;
- Role_Name=SysAdmin, mutex=SecAdmin,cardinality =2, Profiles= Audit_Review,File_Mgmt;
- Profile_Name=Audit_Review, Authorizations=solaris.audit.read;
- Profile_Name=File_Mgmt, [Executable_ID=/usr/sbin/tunefs; Process_Attributes=(euid =0,egid=3)].

The access enforcement process in the RBAC-Solaris prototype is summarized as follows:

1. A valid user logging into the Solaris UNIX system is authenticated.

Table 10.5 Layout of RBAC Database in the RBAC-Solaris Prototype

Database Component	DB Name in the Prototype	Associated Attributes
User	User_attr	User name, list of assigned roles, list of execution profiles
Role	User_attr	Role name, list of execution profiles, cardinality limit, list of mutually excluded profiles
Profiles (permission sets)	Profile_attr	List of authorizations (refer Auth_attr), list of executable objects and associated process attributes (refer Exec_attr)
Authorizations	Auth_attr	Authorization name and its help description file
Executable objects and associated process attrbutes	Exec_attr	Fully qualified executable name, associated profile, type of executable (UNIX command or CDE), value of process attributes

2. The authenticated user can then assume a role by using the traditional su command (after supplying the password associated with the role provided that he or she has been assigned that role).

3. The information in the execution profiles assigned to the role is set up. This information consists of a list of authorizations and a list of executables with their associated process attributes. When an executable file is invoked, the binding of process attributes in the profile with the executable is enabled by the profile execution program pfexec.

10.3.2 RBAC implementation within the NFS

A prototype implementation of RBAC within the NFS (a file system that provides distributed file service in networked UNIX systems) was developed by a group of researchers at Linkoping University [19] (we shall refer to it as the Linkoping-RBAC prototype) in Sweden. Their implementation platform was the Linux User Space NFS server running on a Linux 2.0 system. The implementation was based on a design that modified the NFS server to use the access control information from a role-based security information database to set the access attributes for a file. To understand how RBAC was incorporated into the NFS access control process, we have to take a brief look at some background information with respect to the overall architecture of NFS and how it normally enforces access control.

The NFS is a distributed file system that was introduced by Sun Microsystems to provide transparent access to remote file systems on UNIX platforms. NFS provides file service based on a client-server protocol. The system that requests a remote file system is called an NFS client. A system that makes its file systems available for remote access (exports) is called an NFS server. Hence a single machine can be both an NFS client and an NFS server. Since the file systems on remote machines can be different from the one on client machine, clients use an abstract file system called the virtual file system (VFS). The VFS enables clients to obtain a common view (or interface) of both their local and remote files. Access to files in remote systems is enabled through a network transport mechanism called the remote procedure call (RPC) that uses a platform-neutral representation of data called the external data representation (XDR). Before a client can access the contents (files and directories) of a remote file system, it needs to incorporate the remote file system into its own VFS. This operation is called mount, and the client uses a command of the same name. Through this mount command the NFS client specifies the host name, the name of the file system, and the file type. The NFS server on the remote host on receiving this

10.3 RBAC for UNIX environments

request checks whether the file system is available for export and then returns a file handle to the requesting NFS client. The NFS client creates a node of its virtual file system (called VNODE) with a pointer to another node called RNODE where the returned file handle from the remote host is stored. The NFS client through the newly created VNODE then accesses the contents of the remote file system.

With the above background information on NFS, let us now take a look at how NFS normally enforces access control on the resources under its control—directories, directory trees, and files. When an NSF server receives a resource (say a file) access request from a NFS client, it also receives with each request, the effective user and group identities (UID and GID, respectively) of the caller as well as the file handle. The NFS server uses these identities to authenticate the file handle, the calling machine, and the calling user. It then accesses the file and makes the file available to the client along with file access attributes (generally called the permission bits). The main responsibility for access control still rests with the kernel of the client that allows or disallows access based on the file access attributes, as reported by the NFS server.

The central design idea in the Linkoping-RBAC prototype is to mount the remote file system as usual but then to sidestep the default permission-checking behavior. The sequence of steps involved in role-based access enforcement in the Linkoping-RBAC prototype using the modified NFS server (marked as RBAC NFS server in Figure 10.9) is as follows:

(a) *Activate roles:* The user (through an NFS client) starts out an NFS access request by using a special application (resident in a server called the role state server that is located in the same network domain as the NFS server to which it is making the NFS access request) to activate one or more roles. The list of roles assigned to the user is stored in a user/role database attached to the role state server. Since a user can only activate roles to which he or she has been assigned, the role state module checks with this user/role database to verify whether the user has been assigned that role. The role state module then stores the activated roles indexed by the UID of the user.

(b) *Request NFS:* The user application accesses the contents of a mounted file system. This results in an NFS service request from the NFS client to the RBAC-NFS server.

(c) *Get activated role list:* The RBAC-NFS server contains two modules. The first one is what we call the role retriever (RR) (though not

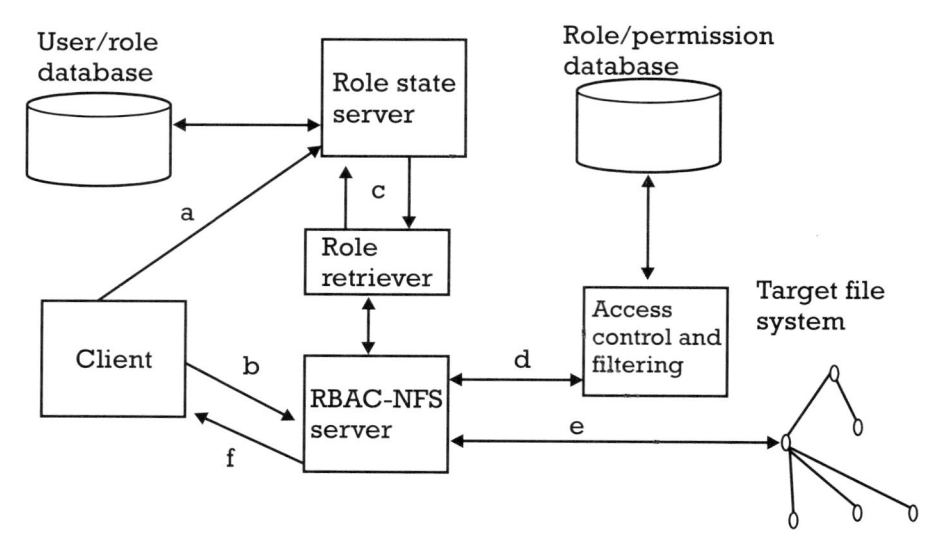

Figure 10.9 Access enforcement in Linkoping-RBAC prototype: (a) activate roles, (b) NFS request, (c) get activated role list, (d) retrieve role permissions, (e) file system access (NFS request and file access attributes, and (f) reply (retrieved file and access attributes).

explicitly mentioned by this name in the prototype), and the second module is called the access control and filtering (ACF) module. The RR retrieves the set of activated roles from the role state server (refer to step a) using the UID of the user.

(d) *Retrieve role permissions:* The active roles retrieved by RR are passed along with the NFS service request to the ACF. The ACF retrieves permissions associated with the active roles from a role/permission database. The permissions are in the form of access modes from a predefined set. These access modes pertain to files, directories or directory trees. Tables 10.6 and 10.7 list the access modes specified for the RBAC-NFS server and sample contents of the role/permission database.

(e) *Obtain file system access:* The RBAC-NFS server maps the access modes obtained from the role/permission database to the format in which the file access attributes are usually specified in UNIX. (Note that the access modes in the role/permissions database are specified in terms of mnemonics, whereas the file access attributes in UNIX are specified in terms of privileges read, write, and execute at owner, group,

10.4 RBAC in Java

Table 10.6 Defined Access Modes for RBAC-NFS Server

Access Mode	Mnemonic
Read file	FR
Create file	FC
Write file	FW
Append to file	FA
Delete file	FD
Execute file	FX
Create directory	DC
List directory	DL
Remove Directory	DR
Toggle execute bit	XT
Create symbolic link	LC

Table 10.7 Layout of Role/Permission Database

Path	Role	Permissions
/usr/apps/dbms/audit.log	DBA	FR:FC:FA:FD
/usr/apps/dbms/audit.log	Db_User	FR
/usr/apps/dbms	DBA	FC:FD:FR:FX
/usr/apps/dbms	Db_User	FR:FX

and other levels.) Based on the access attributes, the RBAC-NFS server performs the corresponding operation on the target file system (e.g., retrieve a file). (Note that the access attributes stored for a file on the target file system are ignored.)

(f) *Reply:* The retrieved file along with the mapped file access attributes are sent in the reply to the NFS client. As already stated the kernel in the client machine enforces access control on the retrieved file using the file access attributes supplied by the RBAC-NFS server.

10.4 RBAC in Java

Java is both a modern object-oriented programming language and a complex software architecture. Java, developed by Sun Microsystems, offers sophisticated solutions for the design of distributed and mobile applications, where the software can be partitioned on distinct network nodes and downloaded from one node to be executed on another. The biggest security problem in such an architecture is to protect the local system from the downloaded executable code (called the applets), especially those from untrustworthy hosts. Hence, successive evolutions of the access control model for Java (also called the Java Security Model) provided through JDK has been code-centric (i.e., associates permissions with pieces of Java code).

Before we take a look at some of the research concepts and prototypes that have incorporated the RBAC model concepts into the Java security model, we need to understand the principles behind the evolution of the successive versions of Java security models. This is the focus of Section 10.4.1. Section 10.4.2 describes the current version of the Java security model (i.e., the Java 2 security model) to provide the proper context for the introduction of roles into the Java 2 security model (also referred to as the JDK 1.2 security model). Section 10.4.2 also briefly describes the salient features of JAAS, a set of Java packages that extend the Java 2 security model to offer services for user authentication and management of access control rights. The following sections describe the two research concepts/prototypes proposed for incorporating the RBAC model paradigms into the Java 2 security model. Section 10.4.5 provides a summary.

10.4.1 Evolution of Java security models

The first security model of Java, the one associated with JDK version 1.0 (JDK 1.0) is based on partitioning the set of Java programs into trusted and untrusted programs. The JDK 1.0 security model considered every local program as trusted and every remote program downloaded (i.e., Applet) as untrusted. This untrusted downloaded code was made to execute in a restricted run-time environment called the sandbox. A program running in a sandbox has rigid restrictions on the set of local resources that could be used (e.g., cannot access files on the local file system) and limits on network access (e.g., can open network connections only if the target host is the host from where the code was downloaded). The concept of trusted downloaded code (also called dynamically loaded code) was introduced in JDK 1.1, where downloaded code that was digitally signed by a trusted code provider (e.g., signed applet) was allowed to execute with the same permissions as local code.

The Java 2 Security Model supported by JDK 1.2 has provided an extensible access control scheme that applies to both local code and dynamically loaded code (in fact, it does not make a distinction between the two). In the JDK 1.2 security model, the sandbox concept has been replaced by the concept of the protection domain. A protection domain refers to a group of programs that come from a specific location or origin (called a code base), signed with a specific set of public keys (signers), that have the same set of permissions. The origin of a program is specified through a URL location, and the association between the origin and the set of public keys is called the code source. In other words, a protection domain can be looked upon as a customized sandbox associated with every Java program that belongs to a particular code source. Figure 10.10 shows a schematic diagram that explains the concept of the protection domain.

10.4.2 JDK 1.2 security model and enhancement

The JDK 1.2 security model requires the definition of a policy file. A policy is a set of rules that permit one to derive the set of permissions associated with a code source (origin and signers). A policy file therefore consists of a set of entries, each of which grants a set of permissions to a specified code source using the following syntax:

```
Grant CodeBase    URL ,
   SignedBy { signer_name1 , signer_name2 ,  .}
{
  permission1;
  .
  Permission2;
};
```

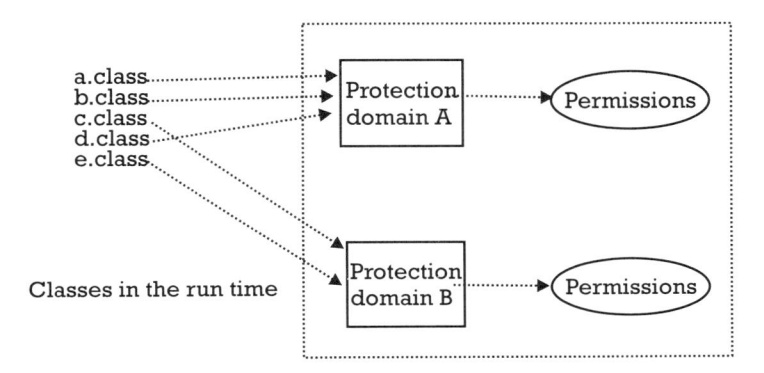

Figure 10.10 The concept of protection domains in the JDK 1.2 security model.

The URL notation (based on a predefined relation) can be used to denote either class files or JAR files (or both) in a single directory or in all subdirectories. Since an origin (code base) plus a set of signers with the same set of permissions defines a protection domain, in effect, each policy entry is a mapping from a protection domain to its associated permissions. It is this mapping relation *P* that defines the policy.

$$P(d) \rightarrow \{Pr\} \tag{10.1}$$

where d stands for a protection domain and {Pr} stands for sets of permissions.

A policy is implemented by subclassing the java.security.Policy abstract class. Permissions are defined using subclasses of the abstract class java.security.Permission. An example of such a subclass is the FilePermission class used to represent access rights on files and directories (permissions of a particular type). There is also a PermissionCollection abstract class that represents a homogeneous collection of permission objects (i.e., it holds permissions of the same type). For example, the FilePermissionCollection class is used to hold FilePermission objects.

The JDK 1.2 security model enforces access controls based on where code came from and who signed it. To enforce similar access controls based on who runs the code, the JDK 1.2 requires additional support for user authentication and requires extension to existing authorization components to enforce new access controls based on who was authenticated. The JAAS framework was designed to augment the JDK 1.2 with such support.

First of all, the JAAS framework defines the concept of *subject* to represent the source of the request. A subject in Java represents a single entity such as a person or service. Associated with each subject is a set of identities and a set of security-related attributes. Each identity is represented as a *principal* within the subject. Hence, a subject could have many principals. Examples of principals include names such as e-mail addresses, employee numbers, group identification headings such as departments, and driver's license numbers.

JAAS facilitates authentication of a subject by providing a *LoginModule* interface that can implemented by the Java application depending upon the type of authentication the application requires (e.g., passwords, smart cards, or biometrics). Once a subject is authenticated, permissions have to be associated with the subject (indirectly though), through the principals associated with that subject.

10.4 RBAC in Java

Recall that a policy entry in the JDK 1.2 policy file only associated code source (origins and signers) with permissions. Now, principals also must be included in these entries. In other words, the concept of a protection domain in JDK1.2 enhanced with JAAS (we will refer to this as JDK1.2-JAAS) now comprises code source (practically a URL+ set of signers) or principals. To define permissions for the JDK1.2-JAAS protection domain, JAAS provides the JAAS policy class. An example of a grant entry then in JDK1.2-JAAS is as follows:

```
Grant CodeBase http://foo.com,
SignedBy "Jim",
Principal UnixPrincipal  "Joe" {
Permission java.io.FilePermission  "/user/Joe",
   "read, write" ;
};
```

Hence semantically a protection domain can now be defined from either a code-centric or principal-centric (by implication user or subject-centric) point of view. In the principal-centric point of view, principals with similar security properties are grouped into protection domains and permissions are granted to protection domains, thus establishing an indirect relationship between principals and access rights.

We have already stated that many principals might be associated with a single subject or user. However, not all principals may be activated in any login session. Usually the activation of principals associated with a subject takes place at the time of login (soon after authentication of the subject), and the logic for activating which subset of associated principals is an application-specific feature.

When a subject logins in and starts a session, a number of principals associated with a subject might be also activated. Then the subject may make a series of method calls. Each of the invoked methods may be from different code sources and hence may be from different protection domains. Hence the execution environment (access control context) for a subject after a sequence of method calls consists of a sequence of protection domains and a set of active principals. When a subject makes a new access request p (permission), the subject is granted access only if permission *p* can be derived from the intersection of permission sets from all the domains crossed under the set of currently active principals. In other words, the access control context is automatically set up by the sequence of protection domains associated with the subject's method call chain. The verification of the permission is done by the checkPermission method of SecurityManager class.

10.4.3 Incorporating RBAC into JDK 1.2 security model with JAAS

A survey of existing research projects or prototypes that have incorporated RBAC concepts into JDK1.2-JAAS reveals that the RBAC model has been incorporated using the following approaches:

- Defining appropriate policy entries;
- A new implementation of the security manager class that contains methods for the enforcement of RBAC constraints.

10.4.3.1 IBM research project

In the research project by Gunter Karjoth of IBM Research [20] (hereafter referred to as the Gunter project), a formal specification of the JDK1.2-JAAS access control model was been developed. The expressiveness of the JDK1.2-JAAS model has been illustrated by using the building blocks of the specification to express role-based authorizations. In the Gunter project a role is treated as a named principal. A user group is also treated as a named principal. A distinction made between groups and roles is that roles can be "activated" and "deactivated" by users (subjects) at their discretion, whereas a group membership always applies. The incorporation of various aspects of RBAC model concepts in the JDK1.2-JAAS model based on specification in the Gunter project is given as follows:

- *Role-permission assignment:* The assignment of permissions to roles that, in effect, is equivalent to the assignment of permissions to named principals is implemented through grant entries in the Java policy file. An entry in a policy file that states that "only somebody who is a manager and a member of project X is allowed to change project X's time schedule" will be:

```
Grant Principal Role    manager ,
Principal Group   project-X {
Permission SchedulePermission   change ;
}
```

Stated in terms of the policy mapping relation (10.1), the above policy entry is:

$$P(<E,\$,\{manager, project\text{-}X\}>) = \{<schedule, change>\}$$

10.4 RBAC in Java

where (<E,$,{manager,project-X}>) denotes a domain with an empty code base (E), a null set of signers ($) and the set of principals denoted by {manager,project-X}. The expression {schedule,change} represents the permission where schedule is the target object and the change is the action.

- *User-role assignment:* The user role assignment (which in our case is association of subjects with principals) is handled by administrators outside of the JDK1.2-JAAS model implementation.

- *Activation of user roles in a session:* The activation of a role in a user (subject) session (which in our case is the dynamic association of principals with the current access-control context) is accomplished using the java.security.auth.subject.doAs method, which adds additional principals to the current access control context. It is thus equivalent to defining a session during which a subset of user roles is simultaneously activated. The permissions available to the user are thus the union of the permissions of all roles activated in that session (i.e., the role principals given to the subject.doAs method).

10.4.3.2 RBAC for a Java-Web application

Luigi Giuri has defined an extension to the JDK1.2-JAAS model [21] to incorporate RBAC model concepts for Web-based server-side Java applications (i.e., Java Servlet). Just like in the Gunter Project, the concept of a role is treated as a named principal. Giuri created a new class called "RolePrincipal" for this purpose. In addition, Guiri has implemented a class called "UserPrincipal." The UserPrincipal class has no semantic significance. It is merely a place holder for assigning RolePrincipal instances (in effect, assigning roles to a user or subject). There is, at most, one UserPrincipal object associated with a subject. The association between a subject and a UserPrincipal object is established soon after the subject is authenticated using the LoginModule by making use of an implementation of a newly created RoleLoginModule:

- *Role-permission assignment:* Just like in Gunter's project, the assignment of permissions to roles that in our case is equivalent to the assignment of permissions to RolePrincipal principals is implemented through grant entries in the JDK1.2-JAAS policy file. An entry for a policy that states, "Only Departmental heads can modify task assignments," will be:

```
Grant Principal RolePrincipal   "depthead"   {
Permission TaskAssignmentPermission
  "modify" ;
}
```

- *User-role assignment (also role-hierarchy creation):* The user role assignment (which in our case is the assignment of RolePrincipal objects to a UserPrincipal object) is accomplished through a new RolePolicy abstract class. An implementation of the RolePolicy class uses a file called RolePolicy file (similar to JDK1.2-JAAS policy file) to store grant entries pertaining to assignment of RolePrincipal objects to a UserPrincipal (in effect assigning roles to users). The same file can also be used to grant RolePrincipal objects to other RolePrincipal objects in effect creating a role hierarchy.

```
Grant principal [RolePrincipal    "role-name"    |
UserPrincipal    "user-name" ]
{
RolePrincipal    "role-name1"  ,
RolePrincipal    "role-name2"
};
```

- *Activation of user roles in a session:* The activation or deactivation of a role in a user (subject) session (which in our case is dynamic association/disassociation of RolePrincipal with the UserPrincipal) is accomplished in Guiri's project through a separate RoleController class. Two methods of RoleController class that are useful for this are described as follows:

1. *ResetDefaults( ):* Enable or activate only a predefined set of default roles associated with the subject;

2. *EnableRole(String rolename):* Add the role identified by the rolename to the set of activated roles.

10.5 RBAC for FDBSs

A FDBS consists of an interoperable layer providing access to data stored in several heterogeneous databases. The individual databases for which the FDBS provides access are called component database systems (CDBSs). The FDBS gives the users the illusion of a homogeneous central database system.

10.5 RBAC for FDBSs

The process of specifying the individual CDBSs and configuring the software at the interoperable layer to enable access to data residing in the CDBSs is called "creating the federation." Depending upon who is responsible for creating and maintaining the federation, FDBSs can be classified as loosely coupled and tightly coupled. In a loosely coupled FDBS, the user is responsible for creating and maintaining the federation, and the FDBS and its administrators exercise no control. In a tightly coupled FDBS, the administrators are responsible for creating and maintaining the federation and actively control the CDBSs.

Although sophisticated RBAC models have been implemented in individual commercial DBMSs (refer to Chapter 12), there are not very many research frameworks and prototypes that have been developed to support authorization and access control in the context of a FDBS. This section discusses the architecture of a role-based authorization and access control system that has been developed as part of the security subsystem for a FDBS called the interoperable relational and object-oriented database (IRO-DB). The IRO-DB is a FDBS that is designed to provide access to several heterogeneous relational and object-oriented CDBSs. The IRO-DB FDBS as well as its authorization and access control subsystem is currently under implementation as part of the IRO-DB ESPRIT-III project [22], a joint project that involves several European union countries. Before we discuss the features of the role-based authorization and access control subsystem of IRO-DB, we need to take a look at the overall architecture of the IRO-DB itself and the services provided by its security system (in which the authorization and access control system is a subsystem).

10.5.1 IRO-DB architecture

The goal of IRO-DB is to provide homogeneous access to heterogeneous and distributed databases. To fulfill this requirement, IDO-DB has be designed with a three-layer architecture—a local layer, a communication layer, and an interoperable layer.

The local layer supports a uniform data model and provides access to heterogeneous component databases through the use of local database adapters. The communication layer provides services for remote databases and object access. The interoperable layer integrates the various local schemata (structure of the database) into an interoperable schema that is able to combine related data from local databases and to overcome inconsistencies in such areas as structure, naming, and semantics.

The IRO-DB security system (ISS) is located at the interoperable layer and performs the following functions:

- Communicates with the user application in providing identification and authentication mechanisms;
- Communicates with the interoperable layer's query processor and object manager in providing access control features;
- Communicates with the interoperable layer's data dictionary from which information about authorization subjects (explained below), objects and rules is retrieved.

10.5.2 RBAC model implementation in IRO-DB

The role-based authorization and access control model in the ISS consists of the following: authorization subjects (ASs), authorization objects (AOs), authorization types (ATs), and authorization rules. Figure 10.11 shows the security metaclasses that implement the model, together with their interrelationships.

Roles are ASs of IRO-DB and represent jobs. Hence authorizations associated with roles should be limited to those required to perform the functions associated with the job. Consequently, it is possible to define a role hierarchy that reflects the organizational and functional structure of the enterprise that deploys IRO-DB. Users are assigned several roles, but they can play only one role at a time. The AOs of IRO-DB are classes that can have one or more of the following structures:

- Relationships (related class);
- Hierarchy (subclasses and superclasses);
- Class composition (comp-class).

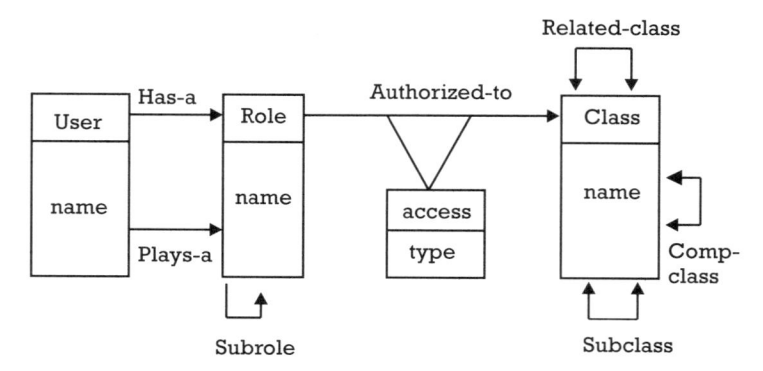

Figure 10.11 Security metaclasses of the IRO-DB security system.

The AT with which a role may access a class can be either read (R), write (W), create (C), and delete (D) for covering relational CDBSs, or method-access for covering object-oriented CDBSs. There is also the ownership (T), which is the most powerful authorization type that implies all other authorization types. Finally, an IRO-DB authorization rule is defined as a triple (s,t,o) where

s belongs to the set of authorization subjects (roles);
t belongs to the authorization types (e.g., R, W, C, T);
o belongs to the set of authorization objects (e.g., class, database).

Both positive and negative authorizations can be specified using the above formalism. The RBAC model in IRO-DB employs a combination of administration and ownership paradigm. In this paradigm, when a role "$r1$" that creates an authorization object "$O1$" becomes its owner with authorization type 'T', a corresponding authorization rule $(r1, T, O1)$ is added automatically to the authorization database. Automatically such a rule is also added for an administrator role making the administrator a joint owner of the object "$O1$." The ownership authorization on object "$O1$" for role "$r1$" does not imply the ability to change authorization rules (i.e., to delegate authorizations to other authorization subjects).

The RBAC model implemented in IRO-DB through security metaclasses is stored in the IRO-DB authorization database. This database can only be edited by one or more designated administrator roles. The administrative features provided in IRO-DB for maintaining the RBAC model consists of the following:

- Adding, removing, and modifying users;
- Associating users to roles;
- Adding, removing, and modifying roles in the role hierarchy;
- Adding, removing, and modifying authorization rules in the authorization database.

10.6 RBAC in autonomous security service modules

In the previous sections, we have seen the research frameworks and prototypes that have incorporated RBAC model concepts into various enterprise IT infrastructures to achieve role-based access enforcement. Dridi, Fischer, and Pernul [23] describe an implementation where an RBAC model has been incorporated into an autonomous security services module called "communication, security, authentication, and privacy" (CSAP) module to provide an access control service called the "RBAC service." The CSAP is a generic and adaptable security module that offers programming interfaces to core security services such as user identification, authentication, access control, auditing, and security management. The CSAP security services module was originally developed to work with Web application system WEBOCRAT, which supports the concept of e-government, although it has been designed in a generic way to work with any Web-based application.

The layered design of CSAP enables an application designer to integrate new security services or to enhance existing security services depending upon the changing security needs of the application system. This is possible since CSAP facilitates the exchange or enhancement of security mechanisms via a plug-in concept based on abstract classes. Before we discuss how the CSAP provides the RBAC service, we need to understand the functionality of the three layers—the API layer, the service layer, and the data layer in the CSAP. The API layer provides a unified access to the security services implemented by CSAP by providing common interface that separates the usage of a security service from its implementation. Applications request services only through the CSAP API. The service layer is built upon the kernel of CSAP and provides the infrastructure for changing an existing security service or plugging in new services. All the security services discussed above are integrated in this layer. The clients (which in our case are applications) use a security service via the API layer. The data needed by the service is provided by the third layer of CSAP called the data layer. The data layer provides the flexibility to access and manage user security information (e.g., permissions and passwords).

The service layer in CSAP contains two kinds of classes—service classes and product classes. A product class is an instance of modeling low-level objects within CSAP, such as user, object, operation, permission, session, and role. The service classes are responsible for creating product classes and implementing security services. For example, CSAP contains a service class called "RBACService." The "RBACService" service class contains all the methods necessary to implement the core RBAC model of the NIST standard. By implementing these methods, an access control service based on roles (called as the "RBAC service" within CSAP) can be implemented. This is what has been exactly done in the European Union–funded Webocracy project.

The functionality of the RBAC service in the CSAP implementation is as follows: On the API layer, the authenticated user requests a certain role from the RBAC service at the service layer. Based on the role data stored at the data layer, the RBAC service presents the set of available roles. After the user has chosen a certain role, the RBAC service verifies, based on the security information gathered from the data layer, whether the user is allowed to activate that role. After the user activates the role, a session object (with a designated session id) containing the user object and the activated role is created by CSAP. When a user invokes an operation on an object within that session, a method called checkAccess containing three arguments (session-id, operation name, and object name) is invoked. The RBAC service then retrieves the user's active role by accessing the corresponding session object based on session id and then determines the permissions associated with the active role. If there exists a permission tuple <object, operation> that matches the object name and the operation name in the checkAccess invocation, access is granted; otherwise it is denied.

10.7 Conclusions

The motivations behind the development of prototypes integrating the RBAC model into the various enterprise technologies are quite varied in nature. A common thread running through these motivations is better policy support and ease of access administration. Hence it is not surprising that authorization management through RBAC is being explored for some emerging enterprise infrastructures like XML repositories.

A research proposal to this effect can be found in [24].

References

[1] Workflow Management Coalition, at http://www.wfmc.org/about.htm.

[2] Lotus Notes Administrator's Reference Manual (1996), Release 4, Lotus Corporation.

[3] Georgakopoulos, D., M. Hornick, and A. Sheth, (1995), "Overview of Workflow Management: From Process Modeling to Workflow Automation Infrastructure," *Distributed and Parallel Databases,* 1995, pp. 119–153.

[4] Botha, R. A., and J. H. P. Eloff, "A Framework for Access Control in Workflow Systems," *Information Management and Computer Security,* Vol. 9, No. 3, 2001, pp. 126–133.

[5] Kang, M. H., J. S. Park, and J. N. Froscher, "Access Control Mechanisms for Interorganizational Workflow," *6th ACM Symposium on Access Control Models and Technologies,* 2001, pp. 66–74.

[6] Bertino, E., E. Ferrari, and V. Atluri, "Specification and Enforcement of Authorization Constraints in Workflow Management Systems," *ACM Transactions on Information and System Security*, Vol. 2, No. 1, 1999, pp. 65–104.

[7] Huang, W. K, and V. Atluri, "SecureFlow: A Secure Web-Enabled Workflow Management System," *4th ACM Workshop on Role-based Access Control*, 1999, pp. 83–94.

[8] Payne, C., et al., "Napoleon: A Recipe for Workflow," *15th Annual Computer Security Applications Conference*, 1999, pp. 134–142.

[9] Joshi, J. B. D., et al., "Security Models for Web-based Applications," *Communications of the ACM*, Vol. 44, Issue 2, 2001, pp. 38–44.

[10] Ferraiolo, D. F., J. F. Barkley, and D. R. Kuhn, "A Role-Based Access Control Model and Reference Implementation Within a Corporate Intranet," *ACM Transactions on Information and System Security*, Vol. 2, No. 1, 1999, pp. 34–64.

[11] Park, J. S., R. Sandhu, and G. J. Ahn, "Role-Based Access Control on the Web," *ACM Transactions on Information and System Security*, Vol. 4, No. 1, 2001, pp. 37–71.

[12] Shim, W. B., and S. Park, "Implementing Web Access Control System for Multiple Web Servers in the Same Domain Using RBAC Concept," *8th International Conference on Parallel and Distributed Systems (ICAPDS)*, 2001, pp. 768–773.

[13] ISO/ITU-T Recommendation X.509 (2001), "The Directory: Authentication Framework."

[14] Chadwick, D. W., and A. Otenko, "The PERMIS X.509 Role-Based Privilege Management Infrastructure," *7th ACM Symposium on Access Control Models and Technologies*, 2002, pp. 135–140.

[15] The Open Group (2000), "Authorization (AZN) API, Generic Application Interface for Authorization Frameworks," http://www.opengroup.org/publications/c908.htm.

[16] Herzberg, A., et al., "Access Control Meets Public Key Infrastructure, Or: Assigning Roles to Strangers," *IEEE Symposium on Security and Privacy*, Oakland, CA, 2000, pp. 2–14.

[17] Oppliger, R., G. Pernul, and C. Strauss, "Using ACs to Implement Role-Based Authorization and Access Control," Swiss Federal Office of Information Technology and Systems, 2001.

[18] Faden, G., "RBAC in UNIX Administration," *4th ACM Workshop on Role-Based Access Control*, Fairfax, VA, 1999, pp. 95–101.

[19] Gustafsson, G., B. Deligny, and N. Shahmehri, "Using NFS To Implement Role-Based Access Control," *6th IEEE Workshop on Enabling Technologies: Infrastructure for Collaborative Enterprises*, 1997, pp. 299–304.

[20] Karjoth, G., "An Operational Semantics of Java 2 Access Control," *13th Computer Security Foundations Workshop*, 2000, pp. 224–232.

10.7 Conclusions

[21] Giuri, L., "Role-Based Access Control on the Web using Java," *4th ACM Workshop on Role-Based Access Control*, 1999, pp. 11–18.

[22] Elmayr, W., et. al. "Authorization and Access Control in IRO-DB," *International Conference on Data Engineering*, 1996.

[23] Dridi, F., M. Fischer, and G. Pernul, "CSAP—An Adaptable Security Module for the E-Government System WEBOCRAT," *A Report on the Webocracy Project Funded by European Commission*, 2002.

[24] He, H., and R. K. Wong, "A Role-Based Access Control Model for XML Repositories," *First International Conference on Web Information Systems Engineering*, 2000, pp. 138–145.

CHAPTER 11

Migrating to RBAC—Case Study: Multiline Insurance Company

Contents

11.1 Background

11.2 Benefits of using RBAC to manage extranet users

11.3 Benefits of using RBAC to manage employees (intranet users)

11.4 RBAC implementation costs

11.5 Time series of benefits and costs

Reference

This chapter documents the experience of a real company in its transition from conventional access control methods to RBAC. This case study was conducted by the Research Triangle Institute (RTI) as part of an evaluation of the economic impact of RBAC on U.S. industry, and this section was excerpted with permission from the RTI report, *The Economic Impact of Role-Based Access Control* [1] distributed by NIST. The case study provides an opportunity to more fully explore the benefits and costs of RBAC from the vantage point of a software end user.

RTI conducted the case study with a multiline insurance company (referred to here as "the company"). RTI selected the company for the case study for two principal reasons. First, the company is implementing RBAC to manage both its employees' access permissions and its extranet users' permissions. The case study was able to capture, with one software end user, insights from implementing RBAC in these two environments. Second, because the company's extranet users are contracting agencies, the case study could also capture insights related to delegated administration and other functionalities afforded RBAC users.

This section discusses the company's line of business and how the company intends to leverage RBAC to enrich its business model and improve employee productivity. The installation and implementation will cost the company an estimated $783,636 over the course of 12 to 18 months. Once fully implemented, however, RTI estimates that the annual administrative and productivity estimates will total nearly $661,330. In addition, the company estimates that its RBAC-enabled e-business strategy will increase its annual amount of new business by 10% to 20%.

11.1 Background

The company's primary line of business is the provision of an array of insurance products, including home, auto, business, and life insurance. Like many multiline insurers, the company does not sell directly to policyholders, but it instead teams with locally operated independent insurance agents. These local insurance agents market and sell products within their area, contracting with the company upon selling a policy. The company's annual revenues are measured in the billions; it has several thousand employees; and it works with hundreds of agencies located across the United States.

The company is in the middle of rolling out RBAC to its internal and external user population; the rollout is occurring in two stages. First, the company is providing electronic services to its customer base, the local insurance agencies, via the Internet. The system will use RBAC to provide systems security and to relieve maintenance and administrative pressures by delegating administration. As this process nears completion, the company will devote more resources to its internal migration from identity-based ACLs to RBAC.

The company expects that using RBAC will increase productivity and increase its amount of new business annually. RBAC will also provide the level of security required by an institution with a large number of users and a wide variety of user types, including potentially competing insurance agents. The company was not able to provide any quantitative information concerning security benefits; however, it openly discussed the other benefits it expected to accrue and costs it expected to incur. These costs and benefits, quantified by RTI, are presented in Table 11.1. The company's strategy should save it at least $661,330 annually, but to reap these benefits it must first outlay $783,636 in labor, software, and hardware expenses.

11.2 Benefits of using RBAC to manage extranet users

The company's client base consists of hundreds of independent insurance agencies located across the United States, each employing approximately three agents and their support personnel. Traditionally, insurance agents

11.2 Benefits of using RBAC to manage extranet users

Table 11.1 Summary of the Company's Costs and Estimated Benefits

Variable	Dollar Value	Economic Metric
Enhanced organizational productivity	$471,040	Reduced paper- and telephone-based workload for insurance claims and policy-processing professionals
Delegated administration of extranet user accounts	$161,086	Avoided cost of corporate systems administrators; maintaining extranet users' accounts
Reduction in new employee downtime	Undisclosed	Reduction in the amount of time an employee is without access permissions
Improved management of employees' permissions	$29,204	The cost difference between RBAC and non-RBAC policies to manager employees' user accounts
Total annual benefits	**$661,330**	
Software expenses	$120,000	Software purchases, including maintenance and support agreements
Hardware expenses	$20,000	Hardware purchases to support systems migration and e-business strategy
Consulting fees	$24,000	Fees paid to consultants to assist in the implementation process
Labor expenses	$608,088	Labor expenses of employees tasked with implementing RBAC systems and e-business strategy
Role engineering expenses	$14,548	Labor expenses related to determining the characteristics of roles to be used
Total one-time costs	**$783,636**	

have interacted with the company through telephone calls and written communication. Agents contact the company directly to determine rates, receive quotes, and obtain other information. After receiving information from the company, agents then recontact prospective policyholders to inform them of the results. The process of contacting the company directly to determine rates and to gather other information translated into a significant amount of time between a customer's inquiry and the sale of the policy. If the customer should choose to purchase the policy, the agent must then initiate a process whereby the policy is enacted and the appropriate forms filed at the agency and mailed to the company. The company would supplement its records with information obtained from agents in the additional mailings and other communications. The process of completely selling a policy, including mailing and final data entry, could take as long as 4 to 6 weeks.

RBAC is the technology enabling the company's strategic e-business initiative. The RBAC software will grant or deny access to users to data and applications as users' roles dictate. In essence, the software is the platform to which data and applications will be linked. Agents will interact with the company over the Internet. Agents will be assigned roles that allow them to enter policyholder information, examine rates, and sell products instantly to customers. The goal is to allow agents to maintain, access, determine, and interact with policy information and details electronically. The company also estimates that the ability to instantly register and sell products to prospective policyholders will increase its amount of new business by 10% to 20% annually.

The company could have selected an alternative access control model, but it would have been more costly, although the extent of the additional cost is unknown. What is known, however, is that a non-RBAC solution would have entailed a larger programming component, which would have increased installation and customization costs. The system would also have been far more costly to operate and less secure for several reasons related to systems administration and maintenance, such as user directory maintenance and user account maintenance (i.e., no delegated administration).

11.2.1 Simplifying systems administration and maintenance

The company will use RBAC's delegated administration capability to establish an administrator at each agency who will be tasked with performing the basic systems administration and role maintenance for its agency. It will take the company less than 1 hour per agency to establish administrators and set up the basic structure, a cost that is included in the labor cost estimates presented in Section 11.4. Delegated administration of the company's agents is expected to decrease the systems administrator's workload by approximately 1.5 full-time employees annually, compared to using an alternative access control model. Based on data from 2000 National Occupational Employment and Wage Estimates published by the Bureau of Labor Statistics, the average, fully loaded wage of the systems administrators performing these functions is estimated at $51.62 per hour. At this wage, the company would save $161,086 annually.

Delegated administration does not push costs further down the supply chain, rather there may be benefits to those organizations to which account administration has been delegated. For example, the cost of having the office manager at a local insurance agency assign a role to a new agent may be outweighed by the benefit of that agent having his or her permissions quickly. If the office manager does not have to arrange account set-up and administration with the company, he or she avoids the labor and lag time expenses. The agent is also able to assume his or her regular duties.

11.2.2 Enhancing organizational productivity

Policy and policyholder information is transmitted to the company securely over the Internet, reducing the company's administrative and data entry burden as well as the amount of paper circulating among its departments. The company currently employs 40 people tasked solely to maintain the communication and data entry associated with managing relationships with agents in the mailroom, call center, support, and data entry departments. It estimated that the new initiative would make available about 20% of their time. Based on information gathered from the Bureau of Labor Statistics, the mean national loaded wage for insurance claims and policy processing clerks is estimated to be $29.44 per hour. The e-business strategy should free up 16,000 person hours annually, given its current level of employment. The value of those hours is therefore at least $471,040.

11.3 Benefits of using RBAC to manage employees (intranet users)

The company is replacing its current, identity-based access control system with a role-based one. The company employs a few thousand people at several offices. IT systems administrators at the headquarters facility currently maintain each employee's access permissions using ACLs. The company estimates that once it implements RBAC, its principal benefits will fall into two categories: reduced new employee downtime and simplified systems administration and maintenance.

11.3.1 Reduction in new employee downtime

The administrative benefits of allowing a new employee to quickly assume his or her duties by having access permissions more quickly are potentially substantial. Being a large insurer, the company has scores of employees in similar job functions. With RBAC, it can create and define a role once and then assign that role to new employees as opposed to adding the employee's user ID to each ACL. The company indicated that the time until a new employee is fully enabled is currently 2 to 3 days, including the routing of paperwork. The role-based system and accompanying administrative policies are expected to reduce the amount of time significantly; therefore, the employee is able to access data and applications more quickly.

Because information on employee turnover and employment at the company is confidential, we do not present the impact estimates. However, if we assume that the amount of downtime is reduced by one-half, and that during that time the employee is 85% productive, we can estimate the approximate benefits. For a new policy-processing clerk, the reduction in new employee downtime would be worth $44.16. [The reduction in downtime (50% of 2.5 days = 1.25 days = 10 hour) is multiplied by the loaded wage rate for policy-processing clerks ($29.44 per hour) and the productivity loss (15%).]. This number is excluded from the total benefits calculation for the company case study because it is meant solely to illustrate the benefit.

11.3.2 Simplified systems administration and maintenance

As explained in the previous section, the company expects that the ability to more quickly assign access privileges will reduce its systems administration and maintenance costs. The time that otherwise would have been spent determining and assigning privileges will be free for other tasks. Alternatively adjusting or terminating privileges for employees that are either leaving the company or moving to new positions internally will be equally facilitated. The aggregate effect is an improvement in administrators' productivity. It is estimated that using RBAC rather than identity-based ACLs to manage user permissions will save the company $29,204 annually. (Results from a survey of firms using RBAC allowed RTI to calculate the number of minutes administrators save by using RBAC rather than other access control models, and estimate the average number of times administrative tasks such as assigning and terminating permissions were performed annually.)

11.4 RBAC implementation costs

The migration to RBAC and the implementation of the e-business strategy will cost the company approximately $784,000. The labor costs associated with installation as well as the software and hardware costs are one-time costs. The company will intermittently incur role engineering costs as its business activities warrant redefining roles over the life of the system. The company's total user population is expected to be 10,000; thus, the implementation cost per user will be approximately $78.36.

11.4.1 Software and hardware expenses

The company's costs included software and hardware purchases, consulting fees, and labor expenses. The access control software, which complements the e-business platform and other software, cost the company $120,000, including a one-year maintenance and support agreement. The company also hired consultants to assist in the implementation at a cost of $24,000. It purchased two additional servers to facilitate the migration and to support the e-business initiative at a total cost of $20,000. Thus, the company's total software and hardware outlay totaled $164,000.

11.4.2 Systems administrators' labor expenses

Three computer systems managers are tasked full time to accomplish both the e-business and RBAC rollout to independent agencies and the internal RBAC rollout. These systems managers anticipate that the entire process will take between 12 and 18 months. Included in these costs are several tasks such as the following:

- Software customization;
- Programming related to Web-enabling applications;
- Software and hardware installation;
- Training and education;
- Defining roles within the software package;
- All other labor activities related to the software rollout.

Using data provided by the Bureau of Labor Statistics, the loaded wage rate of computer and information systems managers was estimated to be $77.96 per hour. The midpoint of the company's time horizon and the number of administrators tasked yield an estimated labor expense of $608,088.

11.4.3 Role engineering expenses

The final labor activity to be included is role engineering. The company has yet to complete the role engineering process and is unsure of the amount of time, and therefore the expense, it will take to complete the task. The company anticipates that several more meetings in the coming months will be required to determine and establish administrative policies and roles and to work out organizational issues. Role engineering is an iterative process and the company will most likely revisit role definitions established during initial rollout.

The role engineering cost is also a recurring cost as the company grows and its organizational structure shifts. New tools and experience with role engineering should make the process less costly in the future. However, it is impossible to hypothesize how the company's future business environment may affect the need to redefine the roles established during the rollout. For this case study we assumed that role engineering is a one-time cost and that the organizational structure of the company is fixed.

At the time the interviews were conducted, the company had held 40 hours of meetings, each with an average of five individuals consisting equally of general managers and computer and information systems managers. The loaded wage rate of computer and information systems managers was estimated to be $72.74, using the 2000 National Occupational Employment and Wage Estimates published by the Bureau of Labor Statistics. Using the wage rates for these two groups of employees, we calculate the cost of these meetings to be $14,548.

11.5 Time series of benefits and costs

The RBAC software and model will be in place indefinitely. Because of the significant capital and labor expense of implementing access control policies and products, it is unlikely that the company will migrate to an alternative model in the foreseeable future. It may deepen or adjust the model it has chosen, which may include further labor and capital investment for software revisions or the creation of new roles or redefinition of existing ones. At present the company has no plans to deepen or adjust its model once RBAC has been fully deployed.

Table 11.2 presents a time series of the company's estimated costs and benefits, based on its current expenditure plans. The time series assumes that real wage rates are constant and that the company's organizational structure remains fixed. All dollars are 2001 dollars. The company's costs are spread over six quarters encompassing 3 calendar years. Because some employees will be managed using RBAC while others are being migrated to the new system, costs and benefits overlap. The total estimated annual benefit to the company is not first accrued until 2003.

11.5 Time series of benefits and costs

Table 11.2 Time Series of the Company's Costs and Benefits

Year	Costs	Benefits
2000	$164,000	—
2001	$501,018	$159,857
2002	$121,618	$659,505
2003	—	$661,330
2004	—	$661,330
2005	—	$661,330
2006	—	$661,330

Expenses are distributed over a six-quarter period. The company purchased the hardware and RBAC software during the final quarter of 2000. The time series assumes the company began implementation at the start of the first quarter of 2001 and completed it 15 months later at the end of the first quarter of 2002. Hence, there was a one-quarter lag between software and hardware purchases and the beginning of implementation. The role engineering process was completed before users were migrated to the new system; therefore, the implementation labor expense is distributed evenly over the five-quarter period, but the role engineering expense was limited to the first two quarters.

The company plans to first bring its extranet users into the system and then its employees. The entire process will take nine months; during three months both extranet users and employees will be migrated. The process began in the third quarter of 2001 and will be completed at the end of the first quarter of 2002. Although some benefits will be accrued in 2001, the total estimated annual benefit does not begin to accrue until 2003.

Figure 11.1 illustrates the net benefits to the company on a quarterly basis. Although the software and hardware costs were incurred solely during the fourth quarter of 2000, Figure 11.1 conceptualizes these particular costs over the entire 2000 calendar year. This adjustment was made because the labor costs were distributed evenly over time, when in reality some months may have seen more labor activity than others. If the software and hardware costs had been depicted as a spike in net cash flows, the resulting data point would have made the curve's cost area difficult to illustrate and understand.

Figure 11.1 illustrates the flow of the company's net benefits on a quarterly basis from implementation to full operation.

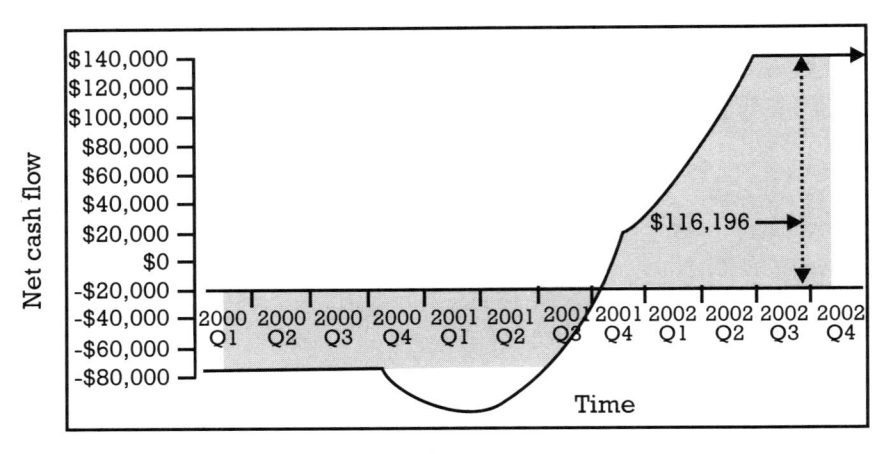

Figure 11.1 Quarterly flow of net benefits.

Reference

[1] Gallaher, M. P., A. C. O'Connor, and B. Kropp, "The Economic Impact of Role-Based Access Control," *Planning Report 01-2,* National Institute of Standards and Technology, 2002.

CHAPTER 12

RBAC Features in Commercial Products

Contents

12.1 RBAC in relational DBMS products

12.2 RBAC in enterprise security administration software

12.3 Conclusions

References

This chapter discusses the RBAC features found in two important classes of commercial software: relational DBMS products and enterprise security administration (ESA) products (also called system management software). The motivations for using RBAC in these two classes of software are different. In DBMS products, the RBAC model forms an integral component of the access control mechanism, and hence the RBAC model data is used for enforcing access control on the various resources (database objects) under the control of the DBMS product. In ESA products, the RBAC model is used as an abstract higher-level model for capturing authorizations to enterprisewide resources resident in various heterogeneous systems (OSs and application systems). We call this the enterprise authorization model (or simply the authorization model based on roles). The authorization model data in ESA products is then mapped to the access control entities (components) in the various systems (called target systems) distributed throughout the enterprise. The actual access enforcement is performed by the native access control mechanisms in the target systems, many of which may not support RBAC. Thus, while the RBAC model is used for access enforcement in DBMS products, it is used for authorization modeling and management in ESA products.

12.1 RBAC in relational DBMS products

More than any other class of commercial application software, DBMSs provide access control at several levels of granularity including provision for content-based controls. An application system developed using a DBMS can contain a large amount of data with highly differentiated access permissions for different users depending upon their job function(s) or role(s) within the organization. Hence it was no surprise that DBMS products were one of the earliest classes of commercial products to support RBAC. Also the set of RBAC features supported in DBMS products far outnumber the features supported in other classes of commercial products.

Our analysis and discussion of RBAC in the context of DBMS products will go beyond the RBAC model features (e.g., the ability to build role hierarchies) to also cover the implementation features relating to certain administrative tasks such as role propagation, role maintenance, and the control of permission sets for roles. Hence, our RBAC model description in various commercial DBMS products is organized in terms of various broad categories of RBAC administrative functions. These broad categories are listed as follows:

- Role creation;
- User role assignments and role propagation;
- Role activation;
- Creation of role hierarchies and constraints;
- Assignable privileges.

We have chosen the following three commercial DBMS products for our discussion. Our choice was not motivated by any commercial factors such as market share but to present to the reader the total set of all RBAC model capabilities (which is in fact a combination of RBAC model features and supported administrative functions) in this class of commercial products. All the information needed for our analysis was obtained from DBMS product manuals or text books.

- Informix Dynamic Server version 9.3 [1–3];
- Oracle Enterprise Server version 8i [4, 5];
- Sybase Adaptive Server version 12.5 [6, 7].

12.1 RBAC in relational DBMS products

12.1.1 Informix Dynamic Server version 9.3 (IBM)

- *Role creation:* In Informix only the database administrator (DBA) can create a role. An example of the CREATE ROLE command to create a teller role is

    ```
    CREATE ROLE teller
    ```

    The role name cannot be a user name that is known to the DBMS server or to the operating system of the DBMS server. No authentication information can be attached to a role.

- *User role assignments and role propagation:* The DBA has the authority to grant an existing role to a single user, a specified list of users or—by using the keyword PUBLIC to all users. Examples for each of these variations are

    ```
    GRANT teller TO Mary
    GRANT teller TO Mary, John, Joe
    GRANT teller TO PUBLIC
    ```

    A user can be granted more than role. A role can be granted to a user with the GRANT OPTION. A user who receives a role with GRANT OPTION can grant that role to other users or to another role. In addition, the receiving user can also drop that role. For example, if Mary receives the teller role with GRANT OPTION through the command

    ```
    GRANT teller TO Mary WITH GRANT OPTION
    ```

    Mary can grant that teller role to any other user or even drop the role using the command

    ```
    DROP ROLE teller
    ```

- *Role activation:* The privileges in the various roles received by a user (through a DBA or another user) are not available to the user automatically by opening up a session through successful login. The user has to activate a role in the session to exercise the privileges in the role's privilege set. At login time all users are, by default, assigned the dummy role NULL or NONE. The roles NULL and NONE have no privileges. The user can enable a role assigned to him or her by means of the SET ROLE command. If Susan has been assigned the role Customer_Rep she can activate that role by the command

```
SET ROLE Customer_Rep
```

The SET ROLE allows for the specification of only one role, so the command can be used for enabling or activating only one role at a time. Moreover, if a user executes the SET ROLE command after a role is already set, the new role replaces the old role. This implies that a user can be active in one and only one role at any point in time during the user session. Informix provides no feature to specify a default active role, other than NULL or NONE, for a user.

- *Creation of role hierarchies and constraints:* As already stated, users who have been granted a role with GRANT OPTION as well as the DBAs can grant a role to another role. This feature enables building nested roles, so it is possible to build a role hierarchy. Informix has no features to designate a set of roles as mutually exclusive roles, meaning that all roles in that designated set cannot be granted to the same user. Hence it does not support static SoD. There is also no support for a cardinality constraint to restrict the maximum and minimum number of users that can be assigned to a role. Informix does in a sense support the dynamic SoD, which is preventing a set of designated roles from being activated simultaneously (within the same user session). However, this is more a side effect of the fact that only one role can be activated at a time rather than an independent feature in its own right.

- *Assignable privileges:* There are seven categories of privileges in Informix. The most important of these are: database-level privileges, table-level privileges, and routine-level privileges. Database-level privileges enable a user to create new objects (such as tables and views) in the database as well perform some administrative functions like granting privileges on objects to other users and allocating disk spaces. Table-level privileges enable a user to perform operations on a named application table (e.g., ledger table). These operations include SELECT (which retrieves rows from the table), INSERT, DELETE, and UPDATE (which update the contents of the table), INDEX (which creates new indexes), ALTER (which changes the table definition—adding or deleting columns), and REFERENCES (which specifies referential constraints on the table). Routine-level privileges allow a user to execute stored procedures. Out of the three privilege categories discussed above, Informix allows only table-level and routine-level privileges to be granted to roles. The object owners, the DBA, as well as users who have been granted these privileges with GRANT OPTION can grant these privileges to roles.

12.1.2 Oracle Enterprise Server version 8i (Oracle)

Role creation   Oracle 8i comes with a set of predefined roles called system roles or default roles. Roles created by DBA or other users for the purpose of controlling access to database objects in various applications are called user-defined roles. The three main system roles and their associated permissions are described as follows:

- *CONNECT role:* log into the database and create a session;
- *RESOURCE role:* privileges to create database tables and procedures;
- *DBA role:* perform any type of operation on the Oracle 8i server including the ability to create roles, assign to users, and assign privileges to roles.

The DBA (a user who has been assigned the DBA role) can create a user-defined role (with an optional password requirement for activating that role) using the command:

```
CREATE ROLE<role name>[NOT IDENTIFIED | IDENTIFIED
  [BY <password> | EXTERNALLY]];
(e.g., CREATE ROLE auditor IDENTIFIED BY
  scrutinize;)
```

The password requirement for existing roles can be added or removed using the following commands by the DBA:

- ALTER ROLE accountant IDENTIFIED BY wizkid;
- ALTER ROLE auditor NOT IDENTIFIED;

User role assignments and role propagation   Oracle 8i allows a role to be granted to multiple users, and a user can be assigned multiple roles. Oracle's GRANT command enables a role to be granted to a user or a role (or corresponding lists) or using the keyword PUBLIC to all users with a single statement. In addition, a role can be granted with the optional ADMIN OPTION. A user, who is granted a role with admin option clause, can grant that role to other users or roles, or to alter (add or remove the password requirement) or drop the role. To grant the accountant role to the user Dora with admin option, the command is

```
GRANT accountant TO Dora WITH ADMIN OPTION;
```

Role activation   In Oracle, a user who has been granted one or more roles can invoke the SET ROLE command to enable or disable roles for the current user session. The SET ROLE statement in Oracle has the following three options:

1. A list of roles can be enabled, optionally giving a password if a role has one (Example 1: SET ROLE accountant IDENTIFIED BY wizkid, financial_analyst IDENTIFIED BY brainy).

2. Enables the user to activate all the roles assigned to him/her except for specific ones. This option does not activate roles with passwords. (Example 2: SET ROLE ALL EXCEPT auditor).

3. Disable all roles for the current session (Example 3: SET ROLE NONE).

It is also possible for the user to set up a default list of roles to be activated at the time of user login. However, roles that have passwords associated with them cannot be part of this default list. The user has to individually activate those roles using the SET ROLE command. The default list of active roles for a user can be built using a single invocation of the ALTER USER command with the DEFAULT ROLE clause. The ALTER USER command with the DEFAULT ROLE clause has the same three options that are available with the SET ROLE command except for the password identification feature. This implies the following:

1. It is possible to specify a list of default roles to be activated (Example 4: ALTER USER Scott DEFAULT ROLE accountant, financial_analyst).

2. One should include all assigned roles in the default set except specified roles (Example 5: ALTER USER Scott DEFAULT ROLE ALL EXCEPT auditor).

3. One should make the default active role set null (Example 6: ALTER USER Scott DEFAULT ROLE NONE).

12.1 RBAC in relational DBMS products

Creation of Role Hierarchies and Constraints As already stated, the Oracle's GRANT command can be used to assign a role (or a list of roles) to another role (or list). This enables building a hierarchy of roles. An interesting feature in Oracle is that the GRANT command with ADMIN OPTION can be used when assigning a role to another role just as in assigning a role to a user. Thus when a junior role is assigned to a senior role with ADMIN OPTION, a member of the senior role becomes a local role administrator since he or she can assign the junior roles or the system privileges (see discussion on Assignable privileges) contained in the junior roles to other users. Oracle does not have features to specify and enforce static and dynamic SoD constraints. It is also not possible to specify the maximum number or minimum number of users that can be assigned to a role.

Assignable privileges Privileges in Oracle fall into two general categories: system privileges and object privileges. System privileges are rights to execute various types of commands. For example the CREATE TABLE system privilege lets you create tables. The definition of a system privilege does not involve a reference to a named database object used in an application (say a SALARY table). Object privileges, on the other hand, allow users to perform a particular operation on a specific table, view, or stored procedure. They include the SELECT, UPDATE, INSERT, and DELETE operations on tables and views, the ALTER, CREATE INDEX operations on tables alone, and the EXECUTE operation on stored procedures and functions. Both categories of privileges can be granted to roles. A system privilege can be granted to a role only by the DBA or by a user who has been granted that system privilege with the ADMIN option. An object privilege can be granted to a role only by the object owner or by a user who has been granted that object privilege with GRANT option.

12.1.3 Sybase adaptive server version 12.5 (Sybase)

Role creation The Sybase adaptive server comes with a set of pre-defined roles called system roles. The roles created for the purpose of access control on the objects (e.g., tables and views) in various databases (where each database has been created for supporting one or more applications) in the adaptive server are called user-defined roles. The three main system roles and their associated permissions are described as follows:

1. *sa_role (system administrator):* performing server-level tasks like managing and controlling physical resources (e.g., disk space allocation and usage) and creating databases;

2. *sso_role (system security officer):* performing all security-related tasks like creating logins, lock, and unlock logins and creating user-defined roles and granting them to users, groups of users or other roles;

3. *Oper-role (operator):* backing up and restoring databases serverwide.

The system security officer (a user who has been assigned the sso_role) can create a user-defined role (with an optional password requirement for activating that role) using the command:

```
CREATE ROLE<role name>[WITH PASSWD < password >]
(e.g., CREATE ROLE auditor WITH PASSWD scruti-
nize )
```

User-defined role names cannot duplicate user names. The password requirement for existing roles (both system and user-defined) can be added or removed using the following commands by the system security officer:

```
ALTER ROLE accountant ADD PASSWD  wizkid
ALTER ROLE auditor DROP PASSWD
```

User role assignments and role propagation   The system security officer can grant a role or a list of roles to a user or a role (or corresponding lists) using the GRANT ROLE command. For example, roles accountant and financial_analyst can be assigned to Susan and John with the following command:

```
GRANT ROLE accountant, financial_analyst TO
   Susan, John
```

Thus, we see that in Sybase a role can be granted to one or more users and that any user can be granted more than one role. However there is no feature in Sybase for granting a user-defined role to a user with the recipient being able to propagate that role to other users.

Role activation   Sybase allows users to activate multiple roles in a user session. Although the SET ROLE statement (the one that activates a role for a user during a session) allows for specifying only one role, by repeated invocation of this statement, the user can activate multiple roles from the set of roles assigned (granted) to that user. The activation process is required mainly for user-defined roles. Sybase system roles are automatically activated, if they do not have passwords associated with them.

12.1 RBAC in relational DBMS products

The usage of Sybase's SET ROLE command is illustrated through the following examples:

- *Example 1:* To activate the accountant role:

    ```
    SET ROLE accountant WITH PASSWD wizkid ON
    ```

- *Example 2:* To deactivate the auditor role:

    ```
    SET ROLE auditor OFF
    ```

It is also possible for the user to set up a default list of roles to be activated at the time of user login. However roles that have passwords associated with them cannot be part of this default list. The user has to individually activate those roles using the SET ROLE command. The default list of active roles for a user can be built by repeated invocation of the command SP_MODIFYLOGIN. It is also possible to delete any role from the default active role set by using a variation of this command. These features are illustrated through the following examples:

- *Example 3:* To add the accountant role as one of the default active roles for John:

    ```
    SP_MODIFYLOGIN John ADD DEFAULT ROLE
        accountant
    ```

- *Example 4:* To delete the auditor role as one of the default active roles for Susan:

    ```
    SP_MODIFYLOGIN Susan DROP DEFAULT ROLE
        auditor
    ```

Creation of role hierarchies and constraints As already stated, the GRANT ROLE command can be used to assign a role to one or more roles. Hence it is possible in Sybase to create a role hierarchy. In addition, Sybase supports a powerful feature of RBAC. This is the ability to define mutual exclusivity of roles. Two types of mutual exclusion can be defined:

- Two roles are *mutually exclusive for membership* if one user cannot be granted both the roles.
- Two roles are *mutually exclusive for activation* if one user cannot activate or enable these two roles at the same time.

The above two types enable definition and enforcement of static and dynamic SoD policies respectively. Examples of commands to define the two types of mutual exclusion are given below:

- *Example 5:* ALTER ROLE accountant ADD EXCLUSIVE MEMBERSHIP auditor (makes roles accountant and auditor mutually exclusive for membership and hence cannot be assigned to the same user)
- *Example 6:* ALTER ROLE accountant ADD EXCLUSIVE ACTIVATION financial_analyst (makes roles accountant and financial_analyst mutually exclusive for activation and hence these two roles cannot be activated by a user at the same time even though both are his or her assigned roles).

Both system roles and user-defined roles can be defined to be in a role hierarchy or to be mutually exclusive. Sybase does not provide support for cardinality constraint to restrict the maximum and minimum number of users that can be assigned to a role. However, the maximum number of roles that a user can activate per user session and the maximum number of roles that can be activated serverwide can be specified.

Assignable privileges Privileges in Sybase fall into two general categories: object access permissions and object creation permissions. Object access permissions regulate the use of certain commands that access named database objects. They include the SELECT, UPDATE on tables, views and columns, INSERT and DELETE on tables and views, REFERENCES on tables and columns and EXECUTE on Stored procedures. Object creation permissions regulate the use of commands that create database objects. Examples of object creation permissions are CREATE TABLE, CREATE VIEW, and CREATE PROCEDURE. Both categories of privileges can be granted to user-defined as well as system roles. Object access permissions can be granted only by object owners and system administrators (users who have been assigned the sa_role). Only a system administrator or a database owner can grant object creation permissions.

12.2 RBAC in enterprise security administration software

This section analyzes and discusses the RBAC model concepts that have been implemented in another class of commercial software called the ESA products. ESA products enable centralized management of access control for

12.2 RBAC in enterprise security administration software

a wide variety of security systems (called target systems) resident in several heterogeneous platforms throughout the enterprise. The various types of target system platforms include the following:

- Server operating systems (e.g., UNIX and Windows NT);
- Web servers (e.g., Apache, WebSphere, and BEA);
- DBMSs (e.g., Oracle and Sybase);
- Mainframes.

Although the term target system refers to the native access control mechanism, since many platforms have only one native access control mechanism (with the exception of mainframes that support many mechanisms like RACF and ACF2), we refer to a target system by its platform name (e.g., UNIX). In general the ESA software does not replace the native access control mechanism in the target systems. In a few cases, it might extend the access control capabilities of the native access control mechanisms by providing add-on modules.

ESA products can be used to perform several enterprise security functions like single sign-on, password synchronization, and delegated administration. For our purposes, we are only interested in the following two general functions:

- Defining an enterprise authorization model and storing authorization data pertaining to all the IT resources in the enterprise in the model;
- Mapping authorization data under the enterprise authorization model to access control entities in the various native access control mechanisms (target systems).

Our interest is mainly in the set of ESA products whose enterprise authorization model uses the concept of roles. Since the design motivation in ESA products is to reduce the administrative complexity involved in managing authorizations for hundreds of users and a still larger number of IT resources throughout the enterprise, it is necessary that the enterprise authorization model based on roles supported in these products should not be complex. Hence the RBAC model features found in the enterprise authorization model of ESA products are not as extensive as those supported in the DBMS products. Many of them support the definition of role hierarchies but do not provide support for constraints like static SoD and dynamic SoD. An important distinction to note is that while the authorization data based on roles is used for enforcing access control on resources in

DBMS products, the authorization data stored under the enterprise authorization model in ESA products is only used for mapping to the relevant access control entities in the various target systems. In fact many of these target systems may not have the concept of roles as part of their access control mechanism. Based on the above observations, our analysis and description of RBAC features found in the various ESA products is organized under the following headings:

- Enterprise authorization model and target system access control entities;
- Connecting users to enterprisewide resources (provisioning).

In addition, we also provide a brief overview of the architecture of each of the ESA products highlighting the functions performed by the product's components.

We have analyzed the RBAC model features found in the following commercial ESA products. Just as in the case of DBMS products, our choice of these products was not based on market positions or other considerations but with a view to present to the readers the total landscape of RBAC features available in the ESA product category. All the information needed for our analysis was obtained from product manuals or published technical reports:

- Control-SA [8];
- DirXMetaRole [9, 10];
- SAM Jupiter [11, 12];
- Tivoli Identity Manager [13, 14].

12.2.1 CONTROL-SA (BMC software)

CONTROL-SA, the ESA product from BMC Software provides centralized security administration through the following main components (refer to Figure 12.1):

- Enterprise security station (ESS);
- Several SA-agents.

The ESS, the management component of CONTROL-SA, communicates through gateways to several SA-agents each running on top of a target system. The ESS uses a central security administration database to store

12.2 RBAC in enterprise security administration software

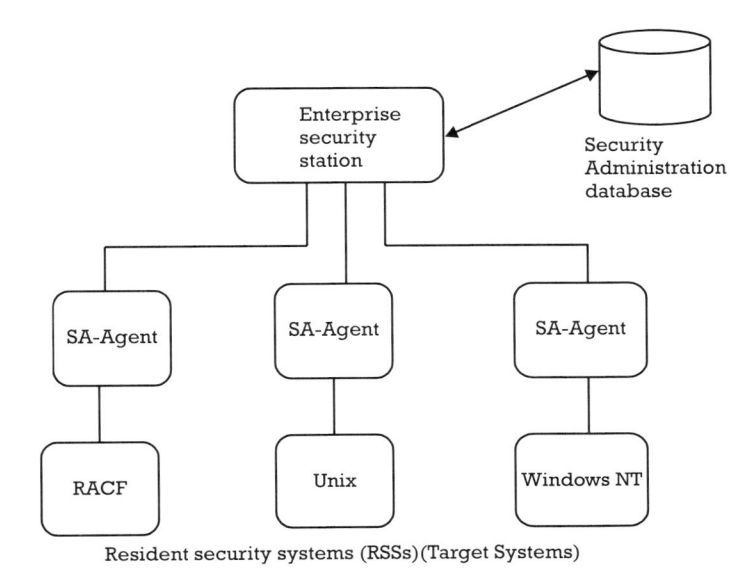

Figure 12.1 BMC'S CONTROL-SA components.

authorization data for the entire enterprise (contents of enterprise authorization model). SA-agents (an instance of which runs on each of the target platforms) receive commands (as well as pass messages to) from the ESS and pass them to the native access control system on the target platform. Each native access control system is referred to as a resident security system (RSS) in CONTROL-SA. The RSS may be the native security kernel of the operating system (e.g., Solaris, HP-UX, or Novell Netware) or any other product implementing access control (e.g., RACF and ACF2).

Enterprise authorization model and target system access control entities
From an administration stand point, CONTROL-SA does not make a distinction between the enterprise authorization model entities and the RSS (target system) access control entities. This is due to the fact that the management component of CONTROL-SA—the ESS—handles the tasks of configuration of even RSS entities (e.g., creating RSS groups and assigning resources to those groups) through its own interface instead of those tasks being handled by an RSS administrator through RSS native interfaces. Furthermore, the ESS itself needs a number of additional entities for the administration of CONTROL-SA. However, for our goal of understanding the structure of enterprise authorization model and the use of the model for access enforcement on various RSS (target systems), consideration of the following entities is sufficient:

- Enterprise user;
- Job code (role);
- RSS user;
- RSS user groups;
- Resources.

Figure 12.2 shows the relationships among the above entities. A brief discussion on the semantics of the above entities is as follows:

- Enterprise user represents a person in the enterprise who may need access to a number of resources resident in several different platforms.
- A job code (role) represents a job function. The definition of the job code itself includes the set of user groups in various RSSs in which the user requires membership to perform the job function represented by the job code. Thus we see that the authorization model in CONTROL-SA does not make a distinction between the concept of a role and the concept of permission since the definition of role (job code) includes the concept of permission (RSS user group memberships). An enterprise user can be assigned to any number of job codes depending upon the job functions associated with his or her organizational position in the enterprise.

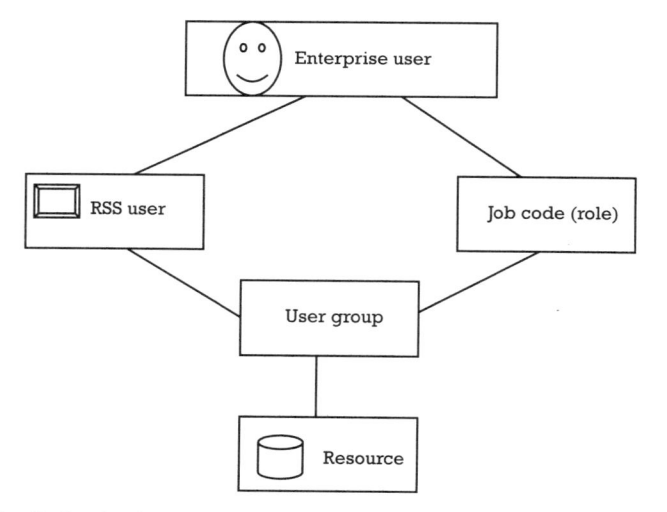

Figure 12.2 Authorization model and access control entities in CONTROL-SA.

12.2 RBAC in enterprise security administration software

- An RSS user represents a single user login ID in a specific RSS (target system). A single enterprise user may be connected to many RSS users in one or more RSSs.
- An RSS user group represents a named collection of one or more RSS users in a specific RSS.
- A resource represents a logical or physical IT asset (e.g., files, directories, and printers) in a specific RSS. An RSS user group may be connected to any number of resources in a specific RSS.

Out of the entities described above, information pertaining to enterprise user and job code (role) are carried in the central security administration database that is an integral component of ESS. The entities RSS user, RSS user groups, and resources are resident in various RSSs, and information regarding these entities is carried in the local RSS databases like the ACL (a table listing the RSS users and user groups with access rights for a specific resource and the type of access for which each is authorized). In addition, one or more template entities can be defined for each of the above entity types. These template entities carry a set of absolute values or rules used to assign default values for fields when a new entity record is created. Please note that the job code definition only contains references to RSS user groups in various RSSs. The actual RSS user groups are resident in the various RSSs.

In CONTROL-SA, two or more job codes can be connected to form a hierarchical structure called as multilevel job code. Also the hierarchical structure can have any number of levels. Thus CONTROL-SA supports role hierarchies. A multilevel job code can be used to either represent a complex job function (with the junior roles representing the simple or basic job functions) or a complete job description (with the junior roles representing the job functions related to the job title).

Connecting users to enterprisewide resources In established enterprises, a set of job codes (roles) would be already defined. Since a job code contains the references to RSS user groups in various RSSs, we can also assume that the RSS user groups in various RSSs would have been defined as well and resources connected to those RSS user groups. Hence the association between job codes, RSS user groups, and resources is relatively static in established enterprises. Hence the major administrative tasks are adding users and assigning them the appropriate job codes.

Let us see the process involved in connecting a new IBM mainframe systems developer John Smith to the IT resources using CONTROL-SA. To start performing his job activities John needs access to e-mail and connection to systems program development utilities. The ESS administrator uses the ESS's GUI interface to perform the following tasks:

- Create the enterprise user John Smith;
- Connect John Smith to CORP_NETMAIL and SYS_DEV job codes to enable John to use the corporate e-mail and invoke systems programming utilities.

The ESS automatically performs the following tasks:

- The CORP_NETMAIL contains references to "Domain_User" group on a NT server and "General" group on Corporate Exchange Server. The CORP_NETMAIL job code has also associated with it "NT_DOMAINUSERS" template and "EX_GENERAL" template. These templates provide the attributes for creating an account for John Smith in the NT server and corporate exchange server, respectively. Using these templates, the ESS automatically creates those accounts (RSS users) and connects those RSS user Ids to the relevant RSS user groups (in our case Domain_User group on the NT server and "General" group on the corporate exchange server).
- The SYS_DEV job codes contain reference to SYS_DEV user group on two different MVS/RACF systems. A template "RACF_DEV" is also attached to this job code. Using this template the ESS creates new RACF accounts and connects those accounts to SYS_DEV groups.

12.2.2 DirXmetaRole version 1.0 (Siemens)

The DirXmetaRole is the main component of the DirXSolutions product suite that enables centralized cross-platform role-based access administration for a variety of security systems (target systems) resident on server OSs, databases, and mainframes. The component products in the DirXSolutions product suite and their functions are described as follows (refer to Figure 12.3):

1. The DirXmetaRole Database (LDAP directory) acts as the data repository for users, roles, and permissions and stores all of the DirXmetaRole configuration and operational data.

12.2 RBAC in enterprise security administration software

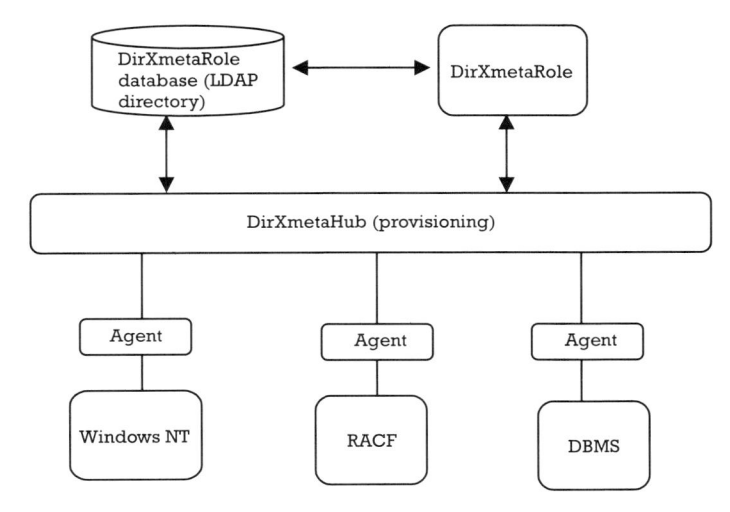

Figure 12.3 DirXSolutions suite for enterprise security administration.

2. DirXmetaHub is the middleware component that enables synchronization of user information in the DirXmetaRole database with corporate human resource (HR) directories as well as security information in various target systems. An important function of DirXmetaHub is the propagation of authorization information defined using DirXmetaRole to the various target systems (provisioning).

3. DirXmetaRole creates the role-based enterprisewide authorization model [called the role-based access management (RBAM) model within the product] and stores the model data in DirXmetaRole database. It then uses the DirXmetahub product to map this information to the target system access control entities.

Enterprise authorization model and target system access control entities The enterprise authorization model in DirXmetaRole is called RBAM. The RBAM model consists of entities user, role, permission, account, and group. The entities in RBAM and their relationship to the access control entities in the target system are shown in Figure 12.4. The semantics for each of these entities in DirXmetaRole are as follows:

- A user in DirXmetaRole represents an employee of the enterprise (or any outside person who needs access to enterprise's resources).

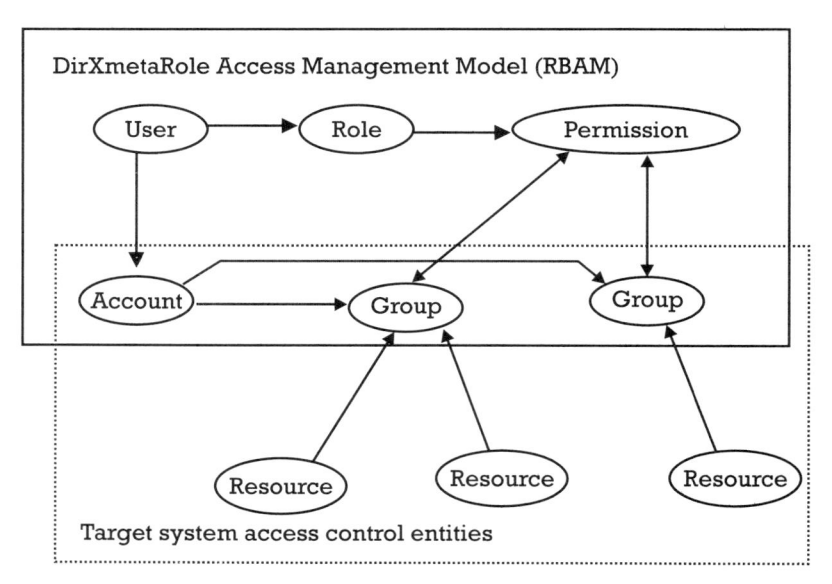

Figure 12.4 DirXmetaRole's RBAM model.

- A role can represent a single task or an entire set of tasks associated with a job title or job description. RBAM allows for building role hierarchies. Using this feature it is possible to build a set of roles each representing a task (junior roles) and then to assign these roles to a common role representing the job title or description (senior role).
- A permission reflects a bundle of access rights (privileges) that are needed to perform a task(s) in the enterprise. A permission is generic and cross-platform with respect to different IT systems (target systems) in the enterprise since it is an aggregation of different access rights from different IT systems.

An account in the RBAM model refers to a user ID in a specific target system. A DirXmetaRole user can have accounts in many different target systems. As shown in Figure 12.4, the account entity is present in both the enterprise authorization model (RBAM) and the target system access control model.

A group in the RBAM model refers to a valid group in a specific target system. Again from Figure 12.4, we see that the group is an entity that is also present in the target system access control model. In fact, it is the group in the target system (and not its reference in the RBAM model) that contains a bundle of concrete access rights pertaining to the resources in that target system. (Contrast this with a permission entity in RBAM that represents abstract access rights and is target system–independent.) An account in the target system is made a member of one or more groups and thus inherits the access rights of the group.

The RBAM model allows a role to be assigned to multiple users and a user to be assigned multiple roles. Any number of permissions can be assigned to roles. In addition, RBAM supports a feature called "role parameter." A role parameter is an attribute of a user that can be used to resolve a generic permission assigned to a role into a specific set of access rights depending upon the user who is assigned to that role. For example, suppose a bank that has branches nationwide, has defined a "teller" role, and this role has the generic "CUSTOMER_ACCOUNT_ACCESS" permission. The access to the exact set of customer accounts (specific access rights) should depend upon the teller's location, even though the role "teller" is common for all tellers. The "CUSTOMER_ACCOUNT_ACCESS" permission bundles all of customer-account access rights necessary for performing the teller role irrespective of where (target system) the customer accounts are located. However when a user Susan in Boston is assigned the "teller" role, her location (Boston) is used as the role parameter on the "CUSTOMER_ACCOUNT_ACCESS" permission to filter into the specific set of access rights (e.g., assignment to relevant groups in the server where Boston area customer accounts are located). Without the "location" role parameter, the bank would have to define a separate "teller" role for each location. With the role parameter "location" (the value of "location" is an attribute of an user), there needs to be only one "Teller" role and one abstract permission "CUSTOMER_ACCOUNT_ACCESS." Other candidates for role parameter are: department, division, and project_group. Thus, role parameters help to reduce the total number of roles required in the RBAM model.

All the entities (or rather entity instances consisting of various users, roles, permissions, accounts, and groups) of the DirXmetaRole's enterprise authorization model RBAM are stored in the DirXmetaRole database, which is a LDAP directory. The synchronization of information pertaining to accounts and groups (since these are part of both the RBAM model and target system access control model) between the DirXmetaRole database and the target systems is performed using DirXmetaHub component.

Connecting users to enterprisewide resources   When a user is assigned to a role, which is related to a permission, not all the groups connected with that permission may apply for that user. We have already seen that a role parameter (a user attribute) can be used to filter the permission-group assignments so that the user gets only those groups that match his role parameter attribute.

This process of identifying the correct groups by evaluating the user's role parameter attributes is called in DirXmetaRole a "role resolution." This process is carried out as follows: The user's record carries the value of the role parameter as an attribute, and the groups also carry the role parameter values for which they are valid. A permission has a user-group matching rule attached to it. A matching rule consists of an expression containing comparison operators involving user and group attributes. When the user is assigned to a role that is connected to a permission that has a matching rule attached to it, the matching rule is evaluated using the role parameter, and the user gets the group memberships that match his or her value for the role parameter. However, there could be some permissions that have no matching rule attached. In this case the user is attached to all the groups that are assigned to the permission. The role resolution described above not only assigns the correct groups for a given a permission but also the relevant target systems.

After resolving the permissions into correct groups, DirXmetaRole creates (through the DirXmetahub component) an account for the user in the relevant target system and an entry for this account in the relevant target system groups (account-group assignment). This process is called "role distribution" in the DirXmetaRole.

The task of assigning access rights to various resources for a group is the responsibility of the target system administrator and is accomplished outside of DirXmetaRole using the target system interfaces. As we have seen, the function of DirXmetaRole is to control which users are entered into and removed from the groups. Thus we see that DirXmetaRole does not replace or bypass the native access control mechanism but simplifies the process of connecting users with various enterprisewide resources.

12.2.3 SAM Jupiter (Systor)

SAM Jupiter is an ESA product by Systor Security Solutions. SAM Jupiter provides a single point of administration for several security systems (target systems) deployed across the enterprise. SAM's support of target system platforms include OSs like MVS, UNIX (AIX), and Windows NT, databases like Oracle and DB2, and standard applications like SAP's R/3. SAM Jupiter's architecture consists of the following components (see Figure 12.5):

- SAM business server;
- SAM repository;
- SAM back end;

12.2 RBAC in enterprise security administration software

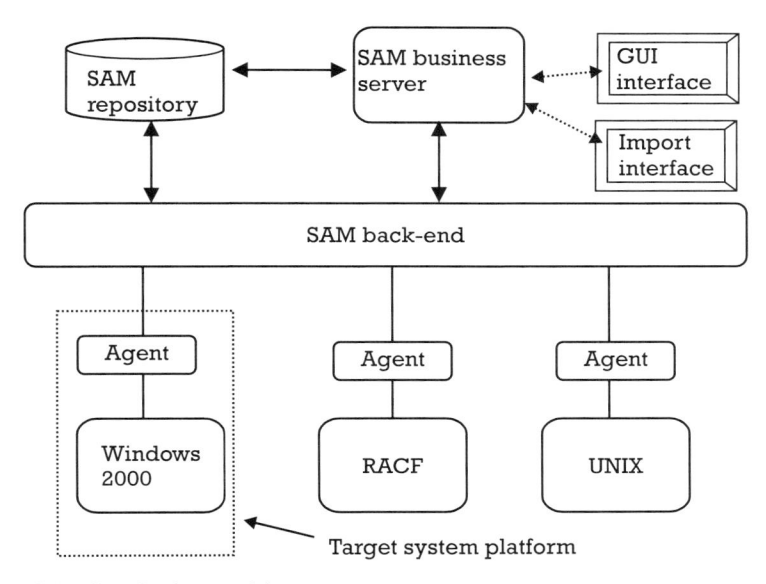

Figure 12.5 Sam Jupiter architecture.

- Agents in target systems.

The SAM business server, the management module of the SAM Jupiter product, is provided with a Web-based graphical interface. The SAM business server is the component used for defining enterprisewide authorization data and rules as well as policies for administration of SAM Jupiter itself. The SAM repository is the location for storing the data defined through the SAM business server. The SAM back-end component acts as a transaction engine for the SAM repository and provides connections to supported systems (target systems) via agents. The agents run on the target platform and propagate the authorization data created through SAM business server (provisioning). The agents can also be used for synchronizing the data in the SAM repository with the information pertaining to access control entities in target systems in case it is out of sync.

Enterprise authorization model and target system access control entities The enterprise authorization model used in SAM Jupiter is called ERBAC (see Figure 12.6). The entities in the ERBAC model are users, enterprise roles, and permissions. The target system entities are accounts, groups, and resources. The semantics and the information carried by these entities are described as follows:

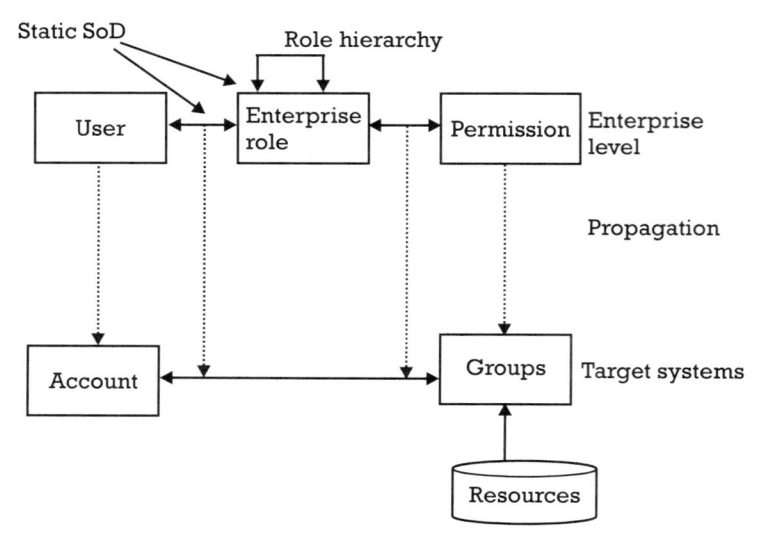

Figure 12.6 SAM Jupiter's ERBAC model.

- A user in SAM Jupiter is an employee in the enterprise. Some common information associated with an employee like organizational unit, location and job description are stored as attributes of a user.
- Enterprise role represents a task or job function in the enterprise. The definition of an enterprise role is target system independent.
- A permission in ERABC is a reference to a group in a target system. If the target system supports the concept of a role, a permission may also refer to a role. Hence the assignment of one or more permissions to a role is nothing but a set of role-to-group connections.
- An account is a user ID in a specific target system.
- A group is a target system entity that bundles permissions. An account that is made a member of a group obtains its underlying permissions.
- A resource is an entity whose definition depends upon the target system platform on which it is resident. A resource may refer to a file (in O/S platform) or a database or database table (in DBMS platform).

The ERBAC model in SAM Jupiter supports the assignment of one enterprise role to another, thus supporting the development of a role hierarchy. The role hierarchy can be of any length. ERBAC implements static SoD by making use of rules defining constraints between roles. These rules are evaluated when assigning users to roles (to ensure that the receiver does not receive two roles that are defined to be in static SoD) and roles to roles (to prevent the static SoD requirement from being circumvented by a role hierarchy). The SAM Jupiter also contains features to define a set of rules associated with the user entity as well. These rules can be used to map the user attributes to roles, enabling the automation of the user-to-role assignment process.

The specific set of access rights a user receives depends upon several of his or her attributes or parameters. Since it is difficult to build separate role hierarchies for each of these parameter values, the ERBAC model in SAM Jupiter supports the concept of parameterized roles. The concept of parameterized roles is enabled by suitable definition of permissions. There are three different approaches used for permission definition:

1. *Generic permissions:* A normal permission refers to a group in a single target system. A generic permission contains a reference to a group in a target system set (say DEV group in SET1) instead of a single target system. Supposing there is a role DEVELOPER that is assigned the generic permission DEV in target system set SET1. The SET1 may consist of target system platforms MVS1, MVS2, MVS3, MVS4, and MVS5. A particular developer Tom may only need access to MVS1 and MVS3. When Tom is assigned to the DEVELOPER role, these values MVS1 and MVS3 are specified. The generic permission is then instantiated into specific permissions with the result that Tom receives permission in the DEV group only in MVS1 and MVS3 (through corresponding accounts) and not in other target systems.

2. *Joker permissions:* A joker permission refers to a named joker group instead of a specific group in a target system. A rule maps this joker group to an actual group in the target system. This rule normally involves a user attribute (e.g., a user's cost center code). Let us suppose that groups corresponding to various cost centers are created in RACF with the prefix "EXP." For example the group EXP554 provides access to expense records for users belonging to cost center 554. A Joker permission is defined that refers to the Joker group "EXP." When a user is assigned to this role, a rule is triggered that computes the name of the correct group for the user by concatenating the fixed string "EXP" with the cost center value (taken from user attributes) and assigns the user's account in RACF to this group.

3. *Constrained permissions:* A constrained permission has associated with it a constraint containing a parameter name (not the value). This type of permission is used in situations where the target system has

parameters for authorization, and these target system-specific parameters are included in the permission definition. For example in a bank there may be many levels of loan officers and limits are set for the maximum amount of loan that each loan officer level can approve. However, there is only one "loan officer" role defined in SAM Jupiter. This loan officer role is assigned a constrained permission by name LOAN_GROUP with the parameter name "approval limit." When a user Susan Smith who is a junior loan officer with an attribute "approval limit" of $100,000 is assigned to the loan officer role, the permission LOAN_GROUP simply passes the attribute value to the underlying target system. The target system then uses its authorization rules to assign Susan Smith to the correct group(s) that prevents Susan Smith from approving any loan higher than $100,000.

Connecting users to enterprisewide resources Let us assume that a new teller John Smith joins as a teller in a bank that has branches nationwide. The set of customer accounts that John Smith can access depends upon his location. The set of all customer accounts is carried in an IBM mainframe (with RACF security system) with separate database views defined for retrieving customer records from a particular region. All the access permissions for a particular view are defined in a separate RACF group. For example the BOSTON_VIEW enables retrieval of customer records from the BOSTON region. The access permissions for the records under the BOSTON_VIEW are included in the RACF group by name BOSTON. The teller also needs an access to an NT account to enter the total cash receipts for the day.

All permissions needed for a teller are included in the role teller in SAM Jupiter. The role teller is connected to two permissions. One permission is a constrained permission with parameter "teller location." The other permission is a normal permission that has the group connection CASH_RECEIPTS in the NT server.

The SAM administrator first defines John Smith as a user in SAM Jupiter with the user ID Smith01. This user ID is then assigned to the teller role. If John Smith's work location is the BOSTON region, this attribute of John Smith is passed on to the permissions associated with the teller role. The constrained permission is evaluated, and John's group connection is determined (i.e., BOSTON group in RACF). John Smith's other group connection CASH_RECEIPTS is directly obtained from the other permission. A user account is created for John Smith (rather for Smith01) in RACF and is assigned the BOSTON group. A user account is created in NT server and the group CASH_RECEIPTS is assigned to that account.

12.2 RBAC in enterprise security administration software

SAM Jupiter eliminates the need for separate administrators for each of the target systems it manages. When these systems are connected to SAM Jupiter and their data loaded into SAM repository, the security administrators need to work only with SAM interfaces. All administrative work is done in SAM Jupiter and automatically propagated to the underlying systems in the format required (provisioning).

12.2.4 Tivoli Identity Manager version 1.1 (IBM)

The Tivoli Identity Manager version 1.1 from IBM provides centralized access control administration for the various systems and applications (target systems) throughout the enterprise using the following components (see Figure 12.7):

- Identity manager server;
- Tivoli user administration version 3.8;
- Tivoli security manager version 3.8;
- Tivoli management framework version 3.7.1.

The identity manager server is the management module of the Tivoli Identity Manager that coordinates with other components. It has a Web-accessible interface. The Tivoli user administration component manages user accounts on various target systems. The Tivoli security manager

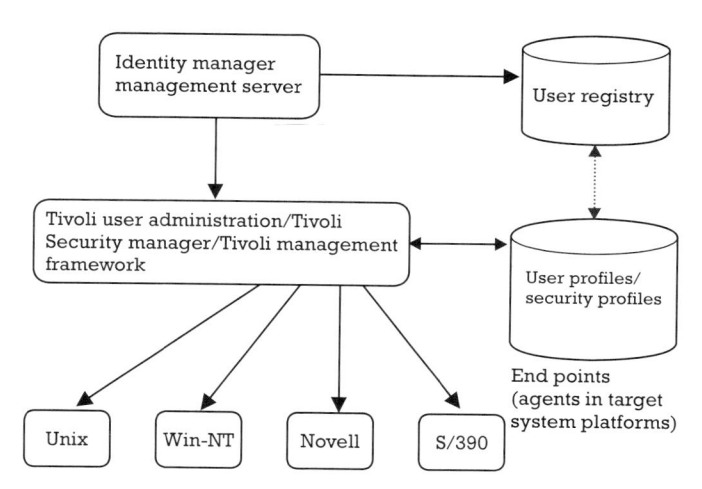

Figure 12.7 Tivoli Identity Manager and its associated components.

provides centralized security policy enforcement for multiple target systems by managing access control. In addition to enforcement of access control rules, the security manager manipulates other security policy aspects like platform password policy, login policy, and audit configuration. An important module of the Tivoli management framework component is the Tivoli management server (TMR). The TMR communicates with agent software (called end points in Tivoli) used to manage each of the native access control systems on target system platforms and thus is able to monitor events in the various target systems. The target platforms for which Tivoli identity manager provides end points include the following: Solaris, HP-UX, AIX, Linux, Windows NT/2000, OS/390, AS/400, OS/2, and Novell NetWare.

Enterprise authorization model and target system access control entities The entities in the enterprise-level authorization model in the Tivoli identity manager are users, groups, roles, and resource definitions (actual resources exist in various target platforms). User IDs, groups, and actual resources reside on target systems. Figure 12.8 shows a schematic diagram showing the relationship among these entities. The semantics for these entities are described as follows:

- A user represents an employee of an enterprise who needs access to IT resources.
- A group (at the enterprise level) represents a set of users within an enterprise. Example groups include divisions, departments, project teams, and job titles. A user can be a member of only one group.
- A role defines a set of capabilities required to carry out a given job. Roles in Tivoli identity manager are system-independent, and the resources associated with them may reside in many different target system platforms. The combination of target systems and roles is called a subscription within the Tivoli management framework. In Tivoli identity manager, it is possible to derive a child role from a parent role object. However, a permanent role hierarchy is not created or maintained in the authorization model. A child role is often used to add new capabilities, override parent capabilities, or subtract capabilities to define a new role. In other words, the role object inheritance is used only for facilitating easy creation of new roles.
- The entity resource at the enterprise level actually stands for resource definitions rather than actual resources since the latter physically exist

12.2 RBAC in enterprise security administration software

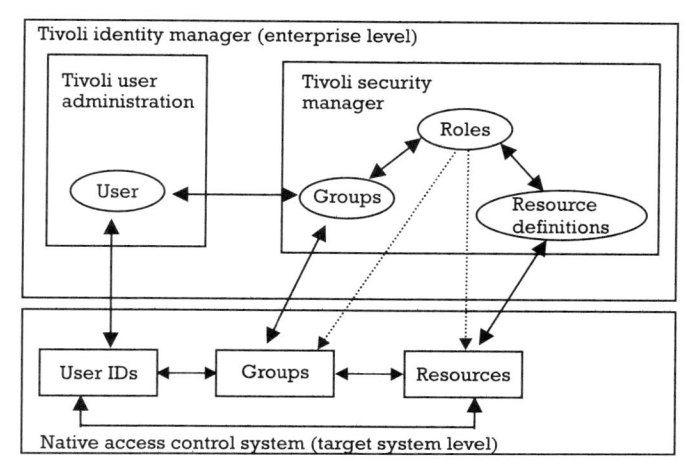

Figure 12.8 Authorization model entities in Tivoli.

at the target system. A resource definition can be a member of more than one role.

- An account is a user ID in a specific managed target (target system). A user can have many accounts.

- A resource at the target system level stands for programs, files, databases etc that need some form of access protection.

- A group at the target system level represents a set of resource access permissions. An account assigned to a group obtains the permissions defined for the group.

Connecting users to enterprisewide resources All security management information in the Tivoli security manager component is stored in security profiles. They contain records using target system–independent formats so that they can be used within an enterprise on many different target system types. The following types of records exist:

- A *group record* contains user, group, and role membership lists. At the target system level they are mapped to UserID-to-groups (target system level groups) associations.

- A *role record* defines the set of capabilities required to carry out a job function within the organization. Groups are given the necessary capabilities by assigning one or more roles to the group.

- A *resource record* defines a homogeneous collection of resource objects in the enterprise that can be accessed by users and groups via their role assignments.
- A *system policy record* provides the ability to define user and resource-related security policy rules that will be applied on a enterprisewide basis to all subscribed (please refer to the definition of subscription in the previous section) endpoints.

The administrator can choose how many and what combination of security profile record types a given security profile will contain. One security profile may contain group, role, and resource records, while another may contain only system policy records. The exact combination of record types in a given security profile is influenced by the security requirements of the target systems that subscribe to the profile manager that contains the security profiles. Security profile management consists of two main functions: population and distribution. Population of security profiles enables discovery of security information from subscribed end points (target systems). Distribution of security profiles enables security information (e.g., user ID-to-group associations) in target systems to be updated. Distribution of security profiles to target systems is enabled through endpoints (agent software) on various target system platforms and is performed by the Tivoli management server.

12.3 Conclusions

We have seen that RBAC model implementation in DBMS products has a rich set of RBAC model features and is actually used for access enforcement. Thus, it supports a rich set of administrative functions defined in the RBAC standard. In the case of ESA products, the concept of roles is merely used in the enterprise authorization model to simplify the management of authorizations. Hence the RBAC model implementation found in ESA products has only a limited set of RBAC model features (e.g., role hierarchy). The main administrative functions in ESA products include defining roles, assigning the relevant target system groups to roles, and assigning users to roles. The functions relating to propagating the enterprise-level authorization information to various target systems is done automatically using middleware products.

References

[1] Informix Guide to SQL: Reference, Version 8.3/9.3.

[2] Administrator's Guide for Informix Dynamic Server, Version 9.3.

[3] Informix Guide to Database Design and Implementation, Version 8.3/9.3.

[4] Loney, K., and G. Koch, *Oracle 8i—The Complete Reference,* McGraw Hill Companies Inc., 2000.

[5] Theriault, M., and W. Heney, *Oracle Security,* O'Reilly, 1999.

[6] Reference Manual Volume 2: Commands (PDF Only) Sybase Adaptive Server Enterprise 12.5 Product Documentation.

[7] System Administration Guide Sybase—Adaptive Server Enterprise 12.5 Product Documentation.

[8] Enterprise Security Station—User Guide (Windows GUI)—BMC Software Inc.

[9] DirXmetaRole Administration Guide—Siemens.

[10] DirXmetaRole Customization Guide—Siemens.

[11] Kern, A., "Advanced Features for Enterprisewide Role-Based Access Control," *Proceedings of the 18th Annual Computer Security Applications Conference,* Las Vegas, NV, 2002.

[12] SAM Jupiter User Manual (2002)—Systor Security Solutions.

[13] Enterprise Security Architecture using IBM Tivoli Security Solutions (2002)—IBM Corporation.

[14] Tivoli Security Management Design Guide (2002)—IBM Corporation.

Appendix A

XML schema for RBAC model

```xml
<?xml version="1.0" encoding="UTF-8"?>
<!-- edited with XML Spy v4.2 (http://www.xmlspy.com) by Ramaswamy
   Chandramouli (NIST) -->
<xs:schema xmlns:xs="http://www.w3.org/2001/XMLSchema"
xmlns:sch="http://www.ascc.net/xml/schematron" elementFormDefault="qualified"
attributeFormDefault="unqualified">

 <xs:element name="Bank_RBAC_Model" type="BankRBACModelType"/>
 <xs:element name="user" type="userType"/>
 <xs:element name="role" type="roleType"/>
 <xs:element name="privilege" type="privilegeType"/>
<xs:element name="role_inherit" type="InheritType"/>
<xs:element name="UserRoleAssignment" type="URAType"/>
<xs:element name="RolePrivilegeAssignment" type="RPAType"/>

 <xs:complexType name="BankRBACModelType">
<xs:annotation>
<xs:appinfo>
   <sch:pattern name="Role Assignment Rules">
     <sch:rule context="Bank_RBAC_Model">
        sch:assert test="UserRoleAssignment[count(role[text ( )='TEL'])= 1]"
           >There should be an assignment for Teller Role
                  </sch:assert>
              </sch:rule>
         </sch:pattern>
  </xs:appinfo>
 </xs:annotation>
```

```xml
<xs:sequence>
        <xs:element ref="user" maxOccurs="unbounded"/>
    <xs:element ref="role" maxOccurs="unbounded"/>
    <xs:element ref="privilege"  maxOccurs="unbounded"/>
    <xs:element ref="role_inherit"  maxOccurs="unbounded"/>
    <xs:element ref="UserRoleAssignment" maxOccurs="unbounded"/>
    <xs:element ref="RolePrivilegeAssignment" maxOccurs="unbounded"/>
</xs:sequence>
</xs:complexType>

<xs:complexType name="userType">
     <xs:attribute name="userID" type="xs:ID" use="required"/>
     <xs:attribute name="fullname" type="xs:string" use="optional"/>
</xs:complexType>

<xs:complexType name="roleType">
    <xs:attribute name="roleID" type="xs:ID" use="required"/>
    <xs:attribute name="rolename" type="validRole" use="required"/>
    <xs:attribute name="cardinality" type="roleLimit" use="optional"/>
</xs:complexType>

<xs:simpleType name="validRole">
        <xs:restriction base="xs:string">
<xs:enumeration value="BranchManager"/>
<xs:enumeration value="Customer_Service_Rep"/>
<xs:enumeration value="Loan_Officer"/>
<xs:enumeration value="Accounting_Manager"/>
<xs:enumeration value="Internal_Auditor"/>
<xs:enumeration value="Teller"/>
<xs:enumeration value="Accountant"/>
    </xs:restriction>
</xs:simpleType>

<xs:simpleType name="roleLimit">
        <xs:restriction base="xs:integer">
          <xs:minInclusive value="0"/>
        <xs:maxInclusive value="10"/>
     </xs:restriction>
</xs:simpleType>

<xs:complexType name="privilegeType">
    <xs:attribute name="privilegeID" type="xs:ID" use="required"/>
    <xs:attribute name="gen_resource" type="xs:string" use="required"/>
    <xs:attribute name="gen_oper" type="operType" use="required"/>
```

Appendix A: XML schema for RBAC model

```xml
</xs:complexType>

<xs:simpleType name="operType">
   <xs:restriction base="xs:string">
    <xs:enumeration value="Open"/>
    <xs:enumeration value="Close"/>
    <xs:enumeration value="Debit"/>
    <xs:enumeration value="Credit"/>
   </xs:restriction>
</xs:simpleType>


<xs:complexType name="InheritType">
<xs:sequence>
        <xs:element name="FromRole" type="validRole" minOccurs="1"
                              maxOccurs="1"/>
        <xs:element name="ToRole" type="validRole" minOccurs="1"
                              maxOccurs="1"/>
</xs:sequence>
</xs:complexType>

<xs:complexType name="URAType">
<xs:annotation>
<xs:appinfo>
   <sch:pattern name="Role Assignment Rules">
     <sch:rule context="UserRoleAssignment[role[text ( ) = 'BRM']]">
       <sch:assert test="count(user)= 1" diagnostics="MUST_BRM">
                          There should be only a single user assigned to
Branch Manager
                     </sch:assert>
                   </sch:rule>
       </sch:pattern>
       <sch:diagnostics>
          <sch:diagnostic id="MUST_BRM">The actual number assigned is:
<sch:value-of select="count(user)"/>
           </sch:diagnostic>
   </sch:diagnostics>
 </xs:appinfo>
 </xs:annotation>

   <xs:sequence>
     <xs:element name="role" type="xs:IDREF"/>
     <xs:element name="user" type="xs:IDREF" maxOccurs="10"/>
   </xs:sequence>
</xs:complexType>
```

```
<xs:complexType name="RPAType">
  <xs:sequence>
    <xs:element name="role" type="xs:IDREF"/>
    <xs:element name="privilege" type="xs:IDREF" maxOccurs="unbounded"/>
  </xs:sequence>
</xs:complexType>
</xs:schema>
```

Appendix B

XML-encoded data for RBAC model

```xml
<?xml version="1.0"?>
<Bank_RBAC_Model xmlns:xsi="http://www.w3.org/2001/XMLSchema-instance"
   xsi:noNamespaceSchemaLocation="A:\BankRBAC.xsd">
<user userID="DrayJ" fullname="Jim Dray"/>
<user userID="GranceT" fullname="Tim Grance"/>
<user userID="VincentH" fullname="Vincent Hu"/>
<user userID="MiraM" fullname="Mira Mouli"/>
<user userID="JansenW"/>
<user userID="TomK" fullname="Tom Karygiannis"/>
<user userID="MellP" fullname="Peter Mell"/>
<user userID="MorganK" fullname="Kim Morgan"/>
<role roleID="BRM" rolename="BranchManager" cardinality="1"/>
<role roleID="CSR" rolename="Customer_Service_Rep" cardinality="3"/>
<role roleID="LNO" rolename="Loan_Officer" cardinality="2"/>
<role roleID="ACM" rolename="Accounting_Manager" cardinality="1"/>
<role roleID="AUD" rolename="Internal_Auditor" cardinality="1"/>
<role roleID="TEL" rolename="Teller" cardinality="6"/>
<role roleID="ACC" rolename="Accountant" cardinality="2"/>
<privilege privilegeID="PV111" gen_resource="DepAcct"  gen_oper="Open"/>
<privilege privilegeID="PV112" gen_resource="DepAcct"  gen_oper="Debit"/>
<privilege privilegeID="PV113" gen_resource="DepAcct"  gen_oper="Credit"/>
<privilege privilegeID="PV114" gen_resource="DepAcct"  gen_oper="Close"/>
<privilege privilegeID="PV211" gen_resource="LoanAcct" gen_oper="Open"/>
<privilege privilegeID="PV212" gen_resource="LoanAcct" gen_oper="Debit"/>
<privilege privilegeID="PV213" gen_resource="LoanAcct" gen_oper="Credit"/>
<privilege privilegeID="PV214" gen_resource="LoanAcct" gen_oper="Close"/>
<role_inherit>
```

```xml
    <FromRole>Teller</FromRole>
    <ToRole>Customer_Service_Rep</ToRole>
</role_inherit>
<role_inherit>
    <FromRole>Accounting_Manager</FromRole>
    <ToRole>Accountant</ToRole>
</role_inherit>
<role_inherit>
    <FromRole>Customer_Service_Rep</FromRole>
    <ToRole>BranchManager</ToRole>
</role_inherit>
<role_inherit>
    <FromRole>Loan_Officer</FromRole>
    <ToRole>BranchManager</ToRole>
</role_inherit>
<role_inherit>
    <FromRole>Accounting_Manager</FromRole>
    <ToRole>BranchManager</ToRole>
</role_inherit>
<role_inherit>
    <FromRole>Internal_Auditor</FromRole>
    <ToRole>BranchManager</ToRole>
</role_inherit>
<UserRoleAssignment>
    <role>BRM</role>
    <user>GranceT</user>
    <user>JansenW</user>
</UserRoleAssignment>
<UserRoleAssignment>
    <role>CSR</role>
    <user>TomK</user>
</UserRoleAssignment>
<UserRoleAssignment>
    <role>LNO</role>
    <user>JansenW</user>
</UserRoleAssignment>
<UserRoleAssignment>
    <role>ACM</role>
    <user>DrayJ</user>
</UserRoleAssignment>
<UserRoleAssignment>
    <role>AUD</role>
    <user>MorganK</user>
</UserRoleAssignment>
<UserRoleAssignment>
```

Appendix B: XML-encoded data for RBAC model

```xml
        <role>ACC</role>
        <user>VincentH</user>
</UserRoleAssignment>
<RolePrivilegeAssignment>
        <role>TEL</role>
        <privilege>PV112</privilege>
     <privilege>PV113</privilege>
</RolePrivilegeAssignment>
<RolePrivilegeAssignment>
        <role>CSR</role>
        <privilege>PV111</privilege>
        <privilege>PV114</privilege>
</RolePrivilegeAssignment>
<RolePrivilegeAssignment>
          <role>LNO</role>
          <privilege>PV211</privilege>
          <privilege>PV212</privilege>
          <privilege>PV213</privilege>
        <privilege>PV214</privilege>
</RolePrivilegeAssignment>
</Bank_RBAC_Model>
```

About the authors

David F. Ferraiolo is a supervisory computer scientist in the Computer Security Division of the National Institute of Standards and Technology (NIST). He has over 19 years of experience in computer and communications security, serving both the government and private industry. During his last 10 years of employment at NIST, he has conducted extensive research in various areas of access control, including formal model development, reference and prototype implementation, and product demonstration development and evaluation. He is the author or coauthor of more than 20 papers in the area of access control. He received a U.S. Department of Commerce gold medal in 2002 and a 1998 Excellence in Technology Transfer award from the Federal Laboratory Consortium for research in RBAC, and has served on the editorial boards of the U.S. Federal Criteria and the international Common Criteria (ISO 15408). He received a combined B.S. in computer science and mathematics from the State University of New York at Albany in 1982.

D. Richard Kuhn is a computer scientist in the Computer Security Division of NIST. His primary technical interests are in information security and software assurance, and he is the author or coauthor of more than 40 papers in these areas. Kuhn, a senior member of the Institute of Electrical and Electronics Engineers (IEEE), received a U.S. Department of Commerce gold medal in 2002, a 1998 Excellence in Technology Transfer award from the Federal Laboratory Consortium for research in RBAC, and a U.S. Department of Commerce bronze medal in 1990 for his contributions to open system standards. In addition, he is a member of Beta Gamma Sigma. He served as program manager for the Committee on Applications and Technology of the President's Information Infrastructure Task Force from 1994 to 1995, and from 1996 to 1999 he was manager of the Software Quality

Group at NIST. He received an M.S. in computer science from the University of Maryland at College Park and an M.B.A. from the College of William and Mary in Virginia.

Dr. Ramaswamy Chandramouli is a computer scientist with the Computer Security Division of the Information Technology Laboratory at NIST. Mouli (as he has been known to his colleagues over the years) has more than 17 years of experience in the design, development, and implementation of information systems both in the commercial and government sector in diverse areas such as international banking, healthcare, energy, and transportation. He joined NIST in 1997. Dr. Mouli's recent research focus has been in the area of RBAC models, security architectures, security functional testing, healthcare IT security, and criteria-based security specifications. He has written more than 12 conference and journal publications in the area of computer security and is the coauthor of the "RBAC Protection Profile," which was the first security protection profile to be formally evaluated and certified by CESG, United Kingdom, under the IT Security Evaluation & Certification (ITSEC) service. He is also the coauthor of the proposed NIST RBAC standard. Dr. Mouli holds an M.S. in operations research from the University of Texas at Dallas and a Ph.D. in information technology from George Mason University in Fairfax, Virginia.

Index

A

Access control
- context-sensitive requirements, 216
- DBMS use of, 27
- defined, 1
- enterprise frameworks (EAFs), 179–208
- forms, 2
- as fundamental security mechanism, 1
- group relationships, 13
- history of, 6–16
- implementation, 202–8
- in mainframe era, 6–8
- military rules, 7
- models, 4–5
- objectives, 27–28
- operating system use of, 27
- *See also* DAC; MAC; RBAC

Access control lists (ACLs), 37–38
- advantages, 38
- defined, 11
- illustrated, 37
- at lowest level, 20
- problems, 20
- *See also* ACL groups

Access control mechanisms, 29
- defined, 29
- support, 30

Access control models, 29–30
- defined, 29
- support, 30

Access control policies, 28–29
- defined, 28
- enforcement, 28
- implications, determining, 29

Access decision function (ADF), 226
Access enforcement function (AEF), 226
Access matrix, 8, 36–39
- defined, 6, 36
- entries, 36
- example, 37
- illustrated, 6
- implementation, 38
- representations, 37–38

ACL groups
- defined, 53
- entries, 13
- roles vs., 53–55

Active role set (ARS), 129
Administrative authority, 165, 177
Administrative functions
- for core RBAC, 146
- defined, 145
- for DSD relation, 152
- for hierarchical RBAC, 147–49
- for SSD relation, 150–51
- *See also* Functional specifications

Administrative permissions, delegation, 173–76
Administrative roles, 156, 184
Administrative scope, 156
- defined, 162, 163
- flexibility of, 163

Administrative support, 55–56
URA02, 158–61
ARA97, 157–58
Assignment(s)
- categories, 133–34

305

306

Assignment(s) (continued)
   privilege, 105–7
Assignment(s) (continued)
   role, 11, 14, 108–11
   role-permission, 217, 218, 244–46
   user-role, 217, 245, 246
   users, 74
Attribute certificates (ACs), 224–30
   issuing/revoking, 230
   PERMIS Project and, 225
   policy, 226
   role, 226
   role-assignment, 225
   role-specification, 225
   types of, 225
   X.509, 224–25
Audience, this book, *xvi*
Authentication
   authorization vs., 3–4
   defined, 3
Authorization
   authentication vs., 3–4
   defined, 1
   generation module (AGM), 220
   RBAC-Solaris, 233–34
   role, 11, 23, 74
   server-pull architecture, 21, 22
   specification model (ASM), 220
   transaction, 11
   user, 74
   user-pull architecture, 21, 22
   as yes/no decision, 3
   See also Access control
Authorization management, 20–23
   solutions, 21
   tasks, 21
Autonomous security service modules, 249–51
Availability
   access control and, 3
   defined, 2

B

Baldwin's privilege graph, 70
Bell-LaPadula model, 7–8, 40–41
   Bell-Nash model vs., 46
   simple security property, 40
   star property, 40
Biba integrity model, 41–42

   defined, 41–42
   integrity star property, 42
   simple integrity property, 42
Brewer-Nash model, 45–46
   Bell-LaPadula model vs., 46
   defined, 45
   rules, 45–46

C

Capability lists, 37–38
   defined, 37
   illustrated, 37
Case study, 255–64
Chinese wall
   defined, 10
   policy, 44–45
Clark-Wilson model, 9, 14, 42–44
   access control triple, 42–43
   application-level controls, 43
   constrained data items (CDIs), 43
   defined, 42
   integrity verification procedures (IVPs), 43
   SoD, 44
   transformation procedure (TP), 43
   unconstrained data items (UDIs), 43
Closed management system, 70
Combiner roles, 86, 87
Common desktop environment (CDE), 235
Communication, security, authentication, and privacy (CSAP) module, 250–51
Completeness, 32, 33
Component database systems (CDBSs), 246–47
Confidentiality
   defined, 2
   preserving, 3
Conflict-of-interest categories (COIs), 45
Connector roles, 76–79
   arbitrary collections, 76–78
   for blocking permission inheritance, 78
   defined, 76, 79
   example role hierarchy with, 76
   See also Role hierarchies; Roles
Constraints
   domain-specific, 189
   duration-type, 115
   dynamic, 103–4, 127–29
   EAM, 186
   inheritance, 103

Index

RCC, 172
role-activation, 115, 218
role-deactivation, 115
role-disabling, 114–15
role-enabling, 114–15
Schematron, 200–202
static, 103–4, 126–27
temporal, 112–17
CONTROL-SA, 276–80
   access control entities, 277–79
   components, 276, 277
   defined, 276
   enterprise authorization model, 277–79
   ESS, 276
   ESS administrator, 280
   ESS tasks, 280
   job codes, 279
   RSSs, 277, 278, 279
   SA-agents, 276, 277
   user connection to enterprise resources, 279–80
   See also Enterprise security administration (ESA)
Cookies
   defined, 222
   RBAC implementation with, 222–24
   in secure cookies set, 223
Core RBAC, 52, 55–59
   administrative elements, 55
   administrative functions for, 146
   administrative support, 55–56
   in all functional specification packages, 143
   defined, 52
   definition, 60
   dynamic component, 58–59
   functional specification for, 146–47
   permissions, 56–58
   review functions for, 147
   role activation, 58–59
   static element, 58
   supporting system functions for, 146
   See also RBAC
Crampton-Loizou administrative model, 162–69
   administrative scope, 162, 163
   decentralization and autonomy, 164
   operations, 162
   RHA_1, 164
   RHA_2, 165
   RHA_3, 165–66

RHA_4, 166–69
See also Role-based administration

D

DAC
   with change of ownership, 122
   defined, 8, 17
   enforcing, with RBAC, 122–25
   with grant-dependent revocation, 123, 125
   with grant-independent revocation, 123, 124–25
   liberal, 122, 124–25
   mechanisms, 35–36
   policies, 17, 35–36
   protection bits, 38–39
   RBAC comparison, 17
   revocation, 123
   strict, 122, 124
Department of Defense (DoD)
   Global Command and Control System, 136
   standards, 8
   Trusted Computer System Evaluation Criteria (TCSEC), 8, 9
Direct privilege inheritance, 69–70
DirXmetaRole, 280–84
   access control entities, 281–83
   component products, 280–81
   defined, 280
   RBAM model, 281–83
   role distribution, 284
   suite, 280, 281
   user connection to enterprisewide resources, 283–84
   See also Enterprise security administration (ESA)
Discretionary access control. *See* DAC
Domain-domain access control table (DDAT), 47
Domain-type access control table (DTAT), 47
Domain-type enforcement (DTE) model, 46–48
   DDAT, 47
   defined, 46
   DTAT, 47
   as enhanced type enforcement (TE) mechanism, 46
DOM API, 203
   element interface, 205
   interfaces, mapping to, 205

DOM API (continued)
   nodes, 205, 208
Dynamically constrained RBAC, 52
Dynamic constraints, 103–4, 127–29
Dynamic SoD (DSD), 94, 98–99
   constraints, 94
   formal definition, 99
   illustrated, 98
   properties, 98–99
   timely revocation of trust, 99
   See also Separation of duty (SoD)
Dynamic SoD (DSD) relations, 98, 144
   administrative functions, 152
   functional specification for, 152–53
   review functions, 153
   supporting system functions, 152–53

E

The Economic Impact of Role-Based Access Control, 255
Eligible subject set (ESS), 220
Enterprise access control frameworks (EAFs), 179–208
   access enforcement mechanism, 180
   conceptual view, 179–82
   data encoding, 193–96
   defined, 179
   distributed system, 181
   EAM, 181, 182–85
   ERBAC model and, 186–92, 197–202
   implementation, 202–8
   policy specification component, 179–80
   privilege specification, 187
   required components, 181–82
   support components, 181
Enterprise access control model (EAM), 181, 182–85
   constraints, 186
   creating/maintaining, 181
   defined, 182
   ease of administration requirement, 183–84
   multiple-policy support requirement, 183
   requirements, 182–84
   specification, 184–85
   as structured representation, 183
Enterprise security administration (ESA), 265
   CONTROL-SA, 276–80
   DirXmetaRole, 280–84
   features, 276
   product functions, 275
   RBAC in, 274–92
   SAM Jupiter, 284–89
   target system platforms, 275
   Tivoli Identity Manager, 289–92
ERBAC model
   constraint representation, XML schema limitations, 198–202
   elements, XML schema specifications for, 187–90
   privilege specification, 189–90
   relations, XML schema specifications for, 190–92
   role inheritance structure, 190–91
   role-privilege assignment relationship, 192
   specification in XML schema, 186–92
   syntactic representation, 199
   user-role assignment relations, 191
   verification of, 197–98
Execution profile, 234
External data representation (XDR), 236

F

Federated database systems (FDBSs), 211
   CDBSs, 246–47
   implementation in IRO-DB, 248–49
   interoperable layer, 246
   IRO-DB architecture, 247–48
   RBAC in, 246–49
Ferraiolo-Kuhn model
   defined, 11
   formal description, 12
   hierarchical roles, 13
Flexibility, 35
Functional specifications, 142–44
   administrative functions, 145
   for core RBAC, 146–47
   for DSD relation, 152–53
   for hierarchical RBAC, 147–50
   methodology for package creation, 143
   overview, 145
   packages, 142–44
   review functions, 145
   for SSD relation, 150–52
   supporting system functions, 145
   See also RBAC standard (NIST)

Index

G
General role hierarchies, 77, 84, 143
    with functional/organizational roles, 86
    See also Role hierarchies
Geographical regions, 81–82
Global users, 62–63, 64

H
Hierarchical RBAC, 52
    administrative functions for, 147–49
    defined, 52
    functional specification for, 147–50
    review functions for, 149–50
    subcomponents, 143
    supporting system functions for, 149
    See also RBAC
History-based SoD, 100–101

I
IBM research project, 244–45
    role-permission assignment, 244–45
    user role activation, 245
    user-role assignment, 245
Immediate descendents, 85
Immediate inheritance, 75
Informix Dynamic Server, 267–69
    assignable privileges, 268–69
    role activation, 267–68
    role creation, 267
    role hierarchies/constraints creation, 268
    user role assignments, 267
    See also Relational DBMS products
Inheritance
    constraints, 103
    direct privilege, 69–70
    hierarchy structures and, 75–82
    immediate, 75
    multiple, 86, 87
    permission, limiting, 78
    permission and user membership, 70–71
    relation, 75, 77
    role graph and, 170–72
    schemes, 69–74
    user containment and indirect privilege, 72–75
Insurance company case study, 255–64
    costs/estimated benefits summary, 257
    employee downtime reduction, 259–60
    employee management, 259–60
    extranet user management, 256–59
    implementation costs, 260–64
    organizational productivity, 259
    quarterly flow of net benefits, 264
    RBAC benefits, 260
    role engineering expenses, 261–62
    software/hardware expenses, 261
    strategic e-business initiative, 258
    system administration/maintenance simplification, 258–59, 260
    system administrator labor expenses, 261
    time series of benefits/costs, 262–64
Integrity
    defined, 2
    preserving, 3
Interoperable relational and object-oriented database (IRO-DB), 247–49
    administrative features, 249
    architecture, 247–48
    authorization objects (AOs), 248
    authorization subjects (ASs), 248
    authorization types (ATs), 248, 249
    defined, 247
    goal, 247
    implementation in, 248–49
    security metaclasses, 248
    security system (ISS), 247–48
Isolation, 32, 33–34

J
JAAS
    authentication and, 242
    framework, 242
    incorporating RBAC with, 244–46
    policy class, 243
JAVA
    defined, 239–40
    RBAC in, 239–46
Java Database Connectivity (JDBC), 206–7
Java security models
    access control enforcement, 242
    defined, 240
    enhancement, 241–43
    evolution of, 240–41
    with JAAS, 244–46
    JDK 1.0, 240

Java security models (continued)
    JDK 1.2, 240–46
        protection domains, 241
    Java-Web application, 245–46
        role-permission assignment, 245–46
        user role activation, 246
        user-role assignment, 246

L

Least privilege
    defined, 5
    enforcement of, 20
    strict adherence to, 5
Liberal DAC, 122, 124–25
    multilevel grant, 125
    one-level grant, 124
    two-level grant, 124–25
    See also DAC
Liberal *-property, 126–27
Limited role hierarchies, 85, 87, 143
Linkoping-RBAC prototype, 237
    access enforcement, 238
    activate roles, 237
    get activated role list, 237–38
    obtain file system access, 238–39
    reply, 239
    request NFS, 237
    retrieve role permissions, 238

M

MAC
    conventional, 10
    defined, 8
    DoD requirements support, 18
    enforcing, on RBAC systems, 125–29
    information flow policies, 121
    liberal *-property, 126–27
    MLS controls, 121
    policies, 39–40
    RBAC comparison, 18
    running RBAC simultaneously, 136–38
    simple security property, 126
    strict *-property, 126, 127, 128
    TCSEC definition, 18
Manageability, 35
Mandatory access control. *See* MAC
Mapping
    abstract permissions, 65
    to DOM API interfaces, 205
    hierarchical privilege, 135
    MLS to RBAC, 134–36
    permissions into privileges, 63–64
    privileges to categories, 134
    privileges to tasks, 108
Migration case study, 255–64
Military access control rules, 7
Modified privilege set, 137
Multidomain architecture, 34
Multilevel secure (MLS)
    categories, 132
    kernel, 136
    MAC controls, 121
    RBAC implementation on, 130–36
    to RBAC mapping, 134–36
    systems, 129
Multiple inheritance, 86, 87
Mutual exclusion, 104–5
    possibilities for five roles, 105
    relationship example, 109
    relationships, 109
    specified by role pairs, 104–5
    specified by sets, 104

N

Named protection domains (NPDs), 10
Napoleon prototype, 219–20
Network file systems (NFSs), 211
    client, 236, 237
    defined, 236
    RBAC implementation within, 236–39
    server, 237
NIST RBAC standard, 141–53

O

Object-based SoD, 100–101
Objects, 58
    defined, 4, 30
    DOM, 204
    as exhaustible system resources, 58
    RBAC control, 57
    resource, 30
    system, 30–31
Operational SoD, 99–100
    defined, 99

policies, 99–100
See also Separation of duty (SoD)
Operations, 137
    Crampton-Loizou administrative model, 162
    defined, 4–5
    RBAC control, 57
Oracle Enterprise Server, 269–71
    assignable privileges, 271
    role activation, 270
    role creation, 269
    role hierarchies/constraints creation, 271
    user role assignment, 269–70
    See also Relational DBMS products
Organization charts
    example illustration, 80
    hierarchies, 79–81
    organizational units (OUs), 80–81

P

Permissions, 56–58
    abstract, mapping, 65
    administrative, 173–76
    assignments, 123
    assignment to roles, 56–57
    as authorized for roles, 23
    creating/maintaining, 22–23
    defined, 5, 233
    inheritance, limiting, 78
    mapping, into privileges, 63–64
    overlapping, 68
    in RBAC-Solaris prototype, 232–36
    selectively assigning, 5
    See also Privileges
PRA02, 158–62
PRA97, 157–58
Privilege and Role Management Infrastructure Standards Validation (PERMIS) Project, 225
    Java-based API, 226
    privilege verification subsystem, 226
Privileges, 59
    assigning, to roles, 107–8
    assignment complexities, 111
    assignment effects, 105–7
    Baldwin's graph, 70
    complications, 106
    indirect, 62–63
    Informix Dynamic Server, 268–69
    mapping, to tasks, 108
    mapping permissions into, 63–64
    Oracle Enterprise Server, 271
    RBAC-Solaris, 233
    Sybase adaptive server, 274
    See also Permissions
Privilege sets, 130
    assignment of categories to, 133–34
    with category labels, 136
    modified, 137
    roles and, 132–33
Protection bits, 38–39
    defined, 38–39
    problems, 39
Public key infrastructure (PKI), 16

R

RBAC
    ACM workshop, 14, 15
    administrative advantage, 19–20, 55
    applications, 14–15
    in autonomous security service modules, 249–51
    commercial product features, 265–92
    concept, 9–10
    configuring, for DAC, 123–24
    configuring, for MAC (dynamic constraints), 127–29
    configuring, for MAC (static constraints), 126–27
    core, 52, 55–59
    core features, 51–65
    DAC comparison, 17
    defined, *xv*
    dynamic constrained, 52
    economic justification, 15–16
    economics of, 18–20
    enterprise and, 18–23
    in enterprise security administration software, 274–92
    for FDBSs, 246–49
    features, 16
    formal description, 12
    hierarchical, 52
    implementation costs, 260–62
    implementation within NFS, 236–39
    integration in Web environments, 220–30

RBAC (continued)
    integration with enterprise IT infrastructures, 211–51
    in Java, 239–46
    for Java-Web application, 245–46
    MAC comparison, 18
    migration case study, 255–64
    on MLS systems, 130–36
    model taxonomy, 52
    modular security administration, 184
    origins, 9–16
    policies, 17
    in relational DBMS products, 266–74
    relationships, 12
    role-based administration of, 155–77
    running MAC simultaneously, 136–38
    static constrained, 52
    static SoD requirements and, 97
    temporal constraints, 112–17
    for UNIX administration, 231–36
    for UNIX environments, 231–39
    Web server access using cookies, 222–24
    Web server implementation, 221–22
    for WFMSs, 212–20
    for workflows, 219–20
RBAC96 framework
    defined, 14
    illustrated, 15
    summary illustration, 156
RBAC/MLS interface, 131
RBAC reference model, 144–45
    components, 144
    subcomponents, 144–45
    taxonomy, 145
RBAC-Solaris prototype
    access enforcement process, 235–36
    authorization, 233–34
    development motivation, 231
    execution profile, 234
    permissions structuring, 232–36
    privileges, 233
    RBAC database layout, 235
    rights, 234
    role semantics, 231–32
RBAC standard (NIST), 141–53
    functional specification for core RBAC, 146–47
    functional specification for DSD relation, 152–53

    functional specification for hierarchical RBAC, 147–50
    functional specification for SSD relation, 150–52
    functional specification overview, 145
    functional specification packages, 142–44
    overview, 141–42
    reference model, 144–45
RBAM model, 281–83
Reference monitor, 31–35
    abstract requirements, 32
    assurance framework definition, 31–32
    completeness, 33
    concept, 31
    defined, 31
    illustrated, 32
    insufficiency, 35
    isolation, 33–34
    verifiability, 34–35
Relational DBMS products
    Informix Dynamic Server, 267–69
    Oracle Enterprise Server, 269–71
    RBAC in, 266–74
    Sybase adaptive server, 271–74
Remote procedure call (RPC), 236
Research Triangle Institute (RTI), 255
Resource objects, 30
Resource provisioning, 22–23
    defined, 22
    requirements, 23
Review functions
    for core RBAC, 147
    defined, 145
    for DSD relation, 153
    for hierarchical RBAC, 149–50
    for SSD relation, 151–52
    See also Functional specifications
Revocation
    grant-dependent, 123, 125
    grant-interdependent, 123, 124–25
Role activation
    Informix Dynamic Server, 267–68
    Oracle Enterprise Server, 270
    Sybase adaptive server, 272–73
Role-activation constraints, 115, 218
Role assignment, 74
    defined, 11
    to users, 108–11
Role-based access control. *See* RBAC

Index 313

Role-based administration, 155–77
    ARA02, 158–62
    background and terminology, 155–58
    Crampton-Loizou administrative model, 162–69
    PRA02, 158–62
    role control center (RCC), 169–77
Role control center (RCC), 169–77
    constraints, 172
    decentralization and astronomy, 176–77
    defined, 169
    delegation of administrative permissions, 173–76
    inheritance and role graph, 170–72
    role views, 172–73
    view display by, 174
    See also Role-based administration
Role distribution, 284
Role graph model, 14
Role graphs
    illustrated, 171
    inheritance and, 170–72
    nodes, 171
Role hierarchies, 13, 67–88
    administrative, 159
    in banking enterprise, 194
    building, from flat roles, 68–69
    connector roles, 76–79
    defined, 67
    definition, 217
    end-user, 159
    equivalent to role type, 84
    functional, example, 69
    general, 77, 84, 86, 143
    Informix Dynamic Server, 268
    limited, 85, 87, 143
    motivation for, 68
    Oracle Enterprise Server, 271
    SoD in, 102–3
    Sybase adaptive server, 273–74
Role-permission assignment, 217, 218
    IBM research project, 244–45
    Java-Web application, 245–46
Role relations, 54, 67
Roles
    ACL groups vs., 53–55
    activation, 58–59
    administrative, 156, 184
    assigning privileges to, 107–8
    assignment, 11, 74
    assignment of categories to, 134
    authorization, 11, 74
    with category labels, 136
    combiner, 86
    connector, 76–79
    defined, 53
    disabled, 114
    enabled, 114
    membership, 75
    organizational, 87
    as permission/privilege sets, 130
    permissions, 61
    privileges, 62–63
    privilege sets and, 132–33
    properties, 54
    in RBAC-Solaris prototype, 231–32
    scope of, 59
    states, 114
    temporal constraints on, 114
    user, 61, 245, 246
Role types
    accounting for, 83–84
    defined, 83
    illustrated, 83
    role hierarchy equivalence, 84
Role views, 172–73
    defined, 172
    defining, 173
    displayed by RCC, 174
    RCC use of, 173
RRA97, 157

S

Safety condition, 107
SAM Jupiter, 284–89
    access control entities, 285–88
    architecture, 285
    business servers, 285
    components, 284–85
    connecting users to enterprisewide resources, 288–89
    defined, 284
    ERBAC model, 285–88
    permission definition, 287–88
    repository, 289
    See also Enterprise security administration (ESA)

SAX API, 203
Scalability, 35
Schematron
    constraint expressions, 201
    constraints, 200–202
    defined, 200
    specifications, 201–2
    Validator, 202
SecureFlow prototype, 220
Security administration, 183–84
    enterprise (ESA), 265, 275–92
    modular, 184
Security kernel, 33–34
    correctness of, 34–35
    defined, 34
    implementation of, 33–34
Security policy
    enforcement of, 33–34
    support, 17
Separation of duty (SoD), 9, 44
    defined, 44, 52, 91
    definitions, 92
    dynamic (DSD), 94, 98–99
    example accounting system, 92
    features, 101–2
    history-based, 100–101
    maintaining, 108, 109–10
    necessary condition, 111
    object-based, 100–101
    operational, 99–100
    in real systems, 101–11
    relations, 94
    requirements, 91
    in role hierarchies, 102–3
    rules, purpose of, 106
    static, 94–97
    sufficient condition, 111
    as "two-man rule," 91
    types of, 94–101
Server-pull authorization architecture, 21, 22
SQL statements, 207–8
Stanford model, 87–88
    abstractions with roles/inheritance relations, 89
    defined, 87
    enterprise/system abstractions, 88
    entitlements, 87
    multiple inheritance and, 88
Statically constrained RBAC, 52

Static constraints, 103–4, 126–27
Static SoD, 94–97
    in a hierarchy, 95
    defined, 94
    formal definition, 97
    illustrated, 96
    implementation, 96–97
    policies, 94, 95, 96
    in presence of a hierarchy, 97
    in RBAC systems, 97
    requirements, 95
    safety condition, 107
    See also Separation of duty (SoD)
Static SoD relations
    administrative functions, 150–51
    component, 144
    functional specification for, 150–52
    review functions, 151–52
    supporting system functions, 151
    See also Separation of duty (SoD)
Strict DAC, 122, 124
Strict *-property, 126, 127, 128
Subgraphs, 72
    complete, illustrated, 110
    selecting, 73
Subjects, 30, 58
Supporting system functions
    for core RBAC, 146
    defined, 145
    for DSD relation, 152–53
    for hierarchical RBAC, 149
    for SSD relation, 151
    See also Functional specifications
Sybase adaptive server, 271–74
    role activation, 272–73
    role creation, 271–72
    role hierarchies/constraints creation, 273–74
    user role assignment, 272
    See also Relational DBMS products
System objects, 30–31
System view, mapping enterprise view to, 59–65

T

Tasks
    authorization management, 21
    mapping privileges to, 108
TE certificate, 227

Index

issuer, 228
mandatory attributes, 228
TE module, 227, 228
Temporal constraints, 112–17
   automatically enforced, 116
   categories, 113
   defined, 112
   duration, 113, 115
   generic form of, 114
   need for, 112–13
   periodicity, 113
   role-activation/deactivation, 115
   role-enabling/disabling, 114–15
   on role-permission assignments, 115–16
   on roles, 114
   supporting, 117
   support requirements, 116–17
   taxonomy of, 113–16
   on user-role assignments, 115
   See also Constraints
Temporal hierarchies, 117
Timely revocation of trust, 99
Time series of benefits/costs, 262–64
Tivoli Identity Manager, 289–92
   access control entities, 290–91
   authorization model, 290–91
   components, 289
   connecting users to enterprisewide resources, 291–92
   defined, 289
   records, 291–92
   TMR, 290
   See also Enterprise security administration (ESA)
Transaction authorization, 11
Trusted Computer System Evaluation Criteria (TCSEC), 8, 9

U

UNIX administration, 231–36
   command executables, 235
   permission structuring, 232–36
   role semantics in prototype, 231–32
UNIX environments, 211
   administration, 231–36
   NFS, 236–39
   RBAC integration in, 231–39
User containment, 72–74

User-pull authorization architecture, 21, 22
User-role assignment, 217
   IBM research project, 245
   Informix Dynamic Server, 267
   Java-Web application, 246
   Oracle Enterprise Server, 269–70
   Sybase adaptive server, 272
User roles, 61
   IBM research project, 245
   Java-Web application, 246
Users
   assignments and authorizations, 74
   defined, 4
   at enterprise level, 62
   global, 62–63, 64
   role assignment to, 108–11

V

Verifiability, 32, 34–35
Virtual file system (VFS), 236

W

Web environments, 211
   with attribute certificates, 224–30
   with cookies, 222–24
   RBAC integration in, 220–30
   Web server, 221–24
Workflow authorization server (WAS), 220
Workflow management systems (WFMSs), 112, 211
   access control design requirements, 214–16
   access control requirements and, 213
   components, 213–14
   components illustration, 214
   as computerized information system, 213
   defined, 212
   design-time component, 213
   RBAC for, 212–20
   RBAC model design/implementation requirements, 216–19
   role-permission assignments in, 218
   run-time component, 213
   support, 212
   workflow engine component, 219

X

X.509 certificates, 224–25

AC, 225
   identity certificate, 225
XML encoding
   enterprise access control data, 193–96
   role inheritance data, 194–95
   role-privilege assignment relation, 196
   user-role assignment relationship, 195–96
XML parser tool, 198, 203–4
XML schemas
   choice of, 185
   EAM specification and, 184–85
   ERBAC, syntactic representation, 199
   ERBAC model specification in, 186–92
   limitations of, 198–202
   specifications for ERBAC model elements, 187–90
   specifications for ERBAC model relations, 190–92
   well-formedness of, 197

Recent Titles in the Artech House Computing Library

Advanced ANSI SQL Data Modeling and Structure Processing, Michael M. David

Advanced Database Technology and Design, Mario Piattini and Oscar Díaz, editors

Action Focused Assessment for Software Process Improvement, Tim Kasse

Building Reliable Component-Based Software Systems, Ivica Crnkovic and Magnus Larsson, editors

Business Process Implementation for IT Professionals and Managers, Robert B. Walford

Configuration Management: The Missing Link in Web Engineering, Susan Dart

Data Modeling and Design for Today's Architectures, Angelo Bobak

Developing Secure Distributed Systems with CORBA, Ulrich Lang and Rudolf Schreiner

Future Codes: Essays in Advanced Computer Technology and the Law, Curtis E. A. Karnow

Global Distributed Applications with Windows® DNA, Enrique Madrona

A Guide to Software Configuration Management, Alexis Leon

Guide to Standards and Specifications for Designing Web Software, Stan Magee and Leonard L. Tripp

Implementing Electronic Payment Systems, Cristian Radu

Internet Commerce Development, Craig Standing

Knowledge Management Strategy and Technology, Richard F. Bellaver and John M. Lusa, editors

Managing Computer Networks: A Case-Based Reasoning Approach, Lundy Lewis

Metadata Management for Information Control and Business Success, Guy Tozer

Multimedia Database Management Systems, Guojun Lu

Practical Guide to Software Quality Management, John W. Horch

Practical Process Simulation Using Object-Oriented Techniques and C++, José Garrido

Risk-Based E-Business Testing, Paul Gerrard and Neil Thompson

Secure Messaging with PGP and S/MIME, Rolf Oppliger

Software Fault Tolerance Techniques and Implementation, Laura L. Pullum

Software Verification and Validation for Practitioners and Managers, Second Edition, Steven R. Rakitin

Strategic Software Production with Domain-Oriented Reuse, Paolo Predonzani, Giancarlo Succi, and Tullio Vernazza

Successful Evolution of Software Systems, Hongji Yang and Martin Ward

Systems Modeling for Business Process Improvement, David Bustard, Peter Kawalek, and Mark Norris, editors

User-Centered Information Design for Improved Software Usability, Pradeep Henry

Workflow Modeling: Tools for Process Improvement and Application Development, Alec Sharp and Patrick McDermott

For further information on these and other Artech House titles, including previously considered out-of-print books now available through our In-Print-Forever® (IPF®) program, contact:

Artech House	Artech House
685 Canton Street	46 Gillingham Street
Norwood, MA 02062	London SW1V 1AH UK
Phone: 781-769-9750	Phone: +44 (0)20 7596-8750
Fax: 781-769-6334	Fax: +44 (0)20 7630-0166
e-mail: artech@artechhouse.com	e-mail: artech-uk@artechhouse.com

Find us on the World Wide Web at:
www.artechhouse.com